The Spine of the Virginias

Journeys along the Border between Virginia and West Virginia

Michael Abraham

[signature]

Pocahontas Press
Blacksburg, Virginia

The Spine of the Virginias: Journeys along the Border between Virginia and West Virginia
by Michael Abraham

Book design by Lindsey Macdonald, Pocahontas Press,
    Blacksburg, Virginia
Cover design by Josh Wimmer, Wordsprint,
    Christiansburg, Virginia

Photographs by the author, unless otherwise noted.

ISBN 978-0-926487-52-9
0-926487-52-3

To Jane and Whitney Abraham,

the two most important people in my life.

Also by Michael Abraham

Union, WV, A novel of loss, healing and redemption in contemporary Appalachia

Harmonic Highways: Exploring Virginia's Crooked Road

For updates and ordering information on books, excerpts, and sample chapters, please visit the author's website at

http://www.bikemike.name/

The author can be reached by e-mail at:

bikemike@nrvunwired.net

Pocahontas Press
www.pocahontaspress.com

In Memory of Bob McGraw, Tazewell

When I met amateur historian and Civil War re-enactor Bob McGraw, he seemed healthy enough. But on my follow-up visit a few months later, he wore a patch on his earlobe and spoke about a touch of melanoma. When I called to ask permission to publish an article about him for *Blue Ridge Country Magazine*, I barely recognized his voice. He said his cancer had returned with a vengeance. Three weeks later he was dead. I feel privileged to have known him and been able to relate his story. Rest in peace, my friend!

Photo by Doug Letteer

Dedication to Stuart McGehee

This book is dedicated to Professor Stuart McGehee of Bluefield, who died on January 11, 2010. Stuart was introduced to me two years earlier by Virginia Tech's renowned Civil War historian, Professor James I. "Bud" Robertson. According to news articles, Stuart committed suicide after being diagnosed with fast-moving, invariably fatal, pancreatic cancer.

In remembrance of his friend and fellow historian and as a favor to me, Robertson provided this dedication:

Photo courtesy of Eastern Regional Coal Archives

> There was nothing usual about Stuart McGhee. Loud, fast-talking, always opinionated (mostly in a wonderfully humorous way), Stuart was also highly knowledgeable, grateful for invitations, and eager to please. A consummate performer on the Stage of Life, Stuart generally gave the appearance of a runaway locomotive. Underneath it all, however, was an introvert who did not want the perimeters of his world to extend too far. When illness threatened to alter that life, Stuart chose to end it.
>
> He was a one-of-a-kind individual, a learned man who made an indelible impression on everyone. He could thrive on controversy, but at the same time he treasured his friendships. When he ended letters to me with "Yr. Obdnt. Srvt." I knew that he meant every letter of that phrase. That is why I miss him so.
>
> — Bud Robertson, February 2010

Stuart's input was absolutely essential to my understanding of the formation of the State of West Virginia, and I do not exaggerate when I say I couldn't have written this book without him! I was only in his company two times, but Stuart McGehee had a profound impact on me and I mourn his death.

Contents

The Spine
of the Virginias

West Virginia

Virginia

BUCHANAN
MCDOWELL
TAZEWELL
BLAND
MERCER
GILES
MONROE
CRAIG
GREENBRIER
ALLEGHANY
POCAHONTAS
BATH
HIGHLAND
PENDLETON
ROCKINGHAM
HARDY
SHENANDOAH
HAMPSPHIRE
FREDERICK

Foreword

The Commonwealth of Virginia was one of this nation's original thirteen colonies and became what was the largest and arguably the most important original state. Its nickname, "Mother of Presidents," is a source of pride for all native sons and daughters. Founding superstars — including George Washington, Thomas Jefferson, James Madison, and James Monroe — were born amidst its verdant, rolling hills and coastal plains.

Many other notable figures in early American history are Virginians: George Mason, Stephen Austin, John Marshall, Patrick Henry, Robert E. Lee, Matthew Fontaine Maury, Meriwether Lewis, and William Clark.

Today Virginia is a vibrant state with a diverse economy. Virginia's population is rapidly growing and nearing eight million people. Its average household income is almost $60,000, in the top ten in the nation.

Wild and Wonderful West Virginia, The Mountain State, is the Rodney Dangerfield of states; it "can't get no respect."

West Virginia has produced no presidents. Its most famous native sons are perhaps Thomas J. "Stonewall" Jackson and Booker T. Washington, both born before the state formed. It has fewer than two million people. Every year since 1997, West Virginia has experienced more deaths than births, the first state in the nation to suffer this natural decrease. Its per-capita income is $38,000, third lowest in the nation, ahead of only Mississippi and Arkansas. Deeply dependent upon extractive industries, for decades it has been described as being in a perpetual recession.

West Virginia was carved, county by county, from its larger sibling state by an act of Congress in 1863 during the great conflict of the War Between the States. It is the only state to have been so created without the parent state's consent.

During my years of travel in the region, I felt something elemental was missing in all the facts and numbers. There was more than meets the eye between these sister states, something I looked to understand. I guess I always sympathized with the underdog. There was something raw, wild, and exotic about West Virginia. I wanted West Virginia to be important, relevant, and, well, normal.

Particularly puzzling was the status of the name itself. There were the Carolinas and the Dakotas, with a North and a South each, indicative of an inherent parity between the two. Why was there no "East" Virginia to match the West? The Virginias seemed to hold no similar equality.

The *World Book Encyclopedia* was the ubiquitous source of reference in my pre-Internet youth. In the maps within its article on the Civil War, it unequivocally placed Virginia in the Confederacy and West Virginia in the Union. A heavy line was drawn between them. Grammatically, the formation of the new state was written about in the passive voice, as: West Virginia was formed from 50 counties that were split from Virginia... I found no explanation of purpose or goal. What caused this irreconcilable riff and who were the architects? Was the divorce amicable? Was a reunification desirable or even possible?

The line drawn between the two states was jagged, arbitrary. Virginia had a linear, horizontal southern borderline separating it from North Carolina and Tennessee, and it followed the mighty Potomac River in its border with Maryland. The Virginia/West Virginia border was inexplicably squiggly. In my mind, it traced the pattern of a ski jump slope, with take-off ramp, jump, landing area, and deceleration upcurve. Who drew this line? Why was it so irregular and why was it where it was?

I was mindful of these paradoxes for years. One day, as I was motorcycling with two friends in Monroe County, West Virginia, I noticed several Confederate flags. How strange this was, I thought, as West Virginia was not in the Confederacy. Sure, there may have been some cross-border sympathizers, perhaps on both sides of the line. But why the militancy illustrated by this flag in a Union state? Why was it still flown, well over a century after the Civil War?

A native Virginian, I realized I had assimilated a greater sense of brotherhood with the people of West Virginia than I had realized. I felt more a product of an Appalachian mountain culture on both sides of the border than of the gentrified, aristocratic, plantation culture of most of Virginia. I enjoyed visiting Monticello, Williamsburg, and Richmond, but I railed against the blue-blooded, cavalier attitude. My heart always longed for the Appalachians. I've always felt uncomfortable in places without mountains on the horizon.

To a greater degree than any place I'd experienced in America, the land of Appalachia had shaped people and the people shaped the land. Mountain people have a visceral sense of locality and place. Mountains make people different, and maybe mountains had made me different. The mountains are strength, permanence, and sustenance. Paradoxically, mountains envelop yet liberate, they insulate yet expand.

Virginia, like many Eastern states, has the Appalachians in the back yard. But West Virginia alone holds the very soul of Appalachia and is geographically entirely within it. Appalachian people feel a sense of freedom, patriotism, and spirituality unmatched in America.

Yet all is not well. Poverty, often extreme, plagues the region. Jobs are scarce. Frequent floods inflict horror and destruction on narrow valleys. In many areas, topography is steep and confining. Land ownership is often held by outside concerns, unfeeling towards the needs of the inhabitants. Cultural traditions are eroding.

I purposely became more attuned to the land and its people.

In farming areas, I saw barns with rusting metal roofs and weathered boards across misty fields, strewn with corroding farm equipment. Small vegetable gardens flanked many houses, and huge woodpiles, some stacked and some not, rested against garages or trees.

I walked through summer rainstorms as loud and dynamic as textile mills and autumn fogs so thick I could barely see the ground in front of me. I gazed from mountain overlooks upon forested hillsides and fields of shrubbery with palettes of green in too many shades to distinguish.

In coalfield towns I saw topography so steep that commercial buildings had half their structure suspended on stilts above sewage-laced creeks below. I saw crumbling structures: mine conveyors and tipples, schools, homes, and businesses.

I gazed in awe at fields in early summer evenings over which lightning bugs dotted the landscape with pixie dust.

I saw uncountable small churches, always the most kempt structures in every town. Seemingly all were Protestant, with a sign outside proclaiming Jesus' love, exhorting new members to worship.

I bicycled along hilly country lanes and watched fog drift over nearby hillsides.

I listened with delight to the soulful twang of Appalachian folk and bluegrass music and the whimsy of storytellers.

I smelled the rich perfume of invasive honeysuckle and the subtle, faint candy smell of wild azaleas. I smelled the dank odor of moist soil in freshly-turned fields. I gagged from the stench of a road-kill deer as crimson-faced turkey vultures circled above.

Who lived in these valleys and hollows? What was the nature of their characters and how did they see their lives?

My curiosity and need to better understand this region launched a quest of two years of traveling the border and meeting the people in order to chronicle their lives, history, culture, and place in America and the world. The Spine of the Virginias became a passion.

My Spine would be confined to the mountainous counties along the border. Virginia's side included Frederick, Shenandoah, Rock-bridge, Highland, Bath, Alleghany, Craig, Giles, Bland, Tazewell, and Buchanan counties. The West Virginia side had Hampshire, Hardy, Pendleton, Pocahontas, Greenbrier, Monroe, Mercer, and McDowell. The West Virginia Eastern Panhandle counties of Jefferson, Berkley, and Morgan, across the line from Virginia's Clarke, also share the border. I left them out of this book because they are not mountainous.

The great Appalachian Mountain chain extends from Canada's Quebec southward through New England, the Mid-Atlantic States, and into Georgia and Alabama. The great peaks within the Whites,

Greens, and Adirondacks to the north and the Smokies to the south are somewhat detached, isolated from the others. Conversely, many of the mountains of The Spine of the Virginias are generally characterized by long trellislike ridges, resembling the tines of a fork. Some — Great North Mountain, Allegheny Mountain, Back Mountain, Shenandoah Mountain, Peters Mountain, Potts Mountain, East River Mountain, and Big Walker Mountain — stretch fifty miles or more in relatively straight lines. Peters Mountain and East River Mountain, the same ridge sliced by the New River, is almost 100 miles long. In the southwest, the coalfield mountains are jumbled and haphazard, like swells in a restless sea.

Many of these long ridges created transportation barriers with the concomitant isolation. There are only two Interstate highways that cross the Spine and only four railroad tracks. The mountains remain formidable barriers.

The metaphor of a spine took shape in my mind as I saw satellite photos of the area and envisioned how the region was held together geographically and culturally the way a backbone supports a vertebrate's body, holding it together physically. Along my way I heard other people use the word "spine" relative to the region, convincing me the metaphor was apt.

Furthermore, the Spine came to represent the fortitude and resilience of a people often beset with tough times and situations.

The border itself is serrated and unwieldy. To get a handle on it, look to two parallel lines. One is indistinct but easy to see, even from space. It is the Great Valley of Virginia. This long, diagonal cut running from northeast to southwest is not drained by a single river, but by many. It has always been a valuable transportation route, first an Indian trail, then the path of The Valley Pike, then of US-11, and finally today of Interstate 81. The three northernmost counties along The Spine of the Virginias — Frederick, Shenandoah, and Rockbridge, are Valley of Virginia counties. Beginning with Augusta County and extending southwestward, there is a continuous string of counties separating the Great Valley of Virginia from the state borderline.

The other parallel line is distinct but difficult to see. It is the line inscribed by the presence of underground coal. The coal line — if we can call it this — is roughly parallel, and to the west of the Great Valley of Virginia, typically about 100 miles away. Hampshire, Hardy, and Pendleton, the three northernmost West Virginia counties along The Spine of the Virginias, do not have significant coal reserves. The coal line clips the western edge of Pocahontas, Greenbrier, and Mercer counties and takes in the entirety of McDowell County. The coal line slices across the border near the West Virginia town of Bramwell in Mercer County and Pocahontas in Tazewell County, Virginia. Buchanan County is the only Virginia Spine county entirely within the coal band.

The rivers meander through these mountains, sending fresh water in every compass direction. In the north, the rivers on both sides of the Spine flow northward, all tributaries of the great Potomac. On the Virginia side, the Shenandoah River, with its lovely meanders, is the primary tributary. On the West Virginia side, the Cacapon and the myriad of forks of the Potomac itself drain the state's highest and most rugged mountains, a far cry from the turgid basins of Washington, D.C.

Further south, from mid-Highland, through Bath, Alleghany, and part of Craig counties on the Virginia side and Pocahontas and Greenbrier counties on the West Virginia side, the Spine forms a true divide. The James River — built by the waters of the Jackson, Bullpasture, Cowpasture, and Calfpasture rivers and many smaller creeks — flows eastward through Richmond to the Chesapeake Bay and the Atlantic Ocean. In West Virginia, the Greenbrier River flows first southward, then westward to its rendezvous with the New at Hinton. The New River flows north from North Carolina through Southwest Virginia and into West Virginia, joining the Gauley to become the Kanawha, an Ohio River tributary.

The New River is the only major river to slice The Spine of the Virginias. It flows through Giles County in Virginia and between Monroe and Mercer counties in West Virginia, draining much of those two counties. Portions of Tazewell County are drained by the Clinch River, a Tennessee River tributary. The rest, along with Buchanan County, is drained by the Big Sandy. McDowell is drained by the Tug Fork River.

The Big Sandy and the Tug Fork are Ohio River tributaries.

This Spine is anything but homogenous and uniform. The vast complexity of water, soil, geology, history, and cultures in this collection of vertebrae makes for one of the most diverse regions on earth. Explore it with me.

Before we take this journey together, I must do some housekeeping.

This book doesn't profess to be a travel guide. Should you choose to explore or replicate my journeys, please have Virginia and West Virginia State maps with you. Both states produce outstanding maps available at all visitor centers and Department of Transportation offices.

Spelling and naming in the Spine area are capricious. Virginia's Alleghany County is adjacent to the Allegheny Mountains; the "a" spelling is more common in Virginia. The river and county of the name Greenbrier are frequently spelled Greenbriar; both are acceptable.

Some names are used in more than one place. The town of Pocahontas is in Virginia's Tazewell County. Pocahontas County is in West Virginia. The town of McDowell is in Virginia's Highland County. McDowell County is in West Virginia. Union is the county seat of Monroe County, West Virginia. "The Union" is the United States of America, or the non-seceding states during the Civil War.

The Shenandoah River runs generally northward in Virginia, as does the Potomac in West Virginia. Thus, "down-valley" is to the north, not south.

Sulfur is a nonmetallic pale-yellow chemical element often found in spring water. Most place names, e.g. White Sulphur Springs, use the British spelling.

The state bird of Virginia is the cardinal. The state bird of West Virginia is also the cardinal, which, interestingly, it chose in 1949, one year before Virginia. However, this book's cover shows a rose-breasted grosbeak on the West Virginia side instead. West Virginia features a rose-breasted grosbeak on its vanity license plate. The male cardinal is a stately, 9-inch long, bright red bird with an audacious crest and a black mask, flanking a thick reddish beak. The male rose-breasted grosbeak is perhaps an inch shorter, a bit plumper, with a dramatic black cape and hood, a snow-white breast and beak, and a cherry red upper breastplate. For my eye, it's the better looking bird. The cardinal is a year-round, common resident of the region, often shown in promotional pictures flashing its crimson brilliance. The rose-breasted grosbeak is an occasional, migratory visitor, typically showing up at my window feeder in May. This, for me, makes it more exotic and welcomed. If it's good enough for West Virginia's vanity plate, it's good enough for my cover.

Most of this book was researched between February 2008 and September 2009. Considerable changes occurred in our nation during that period. Ideally, I would have performed this entire effort continuously, but that wasn't practical. Rather than organizing chronologically, I grouped chapters by geographic regions, starting at the northeastern end of the Spine and moving to the southwest. I hope you will adjust to this time discontinuity without difficulty as these pages are presented in what may seem a random fashion, from season to season.

Preface

This book is about a region, a thin slice of Appalachia, steeped in history, mysticism, and mountain culture. It is a compilation of profiles, stories, anecdotes, and vignettes, linked to one another by a squiggly line placed on a map a century and a half ago by politicians. Because the area encompasses 19 counties with more than 1,000,000 people, this book is necessarily incomplete. Other than perhaps launching a likely futile effort to reunify the nation's 10th and 35th states, it serves no grand purpose.

Acknowledgments

I am deeply indebted to many people who supported my effort. My editors worked countless hours to make sure my book was readable and relevant:

David Abraham, Radford
Jane Abraham, Blacksburg
Joyce Ackermann, Blacksburg
Mary Ann Johnson, Blacksburg
Kate McCoy, Blacksburg
Sally Shupe, Newport

I conducted more than 150 interviews during this process, often unannounced and with strangers. I appreciate the honesty, intelligence, and candor I was shown. Many people sat for interviews but were not included in the book, not because their stories weren't compelling, but because of space and relevancy considerations. Regardless, I thank them. And I give special thanks to Bob Pearsall of Christiansburg, who created the maps.

I also appreciate the special help I was given by:
Jon Cawley, Salem
Jennifer and Dan Copeland, Rock Camp
Ray Froy, Bluefield
Rod Graves, Union
Jim Mead, Low Moor
Craig Mohler, Union

I thank these people for allowing me to use their photographs:
Bob Abraham, Christiansburg
John Adamson, Woodstock
Steve Brightwell, Beckley
Doug Puffenbarger, Blue Grass
Ray Roberts, Sinking Creek
Tracy Roberts, Sinking Creek
Ray Schmitt, Mathias

Part I

Cervical

Virginia gave its permission for West Virginia to form, but everyone knew that the real Virginia had done no such thing, and so West Virginia's right to existence appeared to rest on a sham. [1]

— John A. Williams, historian

The great enemy of the truth is very often not the lie — deliberate, contrived and dishonest, but the myth — persistent, persuasive and unrealistic.

— John F. Kennedy, 35th president

Winter

On a cold Sunday in January, I awoke to find that sleet, as pristine as ivory and as fine as grains of sand, had fallen overnight. The brick steps from our front porch in Blacksburg, Virginia, were treacherously slick. I scraped ice from the car windows.

Leaving town on US-460, I watched the road surface alternate from white to black, as wet asphalt vied with a mixture of sleet and highway-department-applied rock salt. Traffic was scant. The outside thermometer on my dashboard read 29°F.

Brush Mountain and Gap Mountain form the northern backdrop to Blacksburg. I drove over the two parallel ridges into Giles County. The ridges and the land between them are in the George Washington and Jefferson National Forest. The trees, mostly locust, oak, walnut, maple and poplar, leafless, stood like rimy sentinels on the ridgelines, unlike the continuous carpet of green in summer. The forest floor, unhidden by leaves or understory, was a palette of tan earth-tones, interspersed with patches of sleet. The trees, of second-growth stock and generally no more than a few inches in diameter, were ghosts of the virgin forests which greeted the first Europeans.

Over Gap Mountain, I took in the grand view towards Salt Pond and Butt Mountains, dark and foreboding, to the north. Low-hanging clouds blocked my view of their tops, leaving their summits in mystery. At the base of Gap Mountain, the village of Newport lay, looking like a stray vestige from New England, ensconced in winter's grip.

Beyond Maybrook, a fire truck and a police car blocked the right-hand lane and, just past them, a white utility van lay on its side in the road. Ladders that had been strapped to the rooftop rack were strewn across the ditch.

In Pembroke, the speed limit drops from 65 to 45 miles per hour. A Subway restaurant and an older brick building with bright yellow letters "Amish Furniture" dominate the small business district to the left. At the end of the downtown straight-away is a double-decker billboard, the upper screen promoting Wendy's restaurants in Ripplemead and Pearisburg, and the lower promoting SOUTHERN "X" PO-SURE, Gentlemen's Club in Princeton. The latter features a brunette with a seductive stare, munching on her left index finger.

Above the bypass around Pearisburg loomed Pearis Mountain, its summit decapitated by low-hanging clouds. All around were gentle hills with scrub forests and occasional homes and barns. From the bridge across the New River, I watched two squadrons of Canada geese flying in formation, one with five birds and the other with eight.

I passed the complex of a factory the locals refer to simply as "Celanese" whose main product is cigarette filters. The pungent scent of acetone permeated the air. A dozen exhausts of white steam rose into the laden sky, almost as if manufacturing the fog above. I drove through the steep narrows of the New River and left the main highway in Rich Creek. This small town is situated in a 5-mile by 6-mile nipple of land north of Peters Mountain in Virginia, surrounded by West Virginia.

I took US-219 to the north, towards Peterstown. Near the state line is a cluster of gas stations, taking advantage of Virginia's lower gasoline taxes. Here, a large, painted statue of a rooster stands on a pedestal outside a restaurant.

Peterstown has grocery and drug stores, a funeral home, a tax preparer, a lawyer, a flower shop, and a tanning salon.

The first few miles of US-219 are uncharacteristically straight for a two-lane West Virginia highway. The temperature had risen to 33°F. I passed a mix of residential and commercial development, alongside farms and barns. Black cows stood like ink-blots, silhouetted against the frosted, bleached gold pastures.

The unincorporated communities of Linside and Rock Camp each featured a couple of weathered stores and churches. I passed the Salt Sulphur Springs. Two centuries earlier it had been a major resort,

bringing in outsiders, primarily southern flatlanders with their welcome cash, to the frontier Appalachian settlements.

Union is the largest community and the seat of Monroe County, a
county with neither traffic lights nor four-lane roads. The highway approaches from the west, and there is a stop sign where it turns 90-de-
grees to the left, points due north, and forms Main Street. Several picturesque and historic structures line the business district, including a
two-story log cabin on the left with a placard with the number "1810,"
presumably the date it was built. A brick courthouse sits grandly on
the right, its roof festooned with various antennae and a siren. The office of the historic newspaper, The Monroe Watchman, is beyond. Its
front porch is decorated with a period-piece, a horse-drawn wagon.

Main Street is a quarter-mile long. At its end, it makes another
90-degree turn, this time to the right, and heads eastward again. Just
beyond the turn, I pulled into the parking lot of the Union Presbyteri-
an Church, a tan brick structure with four white columns on the front
portico. There were a dozen cars in the lot, half on asphalt and half
on grass. One sported a sticker in a back window that read, "When
Jesus said 'Love your enemies,' I think he probably meant don't kill
them."

At the back of the churchyard were a white fence and a stone en-
tranceway to a paved sidewalk leading up a gradual incline to a monument, perhaps 40 yards away. The sidewalk was as slick as a hockey
rink. The monument is 20-feet tall, with a limestone base, a granite
pedestal, and a marble figure at the top, a statue of an unnamed Civil
War soldier — a generic combatant. The soldier stands with a down-
cast face. He holds his rifle before him with both hands, resting. Chiseled on the monument is the inscription, "Confederate Soldiers of
Monroe County."

A couple of wooden benches and four small cedar trees in a
square yard were surrounded by a white wooden fence. As I arrived, a
herd of 30 crow-black cows trotted towards me from 100 yards away.
Each had a red tag hanging from one ear. They hesitated, came to a
stop, moved towards me again, stopped again, then lost interest and
resumed grazing. I wondered how any creature so vacuous could have
survived the vicissitudes of evolution, before concluding intelligence

was of no value in the longevity of species. A stiff breeze blew from the northwest, and waves of sleet danced on my parka.

I brushed some sleet from one of the benches and sat. To the north, Swoopes Knobs emerged, then hid, then emerged again through the frozen mist. The statue was oriented to look southward, down the length of Main Street and to Peters Mountain beyond.

I found this most curious: Confederate soldiers of Monroe County. Confederates! Civil War maps show West Virginia not in the Confederacy at all, but in the Union. And yet here was a statue of a Confederate soldier, in a Union state, and in, of all places, a town called Union.

In my goose-down parka and a woolen cap, I shivered. Sleet pounded my eyeballs. I looked at the face on the statue. The swirl of frozen moisture around it made it look as if the statue were in motion, its eyes able to take in the grand view and the quiet happenings of Union, so tranquil and serene now, but permeated with strife 150 years earlier.

Again I thought about this Confederate monument in a Union state. Would local schoolchildren visit on field trips and wonder how this happened? What would their teachers tell them?

I had a flashback. I was sitting in an auditorium at Virginia Tech in 1975 listening to Professor Robertson, a pre-eminent Civil War historian, lecture. James I. Robertson, Jr. — "Bud" to all his friends — was talking about an army from Mississippi or Georgia, shivering through a Virginia mountain winter. In his signature Southside Virginia drawl, he made the War more real on a human scale than any history book. I saw in my mind's eye a Confederate infantryman sitting under a grand cedar tree, sleet falling around him. He was from Monroe County, Virginia, writing a letter to a loved one back home. He sat impervious to the cold but stricken by wrenching homesickness and a malnourished heart.

Leaving the Memorial, I turned back along Main Street. Squalls of snow blew across the road. A shiver started in my upper arms and made its way into my neck, and I involuntarily scrunched my shoulders. A lone red pickup truck parked in front of the café. Four pigeons flew from the courthouse roof.

James I. "Bud" Robertson, Jr.
Blacksburg (Montgomery County)

My curiosity about the Memorial compelled me to make an appointment to see Dr. Robertson again.

Bud has piercing blue eyes and grey hair. As medals are given to war heroes, awards are given to academics, and Bud has won many. The author of several books including the essential biography, Stonewall Jackson: The Man, The Soldier, The Legend, Robertson, now well past official retirement age, still teaches upwards of 250 students every semester, just as he did when I attended more than three decades earlier.

Professor Robertson's watchwords were, "If you want to understand America today, you must understand the Civil War." I reasoned that in order to understand Virginia and especially West Virginia today, I needed to understand West Virginia's creation.

Robertson greeted me warmly, adding, "In 1861 when the area that became West Virginia was making waves, people in Virginia including Jackson thought of this as just an uprising.... a little rebellion that needed to be stymied. Jackson begged [officials in] Richmond to, 'Give me an army so I can go over in there and stop this.' And they wouldn't do it. He would have been appalled by what those counties did to create a state. The whole statehood movement wasn't taken seriously until it was too late. When statehood came in June '63, Jackson was dead. He never saw the state of West Virginia as a reality."

West Virginia was created by an act of Congress in 1863, the first and only state created from another state without the parent state's consent. Statehood was precipitated by the actions of businessmen and civic leaders in the northwestern part of the state, primarily in the area around Wheeling. For several decades prior to the War, leaders in northwestern Virginia had had a series of disagreements with the government in Richmond. In their view, the Richmond government was slanted in its approach, favoring the slave-owning plantation farmers of the Tidewater and Piedmont regions rather than the rapidly industrializing Ohio River Valley. The secession of Virginia from the Union provided their impetus to act. I asked about their motivations.

Robertson said, "There are two schools of thought. The West Virginia University school of thought is, 'We are doing the patriotic thing; we are Unionists. We will stay in the Union.' The modern- day school of thought asserts that the state-forming activities were as illegal as bootlegging. At the Wheeling Convention, people appeared and said, 'I'm representing so-and-so County,' when in fact they were representing nobody but themselves."

There were two founding conventions in Wheeling to decide the question of independent statehood. The first was held May 13–15, 1861 and the second June 11–19, 1861. Of all the counties along The Spine of the Virginias, only Hampshire, the northernmost, sent a single delegate. Wheeling was then the third largest city in Virginia, behind only Richmond and Petersburg.

"West Virginia was valuable to the Union simply because the Baltimore and Ohio Railroad ran across the northern tier."

The B&O ran from Baltimore to Harpers Ferry, and then split at Grafton. One line went northwest to Wheeling; the other went west to Parkersburg. When the Civil War began, the B&O was the only railroad in what would become West Virginia and the only railroad linking the eastern and western states of the Union.

Take a look at your map of West Virginia. (Note, if you don't have a paper copy with you, there's always one on your right arm. Take your right hand and face your palm, with your fingers and thumb extended. Roll your pinkie, ring, and index fingers to the palm. Voilà! There's your map of West Virginia.) The northernmost extension is less than 100 miles from the shore of Lake Erie. The boundaries of Virginia in 1861 almost split the Union.

"Nobody tells this story better than my friend Stuart McGehee at West Virginia State University. He talks about the folks who attended that conference in Wheeling, and about how what they did was so blatantly unconstitutional that the whole gang should have been put in jail!

"The northern counties had much more in common with Ohio than they did with Tidewater Virginia. It was easy for them to stay Unionist. But the southern tier counties were culturally aligned with the Southwest Virginia and Piedmont Virginia farmers. [The northern tier counties] had delegates who dragged [the southern tier counties] into the new state."

Robertson is convinced that Stonewall would have never accepted the concept of West Virginia. "Stonewall felt that if there was a presence of the [Confederate] military, they would all fall back in line. He thought the people were being duped by the politicians. Once the Valley Campaign in '62 and all the military campaigns in Virginia, Antietam, et cetera, got underway, Jackson lost touch with the politics over there."

Appalachia

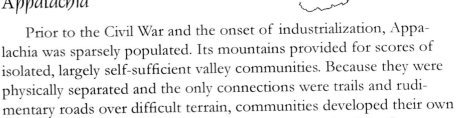

Prior to the Civil War and the onset of industrialization, Appalachia was sparsely populated. Its mountains provided for scores of isolated, largely self-sufficient valley communities. Because they were physically separated and the only connections were trails and rudimentary roads over difficult terrain, communities developed their own robust social systems largely based upon extended families. Communication between settlements was infrequent and sketchy; national and international news took weeks to reach the people.

Much like the Native Americans who populated the region before them, the newcomers of European descent — largely of Scottish and Irish descent — found stability and relative autonomy in the coves and hollows of Appalachia. Households relied heavily on kinsfolk and neighbors for economic, social, medical, and nutritional needs. Community-wide events provided relief from the loneliness of isolation.

Social interaction was most common on Sundays at church, during court, and on election days. Church services, baptisms, revivals, and other gatherings were often organized by itinerant preachers, traveling a circuit of nearby communities. Circuit court was an opportunity for social discourse. These, along with political campaigns, were marked by informality, showmanship, and entertainment. The dynamic of extended families taking sides and staffing various political caucuses and juries led to heated and often violent encounters, exemplified by well-publicized feuds.

Settlements were along the rivers, progressing upwards along tributaries. The most fertile areas along the flood plains were first to be settled, providing the greatest agricultural return. Families were prolific, often producing more than a dozen offspring. Successive waves of offspring moved farther into the narrow valleys, where less productive soils and steep terrain made farming difficult.

Appalachia benefited from an absence of pre-ordained hierarchies. Unlike the lowlands where the prickly issue of slavery festered for generations before the Civil War, mountain communities had settlements of free blacks, old and new immigrants, and even Native Americans. While some residents owned more land than others, limited cash prevented class structures from emerging.

Like the Indians before them, settlers owed their survival to the land. Rudimentary farms, sustained by a milk cow, free-ranging hogs foraging for acorns, chestnuts and other abundant mast, a flock of chickens and a horse, sustained growing families. Rather than bloodline or endowment, personal intelligence, wit, skill, and charisma helped a man (or occasionally a woman) to achieve higher status. An egalitarian ethos emerged, underpinned by a pugnacious and independent spirit.

The Appalachian family farm became the cornerstone economic unit. While agriculture in the Tidewater and Piedmont areas developed with the production of a single cash crop, typically tobacco or cotton, Appalachian family farms were diverse, providing almost entirely the food, shelter, clothing, and energy needs of the family.

Marriage was the key economic partnership. Husbands did the heavy tilling, planting, harvesting, and hunting. Wives did everything else: knitting, sewing, cooking, spinning, weaving, cleaning, child rearing, and preserving foods. Children did whatever their ages allowed. One can only imagine the disarray and tumult should any participant be unable to play his or her part. Youth had comparative freedom. Sexual relations ensued, and sexual roles were imposed at ages younger than customary today. First-time mothers were often in their mid-teens. The stature of authority grew with age, especially since life beyond one's sixth or seventh decade was rare.

The immediate and extended family, the community, and a benign climate provided a healthy, albeit cash-poor, society. The region enjoyed ample water and a long growing season. Much of the land was used to grow corn as food for the family and livestock. Additional crops were oats, wheat, rye, sorghum, fruits, and vegetables. Wild fruits were abundant, as were game animals including squirrels, rabbits, pheasants, deer, and quail. Bottomlands were tilled for crops, and some hillsides were denuded of trees for livestock grazing, although much land was left wooded.

Crops were intermingled with one another to provide maximum output per acreage. Sheep raised on the hillsides provided wool for clothing, rugs, and blankets, in addition to meat. Cattle provided milk and meat. Geese and ducks managed the insect population in addition to providing food and feathers for pillows and bed mattresses. Hounds assisted with the hunt and protected the home, garden, and the other domestic animals and flora from foxes, wolves, groundhogs, and deer. Hunting and fishing were year-around activities. Thick forests of chestnut, oak, and other nut-bearing trees supplied sustenance for free-ranging livestock and an abundance of wildlife unimaginable today.

Log cabins remain the most iconic images of the Appalachian life style. They were constructed of notched pine or chestnut logs, with cracks filled with mud. Roofs were made from shingles of split white oak. Floors were made from shaved chestnut, the region's most available and valuable wood. Chimneys were made from local stones, affixed with handmade cement. Porches often adorned both the front and back.

Most log cabins consisted of a single room with a loft above. Everyone spent considerable amounts of time outdoors. Weather needed to be seriously inclement to drive early Appalachian people indoors.

The location of the cabin was of primary importance, as proximity to water and cultivated fields saved considerable recurring effort. The rugged landscape and sparse population meant that seldom was one cabin within sight of another. Isolation was both a blessing and a curse.

Cabins were sparse and utilitarian. Decorations were generally absent, but there weren't many windows — so vases would have been on tables. Occasionally a quilt did double duty as a decoration and a comforter. There were kettles, cook stoves, washtubs, looms, and spinning wheels. To many outsiders, particularly traveling journalists, the simplicity, spirituality, and connectedness with nature exemplified by these cabins touched a romantic nerve. Writers described this atmosphere in glowing terms in newspaper and magazine articles printed in metropolitan areas.

Occasionally, a farmer cut and milled some trees to provide cash. Harvests were small-scale and returned only a tiny income because of a lack of demand in the marketplace and difficulties in transportation. Specializations in crafts of furniture making, shingle or fence-rail manufacturing, or musical instrument crafting emerged in some families, helping with cash flow. Wild plant products, principally ginseng, galax, and witch-hazel, also brought currency. There was some need for manufactured products or outside commodities such as sugar and coffee, but the bedrock of the economy was each family providing for itself or bartering with neighbors.

There were few banks in Appalachia. The local merchant, the country store manager, was important to the barter system, but much trading occurred family to family.

Pride and self-sufficiency emerged as cornerstone values of mountain peoples. The relationships mountain people shared among themselves and with their land provided a culture and lifestyle marked not by material wealth but by familial and community relationships, consistency, simplicity, and tranquility.

While the foundries of Pittsburgh, Richmond, Cincinnati, Cleveland, and other cities surrounding The Spine of the Virginias produced manufactured goods and monetary wealth, Appalachia remained isolated, ideologically and economically. The need for armaments and other manufactured goods figuratively exploded during the Civil War. The Industrial Revolution reached deeply into the Appalachian Mountains, turning former farming areas into mine camps, mill towns, and factory towns in some cases almost overnight.

The Appalachian ethos fostered an innocence and vulnerability to the rapid changes that would sweep much of the region in the latter nineteenth and early twentieth centuries. The agrarian, subsistence culture of Appalachia was threatened by the exploitive, materialistic wave of industrialization. The adaptations and concomitant conflicts, struggles, and ethical dilemmas placed upon mountaineers, both individually and collectively, still play themselves out to this day and are cornerstone themes of this book.

Stuart McGehee
Bluefield

A few weeks later, Bud Robertson and I were together again, this time on our way to Bluefield to meet with Stuart McGehee. I carried a book on West Virginia history called *West Virginia Stories and Biographies*, copyright 1937, by Charles Henry Ambler. The friend who loaned it to me said it was the definitive textbook in West Virginia high schools during the 1950s and 1960s.

Stuart's office is on the upstairs floor of the Bluefield Public Library building, the home of the Eastern Regional Coal Archives, of which Stuart was curator. Stuart is a tall man with a mop of dark hair.

McGehee said the textbook I was carrying can be credited for what is considered the official version of the formation of the State of West Virginia. "According to Ambler, the evil slave-owning, east-dominated Virginia state government placed the burden of taxation on the noble anti-slavery man of the west." McGehee explained Ambler was chairman of the history department at West Virginia University in Morgantown during the early 20th century. According to Ambler, the western counties that became West Virginia ostensibly railed against this oppression and formed their own state.

"You must understand," he continued, "this stuff was written around the turn of the 20th Century when there were still people alive who had participated in West Virginia statehood. The official story needed to be sanitized for them." Ambler's original work, written about 1910, Sectionalism in Virginia 1776 to 1863, formed the basis for his later work, including this textbook.

"Virginia after Fort Sumter was enthusiastic in its embrace of secession. This included even the Ohio Valley people, where the Confederacy did extensive recruiting. When the War broke out, Congress was not in session. Lincoln did not call it into session until July 4th, after which all the decisions had already been made, fatefully. Fort Sumter was attacked on April 12th. So Lincoln, acting as commander-in-chief, ordered the militias of the Northern states to be sworn in and mustered into service for the federal government.

"Lincoln and his military advisors wanted to protect the B&O Railroad. It was the only way to get troops supplied from the west. So the first action of any consequence of the Civil War was 20,000 Union troops pouring across the Ohio River at Parkersburg to protect the B&O Railroad and its corridor. And that pretty much was the last military action in what became West Virginia."

McGehee said there is a lot of romance about cavalry raids and guerrilla warfare, but the only military objective of any consequence was to protect the B&O Railroad, the only railroad in western Virginia during the War.

"So the Union troops came in and built a screen to protect the railroad. Safely behind Union lines, the political leaders in Wheeling had long been clamoring for a variety of political and economic reforms from the state government in Richmond. There were no elections held. These people simply gathered in Wheeling and expressed their Union sentiments and said, if the elected representatives of the state of Virginia didn't want to do it, they would do it for them. These men were inordinately connected economically and politically with the B&O Railroad. They began to act.

"They first declared themselves to be the legitimate government of Virginia, the entire state. The object of the game at that stage was not to split but to simply represent the entire state apart from the 'renegade' government down in Richmond. They knew they couldn't form another state. The Constitution of the United States says that you can't form a state from another state without the permission of the state legislature involved. The way to become a state is to first become territory and submit a territorial constitution. The president then appoints a territorial governor. The territory then submits a draft constitution."

At this point, there were two governments claiming to represent Virginia, one aligned with the Confederacy and one with the Union.

"They asked to be recognized as the restored, reorganized government. Lincoln was no fool. He had a shaky Republican majority even though the Southern Democrats had left Congress. So he promptly, with the blessing of his congressional handlers, admitted the western Virginia leaders as the legitimate government of Virginia. By acclamation, that gave Lincoln two more Republican senators and two more congressional representatives. The governor of [this restored government of] Virginia, Francis Pierpont, moved to Alexandria after allowing the people in Wheeling to be the state's official legislators.

"Shortly thereafter, the people in Wheeling proceeded to give themselves the authority to form a new state. And they held elections behind Union lines. There were no elections at all held in the southern part of the state, because the Confederates held the New, Tug, and Bluestone River valleys.

"Lincoln didn't heartily approve this. He asked the six members of his cabinet. They split three-to-three. The votes in the House and in the Senate were close because many people feared the precedent of allowing a state to subdivide itself. Many people doubted the constitutional legality. I believe Lincoln's moral purpose for fighting the war was preservation of the Constitution. If Lincoln was fighting a war to preserve the Constitution, he couldn't simply ignore it because he disagreed with the results of an election.

"Finally, he signed the bill. What we see in West Virginia is the only successful example of secession in American history. And Lincoln fought the War because he denied the right of secession! He said to the postmaster, Montgomery Blair, 'This is secession and secession is wrong. While I say secession in favor of the Constitution has got to be more significant than secession against the Constitution, I'm going to sign the bill.' (The new representatives) purported to be representing this entire section [including what became southern and eastern West Virginia] although no elections had been held, and no delegates went to these conventions. It must be said that calling them delegates dignifies the process greatly, because the delegates were self-selected. [The state-makers] put calls in newspapers to those who wanted to come. Two types of people were greatly overrepresented: attorneys and Methodist circuit riders.

"It's often called the Methodist Revolution. Both [attorneys and preachers] rode circuit because the area wasn't populated enough [to employ permanent ministers or lawyers]. The only people who knew a lot of people were those who got around. Those were also the people who had sufficient resources to go to Wheeling. The only people who attended were from behind Union lines, north of the B&O Railroad."

McGehee explained that the representatives were sympathetic to the Union cause, wealthy enough to travel, and sufficiently protected by Union presence to attend. The counties in the southern and eastern part of what is now West Virginia didn't attend because they were generally sympathetic to the Confederate cause and lacked the wherewithal to go. No county along The Spine of the Virginias sent delegates except a single delegate from Hampshire County. McGehee felt that had any Spine counties had elections, all would have disapproved of the new state and would not have wanted to be included in it.

"When the state-makers originally decided to form a state, they were going to call it 'Kanawha,' and the original boundary was relatively fair. It was to include the Ohio Valley and the Monongahela Valley. These were places that had legitimate concerns. The Ways and Means Committee in Congress drew the final map, and nobody knows (how or why they picked the counties they did). They didn't keep minutes or records."

A handful of Congressman sat in a closed-door room looking at a map of the state of Virginia, picking and choosing the counties they wanted to include in the new state. McGehee explained that the state-makers had several conflicting objectives regarding the counties they chose for the new state. They needed defensible borders, because, when the decisions were being made, the outcome of the war was uncertain. They didn't want to include too many southern-leaning counties because of the inevitable shift in political power towards them after the war. When the people in these southern counties learned what was going on in Wheeling, many were appalled. "They hated it! During the war, places like Princeton recruited company after company to the Confederate Army and nobody for the Union.

"All these counties were dragged into a new state against their will. People didn't even know about it in remote areas for weeks. Consider a soldier who fought with the Seventh Virginia Infantry at Gettysburg, mustered out at Appomattox. He returned home to the family homestead but found himself returning to another state.

"A few years later, when the War was over, the guys in Wheeling looked in horror at the shape and population of the state. They were like, 'Oh my God! A fair election would overturn everything we've done.' Jefferson and Berkeley Counties sued for re-admission into Virginia after the Civil War. In 1871 in a Supreme Court case, they were denied readmission into Virginia. By this time the Supreme Court was packed with Lincoln appointees. They were not going to allow that to happen."*

McGehee continued, "The guys in Wheeling knew that they couldn't control the new state because the state had so many Southern and Confederate sympathizers. So they enacted strict voter registration disenfranchisement prescription laws. This was not illegal, as the Constitution says states determine who gets to vote. So for five or six years they held onto their creation [politically] by denying the vote to anybody who served in the Confederate Army.

"As soon as the vote was restored to all men [in 1870], immediately both houses of the state legislature were all Confederates. For the next 30 years, only candidates from the Confederate counties won state offices. They moved the capital to Charleston, indicating the political power shift towards the Confederate counties. They put a statue of Stonewall Jackson on the Capital lawn, a man who never set foot in West Virginia [because he died before statehood was achieved] and

- *Weeks later, I read a book by Michael F. Doran, called, *Atlas of County Boundary Changes in Virginia 1634–1895*. Doran wrote, Because the Confederacy lost its bid to establish a separate federal union, the objections of the occupied eastern Virginians to the loss of western counties were ineffectual and eventually abandoned. In 1866, during the earliest phases of Reconstruction, two last Virginia counties at the lower end of the Shenandoah Valley were transferred to West Virginia despite the fact that they had opted with Confederate Virginia during the war. This transfer was effected by the Federal Government so that the strategic lower Shenandoah would not return to a former secessionist state's control, on the bare chance that there might be a future need by pro-union forces for that area to be securely in hand. This transfer was again objected to weakly but without success. [2]

fought against it. Another statue on the state of West Virginia Capitol lawn is entitled "Lincoln walks at midnight." Lincoln has his head bowed, and he is presumably contemplating whether to sign the bill [allowing creation of the state]. It is significant that the statues, and the capital itself, are in Charleston and not in Wheeling.

"These returning Confederates also set about rewriting the West Virginia State Constitution. The Constitution that the state-makers adopted in Wheeling was progressive, dealing with and correcting all the problems from the Virginia Constitution. It was overturned by the former Confederates, and it has never been rewritten since then. The political backwardness and economic stagnation of West Virginia has its roots in the Civil War and in Reconstruction.

"The technology to access the coal reserves in southern West Virginia was developed during the Civil War. Soon after the War, the C&O (Chesapeake and Ohio) Railroad built lines in from the west and the N&W (Norfolk and Western) built a line in from the east to service the coal mining areas."

The mineral resource companies set about obtaining mineral rights to the land. Often these companies were subsidiaries or were otherwise affiliated with the railroad companies. Today, more than 50 percent of West Virginia's total land — and significantly more in the coalfields — is owned by absentee corporations.

McGehee continued, referring to the Ambler version of West Virginia's history, "First of all let me say that historical facts have no meaning. Placing them into context and interpreting them is what historians do. I'll accept anybody's challenge to my interpretation, but the story in Ambler's textbook is quite different. And the reason is complex because it gets to the nature of history and why we study the past.

"The argument persists that in loyalty to Lincoln, the martyred hero, and the Union, and in opposition to slavery, the evil of human bondage, a new state was created, born in freedom and patriotism. Ambler doesn't tell at all the story of Reconstruction or the long-term ramifications of West Virginia having a constitution rooted in Virginia's 1851 convention while rapid forces of industrialization were seizing control of its valuable natural resources. West Virginia is richly endowed with natural resources. Few native West Virginians profited from the incredible industrialization that occurred rapidly after the Civil War, as soon as the technology could get to it.

"Anyway, Ambler and his successors built this edifice of patriotism, pride, and anti-slavery that just won't move. They wrote biographies of the state-makers that painted them as brave patriots, not as shrewd railroad lawyers. And it raises the disquieting question of why we study history. Do we teach history so that people will take pride in the state of West Virginia? Or do we teach history to find out what happened in the past in order to understand the present and shape a brighter future?

"The facts are so clear and are manifested in so many ways. What is unique about my assault [on Ambler's interpretation] is that I've tied West Virginia's current poverty — economically, politically, and socially — back to the statehood movement and the reconstruction processes that created the state constitution. But that's not fun and sexy. John Brown's gang's raid on Harpers Ferry, now that's sexy.

"Once Lincoln was assassinated and the country began to turn its back on his idealism about race and American morals, nobody was going to question West Virginia statehood. There were more serious issues of Reconstruction that needed to be addressed.

"The returning Confederate soldiers were disenfranchised in the new state unless they signed an oath of loyalty to the reunited nation. Once these Confederates got the right to vote in 1870, West Virginia was again, in its thinking, a Confederate state. Many of these new legislators wanted West Virginia to rejoin Virginia. They wanted what they called 'Restoration,' restoring the former boundaries of the state of Virginia. The Supreme Court would not let them.

"The ordinance of October 1861, passed by the voters which created West Virginia, included the watersheds of the Big Sandy, Guyandot, Coal, Elk, and Gauley rivers to the original Ohio River and Kanawha River Valleys, reaching a total of 39 counties. Finally, the Constitutional Convention decided to take 11 more, reaching an even 50, including Mercer, McDowell, Summers, Monroe, Greenbrier, and Pocahontas. [West Virginia's current count of 55 includes 5 counties carved from the original 50.] These seemed to provide a nice, rounded border suitable to the Kanawha delegates. However, the Unionists around Wheeling would not have wanted these counties because they recognized that if these counties were to be included in the state, they, the Unionists, would lose their majority and power in the new state legislature. The inclusion of these counties has affected the policies of statehood ever since. These southern counties dominated state government all the way through the end of the 19th century.

"As far as I know, the House Ways and Means Committee simply took out a map of Virginia and pointed at it, selecting each county they wanted for the new state. When they returned that to the people in Wheeling who had applied for statehood, [the Wheeling people] said, 'Oh fuck!' The plan was to have a modern industrial-styled constitution in the Ohio Valley to oversee the economic modernization of that area. Instead, they got a big hunk of southern Appalachia that soon dominated them politically.

"The foundation of the state of West Virginia wasn't that long ago. The creation of West Virginia is a story that people have told me their grandparents remembered. I have met people who are living on land that was divided up and mostly stolen away from them at the end of the Civil War. What happened 150 years ago is still a part of the lives of people along The Spine of the Virginias today. It ain't over.

"My bottom line is that in this part of the country, we are all still prisoners of the Civil War. Reconstruction determined the politics of West Virginia, and we are still living the legacy today. To create pride in this state, historians who came before me created an historical myth. To a certain extent, all history is a myth. But this one has been particularly toxic because it has prevented social change."

I asked Stuart what he would do if he had a magic wand to set things right.

"We would still be West Virginia, but we would immediately call for a new state constitutional convention. We would build a new state government that is specifically designed for the state as it is now, which is rich in natural resources, fraught with transportation problems due to the difficult topography, landlocked, and without much publicly owned land. We would reevaluate the way land is assessed and taxed in an equitable and fair way. [Instead of] being the equivalent of the Congo, a place to exploit for its resources and labor, we would model it after Switzerland where the symbol of mountains is not of poor hillbillies but is of the people of Mount Olympus.

"I don't have any problem with West Virginians staying West Virginians, but we need to view ourselves, behave, tax, and educate ourselves differently. Everything relates back to the Civil War."

Civil War

As Bud and I drove home, my head swam. I neither profess nor pretend to be a historian nor do I disparage or criticize the work of historians. But I began to wonder…

Is the Stuart McGehee version of the creation of the state of West Virginia the final word? It seems unlikely. Several aspects of what he said are intensely controversial. Did the West Virginia statemakers have the legitimate right to form a new state? The federal government, all three branches, said yes. Therefore the answer is yes. The Union, in winning the War, crystallized that legitimacy. Should Virginia's Confederacy-aligned government have had a right to participate in the question of a new state if it chose to leave the Union? If leaving the Union was a traitorous act itself, didn't Virginia abdicate any rights it may have to the Western counties? Slavery was blatantly counter to the Declaration of Independence, yet Virginia persisted in allowing it for decades prior to the war. The West Virginia statemakers were assuming the moral high ground in righting that eternal wrong. My conclusion is that during the War, there was ample constitutional illegitimacy on both sides with the final determination set by the winner, the Union.

McGehee asserted the statemakers were "inordinately connected economically and politically with the B&O Railroad." To what degree was this true? This remains a contentious battle amongst some historians today.

History is first written by the triumphant. Then it is re-written time and time again as societies and social mores evolve. Hyperbole, spin, and civic pride all enter into the equation. Every adult in America watched coverage on television on September 11, 2001 as the World Trade Center towers collapsed as a result of impact from jetliners. But opinion polls have shown that literally millions do not believe the official government commission report on how it happened. How can we expect to have a clear consensus on events that transpired nearly a century and a half ago?

Perhaps if history is written by the winners, memory is dominated by the losers. Those of us who played sports in high school always remember the losses with better clarity than the wins. I'm confident much of what I've reported here will be challenged. The definitive word on historical events can never be unequivocally written. For many, the wounds are still fresh.

These things are undeniable: Virginia had been split in loyalty, with pockets of Union sympathy amidst a generally Confederate state. There were Confederates all the way into the Ohio River Valley counties just as there were Union sympathizers in the counties that stayed in Virginia. There was not a collective uprising in the counties of present-day West Virginia in support of the Union. The Greenbrier Valley, for example, was strongly Confederate, yet it was taken by the statemakers into West Virginia.

The economy across the entire state of Virginia prior to the War was interdependent. There were slave-owning plantations in the Ohio River Valley in what became West Virginia. There were poor mountaineers in the hollows of the Appalachians east of the Spine, including the Blue Ridge. Stuart proffered the inclusion of the Spine counties of McDowell, Mercer, Monroe, Greenbrier, and Pocahontas was made to achieve a nice, rounded border, but this is likely an incomplete answer. Perhaps the statemakers were learning about the incredible natural resources these counties possessed. If the War were to end in stalemate, these counties could have been bargaining chips in a negotiated armistice. The plebiscite was held under wartime conditions with many eligible voters away on the battlefield and extensive intimidation at the polls. The results, as an indication of true public sentiment, can never be definitively assessed.

It seems unlikely that in 1861 most of the people in the West Virginia counties in the Spine wanted to be in the new state. Even today, many proud Mountaineers look to the east for commerce and identity. Many admitted to me they would be happier if the Virginias were to reunify. This area had then and has today significant Confederate leanings, thus the Confederate monument in Union and the widespread display of Confederate flags. In that regard, political lines drawn over a landscape and color-coded areas on maps in history books are irrelevant.

What is relevant is that political lines affect policy and policy affects economies and lifestyles. From relatively inconsequential issues, like alcoholic beverage laws to substantial issues of taxation and economic development, differences across the state line have benefited Virginians relative to West Virginians with regards to the ability to seek prosperity. For this reason as well, the Civil War really isn't over.

The Civil War was injurious in more ways than we can count, but here's a start:

- Many of the region's able-bodied men either never returned or were incapacitated to the point where they were a liability rather than an asset to their families.
- Many simmering animosities remained and plagued individuals and families for generations to follow.
- Much public infrastructure was destroyed.

But the two most profound impacts that would lay the course of history along The Spine of the Virginias were these:

- Many soldiers, commanders, and surveyors became familiar with the remote regions and wilderness areas and were able to gauge the stores of timber, iron ore, and coal therein,
- The War spawned a thirst for these kinds of raw materials never before known.

The arrival of industrialism into an area previously agrarian, self-sufficient, and independent would change the area forever. In the decades following the Civil War, The Spine of the Virginias was on the cusp of an era of exploitation and development to such an astonishing degree that the fallout still haunts descendents of hapless mountaineers today. The Appalachians presented an irresistible wealth of resources unique in their extreme value, proximity to burgeoning markets, and inexpensive procurement. Many factors conspired to make existing residents vulnerable to abuse and exploitation.

Industrialists, journalists, and politicians began to publicize and foster development in the mountains. Enormous stands of virgin timber and vast coal seams were known in colonial days. But prior to the War, there was neither means for their removal from remote areas nor demand for them in the marketplace. After the War, the area was depressed. Mountain people longed for the betterment of their standards of living. In a vivid example of what in contemporary language is termed "public-private partnerships," government agencies collaborated with and monetarily assisted industry to survey and catalog natural resources to entice buyers and investment. In an unprecedented effort to foster economic development, creative incentives were made to lure immigrants and capital to the region. The state's leaders who were encouraging development were unmoved by the stresses on the people or the natural environment caused by that same development.

Private speculators were first to arrive on the scene. Hospitable mountaineers generally greeted them warmly. The guest was often invited to a family dinner, even asked to share accommodations for the night. The buyer would offer cash, a rifle, or some other item of value, to the landowner for the mineral or timber rights to a selected spot of land or in some cases to the entirety of the resident's tract. With cash so scarce, these offers were difficult to resist. The landowner was invariably the loser. The negotiated rights were usually for the minerals under the land only, which left the tax liability to the owner. The scope and scale of exploitation were unfathomable to the owner, having never experienced the insatiability of the emerging industrial infrastructure. Buyers routinely won disputes because the owners had limited knowledge of the law and limited access to legal help.

As a result, billions of dollars of wealth transferred from the hands of residents into those of distant investors and corporations. Mountaineers consistently devalued their land. Ownership of a watershed of a small stream, for example, never precluded common usage among the residents of the area. Cash-poor mountaineers could not fathom the enormous wealth beneath their feet, nor the utter destruction the removal of timber or minerals would entail in the loss of wildlife, the pollution of the waters, and the spoilage of the air. Entire mountains rich in coal were known to have been sold for a horse, a mule, or some other item of temporal value.

The independence of the mountaineers acted to their detriment, as few efforts were made to organize citizens to resist the onslaught. The cornerstone of their independence, the land, was being transferred away.

Although some riches were locally held, most fell to outside control. Along with the transfer of land ownership, the transfer of power to control the region's economy left local hands and landed upon the conference tables of Pittsburgh, Philadelphia, and Richmond corporations. So egregious was the transfer that a West Virginia Tax Commission Report of 1884 asked, "… whether this vast wealth shall belong to persons who live here and who are permanently identified with the future of West Virginia, or whether it shall pass into the hands of persons who do not live here and who care nothing for our State except to pocket the treasures which lie buried in our hills." [3]

This exploitation would not have been possible without the railroad. The iron horse's impact embodied the power and energy of the emerging economy. It became, and to some degree remains, a symbol of industrial might. The Civil War gave dramatic evidence of the railroad's importance in its ability to move huge amounts of materiel and troops.

The first rail to cross The Spine of the Virginias was part of the Chesapeake and Ohio's link to the grand transcontinental railroad. Built in the early 1870s, this line left the east-flowing James River watershed near Covington, tunneled into West Virginia under Allegheny Mountain, then along the west-flowing Greenbrier River near Caldwell to its confluence with the north-flowing New River near Hinton. The populations of the communities adjacent to the railroad — Covington, Clifton Forge, White Sulphur Springs, Ronceverte, Hinton, and Thurmond — grew more than 60 percent in a decade.

The exploitation of timber or mineral resources could not occur efficiently without the proximity of the railroad. In many other areas of the nation, navigable watercourses made barge conveyance of heavy minerals more cost effective than rail. But the area along The Spine of the Virginias was almost bereft of navigable waterways. So, encouraging railroad development into previously untrammeled areas was as important to speculators as the acquisition of mineral rights themselves.

After the Civil War, the C&O began expanding its reach into south-central West Virginia, while the Norfolk and Western branched from its main line northward along the banks of the New River and into Bluefield and Pocahontas, to what quickly became the nation's richest and most productive coalfield. The ensuing rush of trading, speculation, and development would rival the gold rushes of California and the Yukon.

By 1888, a 3,100-foot tunnel under Flat Top Mountain opened access to the McDowell County coalfields, rapidly transforming it into the most productive county in the state. This formerly sparsely settled county of deep hollows and rushing streams increased in population from 1890 to 1900 by an incredible 600 percent! In the following decade, McDowell County absorbed 30,000 new residents, housed densely in its tight confines, forming scores of tiny, intensely urban environments. The history of the transfer of ownership of McDowell County, as well as many neighboring counties, from the hands of a few hundred homesteaders into enormous land companies is unprecedented.

After historians Bud Robertson and Stuart McGehee set the stage for my understanding of the creation of West Virginia from Virginia, I began my journey of discovery into the people and culture, working from northeast to south-west.

Part 2
Thoracic

Watersheds of the Potomac and Shenandoah Rivers
Counties of Frederick, Hampshire, Shenandoah, Hardy,
Rockingham, Pendleton, and a smidgen of Highland

"Appalachia," once a specialized term used by geologists, became a
code word that summed up all things that made West Virginia different
from the rest of the nation, the good things as well as the bad.[4]

— John Alexander Williams, historian

It always rains on tents. Rainstorms will travel thousands of miles,
against prevailing winds, for the opportunity to rain on a tent.[5]

— Dave Barry, comic

Spring

M.G. and I left my house on our motorcycles on a chilly early spring morning under an uncertain sky. We headed northward and entered Giles County. Our destination was Cacapon State Park, at the northeastern tip of The Spine of the Virginias.

M.G. are the initials of Mike Gunther, my friend and frequent riding partner. He came to Southwest Virginia in the late 1960s to attend school at Virginia Tech, and he never left. He's polite, thoughtful, and even-tempered: a great traveling companion.

After cresting Gap Mountain, we descended into tiny Newport, a village that once hosted a bank, a general store, and a service station. The bank is long gone, its vault moved into a museum in Pearisburg. The post office is now in a modern building up the hill near the highway, beside the convenience store.

The village is pretty, with nice houses and a white-framed church with an impressive steeple. Yellow daffodils bloomed in the churchyard. The grass was an eager brilliant emerald, having turned from the bleached gold of winter just a week before. The Bartlett pear trees were white. The leaves of the hardwood trees of the forests still slumbered.

The Sinking Creek valley runs from the east-northeast, like a long, slender finger. It is two or three miles wide for most of its 25-mile length, but never truly flat. In a region known for lovely valleys, Sinking Creek valley is among the loveliest. New homes in log and clapboard coexist with older homes mostly in brick. An abandoned farmhouse near Huffman has a full wrap-around porch and intricate trim. The road that traverses the valley, SR-42, flows with the land as gracefully as a calligrapher's pen over parchment. Sinking Creek, running fast and clear, is a New River tributary, draining three-quarters of the valley to the southwest. The northwest quarter is drained by Meadow Creek, which flows northeastward to the James River. This is part of the Great Eastern

Divide, separating Atlantic from Gulf of Mexico waters.

As we descended dramatically into New Castle, I was on full attention alert, because handling a high-powered motorcycle on this twisty road required all my faculties.

New Castle is timeless and picturesque. There are several fine houses in town, remnants of an era when the economy was more favorable to smaller communities. The courthouse on the block-long Main Street was built in 1852.

M.G. and I turned north on SR-311 towards Potts Mountain. The road ascended in broad, graceful turns. Our speed was brisk and riding was fun! Mountains in the distance on the left were backlit and dark against the horizon. No other vehicles were around. In Paint Bank, we stopped briefly for gas. We rode SR-18 northwards towards Covington. Sun breaks illuminated fresh grass and blossoms.

As we passed a man with a chainsaw, slicing a log, the scent of pine permeated the air. A flicker fled into the woods, his white rump flashing above the yellow of his under-wings.

On the approach to the city of Covington, clapboard homes of working-class people lined the road. Plastic toys and swing sets revealed the homes with children. The Westvaco paper mill came in sight to our left. It produced a pungent, disagreeable smell.

We continued northward from Covington and ascended past Falling Spring Falls into the exquisite Falling Springs Valley, a high-elevation valley sandwiched between Warm Springs Mountain to the east and Little Mountain to the west. Across the Bath County line, manicured golf courses and lawns flanked the road. We drove past the magnificent resort of The Homestead, with its 12-story grand hotel.

Five miles later, we passed the Jefferson Pools. Here, crystal clear 98°F water is piped into two gender-specific octagonal wooden structures. The men's pool hous, constructed in 1761, is the oldest spa structure in America. Thomas Jefferson reputedly visited in 1818.

M.G. and I continued northward on US-220 through Monterey and crossed into West Virginia. The road paralleled the South Branch of the Potomac River. In various places, fishermen tried their luck in the swift-running water. Two deer crossed the road. Sometimes the valley was tight, pinching the road against the riverbank. Other times it was wider than a football field. There was emerald grass by the road, brown fields, and bare forests. Buzzards circled in the air.

We drove through quaint Franklin, the seat of Pendleton County. Franklin has nice homes lining Main Street, plus an active downtown, something too rare these days. We waited for the traffic light at the intersection of US-220 and US-33, the only light in Pendleton County.

After Petersburg, with its food processing plants and tractor-trailers, we entered a lightly-traveled four-lane superhighway, "Corridor H," that had deep cuts into the mountains and crossed long and high curving bridges. Signs proclaimed "Bike Route," but there were no bicycles to be seen on this bitter, windswept day. We exited the highway at Baker and took SR-259 North into Virginia. For a few miles, the road hugs the ridgeline that separates the two states, with Virginia on the right and West Virginia on the left.

We re-entered Virginia and found our destination, the lodge at Cacapon State Park. After I checked us into the lodge, we got back on our bikes and rode to the lookout at the top of the mountain. The access road angled up without a curve or switchback. The forest, still bare of leaves, had thousands of downed trees, perhaps the remnants of a winter windstorm. At the top were two impressive communication towers, one with large, gourd-shaped antennae in each of the four corners.

Cacapon Mountain is unimpressive by the standards of Craig, Allegheny, Bath and Highland counties, but there is a sweeping view to the east. Sporadic settlements dotted the valley. A few clouds cast dark shadows on the valley. Visibility was good in the clear air. Being at the northern extreme of The Spine of the Virginias, most of our view was of West Virginia.

Mike Gunther on Cacapon Mountain

West Virginia

HAMPSHIRE

FREDERICK

🏛
Winchester

HARDY

Middletown
.

SHENANDOAH

Virginia

Frederick County, Virginia

Frederick is Virginia's northernmost county. It is the lowest in overall elevation of The Spine of the Virginias counties. Most of the county is in the relatively flat lower Shenandoah Valley. The far northwestern corner straddles Cacapon Mountain. Great North Mountain is in the southwest, but the county loses elevation rapidly.

Frederick County has 416 square miles.

The city of Winchester is wholly within the county and is the county seat, although as a city it has an independent government. Incorporated towns include Stephens City and Middletown.

Population

Frederick County's population including Winchester has steadily increased over the last century, from 18,000 in 1900 to 96,000 now, making it The Spine of the Virginias' second-most populous county.

Institutions of higher education

Lord Fairfax [Middletown] Community College is in Frederick County. Shenandoah University is in Winchester.

Traffic

Frederick County has many miles of four-lane roads, among them 23 miles on Interstate 81, the busiest highway along The Spine of the Virginias. Traffic is typically heavy, and there are dozens and dozens of traffic lights.

Today's...

Frederick County, once known for its apple production, has in recent decades seen a diversification that includes tourism, industry, health care, and transportation. The influence of Washington, D.C., is increasing because of commuters and weekend visitors.

Attractions

- Abram's Delight, Winchester. Built in 1754, the oldest home in the county.
- State Arboretum of Virginia Museum, Boyce.
- Belle Grove Plantation, Middletown.
- George Washington's Office Museum, Winchester. Once Washington's log cabin office.
- Museum of the Shenandoah Valley, Winchester. Regional history complex featuring furniture, arts, paintings, and artifacts.
- Old Court House Civil War Museum, Winchester. Located in 1840 courthouse.

Thomas T. Byrd
Winchester

My journey to become acquainted with Virginia's northernmost county led me to the office of the Winchester Star and to one of Virginia's most influential political dynasties.

The Star, a daily newspaper, was started on the Fourth of July, 1896, by 23-year old John I. Sloat. The Star's first edition covered the nation's gala 120th birthday celebration. The newspaper reported that many Confederate veterans were in attendance in a crowd of 10,000 people, double the town's population.

In October 1897, lawyer Richard Evelyn Byrd bought The Star. Byrd was from one of Virginia's first and most notable families, tracing its ancestry to the earliest days of English settlement. His ancestry included William Byrd and the Powhatan Indian, Pocahontas. The Byrds to follow, Harry Sr., Harry Jr., and Thomas, provided a line of succession that continues to this day.

Richard "Dick" Byrd was reputed to be a better lawyer and editorialist than businessman. Within six years of his purchase of the paper, it was in dire financial straits. Dick's son, Harry Flood Byrd, 15 years old at the time, convinced his parents that he should quit school to resuscitate the flagging newspaper. Showing a business acumen his father lacked, Harry returned The Star to solvency within two years. This experience molded Harry's aversion to debt that continued throughout his life. And because he became a powerful leader in Virginia, his philosophy has influenced his state ever since.

Youthful and ambitious Harry was not content with merely running a newspaper. By his late twenties Harry owned interests in the fledgling local telephone company, the local turnpike company which owned what became U.S. 11 up-valley to Staunton, other newspapers, and several apple orchards.

Meanwhile, Harry was bitten by the politics bug. By 1915, when he'd turned 28 years old, he had been elected to the Virginia Senate. Ten years later, he was governor. His pay-as-you-go fiscal policy was his hallmark. The state, still burdened by Civil War debt sixty years after the war ended at Appomattox, adopted a policy wherein new public works projects would only be started when state coffers had money on hand to fund them.

After serving as governor, Harry was elected to the United States Senate from Virginia, a post he held from 1933 until 1955. His fiscal and social conservatism continues to influence the national political environment.

Harry and his wife had two children. The first, Harry Jr., inherited his father's political aspirations. After serving as a state senator from 1948 until 1965, Harry Jr. was appointed to succeed his father when Harry Sr. retired for health reasons. Harry Jr. won his own election in 1966 as a Democrat, but left the party in 1970 when asked to sign a loyalty agreement, which he found distasteful. Harry Jr. was never seriously challenged and kept his Senate seat until he decided not to run again in 1983.

Like his father, Harry Jr. was fiscally disciplined. The era of Byrd leadership spanned a half-century and was so dominant that for decades it was described by supporters and opponents alike as "The Byrd Machine." All the while, both men continued to have a hand in running the Winchester Star and in particular, contributing to its editorial content. Byrd Jr. was chairman of the board until 1990.

Harry Jr.'s son Thomas Taylor Byrd worked in a number of departments of the newspaper as a young man. After serving in the Marine Corps in Vietnam and earning a degree from Lynchburg College, he began full time at The Star in 1971. Within ten years, he was publisher.

On a windy spring day, I walked the flat, rectangular grid of city streets in Winchester's historic and stately downtown. I strolled along the delightful pedestrian mall on Loudon Street, what the city has called "Historic Old Town Winchester." I crossed Cameron Street where the Federal army of General Nathanial Banks retreated from the aggressive advance of Stonewall Jackson in late May, 1862. Legend has it that Banks, believing Jackson would stop his advance at nightfall, began a hot bath at his headquarters in Winchester. The sound of gunfire roused him from his indolence and convinced him otherwise.

I entered a brick two-story office building, home of The Star. Thomas Byrd welcomed me in and told me about his family's rich history and the newspaper business. "One of my ancestors, Thomas Taylor Byrd, an offspring of William Byrd III, migrated across the Blue Ridge Mountains to the Shenandoah Valley. I believe I am in the 10th generation of the

Byrd family in Virginia. I have spent my entire life working in the newspaper business. I am the fourth generation, and my son, Tommy, is the fifth generation in this family business.

"In the 1960s, the city fathers wanted to diversify the economy because it was predominantely agriculture. So in the 1960s we started to develop industrial parks. They were successful and, through the years, they have been expanded. We are not deeply involved in smokestack industries but things like manufacturing of furniture, food cans, and lightbulbs. The politicians in the city of Winchester and in Frederick County which surrounds Winchester have worked closely together to build these parks and recruit these industries. That has provided diversity which has softened the blow of the economic downtimes. Agriculture has become less of an economic factor. Much of the real estate that once cultivated the production of apples is now in subdivisions and housing developments.

"Water is becoming a big issue. Both the city of Winchester and the County of Frederick use the Shenandoah River as their primary source. Will the river alone support the growth we expect? If not, will we be able to tap into other sources, such as deep wells?

"We are advocates of a diversified business community. We are advocates of less government intervention and as much creativeness as possible for free enterprise to thrive and be productive in the area. We have taken pro-positions on several potential incoming businesses where many of our readers have been opposed.

"Winchester is at a crossroads geographically. It is towards the northern end of the Shenandoah Valley and on the corridor of Interstate 81 which parallels U.S. Highway 11. These highways go through the entire state. Two main roads bring traffic from the east, Highways 50 and 7. Now we also have Interstate 66 that brings traffic from the east. Two roads extend to the west, Highways 50 and 522. We are at the hub at the center of a wheel. Winchester is only 70 miles west of Washington, D.C. We have great weather. We have a great mix of business and industry. We have good government and a good school system.

"The city and the county are working together to preserve green spaces and to build bicycle and walking paths. A new $10 million Discovery Museum will be made with environmentally friendly materials and green building techniques. We recycle here at the newspaper. The legislature has worked with our Press Association to increase the consumption of recycled paper. The city and county work collaboratively. The landfill, library system, water system, and sanitation system are joint efforts. We are trying to combine the recreational departments of the city and the county.

"Virginia is the only state that has independent cities and counties. Winchester is grateful for the leadership of the mayor and of the board of supervisors of the county working towards common objectives. The ultimate objective is to become one community, but I do not know whether that will occur or not. Winchester may at some point decide to revert to town status so there won't be two separate governments.

"Winchester is the oldest (English) city west of the Blue Ridge Mountains, dating back to 1752. Our city changed hands something like 72 times during the Civil War. Cedar Creek was the scene of an important battle in 1864. We have a strong organization working to preserve historic Winchester. The newspaper's building is in the preservation area. Battlefield preservation is a huge issue."

He said the nearness of West Virginia plays a role in economic development. "West Virginia's consumers are certainly welcome here. Winchester and Frederick County have benefited from the business that West Virginians have brought us.

"Our circulation includes about 1300 or 1400 customers in West Virginia. Many people from those areas come into Winchester to work or shop."

Jim Hammond
Lois Tate
Gainesboro

Tom Byrd represents a man and family of unparalleled responsibility and public profile. Looking for a yang to Tom's yin, I called on a couple of hermits. Jim Hammond and Lois Tate live in an underground house they designed and built themselves near Gainesboro. It is said that you know you live in West Virginia if the directions to your house include the phrase, "After you turn off the paved road..." This applies to the Hammond/Tate residence in the northwestern part of Frederick County.

Leaving Winchester, a series of turns took me onto increasingly narrower and rougher roads past old homes and new developments with designer names like Orchard View and Ravenwood.

As I drove down their long gravel driveway on a brisk, clear winter day, I saw a tiny log cabin to my right and a wooden outhouse on the left. Lois emerged from it and walked over to greet me. She explained the cabin was their first home on the property, but the underground house was where they now lived. With the driveway situated at a higher elevation than the house's roof, and it being covered with the same grass as the surrounding lawn, I hadn't even noticed it. As I entered and Jim began to tell me about his life, I scanned their living space, a combination living room, bedroom, kitchen, and library. Large windows were on the east and south walls, the tops adorned with stained glass panels. Heavy rectangular wooden beams held the roof.

Jim Hammond told me that he was protective of his privacy. In order to tell his story, he asked me to use pseudonyms for both he and Lois. These are not their real names.

Jim is from the Washington, D.C. area. He said, "I was an engineer, so I have been in the field of science all my life. In the late 1970s and early 1980s, city life became increasingly uncomfortable and unfriendly. I began to have urges to move towards something more real, not so crazy and competitive. When I decided to move to the country, I was in my 40s. I just walked away from my career, cold turkey. This was more than 20 years ago.

"Lois and I were in the war machine; another yuck factor. It was not right for either of us. Both of us were looking for an alternative life. She talked to me about her goals, and I talked to her about mine. Doing something like this alone is a whole lot tougher than doing it with a partner. I bought 30 acres. The price was reasonable in those days because I had to ford a creek to get here. It is steep and inaccessible. The inaccessibility was something I wanted. I wanted to be able to get away and not see any people."

Lois said, "We quit good jobs. We were careful and saved the money we'd need to make the move. We lived well below our means."

Jim said, "We wanted to be able to live with the least amount of money possible. We established a budget of $6,000 per year per person. For most years we've been here, we've stuck to that budget.

"When we began to develop this dream to move here, I began to learn about underground houses. These houses are cool in the summer without air conditioning. They are easier to heat in the winter because they are better insulated. We have a wood stove in the house, but it does not burn much wood. The north and west sides are sunk into the embankment, and the east and south sides are covered with double-pane windows to allow for optimal passive solar heating.

"We took a building class together to learn many of the techniques we would need. For an underground house which is covered by sod, the roof structure must be strong. It has an unusual type of construction."

They described the home in detail. The ceiling has large timber beams. Above that are several sandwiched layers of shingles, gravel, 6-mil black poly plastic sheeting in three alternating covers of sheeting and Styrofoam, and finally six inches or eight inches of dirt on top of that. The dirt supports vegetation. The walls are of poured cordwood construction, a technique that originated in northern New England and Canada about 150 years ago. Eight-inch logs were laid endwise and encased in mortar. Jim said building the house took longer than expected. "We thought it would take a few months, but it turned into years."

Lois said, "We have an outdoor composting privy. I have a laundry sink, and I wash our clothing by hand. I hang the clothes on a clothesline."

Jim said the neighbors are wonderful. "They are not standoffish. We felt immediately welcomed here. On our first drive out this way, we drove down a narrow, two-lane country road. Somebody in her yard waved at me as I drove by. That told me quite a bit about the culture. But we are still outsiders. They have roots that are deep and strong."

Lois described her lifestyle. "We grow a garden and raise most of our food. We can and freeze a significant amount of food. We are generally vegetarian. We are able to buy some grass-fed beef products, and we eat game if it is given to us."

Jim said, "I have never owned a gun. It has only been within the last few years that we've become comfortable with neighbors that have guns. Now that we've been here for decades, we see the rationale and the history of hunting.

"In moving here, our surplus time was a huge factor. What I began to see was that people can either put in their money or put in their time. We put our time into creating things, building houses, and growing food. Making the decision to do the latter changed my life dramatically because much of my time involved work that was drudgery. I spent hour after hour weeding the garden. I spent hours trimming the grass because I did not have a gas-powered lawnmower. The constant question about every household task was whether to buy a machine or find a way to do it by hand. We always tended to go the route of doing things by hand because it was cheaper and more sound ecologically. Cutting the grass with a lawnmower might take 20 minutes whereas cutting it with a scythe may take two hours.

"I found myself doing more intense thinking and re-evaluating my life. I asked myself the elemental questions, What is it that I am here to do? How am I paying rent on my space on this planet? That got me into the social justice movement, and it got both of us into searching for the spiritual meaning of existence."

Jim said he began to feel a kinship with the people who lived in this region 100 and 200 years ago. "They lived lives of integrity, honesty, and truth. They had a kinship with the land, a day-to-day existence that modern Americans have lost. How can we parallel that or get in touch with that today? We cannot go back to it. I have tried to put down on paper these thoughts in a way that is coherent and makes sense. Am I writing for someone else? Am I writing for my own development? I don't really have answers to these questions.

"I started a blog about six months ago. I began to realize it could be a good discipline for me. It is a good way to force myself to be succinct and coherent. It is an outlet for my feelings, especially about the social justice movement. The local newspaper is a mean-spirited, strongly right wing, hateful institution. I write frequent letters to the editor about social justice issues. What I often read in the editorial page of the Winchester Star will piss me off, get me going."

"So you are not as much of a hermit as you would make yourself sound," I noted.

He said, "There is an interesting dichotomy at work here. I e-mail frequently. I am on the Internet as much as two hours each day. I make a lot of communications. My hermit-ness is more of a physical thing."

West Virginia

Romney

HAMPSHIRE

Capon Bridge

FREDERICK

HARDY

Virginia

Hampshire County, West Virginia

Hampshire is the northernmost county along The Spine of the Virginias and is West Virginia's oldest.

It is characterized by three rivers, the Cacapon to the east, North River in mid-county, and the South Branch of the Potomac River to the west, all of which, along with several other smaller streams, flow north to the Potomac. A series of parallel ridges, large and small, mark the County. The valley supports the agricultural production of corn, poultry, cattle, and fruits.

Hampshire County has 584 square miles.

The city of Romney is the county seat. Capon Bridge is the only other incorporated town.

Population

After languishing at about 11,000 residents from 1870 until 1970, Hampshire County has doubled to approximately 22,000 since, primarily from influxes of urban escapees.

Institutions of higher education

Hampshire County has no colleges or universities.

Traffic

There are no four-lane roads in Hampshire County. The town of Romney has a few traffic lights.

Today's...

Hampshire County, like Hardy to the south, is beginning to see the influx of new, wealthy landowners.

Attractions

- Potomac Eagle, Romney, Scenic rail excursions
- Taggart Hall, Romney, Civil War Museum
- Davis History House, Romney, Civil War Museum
- Fort Edwards, Capon Bridge, Archeological site of early settlers and French and Indian War fort
- The Trough, Glebe, River gap
- Fort Mill Ridge, Romney, Civil War site

Tom Austin
Jonathan Bellingham
Capon Springs

I am always of a mind to put as much space between myself and interstate highways as possible. So after my journeys through Frederick County, I was ready to head for the hills. A friend had mentioned a hidden, quirky resort, Capon Springs, just across the border in West Virginia's Hampshire County. I called Tom Austin, one of the managers, to arrange a conversation. Before departure, I studied the waters of The Spine of the Virginias.

European immigrant settlement patterns followed the watersheds. As pioneers moved into the area, they found Indians had already established routes to the interior. The main transportation route through the Appalachian Virginias is northeast to southwest along the great Valley of Virginia. There were difficult problems getting further west because of the mountains. Generally the rivers run northwest to southeast, except the New River, which flows northward through the region, allowing travel into the interior.

The Potomac crosses the spine. But because of the ruggedness of the mountains to the west, crossing further and linking with the Mississippi system is difficult. The Potomac is more effective for travel from coastal plains to the highlands.

In the coastal plains of the eastern states, the Europeans built fall-line cities as coastal ports to allow access to the interior. These were the last places oceangoing ships could negotiate. Petersburg, Richmond, Washington, and Philadelphia are fall-line cities. In the earliest days, settlers used dugout canoes like those made by the Indians to transport raw materials.

Five brothers named Rucker were tobacco farmers in Amherst County, Virginia. In 1775 they recognized a need to transport large barrels called hogsheads of tobacco to the markets in Richmond, and they invented the James River bateau, a cross between a dugout canoe and a Venetian gondola. Bateaus were typically 56-feet long and were propelled by bateaumen pushing long poles. The hogsheads were 48 inches long and 30 inches in diameter and could hold 1000 pounds of tobacco. A typical bateau could transport up to ten hogsheads at a time.

With this new shipping technology, a river culture emerged. Many of the boatmen were trustworthy blacks, some buying their freedom. They built bateaus over the winter, loaded them, and took them down the rivers during the spring freshet (floods). They knocked the boats apart and sold the lumber. Then they walked home.

Bateaus were used on most of the Spine rivers. Later on, canals were built in strategic places along the rivers. The canals didn't get all the way to the Spine before the railroads took over. The River and Plantation Culture extended as far as the boats could go. Higher in the mountains, a Hill Culture took over.

The soil quality was as diverse as the watersheds, with a mix of limestone, shale, sandstone, quartzite, and metamorphic rocks. The smart Virginia or Pennsylvania big landowners settled on limestone because they understood its value to crops. They could literally pick up the soil and taste it and know if they were on good soil. If so, the farm would be successful and profitable. Poorer Irish and Scots immigrants had come from a situation in which they were unable to own land, so they felt privileged to be able to own any land.

Places of mixed geology have a tendency to produce springs, sinks, and caves. Cave fauna plays into the culture. The springs of the region issue from Oriskany sandstone and Helderberg limestone and emanate from fissures in the rock strata. Falling water enters permeable soils at high elevations and filters through the strata at outcroppings further downslope. The chemical composition of the water is a reflection of the type of rock through which it filters. The temperature is dictated by the rock temperature, with hotter waters emanating from deeper seams. The heating of the water varies from place to place because the geology is complex. The Spine region has world-class springs, pristine and clean, varying in temperature from 120°F to 70°F.

Several springs along The Spine of the Virginias became legendary resort spas because of the wonderful taste and/or mineral quality of the water. Well-heeled lowlanders flocked to the mountains each summer to escape oppressive heat, swarming clouds of mosquitoes, and unhealthy sanitary conditions and to "take the waters." Typically taking the waters meant sitting or bathing in it. Developers built bath houses, segregating the sexes. Early on bathers were nude. During the Victorian era, social mores dictated that clothing be worn. Businessmen used these visits to make deals and to oversee current operations. The resorts brought cash profits during the summer and closed over the winter. It was a valuable interaction with the outside world for people who lived in the mountains.

I arrived at Capon (pronounced "kay-pin") Springs on a cold, windy winter day. The road I took over the border and across Great North Mountain involves about three miles of dirt driving from Virginia and seems impossibly long. The resort was closed, but cousins Tom Austin and Jonathan Bellingham met me in the small office they share with other family members. The Main Building is large, with an expansive porch and lots of places to sit and relax. The lodge contains a spacious dining room where guests eat family style. There are spas, guest cottages, tennis courts, swimming pools, and a golf course.

Tom told me his grandparents bought the property of the former Capon Springs and Baths resort in 1932. Since then, his family's steward-ship has continued into three generations. "Their primary objective was to obtain the water rights to the spring itself. They ended up getting the resort with it, but they were primarily interested in the spring water."

Jonathan said, "Doctors prescribed spring water for various ailments. Capon Springs' water is known for its alkalinity. Most of the stresses that we take on in our lives increase the acidity of our bodily fluids. Because this water is alkaline, it helps to neutralize all that."

Tom said, "Most of our guests are from Virginia. From the stand-point of running a business, I believe that our location in West Virginia is a benefit because it gives us more of an exotic flavor."

Jonathan said, "The type of business we run would not be possible without the openness and friendliness of our coworkers. In an interest-ing way, they are much like our guests. Many of them have mothers or fathers who worked here and their grandmothers or grandfathers as well. There is that kind of legacy. Guests enjoy seeing the same workers year after year. The recipes the cooks use in the kitchen are passed down year after year. We have been fortunate to have found a great number of people who are friendly and who interact well with guests."

Tom said, "We will have weeks during the summer where upwards of 95 percent of the people who are staying here are exactly the same people who stayed here that week the year before. There is not just conti-nuity in the food, the schedule, and the coworkers; there is also a continuity of guests. It becomes a community."

Jonathan said, "It is a throwback to a kinder, gentler time where people were civil towards one another. People routinely watch out for other people's kids. Kids often drive the decision process in coming here. Many parents have told us they will give their kids an opportunity to choose between Disney World and Capon. The kids say, 'Oh, we are going to Capon.' I believe it is because of the freedom they have here."

Jonathan spoke about the familial responsibilities of owning such a special place. He said, "We did not choose to be born into this family. It is an intense privilege, but it comes with responsibilities. All of us take that seriously. Capon Springs does not belong to us; we belong to Capon Springs.

"The water is still the lifeblood of the resort. It is the connection that all of us who work or stay here have to this earth. Guests describe a feeling they get when they come through the gates. People become attuned to the spiritual quality of Capon. This is not just a family recreation place, it is a sacred place. Our remoteness helps to create a feeling of being separate from the outside world. There is something deeper here than meets the eye."

Robert Lee
Romney

Busy US-50 is the Main Street of Romney. There is plenty of traffic, including rumbling trucks. The Koolwink Motel is a charming, old-style family motel on the eastern edge of downtown. It was nicely maintained. My room had new bedding and carpet. It was opened as a tourist home in 1936 when Nora and Henry Klein rented rooms within their residence.

I spoke with Robert Lee, the proprietor. "My in-laws have been in the motel business for 53 years. I came to help them about 10 years ago.

"When my in-laws opened this motel, there really weren't many franchises at all. People built these little mom-and-pop motor lodges, as they called them back then, in just about every small town and city across the country. People were beginning to travel more in their own cars, and so this particular segment of the hospitality industry was born.

"We have been lucky enough to survive. We have been able to generate enough revenue to reinvest in the motel, to keep our rooms in good condition, to purchase high-quality furniture, and to maintain the grounds. Many mom-and-pop motels haven't been so lucky.

"Tonight we have 15 of our 24 rooms booked. With occupancy at 50 percent or better, we generate enough revenue to continue to invest in the motel. The best time of the year for us is summertime. And weekends are busy. We're almost always full on the holidays because more people are traveling. There is an excursion railroad here in Romney which brings lots of tourists to town. People come for family reunions. A number of our guests are looking for land to purchase. One of our guests is taking care of family matters. We get some business travelers. Also, hunting is big. The week of Thanksgiving begins rifle season, so we are typically full.

"It's always been an economically depressed community in that there have never been many jobs. If you wanted a decent job, you either had to go to Winchester or further to Washington, D.C. Winchester is 40 miles away, and Washington is 120. Some people actually make a regular commute to Washington, especially if they work in an outlying area like Leesburg or Manassas.

"You take it for what it is: rural. For several years I worked as a union painter in D.C. When I came back here I took a big cut in pay, but I like the rural aspect of it.

"Within the last three or four years, there has been an explosion in the sale of rural land. It seems like it is primarily people from D.C. or Baltimore or New Jersey who are coming to get away from the problems of urban life. Yet the first thing they ask is, 'Where is your Wal-Mart?' And I think to myself, 'Was there a Wal-Mart where you came from? Then go on back.' The people say they want to get away from the rat race but then they want to bring it with them. These people are putting up multimillion-dollar homes. That has increased land value and, of course, increased assessed values. My assessment went up 90 percent. I told the assessor, 'Frank, if John Henry wants to come up here from D.C. and pay $10,000 per acre and can pay the tax on it, fine. But I can't pay the tax if my land is assessed at $10,000 per acre.' I'm never selling it. They're going to bury me in the ground here.

"West Virginia is beautiful. I can't blame anybody for wanting to come here. But they have to recognize that we've been here for a long time, and we have pride in this area and what it offers. They need to leave their city mentality behind and not try to make this area more like what they left.

"People in Romney are of modest means and are self-reliant. More of them are growing their own food, hunting deer, and living off the grid. People stockpile food and supplies. When people go shopping, they make sure they get plenty of everything. With gasoline costing more, people make fewer trips and buy more with each trip.

"This used to be big orchard country. Most of these orchards have been sold off into lots. There are still a couple of old boys making money growing fruit, typically apples or peaches, but not many. There was an orchard out in Levels where I live. They probably grew 250,000 bushels of peaches a year. When it went out of business, lots of people lost their jobs."

Steve Dawson (l.) and friends serenade Main Street in Romney
on summer Friday evenings

Steve Dawson
Romney

On a pleasant spring evening, four men were playing traditional music on a guitar, a mandolin, a fiddle, and harmonicas in front of a downtown music store. When they stopped for the night, I spoke with one of the musicians, Steve Dawson, who ran the store, called Potomac Music.

"I was born here in Romney and lived here for much of my life. When I got out of school, I wanted to coach football. I was actually a pretty good athlete in football and track, if you can believe that. But coaching didn't work out. So I got a job working for the Welfare Department for about 15 years. After that I got a job with the Rehabilitation Services where I worked until my retirement. I'm 57 years old now. I retired two years ago.

"I opened up Potomac Music about twelve years ago. There are a lot of good musicians here in Hampshire County. Many of the older folks did music for entertainment when there was nothing else available, or they couldn't afford anything else. There are always parties and picnics going on where local people will play music. We have an incredible musical heritage.

"There was a time when you could sit out on that street and probably for ten or fifteen minutes you may not see a car. Nowadays the highway is busy. We often ask ourselves where the hell they are going, and what the hell they are carrying."

Shenandoah County, Virginia

Shenandoah County is a rough rectangle, with its longer axis running north-east to southwest. To the west are the Allegheny Mountains, with Great North Mountain predominant. To the east is the northern part of Massanutten Mountain, a fifty-mile long ridge which divides the expansive valley between the Alleghenies and the Blue Ridge Mountains. Down the center of the county is the North Fork of the Shenandoah River. A string of communities line the corridor from Strasburg in the extreme north to Toms Brook, Maurertown, Woodstock, Edinburg, Mt. Jackson, and New Market at the south.

There are 513 square miles.

Incorporated towns include Strasburg, Mount Jackson, Woodstock, New Market, Toms Brook, and Edinburg.

Population

Shenandoah County's population was 20,000 in 1900 and stayed essentially flat until 1970, after which it grew rapidly to today's 40,000.

Institutions of higher education

There are no universities or colleges in Shenandoah County.

Traffic

Shenandoah County has about 36 miles of Interstate 81, the busiest highway along The Spine of the Virginias. There are a handful of traffic lights throughout the county.

Today's...

Shenandoah County is the least populated county in the Shenandoah Valley. Most of the roads run north-south along with the Shenandoah River. The County is seeing the urban flight effect from Washington, D.C.

Attractions

- Crystal Caverns, Strasburg
- Museum of American Presidents, Strasburg
- Stonewall Jackson Museum, Strasburg
- New Market Battlefield State Historical Park, New Market
- Bryce Resort, Bryce, skiing and golf

Strasburg

In a valley that looks surprisingly linear on the map, the North Fork of the Shenandoah River makes a myriad of drunken bends as if in defiance, not wanting its picturesque and clean waters to be in any hurry to join the inexorable flow to the turgid Potomac estuary that is now our nation's capital. Lyrical and romantic, the Shenandoah is one of The Spine of the Virginias' most lovely rivers.

Strasburg has always been a strategically important transportation hub because of its location at the north end of 50-mile long Massanutten Mountain.

The Manassas Gap Railroad extended from Washington, D.C, to the Blue Ridge at Manassas Gap and into Strasburg in 1854 and joined there with the Valley Turnpike, now US-11. Prior to the Civil War, the line was important for transport of Shenandoah Valley goods to the markets on the East Coast. The route of the Valley Pike now parallels Interstate 81 along its entire length through Virginia. The route of the Manassas Gap railroad is closely paralleled by Interstate 66, stretching to Arlington and the D.C. metropolitan area. It surprised me that Strasburg, this crossroads of commerce, has remained a small, quaint town relative to sprawling Winchester. Strasburg's central business district is but three blocks long on an east-west main street called, simply, Old Valley Pike.

The original non-native settlers were of German descent, migrating south from Pennsylvania. Throughout the 1800s, the town gained a reputation for its exceptional pottery, used as food storage crockery and decorative pieces, giving the town the nickname, "Pot Town". In 1891, a stately building was constructed beside the rail line as a pottery factory, the Strasburg Stone and Earthenware Manufacturing Company. In 1913, the business succumbed to competition from other potters and a switch to glass for food storage. The building was sold to the Southern Railway, which converted it into a depot. It performed this function until the early 1960s, at which point it stayed unused until 1970 when it became a museum. The building is made of brick and has an expansive interior room with exhibits throughout, including a great display of local pottery and pottery-making equipment.

A view of Signal Knob at the north end
of Massanutten Mountain

Richard Fink
Woodstock

Woodstock, another of the string of towns on the original Valley Pike, has perhaps 4000 people and is the county seat of Shenandoah County. The main street is, unsurprisingly, Old Valley Pike. A small sign on a storefront, "Finks' Jewelry," compelled me to pull over and park. Fink's Jewelers is a large, multi-store corporation based in Roanoke. This appeared not to be one of their stores.

Inside, I spoke with a woman behind the counter and told her about my project. She said, pointing to a man in Carhartt overalls who had just entered, "That's my son, Richard. He owns the store."

I introduced myself to him and repeated my mission. He told me, "My family came from Germania in the 1700s. The Roanoke family is "Fink." We are "Finks," with an 's'. There is no relation. We are just, coincidentally, in the same business. Finks is an Austrian word that means little bird. Our family crest has a thrush in it.

"Dad bought this business in 1947 from a cousin. The store actually opened in 1937. It has been in this building since its inception. It was a family business, and it still remains one today. I retired from the business at 50 years of age.

"We are probably the only jeweler within a 100-mile radius. We are kind of in the middle of nowhere. Sometimes that is a good place to be. Winchester is 30 miles to the northeast. Harrisonburg is 30 miles to the southwest. In terms of people who do watch making and repair of watches and jewelry, we are about it.

"I took on an apprentice 21 years ago, and he is still working for us. My degree is in watch making from a technical school in Lancaster, Pennsylvania.

"The Internet has helped us to broaden out clientele. Perhaps 70 percent of our business is done in retail sales. The other 30 percent is in jewelry making and repair. The jewelers you'll find in the mall do almost no repair or manufacturing. They will send that work out."

The Finks enjoy living in Woodstock. "It is not too hot in the summer, and I am not working in piles of snow and ice in the winter. Today is a beautiful day, so I have spent most of it outdoors, working on my farm. When it is really cold or really hot, you might find me here at the store."

Richard left the store, but I stayed for a few moments to talk with his mother, Dorothy. She said about him, "He is a hard-working boy. His father was always tough on him, but he has always thought about the other person. I have never met anyone who does for other people the way he does."

A customer whose name I didn't catch came into the store. I asked her why she was here rather than in the mall. She said, "Shopping here has been carried down in my family. My grandparents shopped here. So did my parents. Gasoline is expensive, and it is a long way to the nearest mall."

Perhaps high fuel costs will fuel the next boom in small towns.

The North Fork of the Shenandoah River near Strasburg

John Adamson
Dennis Atwood
Edinburg

Being a Rotary Club member, I attended a make-up meeting in Strasburg. I found myself sitting next to John Adamson, who wore a shirt with a Virginia Tech monogram. John invited me to Edinburg, a dozen miles south on the Valley Pike, later that afternoon where he and a few other volunteers were working to catalog and restore the photographic collection of Hugh Morrison, Jr., a professional photographer in Woodstock from 1899 until 1950. John had become so enthralled by Morrison's photographs that he had assembled a collection of them and had them printed in a soft-bound book.

Edinburg is a community of around 1000 people. John and I met in a classroom of a building that originally opened as a high school in 1933 and had been converted into a Community Center. Three other men, all of the bifocal set, sat before computers and stacks of files. He introduced me to Dennis Atwood while he attended to other work. Dennis told me about himself.

Dennis said, "I live just north of here in Maurertown. It's pronounced 'maury-town.' I think "Maurer" is German for brick maker. We moved here in 1978 from Columbia, Maryland. I was born in D.C., and I worked for the federal government. My wife and I decided to find a more rural setting, so we ended up moving here. I never quit my D.C. job. I operated a van-pool for most of that time, and I actually commuted into the Washington area from here. The van carried 14 people, and four people alternated driving. It was an efficient and cost-effective way for us to commute. It took two hours each way, every day."

I said, "My understanding is that you are working on cataloging the photographic library of Hugh Morrison, Jr."

Dennis said, "Yes. Hugh Jr. learned the trade from his father and then moved down the valley to Woodstock to open his own business. Approximately 30,000 glass plate negatives from Mr. Morrison's work were donated to the Shenandoah County Historical Society. I have been involved with the cataloging of photographs."

John joined our conversation, saying, "I moved from Fairfax in 1999. Like Dennis and many others, I was motivated to seek out a more rural setting with a quieter lifestyle and a lower cost of living. This is a good landing zone."

We talked more about Morrison's photographs. Dennis said, "For me, working on this project has been arguably the best way to see this county's history. It is photographic forensics. We have tried to identify what Morrison is showing us. Many townspeople have worked with us to help identify the people."

John concurred, "Morrison's repertoire became more varied over the years. In the beginning he may have been itinerant, working around the town from his wagon. But it appears to have not taken him long to realize that he could run a studio. He rented a place on West Court Street near the courthouse and stayed there for 50 years. Most of [Morrison's customers] were people he knew.

"He was smart, curious, intellectual, and friendly. We know this anecdotally and have found various newspaper articles written about him. He was elected mayor of Woodstock for three consecutive four-year terms.

He was a good looking man. He liked the scenes and vistas. He kept a journal, writing whatever he happened to be thinking about. I feel like I know him.

"He kept the same studio for his entire career. These were negatives, not even photographs. What would we do with literally tens of thousands of plate glass negatives? We bought a computer and a scanner and then began to print positives. We found a window into the culture of the County more than the history, although there were elements of both."

Adamson's book of Morrison's photographs is called A Pictorial History of Shenandoah County.

Dennis said, "I actually felt as if I could be transported back to that era through the collection of these photographs."

John said he thought they had a true treasure. "As I began to look at these plates for the first time, I thought, 'God, I said to myself, look at what we have got!' Morrison was highly skilled. He cared about his county. I tell people that I feel that I was Morrison's agent fifty years after his death. We are still inundated with the task of scanning and cataloguing these photographs. This project will extend well beyond our lifetimes."

West Virginia

HAMPSPHIRE

Moorefield

Wardensville

HARDY

SHENANDOAH

PENDLETON

ROCKINGHAM

Virginia

Hardy County, West Virginia

Hardy County contains the wide valley of the South Branch of the Po-
mac River, which flows north through Moorefield, the largest community. The
stern border is along Great North Mountain, with Shenandoah Mountain,
uth Branch Mountain, and Elkhorn Mountain to its west. The western border
ns primarily on Patterson Creek Mountain. The valley supports the agricul-
ral production of wheat, corn, poultry, cattle, and fruits.

Hardy has 584 square miles.

Moorefield is the county seat. Moorefield and Wardensville are the only
corporated towns.

opulation

Hardy County, as primarily farming-based, has grown slowly from about
00 in 1900 to about 13,000 today.

stitutions of higher education

Hardy County has no colleges or universities.

raffic

An Interstate highway-quality road, Corridor H, slices through the northern
r of the County, although as yet neither end connects with any other four-
ie roads. It is currently about 20 miles long. Moorefield has several traffic
hts.

oday's...

Hardy County is beginning to see the influx of new homeowners from the
ashington, D.C., area.

ttractions

• Lost River State Park, Mathias

Lulu and Bibi Ferrenbach
Lost River

The first people I met in Hardy County were newcomers. In fact, Lulu and Bibi Ferrenbach were from France. This freewheeling, fascinating couple has been all over the world, living lives of art and adventure that many of us only dream about.

Their home is in an area the locals call The Cove, off State Highway 259 near Lost River. Lower Cove Run Road is a typical West Virginia layover road, with one lane of narrow pavement in the center of the road, flanked by gravel shoulders. Whenever two cars meet, each must "lay over" one set of wheels on the gravel.

Along the road were several hand-painted protest signs, spaced apart like old Burma Shave signs, with ongoing messages from one to the next. These were railing against a proposed dam, which would, in the mind of the sign-painter, negatively impact the valley.

The Ferrenbach's residence was surrounded by trees, about 60 feet from the road, a mobile home with an addition as large as the trailer attached to the front. Below a blue tarp at the end of the driveway was an upturned hull of an unfinished boat. A dog barked from behind a wire mesh fence.

Beatrice, "Bibi," came outside to greet me on a chilly sunny day. She appeared to be in her 60s with graying hair. She introduced me to Lucien, "Lulu" to all who know him. I guessed him to be in his late 70s or early 80s. He had disheveled hair and crooked fingers but a firm handshake. The addition to the house was a studio with many paintings and tapestries on the wall. Everything, from walls to furniture, appeared to be painted, all in flamboyant colors. A woodstove provided ample heat.

Lulu spoke in clear but accented English about his life, starting in the Alsace region. "For many years I went to art school. During the war, I was not a soldier. I was in prison for a time, and I fought with the resistance."

I learned that Lulu had been brutalized by the Nazis. Additionally, he had had a serious bicycle crash that left him paralyzed for several months.

Bibi told me her story as well. "I also went to art school, although I am much younger than Lulu." She laughed and winked at him. "I was born in Vendee. I attended college in France and England. Lulu had a boat that he had been sailing around the Mediterranean. I met him in 1975 while he was anchored on the island of Lefkas where I was studying. He left, and we did not meet again for four more years. This was in 1979, and we began to travel together, including crossing the Atlantic."

She and Lulu made money in their ports of call by selling watercolors. "We stayed a year in British Columbia and got married there in 1987, because the government did not want to let me stay unless we were married. After that we sailed south to Costa Rica and stayed there for four years. We made our way to the Atlantic side of Panama and rented a house on an island."

They met Dr. Anthony Coates, formerly the director of the center within the Smithsonian Institution that studies the tropics. Tony had a vacation home in Hardy County. Bibi and Lulu came to visit and moved into his vacation home. Eventually, they moved into their own place across the road.

Lulu said, "It is safe here. We have wonderful neighbors who welcomed us. When we arrived, it was in September. On November 28th, we were wearing shorts and T-shirts. The next day it was −15°F. Dave, the farmer up the road, came by and saw that we were collecting firewood. He brought his chainsaw and splitter, and he helped us. A week later, he broke something on his tractor. I told him to bring it to me, and I fixed it for him. I can fix anything in steel."

Bibi said, "It was a pleasant surprise and interesting that I found a link between the farming culture of this area with my own family and their farming roots in France. Farming is universal in the affinity with the land and with the reverence of nature."

Lulu said, "I was surprised to find such nice people. We made friends quickly. I am adaptable and can adjust to any place fast. The first thing that made me feel at home was the wonderful scenery. I am a painter and a sculptor, so living within a beautiful place is always important. The scenery is inspiring to my artistic side.

"The people here have practical minds. I like that because I have a practical mind, too. One of the things we do not like about the United States is that everyone seems to throw things away when they break. People here in The Cove know how to fix things."

When I left, the Ferrenbachs gave me a CD of a film that had been done about their lives. The film, called "Lulu, Triumph of the Human Spirit," had won the prize for the Best Individual Profile Documentary at the West Virginia Film Festival in 2004. The filmmaker, Ray Schmitt, lived just a few miles away outside Mathias.

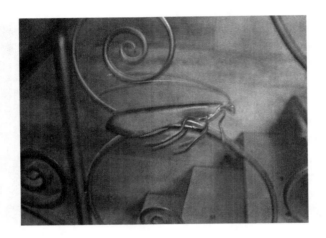

Detailed metalwork of Lulu Ferrenbach

David Wilkins
Lost River

David Wilkins was the old-time resident who had helped the Ferren-bachs with firewood the year they moved in. Dave was born and raised less than a mile away.

"I am a fourth-generation farmer. My wife died two years ago, and we had no children. Farming is all I know. I grow hay and pasture. The soil is too rough and rocky to grow much of anything else, so it has been an area for cattle and sheep. I have 22 ewes and one buck.

"When I was a boy, we used to plant and harvest corn with horse-drawn equipment. Nowadays I use a tractor for everything. I can cut and bail my own hay. Everything I cut and store I use myself. The equipment costs a lot of money.

"I have a cousin who helps me with some of the work. There is no money exchanged; I help him and he helps me. He is a mechanic, and if something breaks down, he will fix it for me. Lulu is a welder, and if something breaks, he can weld it. Bibi is the cook, and she often fixes food for me. I bring her potatoes and vegetables from my garden.

"We help each other however we can. I couldn't make it without the help of my friends and neighbors. A dollar bill really has little meaning for me. As long as I can keep my bills paid, I don't think much about money at all."

He said few farmers made much money. "Obviously, a farm needs to take care of itself or the owner must get rid of it. It needs to make enough cash to pay for the equipment and maintenance. But if I wanted to have money for spending or for enjoying myself, I would go out and look for a job.

"I do some construction work in the summer time to make enough cash to carry me through the winter. My brother and I lease some hunting rights on our land. There are not many people who can make a go of it working on the farm full-time. Most people have either part-time or full-time jobs elsewhere. Sometimes they work in the school system. Some of the women work as nurses or teachers.

"Since my wife died a couple of years ago, I have lived by myself. This is probably the worst time in my life. There are not many eligible

Stained glass art hangs in the Ferrenbach home

women around here. When you are younger, you are more desirable and less particular. At my age, I am less desirable and more particular. My church and friends have been the biggest part in my life.

"In many ways this area is going to change. But change is part of the natural order. The older people are passing away. We are losing a lot of our young people because there is not enough work to do around here. But many of our young people end up moving back. Sometimes they find work, and even if it does not pay as well, they still prefer to live here. Money isn't everything, and people don't really know what they can live without until they try.

"I have been blessed. All of the newcomers have become good neighbors. Lulu and Bibi are from another country, but they moved here wanting to get along with everybody. The first winter they almost froze. We locals got a good laugh out of this. But we helped them with firewood. They managed to survive the year."

Ray Schmitt
Mathias

Filmmaker Ray Schmitt, who had done the film about Lulu, rusticated to a restored farmhouse on a knoll near Mathias. He is a slender man with a salt-and-pepper beard and the long, expressive fingers of a guitarist.

His living room was filled with fine artwork. He said, "I went to college in southwestern Pennsylvania in the early 1960s. I began making the first of many trips into West Virginia.

"Sometimes my wife, who was my girlfriend in college, and I would drive on the weekends just for pleasure. We would head down this road or that with no particular destination. We went down lots of dirt roads. Dirt roads were something new to me. We saw some kids in what seemed like tarpaper shacks, running around barefoot playing outside. It was the first time I had ever experienced anything like that.

"I graduated from college in 1964, and I went to work for the government in Washington, D.C. I also moonlighted playing traditional Bluegrass music. By 1973, my wife and I began to look for rural property.

"The place we bought was advertised as having 32 acres, a small stream, and a barn. Other than needing a new roof, the barn was structurally sound. So we bought it.

"Over the next few years we continued to come to Hardy more and more. By Columbus Day in 1974, we threw a party for all of the friends who had helped us fix the place. Since it was October, we naturally called it our Oktoberfest. Thirty-four years later, this event is still happening annually. People come from all over the country. The largest crowd we ever had probably numbered 200 people. It got so big that we would smoke a pig or cook a side of beef. We asked everybody to bring some food and had a huge potluck dinner. It is a wonderful time, and it has introduced a lot of people to West Virginia.

"In my career, I was a retirement specialist. So I did all my planning and calculations, setting a goal that at age 55, I was out of there. And that is what I did. During this period, my passion switched from music to filmmaking.

"We finally moved here in 1997. I knew just a few of my near neigh-

Photo by Ray Schmitt

Helmick Rocks,
Hardy County

bors, but during all those years of just visiting, I wasn't trying to get to know the community. In more recent years I have joined the Ruritan Club and have become more involved in community activities. I feel that I have gained the respect of local people and that has given me a great deal of pleasure.

"This is my spiritual home. I could never again live away from West Virginia. It wasn't long after we moved here that my wife and I decided to have our ashes interred on the hill above the barn. My wife's father came out for the first time in 1975. He died in 1976 and his ashes are now on the hill. My wife passed away a year and a half ago, and her ashes are now on top of the hill. The following February her mother died, and her ashes are up there. The following April, my father died."

About his filmmaking, he said, "I make films professionally. I was West Virginia filmmaker of the year in 2004. The stories I like to tell have some sort of inspirational vibe to them. Early on, I came to realize that I was doing films in order to learn. The stories all become part of me. I get great satisfaction out of it.

"I have often thought that every person is worthy of a documentary. Whenever I am able to encapsulate a person in 30 minutes, it is quite impressive. I wish everyone had a documentary of their life so they could realize how rich their life has been. I am looking for ordinary people, perhaps offbeat ordinary people.

"If you break down on your way out of here today, someone, likely

Harper Barn,
1845

Photo by Ray Schmitt

the first driver by, will stop and offer to help. These are honest, proud, caring, self-sufficient, hard-working people. They do not like a lot of regulation and resent governmental intrusion. Through my filmmaking I have tried to help local people find pride in their lifestyles and lives. They are not prone to boasting, but they see the importance in their own lives through my films."

Rockingham County, Virginia

Rockingham County is in the Appalachian Ridge-and-Valley topography of limestone mountains. Most of the county is in the relatively flat Shenandoah Valley. The eastern edge of the county abuts the Blue Ridge Mountains and the Shenandoah National Park.

With 853 square miles, it is the largest Virginia county on The Spine of the Virginias.

Incorporated towns include Bridgewater, Timberville, Elkton, Dayton, Broadway, Grottoes, and Mount Crawford. The city of Harrisonburg is wholly within the county, and it is the county seat, although it has an independent government.

Population

Rockingham County's population (including Harrisonburg) has steadily increased over the last century, from 37,000 in 1900 to 115,000 now.

Institutions of higher education

James Madison University and Eastern Mennonite University are in Harrisonburg. Bridgewater College is in Bridgewater.

Traffic

Rockingham County has about 80 miles of four-lane roads and several dozen traffic lights.

Today's...

Rockingham County, with a mix of agriculture, tourism, industry, health care, transportation, and higher education, is The Spine of the Virginias' fastest growing county.

Attractions

- Shenandoah National Park and Skyline Drive, eastern border of the county
- Massanutten Resort, Elkton, skiing, mountain biking, water park
- Hone Quarry Recreation Area, Bridgewater, camping, hiking, fishing

Ron and Peggie Turner
Fulks Run

South of Mathias, Highway 259 crosses the border into Rockingham County, Virginia, as it curves around the southern end of Church Mountain. Fulks Run is a small, roadside community with few commercial establishments. One belongs to Ron Turner and his wife Peggie.

Ron and Peggie run a country store and a ham-curing house. When I met with him, he wore a bright orange t-shirt that said, "Virginia Basketball." I asked him about their business.

He said, "The store was built in 1949 by my dad. When it was built, it was only about one-fourth the size of what is now. When customers came in, they gave a list of what they wanted to my mom, and she pulled their products down from the shelf. My parents lived in the basement of the store and had three kids. In 1959, they built a house next door, and that was where I was raised as their fifth child. They built one addition, and then in 1963 they built another addition, which completes the store as you see it today.

"It was one of the first stores in the area that became self-service with shopping carts. They sold fresh meats, including ground hamburger and chuck-roast that was raised by local farmers. There was a slaughterhouse in Timberville that sold the meats to the store, and all the fresh produce was purchased from Harrisonburg. The store also served as the Post Office for the village of Fulks Run. There were 90 to 100 addresses. We still have the old-style in-store mailboxes. They would sort the mail on one side and shove the letters into slots, and the customer would come by on the other side and open it with a key. Peggie and I bought the store in 1996 and have been working it together since then.

"We have a second business called Turner Hams. We bought that from my parents in 1991. Every Friday in January, [our supplier in Indiana] brings us a shipment by truck."

Ron described a detailed process for rubbing, curing, and selling the hams. Most of their clientele is local. Peggie said, "We also do some mail-order business that we have developed through word-of-mouth. The Washington Post did a nice article about us a few years ago and that brought in new business. There are not a lot of sugar- cured ham pro-

Ron and Peggie Turner in their store in Fulks Run

ducers anymore. Some people will come in and say, 'you make hams the way my father used to make.'"

Ron continued, "Dad always liked to try new things. He started the ham business in the basement of the store. His customers asked for hams. He had no supplier, so he decided to cure his own. He did 20 or 25 hams the first year. Before he knew it, he was doing 300 and then more. Curing and selling hams has been part of my family heritage. We've been doing it for my entire life.

"The store has changed quite a bit. When we first bought the store, we sold groceries. There was no way we could compete with Food Lion and Wal-Mart. We stock the things that are typical for country stores these days.

"It's a good life up here. I can be in Roanoke in two hours. I can be in Richmond in two hours. I can be in D.C. in two hours. Two hours is sort of the magic number."

Peggie said, "My sister lives in Richmond. My kids go to a school that is obviously smaller, but they don't seem to have as much stress. I don't think my kids miss out on much, living in a rural area."

Irene Yankey
Kenny May
Gale Hupp
Criders

Irene Yankey lives in the small mountain community of Criders, a few miles from Fulks Run. She and two friends, Kenny May and Gale Hupp, were at her modest home on a knoll. Irene said, "Criders is on the eastern slope of Shenandoah Mountain, but I was born on the western slope in the town of Milam. My grandparents grew up on Hinkle Mountain, above Milam. My mother was raised on Hinkle Mountain, and my father was raised on this side of the border. Mom and dad met at the one-room schoolhouse they attended near Milam.

"During the weekends we walked from our house here in Criders over the mountain to Grandma and Pappy's house. It was about a 2½ or 3-hour walk. We went over rough trails that we kids made or we followed wildlife trails. The hunters used these trails as well.

"I went to school in a one-room schoolhouse on Bennett Mountain. The schoolhouse was actually in West Virginia, but many of the kids who attended were from Virginia. Rockingham County paid Hardy County for each student that attended. We walked about a mile to school every day. I don't ever remember it being closed in the winter. We studied the basics: reading, writing, and arithmetic. We also studied science and government."

I estimated her age at 70, so this situation existed in the late 1940s.

"The school had perhaps 30 or 40 students in eight grades, typically three or four children per grade. We were not separated and everybody heard the same lesson. The teachers were strict and didn't allow for anyone to interrupt. I think I got a better education than most kids get today."

Irene said she married at age 16. Her husband was 23. "My father-in-law walked from his place to the Allegheny Mountains [in West Virginia] to work in logging. I imagine this was a two or three day walk. He stayed for several weeks at a time. It didn't pay well, but it did provide some cash.

"Each family was self-sufficient. We grew taters, beans, cucumbers, carrots, tomatoes, peas, and squash. We had fruit trees as well; apple, peach, and pear. Most of the vegetables we canned. Apples were turned into applesauce and apple butter. Daddy raised hogs, typically six or eight at a time. Hogs ate table scraps or the inedible garden crops. Hogs free-ranged the forests and ate nuts and roots. Most people had dogs to round up the hogs."

Irene's friend Gale said, "I was born and raised here, too, as were my parents. When I grew up, this area was predominantly small farms. Nowadays many of the farmers have large chicken or turkey operations. Years ago, turkey growers had small flocks. Turkeys were set outside to range-free during the day and were kept indoors at night. Nowadays they are confined 24 hours a day. I am more familiar with chicken operations. Chicken companies like Perdue or Tysons have their own hatcheries. They contract with the growers. They take hundreds of chicks to each grower, along with the feed. The company has its own processing facility. The grower takes the chicks which are one day old and raises them until they are ready to be processed, which takes about six weeks. Chicks grow from a few ounces to about 4 pounds. Each grower will get a load of chicks each cycle. They are all raised at the same time in the same size, and they are all processed at the same time. This cycle repeats itself, year-round.

"The houses are heated and cooled, and fully insulated. Modern broiler houses are 42 by 400 feet. Years ago, the chicken houses were smaller, and each farmer hatched his own chicks and raised his own birds. There is one turkey operation here in Criders that raises more than 30,000 turkeys. I am not sure whether this region is any better suited to growing poultry than other areas around the state, but it got its start here and the industry has done well. Poultry feed is primarily corn, but it also contains animal fat and many other grains. Much of the agricultural land in the Shenandoah Valley is cultivated in the production of grains for poultry feed."

Kenny May joined the conversation. "Unlike chickens, hogs have an indeterminate lifespan. A man grew his hog until he needed the meat and then he butchered it. Hogs were typically one year old when butchered. Many people raised piglets for a few weeks, weaned them, and then sold them to someone else to raise them. A man raised a litter and kept what he needed for himself and then sold the rest. Most hog production was done for the family's own consumption. There were eight of us in my family, and we typically butchered three or four hogs each year."

Gale said, "There were few hospitals. I had a sister who died when she was five or six years old. The last child was a boy, and he died at birth. Six of us lived to adulthood. It was common for a child to either be stillborn or die in infancy, but less common for the mother to die as well."

Kenny said, "You will be surprised to hear this, but the mountain areas had telephones before 1900. Broadway is down in the valley, but we had telephones before they did. In those days, telephone companies were small, entrepreneurial ventures. Ours bought a switchboard and connected several area houses. They ran a telephone line in a big circle all the way around the Criders and Bergton area, even up on Shenandoah Mountain. Two sisters ran the switchboard.

"When we were growing up, we lived in a subsistence economy and people struggled. I don't mean to imply that people starved to death. Everybody had enough to eat. Living here wasn't easy, but I don't think it was easy anywhere in that era."

We talked a bit about hunting which, it seemed, everyone did. Kenny said, "There were some 250-pound Whitetail bucks checked in back during the 1940s and 1950s. Deer hunting has been exceptional on both sides of the border for many years. The bear hunting is unreal. Some of the bears weigh up to 500 pounds. A hunter will hunt with dogs or simply wait in blinds. Some people hunt with rifles, but many use bow and arrow. Turkey hunting is also popular. During the spring the hunter calls in the turkey by imitating the call of the hen either by voice or by a mechanical turkey call. A good turkey caller can bring the gobbler right to him. [Hunters] shoot turkeys with either a 22 gauge rifle or with buckshot.

"People also occasionally hunt squirrels or rabbit. Some people even kill and eat snakes. You can kill a snake by just hitting him in the back with a stick. One year I killed over 100 rattlesnakes."

Irene said, "We have a fire department, a community center, and a recreation center. We have a library. We have everything that anybody could want."

Kenny said, "I think the generosity of the people [defines us]. Anyone in need gets help. I don't think there is any better comment that anyone could make about a community."

Gale said, "Living in the mountains, it seems to me that your burdens are lifted. We don't deal with noise, traffic, and crime."

Irene said, "Everyone is close-knit. There is a freedom here that we all feel."

Paul Roth
Broadway

Further east on Highway 259, the road shoots a gap of Little North Mountain, guarded by impressive rock outcroppings called Chimney Rocks, likely a prime location for rock climbers.

Back into the Shenandoah Valley, the mountains ended abruptly and gave way to larger and more prosperous farms than I'd seen in the mountains. I waited behind, and then eventually passed a horse-drawn black buggy, the fluorescent triangle attached to the rear signifying a slow-moving vehicle. There was a Mennonite Community in the area.

I entered the town of Broadway, just a few miles north of Harrisonburg, and called on Paul Roth, pastor of the Linville Creek Church of the Brethren to ask about the influence of Christianity in the area.

"I have been here for almost 14 years," Paul Roth said. "I knew this was the home congregation of church elder John Kline. He was an important figure in the history of the Church of the Brethren. His home and the remnants of his homestead are nearby. We are doing what we can to preserve what is left of the homestead. Kline was born in 1797 in Dauphin County, Pennsylvania, not far from where I grew up. Kline moved here with his parents during a migration of German Baptist Brethren and Mennonites. Many of the Germanic groups came here to settle in the 18th century. Land was already overcrowded in central Pennsylvania, so they came here.

"Kline was called into the ministry. Part of his ministry took him into missionary travels through the Brocks Gap into Western Virginia. He wrote in his diary about his concern for the poor, not only for their economic status but for their overall health. He learned about their home remedies and herbal cures. Many of his missionary travels began to focus on finding medicinal herbs. Many of these herbs are still around and people continue to use them.

"Several congregations of Brethren churches were formed by him in Western Virginia. During the Civil War, he was called upon to be the moderator for annual meetings of the German Baptist Brethren. So he would go to Maryland, Pennsylvania, Ohio, Indiana, Western Virginia, Kentucky, and Tennessee and then loop back home. He always came back through Western Virginia. He discussed in his diary their growing sentiment not to secede from the Union as the seccession movement swept through the rest of Virginia.

"When the Western, mountainous section of Virginia began its split from Virginia to form its own state, Elder John Kline wrote about it extensively. My understanding comes through his eyes.

"He gave land from his farm to build the first meetinghouse, which stood in the grove of trees on the west side of the current building we are now sitting in. In those days, meetinghouses were private residences that often were equipped with partitions. Lightweight, non-loadbearing walls had pegs in the floor to hold them in place. When it was time for worship, these walls were swung upwards and hung on hooks to the ceiling. These were successors to earlier places of meeting which were often in barns.

"The history of Christianity, from Christ's followers to the modern Anabaptist or Mennonites, started with a Dutch priest named Menno Simons. He felt he needed to take these scriptures more literally and to follow Jesus in a more literal way to re-create the original First Century followers. He felt parents should create a path of service to one another, and their children should make a decision on their own to follow that same path. They began to have adult confession baptisms. His church called for more obedience and discipline to the teachings of Jesus and in living more communally with fellow church members. They also moved towards nonresistance because that is what Jesus taught.

"So this early group eventually became the Brethren or Dunkards, because of their method of full immersion under water in an outdoor setting during baptisms. Because of this public act of adult baptism, these early Brethren were in fact breaking laws, and they were persecuted for it [in Europe].

"Eventually both groups found out about the New World and decided to emigrate. Coincidentally, both arrived in the same place, Germantown, which is now within Philadelphia. In the early 1700s the Amish began to withdraw from mainstream Anabaptism toward a more insular and withdrawn society where purity of thought was reflected in lifestyles and even in clothing. They shunned governments, refused to pay taxes, didn't vote, and didn't take up arms.

"We have these same things exhibited by old order groups of Mennonites and Brethren. Some use horse and buggy for transportation. Some of them use cars, but they have black rather than chrome bumpers. They may have radios but not televisions. It may be okay to use a computer but only for doing business. These people still interact with the general public on a commercial basis, buying and selling on the market. However, they are a much tighter community, and they continually work towards self-reliance.

"My church is more in tune with mainstream American life. Our denomination just celebrated its 300th anniversary last year. We once felt separate, but now we feel integrated into American culture. If you saw one of my members walking or driving the street of Harrisonburg, they would not look any different from anyone else. However, I would expect them to define themselves by the way they approached things. My members would not produce tobacco. Few smoke or consume alcohol. I do not specifically preach about that, but some congregations within my denomination do. We work for justice issues. We respond to the poor and downtrodden. We work with immigrants on family issues, assimilation, and disaster response. It is visceral and natural for us to be involved. We also try to not overconsume and to recycle our resources.

"Just prior to the Civil War, John Kline was an Elder, meaning he was an overseer of many congregations. He did not preach, and I do not preach politically, but we take faith positions that have political implications. Elder John Kline spoke against slavery. Statements were recorded during early gatherings in the 1700s that the Brethren and Mennonites were opposed to the trafficking of souls, as they called it. You could not be a member of the church if you owned slaves.

"Since Kline spoke about this often, his preaching missions across the Blue Ridge Mountains into the Virginia Piedmont and Tidewater never went anywhere. These people, because they owned so many slaves, were not receptive to his message.

"Here in the Central Shenandoah Valley are perhaps 20,000 members of either a Mennonite or a Brethren congregation. These people often take political roles in the community. There were many letters to the editor in our local paper during the buildup to the Iraq War that expressed opposition to it. There was a backlash from outside our church of people who were calling us unpatriotic. These critics did not understand how our faith led us to this political posture. During the Iraq situation, our people felt like they were being beaten up in the editor's column as not being practical or patriotic. To us, it was not a question of patriotism. It was a question of whether it was right for us to be the intruders into another nation and culture without adequate provocation.

"[My church sends] people into war-torn countries on humanitarian missions in order to respond to human suffering. We are at risk simply because we are Americans from birth, and we are tainted by the movements and actions of our government against the people we are trying to serve. Through the Brethren and Mennonite volunteer services, our young people serve humanity throughout the world. I have many here in my congregation who ascribe to a more mainstream path in American life. But some of us are somewhat radical. For many years, I only paid a portion of my income taxes. I did not want to contribute to the large portion that pays for war. We were fined for that. We had some friends who were regular tax resisters. The bottom line is that we are inherently concerned about the way we treat each other, not only in this nation but around the world. How can we be better global neighbors, and how can we be better neighbors with the earth? The abuse of the earth's resources is hugely important to us.

"It is easy for us to assail the basis of our culture which is to accumulate bigger and better things rather than to create ways where more people can live with their basic needs met. I think we need to spread a culture where living with less is valued and where sharing is endemic. This is one of the values that we must cultivate.

"There are people here in this area, not even necessarily from our Anabaptist tradition, who have a close relationship with the land and all the responsibilities that go with that. This economic crisis may actually be a gift to us. It may bring us back to the core beliefs that we have about life and how we relate to one another. I believe that we will see a great sense of generosity emerge from this adversity. My hope is that in the Shenandoah Valley and elsewhere across the nation, we will look to become more self-sufficient but at the same time be supportive of our community overall so that nobody ever goes hungry."

Jack Wenger
Broadway

I drove back through the small downtown of Broadway, with a smattering of shops along the main street. One of the establishments that caught my eye appeared to be an antique car repair business. Jack Wenger, owner of W. W. Antique Motorcars and Parts, was kind enough to visit with me. His office was filled with antique car memorabilia, signs, hats, and models of all things automotive. Jack told me, "We restore antique cars and trucks. We also buy and sell antique cars and other vehicles.

"People bring cars from all over the world. We have a good reputation. We do a lot of show cars. We have had our cars on the cover of automotive magazines. We have had television specials about us.

"I have always been interested in cars. I had my first hobby car when I was 16, and I am 61 now. I taught school for 14 years, and I was in engineering for five years. So I have not been doing automotive restorations full time for all those years.

"You do your first one, then another. Somebody sees you working for a friend, and they ask you to work for them as well. We work with older tools on older cars. One example is a hammer former. We use this type of tool to shape a fender. When we need a fender that cannot be obtained on the market, we must make our own. It is similar to a wheeling machine where one side shrinks and the other side stretches as the operator rolls a piece of metal between two wheels. It takes hours to build a fender this way, but we do quite a bit of it."

Jack said he'd worked for many interesting and famous people. "We worked for Richard and Kyle Petty. We have people who, as part of the contract, will not allow me to tell you who they are. We put an engine in Bill Clinton's Mustang. We have done some charity work for museums and nonprofit organizations.

"We may refurbish a car like a 1957 Pontiac that a man had when he was in school. He wants to re-create the memories he had when he was a teenager. We help people relive their memories. If a guy always wanted a GTO convertible or vintage Corvette, we can fulfill that dream. We have done several Packards including Marilyn Monroe's. The owner was offered one-half million dollars for that car when we finished with it.

"Up until the last two or three months, business was booming. We are finally catching the tail end of the stock market crash. Our primary customers are wealthy people. A typical restoration will cost anywhere from $20,000 or $25,000 to $100,000 or higher. It depends upon the car and how much work needs to be done to it.

"We employ 17 people now. We subcontract our chrome plating and our machining. Everything else, including engine rebuilds, transmission overhauls, painting, bodywork, upholstery, glass, and wiring we do ourselves. We have many exceptional skills here, and we have a lot of fun."

Wegner trains most of his employees. They have a four-day work week, working 10-hour days. "Our employees like this, and it is easier to hire people. So we do not have any trouble staffing. We do not have a lot of turnover.

"We are here because this is where I was born and raised. I want to live here. If I were to move the business to Northern Virginia, I could double my prices and double my workload. But we have reached a point where our reputation is such that people are willing to travel to see us and to ship cars here from wherever they are. It has been four or five years since we advertised. We have had occasions where people have bought a car from us, sight unseen, had us refurbish it, and delivered it to them in a foreign country without ever having met us.

"This area has always been a major transportation corridor. We have unique people in the community who have had a lot of interesting cars. Racing has always interested me. I have done quite a bit of vintage race car driving. I have had 15 vintage race cars.

"I have a lot of pride running the business. People recognize me, and they know who we are and what we do. I hear people brag about our shop. People tell me that they hear other people say, 'Oh, you live in that town where that car restoration shop is.' When local people have visitors from out-of-state, they will bring them here to take a tour of our facility. The town has taken ownership in the business too, in the sense that visiting dignitaries are often brought by.

"In the mid-1990s when the antique car market was steaming hot and everything was rolling, Broadway was perhaps the most car-oriented town in the state of Virginia."

As a businessman, he said, "I learned my first year in business not to talk politics with anybody because you never know who you are talking to. Many of our customers are politically connected.

"Democrats. Republicans. So what? We are all Americans. All of us are faced with the falling of the economy. This country is far weaker because of the great divisions between Democrats and Republicans. We are all in this together, and we have a lot more in common than we have to separate us."

Carole and Dan Downey
Harrisonburg

Just a few miles south of Broadway lies Harrisonburg, the dominant city and county seat of Rockingham County. It is the home of James Madison University and Eastern Mennonite University, so there is a large student population. I began my tour at the Hardesty-Higgins House downtown, talking with Carole Christopher Downey.

The Hardesty-Higgins House was the home of the first mayor of Harrisonburg, Isaac Hardesty. The house bears his name and that of Henry Higgins, a Harrisonburg physician who also lived there. The city of Harrisonburg acquired the home in 2001, and it now serves as a community center, visitor's center, and museum.

Carole works there part-time. She said, "I was born in northern New Jersey near Newark. When I was a senior in high school, we took a vacation trip to the Skyline Drive in the Shenandoah National Park in Virginia. On our way home we were driving on US-11, headed back north. We drove through Harrisonburg and passed Madison College, what is now James Madison University. I took one look and fell in love with it. I had never even heard of it before, and I immediately knew I wanted to go to school there. It was October during the peak of the leaf season. So I applied to Madison College, and I was accepted. I met my future husband Dan Downey on my first day of freshman year. We have now been married for almost 34 years. He was a sophomore at that time, and he was from nearby Strasburg. He was excited about me because I came from the north, and I had seen tall buildings.

"We moved to Louisiana for five years. Dan got his Ph.D. in Chemistry at LSU. We then moved to Morgantown, West Virginia. We then moved back here because we both loved it so much. He is now a chemistry professor at James Madison University.

"Harrisonburg calls itself the Friendly City, and I always felt that was true. Everyone I met was just full of love for the area. People came for many different reasons. But once here, everyone wanted to stay. I have never seen skies as blue as here in the Shenandoah Valley. I never saw mountains when I was growing up. I did not know what cows were for.

"Back during the 1970s, if we walked down the street of downtown we would literally have to carve our way through all the people. In the years that followed, Harrisonburg, like so many other small towns, lost its retail core to the malls and big-box stores on the perimeter of town. The downtown, the heart, was gone. We are lucky because downtown Harrisonburg is in the midst of a renaissance and is being revitalized. It is exciting for me to work in downtown Harrisonburg.

"Tourism is alive and well. I have waited on people from Ecuador, Guyana, Great Britain, France, Germany, South Africa, you name it. We have visitors from every state.

"They come looking for history, mountains, fishing, and hiking. They are looking to get out of the cities and be in a more wholesome, country atmosphere. A lot of our visitors stay at Massanutten resort in one of the timeshares. Within two to three hours is a wealth of experiences, even including our nation's capital.

"A lot of our work is sharing information not just with vacationers but with people interested in relocating here. People are looking to move here from all up and down the East Coast. Sometimes people who live in New York have gone to Florida on vacation and have driven through here on their way. This is becoming a big retirement area."

Carole suggested I meet Dan because of his interest in history. Dan told me, "I was born in Winchester, but I grew up in Shenandoah County."

He was enthralled by my project. "I used to teach at West Virginia University. Chemistry is what I do for a living, and history is what I do for fun. On my mother's side, my family dates back to the original settlers in the Valley. My father's side was of relative newcomers from Pennsylvania.

"Most of the people who settled the Shenandoah Valley came southward from Pennsylvania. That is why the Mennonites and the Brethren were so prevalent here. Later on was a Scots Irish influence. Eastern Virginia, by contrast, was settled from the coastal areas by people from England. The mountains presented a formidable barrier which also limited the mixing of the ethnicities."

Dan told me his passion for history was driven by his upbringing on a farm near Strasburg. "In farming you do many things that are close to nature. I am 56 years old. This past Saturday night my brother and I pulled a calf. The cow was 16 years old, and she had had many calves in the past. She was obviously in labor Saturday afternoon. When we checked on her, the nose and one foot of the calf had emerged from the birth canal. You want to see two feet. The cow was lying down. The calf had a foot buckled underneath to the point where it could not be moved. We managed to get the cow to a standing position where her body was more flexible. My brother pushed the calf's head and foot back into the cow with his hand to the point where he could feel the other foot and clear it. We got both feet outside of the cow's body. We tied a chain to the feet and then tied it around a stick where we could both yank on the stick. The cow worked with us to push from her inside. We finally yanked the critter out. We held him upside down where all the blood and goop drained out. We carried him to the barn lot with the cow in order for her to claim him. Within 10 minutes she had him cleaned up, and both were doing fine.

"This is the sort of thing that brings you back to reality. Someone in my family likely performed this same chore many times in his life 100 years or 200 years ago. Most of the kids I teach at James Madison University think food comes in cellophane wrappers and grows at Kroger.

"When I worked at West Virginia University, I did a lot of field work in the smaller communities. It really felt to me like stepping back in time. This was 30 years ago, and I met some people in their 60s and 70s. They were true mountain people.

"I worked on a research project, a greenhouse gas measurement experiment, in a place called Big Run Bog near Parsons, West Virginia. It is a glaciated area on top of a mountain. We were planting devices in a peat bog to measure gas production. One day we were approached by a man and a woman who looked as if they were right out of the movie Deliverance. I mumbled under my breath, 'Oh crap.' The man began to chat with us about the work we were doing. It turned out we were talking far beneath his knowledge level. He began to tell us about the native plants with their Latin names and the various aspects of the physical environment of the area. Our jaws dropped. I never use the expression, 'dumb mountaineer,' because I know how sharp many of those people are.

"Because of their isolation, they continue to use certain types of terminology and expressions that date back to the original pioneers. It makes them seem unintelligent, but they are not. They are simply well attuned to their environment."

Rodney Eagle
Harrisonburg

Rodney Eagle was a three-term former mayor of Harrisonburg. He was born and raised there. He ran his own business and did real estate development.

"I am in my early 70s. I have watched many changes, some for the better and some not. I have always been pro-development and pro-growth. When I was growing up, we were called the Turkey Capital of the World. That was about the sole industry back in those days.

"When I was a child the city hosted a Turkey Festival. The townspeople dressed for the occasion. The men wore hats and ties and the women wore bonnets. Court Square was so crowded you couldn't elbow your way through. My father was in the poultry business. About 1948 when I was 10 or 12 years old I rode in the Festival Parade on a float. One of my most vivid memories was that organizers would take turkeys in cages to the upstairs windows in the bank buildings over the parade route, and they would release these birds to fly down to the awaiting crowd below. The people would just go crazy trying to catch these birds to take them home to slaughter them for dinner. In my mind I can still see those big wings flapping."

He added his favorite story about the town. "A band of gypsies came through this area during the 1960s. While they were camped here, the queen died. They had a number of big celebrations. She was buried in our town's cemetery. There are many old-timers that still claim that on certain nights you can still see a visage of this queen riding her white horse through that cemetery."

West Virginia

HARDY

PENDLETON

🏛
Franklin

ROCKINGHAM

HIGHLAND

Virginia

Pendleton County, West Virginia

Pendleton County is entirely within the Appalachian Ridge-and-Valley topography of limestone mountains. Major mountains are Shenandoah Mountain along the eastern border, Jack Mountain, North Fork Mountain, Spruce Mountain, and Allegheny Mountain on the western border. The entire county is deeply mountainous and boasts West Virginia's highest peak, Spruce Knob.

Pendleton has 698 square miles.

Franklin, the county seat, is the only incorporated town.

Population

Pendleton County's population has remained steady between 7000 and 10,000 for the past 100 years. Current population is just over 7000.

Institutions of higher education

Pendleton County has no colleges or universities.

Traffic

Pendleton County has no four-lane highways and one traffic light in Franklin.

Today's...

Pendleton County is easily accessible from Harrisonburg. There are many tourists, and it has many vacation homes.

Attractions

- Spruce Knob, Judy Gap, West Virginia's highest peak
- Seneca Rocks, Seneca Rocks, grand limestone outcropping
- Brandywine Lake Recreation Area, Brandywine, boating

Andy Hinkle
Franklin

US-33 snakes its way over two mountains between Harrisonburg and Franklin, the county seat of Pendleton. Franklin is a charming town with one traffic light at the corner of US-33 running east-west and US-220, running north-south.

I wandered downtown on a cold, windy but sunny day. I decided nobody would know the county better than the sheriff. So I walked into the courthouse where Sheriff Andy Hinkle stood, chatting with office staff. He ushered me into a conference room.

"I was hired as a deputy in 1997. At that time I was the only deputy. There are three deputies now who work for me. There are also three state police who work in our county.

"This is a large county for this small group of officers to cover. We burn through about $1500 per month in fuel. We are chronically under-staffed and underfunded. We need better vehicles. Law enforcement is a

Pendleton County Courthouse, Romney

demanding job with lots of stress, and it pays poorly. My deputies make only $18,000 to $28,000 per year.

"I have always lived here, so I have a reputation in and a familiarity with the community. The community is filled with great people, and they go out of their way to help law enforcement. They will tell us if they see a crime or even suspect one. My officers and I are always careful not to burn our confidantes. You may not believe this, but I have actually arrested people who later thanked me for saving their lives. I am always impressed by the willingness of people to give us information that will help us solve a problem.

"We take our scenery for granted. I travel past that wonderful overlook with the view of Germany Valley twice every day, on my way to and from work. Maybe once or twice a year, I will actually pull over and take in the view."

Jeff Bowman
Tom Bowman
Franklin

Leaving the courthouse, I walked the sidewalk northward and entered what looked to be a locally run hardware store, Bowman's Hardware. The owner, Jeff Bowman, is a large, healthy-looking man in his mid-eighties. He wore a flannel shirt and a leather vest.

"My grandfather came from near Mount Jackson in the Shenandoah Valley of Virginia. He and his father fought in the Civil War as Confederate soldiers. My grandfather came through Franklin when he fought in the War, and he liked the area. So after the War was over and he was released from his duties, he moved here and bought into this business.

"We say this business was established in 1860, but it was likely an ongoing concern before that. I was raised here in Franklin. Other than the time that I was serving in the Marine Corps in the South Pacific, I have lived in the same house my entire life. Fortunately, I escaped the War without any major injuries. I did hurt my knee once when I fell, running through a bulkhead on my way to my battle station. I was told I was eligible for a Purple Heart. But the guys I served with told me that if I got a Purple Heart for that they would throw me overboard.

"I live in a nice house that my grandfather built. There are many nice houses. Some of them are for sale now and seem overpriced to me. One of the old mansions has a price of $350,000. It will take a lot of work to get it in good condition, and it takes a lot of energy to heat it.

"When I first started at the store, it was run by my dad and my uncle. We had everything in those days: groceries, hardware, men's and women's clothing, and dry goods. We did a lot of bartering with our customers. Starting in the spring, we would buy maple syrup and maple sugar and beeswax. We bought hides and wool. We bought live poultry, hams, lard, and side meat. We gave credit on our ledgers to the customers who brought these things in. There were hucksters, people who trade goods from one store to another, who would come by here at the end of the week, and we would sell them say, 20 cases of eggs. They would buy chickens, walnut kernels, and hides and would take them to the cities on the east coast. The ones who worked in this area primarily served Baltimore. Much of our business was done by barter.

"We now trade primarily in hardware, appliances and housewares. We do more business now dollar-wise than we have ever done before, but the profit is narrow.

"Franklin is in the South Branch Valley of the Potomac River, east of the Alleghenies. This county should never have left Virginia. The western part of our state has its economy founded in coal and gas. We have none of that. Our mode of life is more affiliated with Virginia than West Virginia. All of our trade is with the Shenandoah Valley. We do not have a view towards the west and the remainder of West Virginia. When I think of the primary cities of the region, I think of Harrisonburg and Winchester. I would certainly be in favor of reunification.

"When I was a boy, it seemingly took all day to get to Harrisonburg and back in a Model T or a horse and buggy. When we drove a Model T, if we encountered another car on Shenandoah Mountain, one would have to back up to find a passing place. I even remember before there were bridges over the streams. Now we are so close that we have become a bedroom community for Harrisonburg.

"We have had several floods. The worst one in recent memory was in 1985. It knocked out all of electrical power and municipal water. All of the roads into and out of town were impassable for several days. Fortunately, the downtown does not flood. The main problem was that it washed out our water supply."

A younger man walked into the small office, and he was introduced to me as Tom, Jeff's son. Tom said, "Did dad tell you that he was a descendent from one of the legislators, Henry Hille Masters, responsible for Highland and Pendleton counties? His ancestors were already living this far west in the early 1700s. Franklin itself was founded in the late 1700s. The Masters side of the family has been here as early as anyone."

Tom did not work in the family business. "I formerly worked in mental health in the Charlottesville area, affiliated with UVA. I retired several years ago. I left Franklin when I was 17 years old, and I couldn't wait to leave. By the time I was retiring, I couldn't wait to get back. Who would have guessed it? There are some rough edges in the move back as I miss my Charlottesville community. It is only 100 miles away, but there are light-years of differences. I have been back [in Pendleton County] five or six years now.

"This is the frontier, still today. A pioneer attitude is prevalent. The ruggedness of the personalities reflects the terrain and the hardscrabble beginnings. Charlottesville's culture is dominated by the landed gentry. It became a bastion of higher education and elite culture, music and literature. There is a strong sense of manners and social structure and what are acceptable and unacceptable behaviors in social settings.

"There is a lot of music here in Pendleton as well, but it is totally different. And the culture is dominated by the Germanic influence and the agrarian lifestyle.

"The best of Pendleton County is that it is relatively pristine in a world that no longer is. Creation has blessed it. It is not as bountiful as it once was, but it is still unique. I feel its bounty is being absorbed by business interests. Boone Pickens has recently insisted that every ridge have a wind turbine on it. I am not so sure that that is what these ridge tops are meant for. I am particularly sensitive to the abuses that happened in the coalfields when out-of-towners came in and brought technologies that undoubtedly benefited the nation, but are still creating havoc for the people who live there."

Jeff had the final word. "Everything here is about recreation now. Nobody can afford to buy farmland and pay for it with the profits from agriculture anymore. Prices for land are too high, and the profits are too meager. People who already own their land or inherited it can make it. There are a few bottomland farms that are big, and they do well. Consider a 100-acre farm where in years past a family may have raised several children. They may have had 10 cows and 40 sheep and were able to make ends meet. Nobody can do this anymore."

Claudia Spohnholz
Franklin

Across the street from Bowman's Hardware was the Pendleton County headquarters for both the Republican and Democratic parties for the upcoming 2008 presidential election. I walked inside the latter. It was staffed by a woman who introduced herself as Claudia Spohnholz. She said, "I'm a 'from-away.' I moved here from Washington, D.C., and live about two miles from Franklin.

"My husband and I bought a cabin for me as a retreat in 2001. At first we did not want to come this far from Washington, but we couldn't find the remoteness that we were looking for any closer to the city. A realtor in Harpers Ferry gave us a couple of listings catalogs, and my husband was flipping through the pages while I was driving. Suddenly, he pointed at the page and said to me, 'This is what you are looking for!' Sure enough, it was a cute little cabin, wood with a stone base, and what we call a moon-bridge arching over a mountain creek. So we drove until we found it.

"Our cabin sits right on the rocks above the creek. I do some writing. The only interruptions are Mother Nature's wild animals and scenery too beautiful too ignore.

"We fell in love with the community here, the friendliness and politeness. In Washington, rudeness has come to dominate public interactions. There is incivility everywhere you turn — on the subway, the sidewalk, in stores, and in offices. We owned a home less than a mile from the U.S. Capitol Building. But that townhouse was too small for two people going into retirement, and I'd had my fill of city life.

"So, we built our dream house and retired here. My husband took a little longer to make the adjustment to full-time country living, but he is happy now that we are living here. He retired as a professor of American studies. I did anthropology. Franklin is in the heart of Appalachia, and we were both charmed by it."

They had a home built, and Claudia did the contracting herself. "Building here was one of the most exciting, fun, and positive experiences I have ever had because of the terrific crews. They were all local people. They never looked down on me because I didn't know what the heck I was doing. People think of Appalachians as being insular and standoffish. It is one of the most welcoming places I have ever been.

"There are so many jokes about hillbillies and West Virginians and so forth. I've heard many from the locals, who are quick to parody the jokes told about them by cosmopolitan types. Many engage the role of backwoods fool and tweak it into a performance art. There is a fierce pride on being self-sufficient in all things, and when you can't do for yourself, to try to get it through an old-fashioned barter system.

"I sympathize deeply with the farmers' struggles to sustain their enterprises. I have equines and buy feed and hay from various farmers. Many of them have 'day jobs' off the farm, the equivalent of two full-time jobs. The farmer I buy hay from told me, 'Come any old time and help yourself. Jus' keep a record of it and pay me every so often.' Everybody is so laid back here. Such trust is refreshing. This type of arrangement I'm sure is common still in many rural areas in America. But when you come out of a city you really appreciate it, to the point your eyes get moist. You feel like you've gotten back to an earlier, more honest and innocent time."

Pauline Harman
Franklin

Pauline Harman is a matriarch of Franklin. She lives in an attractive ranch house situated in the river plain of the south branch of the Potomac River. She is a small woman, approaching her nineties. "I have lived in this area for my entire life. When I was a child, I lived in a village north of town called Ruddle, which was my maiden name. I have always been interested in the history of our area. I was president of the Historical Society for a number of years, and I worked on several books.

"Franklin is not involved with coal mining or other energy fuels. We are more like the counties that we adjoin in Virginia than like most of West Virginia. Pendleton County was formed in 1788. The initial settlers were primarily German and Scots-Irish. Fortunately, this area did not see any major battles during the Civil War. The Union Army, however, did stay in Franklin, and they did a considerable amount of damage. They killed every cow and every farm animal they could in order to have food. Several wounded troops were hospitalized here. Their actions really had a negative impact on local public support.

"Pendleton County was divided in its sympathies. Some areas in the northern and western parts of the county were almost solely Union in sympathy. Here in Franklin and in the south county, most people were Confederates. It seems to remain somewhat divided even today. The Franklin area is Democratic, politically. The North Fork and the northern part of the South Branch area are Republican.

"I think the era of my childhood in the 1920s and 1930s was interesting. I was still living at home through the Great Depression. There was so much poverty. Many people lost their jobs and homes. All of our banks closed. My church was so financially strapped we could hardly pay the minister.

"Nobody had any money, but we all managed. In living on a farm we were fortunate; I never went hungry. We still grew everything we ate except for things like coffee and sugar. We all worked together.

"My father butchered at least seven pigs each fall. He had wheat ground at the grist mill so we had flour and bran. We also grew corn so we had cornmeal. Father fed table scraps from the end of our meal to the hogs. Nothing was ever wasted. The pigs spent some of their time foraging in the woods for acorns and other food. I remember also having loads of chestnuts. We would pick bushels of them and eat them as snacks. The chestnut blight did not sweep through our area until after the Great Depression.

"Schools had abbreviated terms. This was done partially to help free up the children to assist their parents with farm work but also because the school system could not afford to pay its teachers.

"World War II was a difficult time. I taught school for eight years until my husband got out of the service, and we had our first child. My son is now an optometrist in Franklin. My oldest daughter is a counselor in Pennsylvania, and my other daughter is an attorney in Franklin. All of my children got good educations.

"Many citizens drive over the mountains to Harrisonburg for jobs every day. It is a difficult drive, particularly in the winter. This county has never had a railroad, an interstate highway, or even a primary four-lane road. When I was young there was a movie theater in town, but there is none today other than the drive-in, open only during the warm weather months.

"I am proud to be a West Virginian, although I think nationally it has been something that has been made light of. Some of the areas of the state are backward, if you might use that word. I think our state has gotten a bad reputation nationally. The eastern part, where you are now, is mountainous and isolated, but it is not depressed.

"Recreation is popular in Pendleton County. On opening day for fishing, we opened the gates to our farm and let people come in to fish in the pond and the river. In hunting season, people hunt deer, bear, and squirrels. I saw at least 10 deer in my backyard yesterday. They eat my shrubbery. A woman I know told me that she saw a bear near my house just the other day. We also have quite a few eagles."

Living on a river bottom, Pauline has seen her share of floods. She said, "We had a serious flood in 1985. Sixteen people in the county drowned. Water literally went through our whole house, up to eight inches of water on the main floor. I think about nine inches of rain had fallen during four days. It is amazing how destructive running water can be. We moved all of our vehicles out of the garage and parked them at the top of the hill. You never know what to expect when a flood is building, but we feared the worst. The next morning, we were able to get back to the house. My husband was a good organizer, and we were able to get a great deal of help. The flood was on November 4, and by Thanksgiving the house was in good shape, and we were able to have Thanksgiving dinner.

"Franklin got so much help. The Salvation Army was here. The Brethren and Mennonite communities came and worked long hours. The National Guard brought water and provided meals. FEMA was here and many others. More clothing was brought than could be used."

Her cousin Raymond (Gary) Swadley, who was listening to her recollections that day, said, "This kind of sums up the quality of the people here. This is the embodiment of the American spirit. I'm sure it is evident in lesser and greater amounts elsewhere in the country. If this nation enters a serious depression, it will obviously affect this area like any other. But I believe that mountainous areas in the Appalachians will fare better than most."

Pauline said, "A lot of people here in Franklin hope we are not discovered. People have weekend places here or plan to retire here, and I welcome them all."

Ray said that Pendleton County is what John Denver must have been thinking about when he wrote about West Virginia being almost heaven. "I would rather go here than to go to heaven. This area has a tight string around my heart."

Philip Wright
Franklin

Philip Wright does carpentry work for a living. A black man, he belongs to a tiny racial minority in Pendleton County. He lives in a pleasant pre-manufactured home on the hillside to the west of the town, where he has a commanding view from the front porch. The hillsides were brown in winter's earthtones.

"I have lived here all my life," he told me in his soothing baritone voice. "Not only did I grow up here, but my parents grew up here as well. My wife grew up in the Moyers area. Her family, the Moats, were indentured servants. After the Emancipation Proclamation, they were set free just like the slaves.

"They lived on the squatter's property in the Moyers area one mile south of the Blackthorn Valley. These people were of German and Dutch descent. After the Emancipation Proclamation, they were considered poor white trash. The only people who mingled with them were the freed slaves. So that is how we now have a mixture of dark and white.

"There has always been a lot of intermarriage along what you're calling The Spine of the Virginias. Back in the day, if you wanted any type of compassion or love you had to go where that was being shown. Pendleton County is the perfect place to raise our three children.

"One of the wonderful things about living in this area is that it is essentially free from drugs and violence. As a child I probably should have realized that some people were prejudiced, but I just never acknowledged it. The schools were integrated in 1964, and I was in one of the first fully integrated classes.

"I am interested in the history of our county. I have wondered why the black experience is not taught in our school system. My family obtained the land where we are now on the uphill side of the road. It was intended to be split up amongst the black families over the generations, which has happened. After emancipation, many of the freed slaves stayed on with their slave-owning families but were then paid for their work. They were able to obtain property for almost nothing. They also had the freedom to seek better employment or living conditions elsewhere. Sometimes they would be given a small section of a garden to grow their own food in exchange for free labor."

He told me that many blacks from outside were amazed to find a congeniality and a lack of physical confrontations among the races. "I feel comfortable and safe here. I think all of my neighbors feel the same way.

"I have always believed in treating people like I want to be treated. Some of these people in these hollows have probably only seen a few black people in their life and are really amazed by me. I always try to handle myself in a respectful manner. I approach everybody the same way. There will always be some bigotry wherever you go.

"It is hard to make a living. I dropped out of college after two years. I got a good job working at the Hanover shoe factory. I worked there for 17½ years. I loved the job and the people. Then one day the factory was closed. NAFTA did this to us. That was 10 years ago, and I have been doing odd jobs and carpentry ever since.

"My wife and my cousin are the only two blacks that work in the public sector. My wife is a registered nurse, and she works at the clinic. There have been job openings here in the county that I have applied for, but I have been turned down every time. I would prefer to work in a government job than working for myself. I have noticed that on different applications for jobs that I have applied for, they will say that I am unqualified, and they found somebody else for the position. But I know I am qualified. I know how to plan things. I know about safety and quality control.

"In my carpentry business, I talk to people and try to let word-of-mouth bring me new business. I am constantly working to build up my clientele. Chivalry is not dead here. I open doors for strangers. Outsiders may have formed stereotypes about black people from television. But I never want to offend anybody.

"I am proud of being a West Virginian. Living in Pendleton County, whether you are black or white, you will have friends and they will help, protect, and respect you. Our children grow up with morals and with respect for each other. It has everything to do with religion and God."

We shared photographs of our children. Of his three kids, one had light skin, one had dark skin, and one was in the middle. He said, "Our children are tan, butterscotch and chocolate. There is a level of acceptance and respect here in West Virginia for that type of diversity that is as great as anywhere else."

Joshua Nease
Dave Martin
Spruce Knob

The Mountain Institute, an educational center for ecology and natural sciences, was founded in 1972 in Franklin and has since moved to the slopes of Spruce Knob, West Virginia's highest peak. Originally, it worked on leadership programs for the youth of West Virginia. Through the 1990s, its work expanded around the globe, focusing on preservation of traditional mountain cultures and enhancement of economic development in the world's oldest, longest, and highest mountain ranges: the Appalachians, Andes, and Himalayas. An international headquarters was established in 2002 in Washington to provide logistical and financial support to the field offices.

Joshua Nease, a program coordinator, appeared to be about 30 years old. He wore a fleece jacket and a stocking cap. We met inside an octagonal-sided building with a complex, curving roof, draped in sparkling snow. Over a cup of herbal tea, Josh said, "The Mountain Institute was started by two Ivy League students who wanted to find a special place in the mountains to use wilderness experiences to strengthen family relationships. The preservation of mountain environments has come along as a spin-off from their earliest intentions. They were looking around the mid-Atlantic for a place to make this happen. After an extensive search, they found this area and loved it. It is within a day's drive of two-thirds of the population of the United States. Since then, our name has changed a few times from the Woodlands and Whitewater Institute, to the Woodlands Institute, to the Woodlands Mountain Institute, to what we call now The Mountain Institute (TMI).

"We run educational programs. Once our students arrive, we outfit them with all the hard gear they need. Each student gets a backpack, a sleeping bag, and all the necessary backpacking gear. We divide 100 students into seven or eight groups and send them into the backcountry.

"Let me give you a typical course schedule. On the first day we are concerned with setting up our campsite, outdoor skills, and talking about wilderness ethics. We talk about how to find a suitable site for a tent and setting it up and how to cook. The second day we talk about map reading and orienteering. We talk about the use of a compass and how to find one's way in the woods. We then have discussions about forest succession. We talk about how the forest differs with increases in elevation. We talk about the transition from a deciduous forest to a boreal forest, like what is found at the top of Spruce Knob. We talk about geology. We discuss the transition through several different layers of geological formations.

"We teach geology, weather, and climate up there in a way that makes an impression on our students, more so than in a classroom, because at the top of the mountain they can see these things. We point out that the western slopes have already lost their leaves while the eastern slopes still retain some fall color. The lectures from Spruce Knob always have a dramatic impact because the weather is so intense. It is really cold this time of year, but even in the summer it can be windy and rainy. If it is too cold, we simply return to camp. We always do what we need to do to keep our group safe and happy.

"Then we go caving. We have all the safety gear, lamps, and helmets dropped off for us at the cave. We do a safety talk before we go in, and we let the kids know what we expect of them. They stay together and follow instructions. It is a place that virtually all of them have never been

Octagonal meeting room at The Mountain Institute

in before. They listen and respond well. The perceived risk is greater than the actual risk. The physical challenge is definitely part of our programs but not our primary goal. Some kids are in better shape, just like adults. We walk for 2 miles to the summit of Spruce Knob whether it is 75° and sunny or 25° and snowing. Our instructors are good at making these adventures positive experiences no matter what.

"They hike out the first day and set up a camp to use as a base for the week's explorations. Typically one day they will climb Spruce Knob using a map and compass and their newfound orienteering skills. They may hike to the Sinks of Gandy, where they will enter a cave and do some exploration. They may explore the Big Run Watershed, part of which is on our property. It is the highest headwaters in the entire Chesapeake Bay watershed.

"We have been working with some of the schools for more than 30 years now. So the original intent, to educate school kids in nature, the environment, and preservation, is ongoing. We have, of course, developed and refined our ideas over the years for ways to best achieve that. We do youth empowerment and character building, and we teach backcountry skills. We are a nonprofit organization, and we have to cover the costs of our activities and our staff with tuition and contributions. We try to keep our costs reasonable and affordable, lower than a lot of similar programs out there. We do not focus specifically on troubled youth. There are many other programs that deal with that.

"All of our instructors are college graduates. We have instructors with biology, environmental science, and public relations degrees. We have instructors with English degrees and philosophy degrees. These diverse backgrounds bring a lot of skills to the table.

"We do new staff training for our instructors early in the spring before our students arrive. Some work just the spring session and some work just the fall. Some are on staff year-round. We have a high rate of returning instructors. I think this says a lot for what we do and how we do it. Many instructors will come back for two or three years in a row, or they will work for several years, and then do other things and then come back later in their lives.

"We know we are doing good things from the reaction of our students. These are primarily middle school students, especially eighth-graders.

"Many of our students have never been out of the city and in an environment like this. Sometimes they are uncomfortable or anxious about the experience they are about to have. We put them in positions and give them tools to be successful on their own terms. We try to impart the confidence they will need.

"The kids have a great time, they learn a ton, and they are more confident people when they are done. They have a better sense for their responsibilities as citizens of the world and positive experiences in the out-of-doors. If someday they become senators or congresspeople, they will remember the mountain in West Virginia where they learned so much. They will want to make sure it is not destroyed. They gain a preservation ethic.

"Much of what I have been talking about has to do with the programs that we do with private school students. But we also do a lot of work with public schools, either here or going to their classrooms. Historically it has been difficult for us to work with public schools, because many simply do not have the money to pay us to instruct and provide transportation. In the past we have scrounged up what we could, primarily from individual donors who feel that it is important for us to speak with school children in West Virginia. So every time we wanted a particular school to visit, it took lot of time and effort to find and piece together adequate funding."

Josh said they had recently received new funding that makes them able to serve more schools. "We have teachers now who are telling us that their classes' test scores have gone through the roof since they started bringing their students up. Our nearest school program is in Circleville, which is at the bottom of our mountain. We work with their fourth, fifth, and sixth grades every year. Each grade comes up for two days. Their sixth-grade teacher is one of our strongest advocates.

"Students from Pendleton County are different from students elsewhere in the state. They know so much about the forests around them. On a cold and snowy day like today, the weather would not faze them. They are aware of the changes in the forest, when the apples ripen, and when the acorns fall. They know the activities of the squirrels and the deer. They know which trees turn which colors in the fall. They may not know the names of all of the trees, or why they change colors. We work to enhance their understanding of what they already recognize. Kids from throughout the state of West Virginia are comfortable and confident in the out-of-doors. When we bring someone from metropolitan areas, they have a different perception of the forest. While we do help instill pride in these kids, the mountain kids are proud people anyway.

"We want these kids to be proud of West Virginia. We want kids to conclude that it is okay to stay here once they finish school and to help them understand what things they can do for a living. If they don't want to run a farm, there are still other things they can do.

"Being a West Virginian myself, the public school programs are important to me. When I was growing up, I did not have the opportunity to attend a TMI program. I feel a close affinity to West Virginia students. I want West Virginia kids to realize that there are many other places that do not have the amazing mountain wilderness that they have. I want West Virginia students to better understand the way things work and to respect the way things work and to understand how we can improve the way things work in mountain environments. People can live sustainably in these mountains; they have been doing it for generations. But there are some ways things should not be done, and I want my fellow West Virginians to understand this. There are simple things like not over-fertilizing your fields, which causes pollution in the streams, or why it is important to keep cattle out of the streams. I want our students to understand that the things we do here in the mountains affect literally millions of people downstream in the watershed. We as mountain people and as West Virginians are not as isolated as we think. We have a place in our nation and in our world. People throughout our nation have always been affected by the ecological decisions we have made in West Virginia.

"The history of West Virginia since day one has been characterized by outside exploitation of the people and resources here. This is at the core of the worries that people have even today. Every new proposed idea or project is overwhelmed by the roots of suspicion and fear over being taken advantage of again and again as they have been for over 140 years."

Dave Martin, the program officer heading the facility, described the mission of the Institute. "We are looking at this as a holistic watershed model. You can't really separate the downstream folks from the upstream folks. What we do up here has an impact on the water quality, the quality of life, recreational opportunities, and all those types of things for the people downstream. At the same time, decisions that are being made in Washington have an impact on our lives.

"The idea is that our graduates will be able to think for themselves. We are not espousing any particular agenda. There is a lot of value for these kids to be outside of their normal environments and to take the time to have a meaningful conversation and think critically about things. We think that being out here enables us to facilitate that.

"The area along the border here between Virginia and West Virginia is seeing development pressures. It is not in close proximity to large population centers, but it has been discovered by urbanites. We are now seeing property values skyrocket without any real basis in the economy here. We see the same types of problems that all mountain areas near urban centers are having.

"The challenges here are economic. From my experience in life, most people spend what they make. People who come here need to expect to make less money. The people who are successful at living here have found ways to live a happy life that involves less money. I won't sugarcoat it. It is a tough place economically."

Joe Morris
Spruce Knob

There was a dome-shaped building across the snowy field from the Mountain Institute. It resembled the Mt. Palomar Observatory in California, only in miniature. It was owned and staffed by a man named Joe Morris, who lives in Maryland but comes often to view the sky, typically four or five days each month during the new moon. "So every 28 days I am here, from April until early November.

"The dome is a 14-foot diameter homemade fiberglass dome. The telescope has a 16-inch mirror. It is a classical Newtonian type telescope. It is also handmade. The tube is made of carbon fiber to cut down on the weight and to keep it from shrinking or expanding and changing in focus as the temperature changes. The telescope is positioned independently of the dome."

He pointed out the various aspects of the telescope, showing me where the mirror was, where the focal point was, and all the positioning equipment. His laptop computer has a program that positions the telescope to view a star of interest to the viewer.

"Observatories are near mountaintops so astronomers will be looking through less atmosphere. The atmosphere acts like thermal waves that you see coming off a hot asphalt road, making the image behind jiggle. Here on the slope of Spruce Knob we are at about 4100 feet. I worked that out one time and found we were able to cut out about 18 percent of the atmosphere. That is certainly not as good as Mona Kea on Hawaii where the professional astronomers work at 14,000 feet, but this is much easier to drive to!"

Joe told me he was strictly an amateur astronomer. "I am a retired orthopedic surgeon. I have always been interested in astronomy. Back in high school I made mirrors for telescopes for science fair projects.

"I was born and raised in Morgantown. I went to WVU for undergraduate studies and Yale for medical school. Then I went to the University of Florida for the orthopedic training. Then the Navy got me, and I worked at the Bethesda Naval Hospital for two years.

"After Bethesda, we stayed in the Maryland area. Once we got settled in the place that we live now about 30 years ago, I built a small observatory behind my house. It has a dome that is about two meters in diameter. I used it for many years and did photography until light pollution emanating from Baltimore and Washington became a problem.

"Fortunately, it is really dark here on the mountaintop. By East Coast standards, this is about as dark as it gets. I have seen satellite pictures taken towards the United States at night and you can pick out even the smallest towns like Elkins and Franklin and the resort at Snowshoe where the ski lifts are illuminated for nighttime skiing. The biggest threat we have here in terms of light pollution is Snowshoe Resort.

"As a native West Virginian, I always felt guilty about leaving the state. We always talked in college that the biggest export from the state to the rest of the nation was college-educated kids. I am not going to be around forever, so I thought this observatory would be a good chance to give something back to the kids of West Virginia.

He pointed at a picture, and said, "That is the Orion nebula." It had all the color and clarity of a photograph taken from the famous Hubble telescope. He showed me another picture of a spinning galaxy, saying galaxies have always interested him.

"One of my most memorable evenings here was the Leonid meteor shower in November 2001. The staff was out here looking at the sky. Everyone was dressed warmly. I was lying on a lawn chair, looking through a smaller telescope. All night long the meteor shower was spectacular.

"There was an article recently in one of the sky telescope magazines. A professor of physics wrote an editorial, saying we need to get young people into the sciences. Many people who today are interested in the sciences remember being inspired as children by looking through a telescope. That experience helped them see that there was something out there beyond our everyday realm that they could in fact visualize for themselves. I think this astronomy dovetails nicely with the environmental science education that is happening here at the Mountain Institute.

"When I was in college, my classmates couldn't wait to get out of this state. I started coming back to visit my parents. I come back frequently now. I followed the cliché that says 'You can take the boy out of the mountains, but you can't take the mountains out of the boy'. I hope to contribute something back to the people, and particularly to the children, of West Virginia."

Seneca Creek rain

When I met my wife, Jane, 25 years earlier, she was an avid backpacker. But time, aging, and surgeries have taken a toll, and we had not hit the trail with fully loaded packs for many years. Jane and I decided that perhaps this was the time to go. She, our teen daughter Whitney, and I loaded the 20-year old Colt Vista Wagon for what would turn out to be its final voyage.

We set our sights for the Seneca Creek Wilderness, not far from the Mountain Institute at Spruce Knob. The weather report for the early July departure said there was a 30 to 40 percent chance of afternoon thundershowers. When we reached the trailhead, 12 miles from pavement on a dirt road, it was already raining, but it soon stopped. The trail led gently downhill on what appeared to be either an old railroad grade or an old roadway. The trail forced us to ford Seneca Creek on several occasions, but the stream was small enough that we could hop from rock to rock without getting our feet wet. The woods were lovely with many ferns, mosses, and other wet-locale plant species, reminiscent of some of the temperate rain forests of the Pacific Northwest. Spider webs glistened with raindrops.

It rained again. By the time we reached the Judy Springs, where we planned to camp, we were soaked. We crossed Seneca Creek on a footbridge and pitched our tents in an established camp. Several flat rocks were stacked to form tables and chairs. Jane and Whitney took the older, larger of our two tents, with single-walled fabric, and I took the newer, smaller tent. Various campsites were on both sides of the Creek, and another group of two men and two women camped across from us. They had a campfire going in the wet air and were struggling with a tarp.

Around dinnertime, the rain stopped. Judy Springs was a gushing force with a volume rivaling Seneca Creek itself, emanating from a hole in the side of the mountain at the base of an alcove. It was a lovely place. After dinner, the rain began again and continued for most of the night. Even after it stopped, water continued to fall in drips off the trees. Fortunately, our tents kept us warm and dry.

The next morning dawned bright and clear. Because we were planning to return to the same campsite at the end of the day, we hiked without our packs upwards on the hill just to the north. After a mile or so, the forest gave way to an open grassy slope, giving us our first wide view of the area. The entire area was carpeted in a thick cover of green trees, and the topography was gentle. Seneca Creek flowed downhill towards the north. We hiked upward until we re-entered the woods and reached a junction where the main trail ascended Spruce Knob. We decided the climb to the peak would be too many miles for us, and we chose another, unmaintained trail instead. The trail contoured along the ridge and led us through many swampy areas.

We pursued this course for perhaps an hour. Since the scenery wasn't changing, disappointingly, we decided to backtrack. The sky was partly cloudy, and we hoped it would remain that way.

Rather than descending to camp the way we'd come, we decided to take an alternate trail that led to Seneca Creek downstream of where we had camped. The trail was rocky and steep, but the forest canopy was high with sparse understory. Nearing Seneca Creek, we walked alongside a rivulet with attractive cascades. At the Creek there was a 20-foot waterfall and several people milling around. The sky had turned cloudy, and it began to rain again.

We discovered much to our dismay that the bridge had been washed away. We could see abutments but no sign of a structure. The stream was deep and could not be forded without water spilling over the tops of our boots. We marched across and continued. The rain had picked up. This time, we put on our raincoats, but on the trek back upstream there were several more creek crossings. In camp, we discovered that water was streaming from the hillside under the tents. Jane and Whitney's tent floor had already leaked through. The tent was 27 years old. I thought to myself, I should trade this in on a newer model.

For the next two hours, we fought to keep our stuff as dry as we could by working on the outside to divert the streams of water away from the tents and by working on the inside to put things on top of air mattresses and packs. The effort proved largely futile because most of our stuff was already wet. I forlornly sat outside on a rock, head down with my parka hood overhead, cursing the rain and imploring it to stop. Depressing.

Again, by dinnertime, the rain had stopped, and we were able to cook and eat without being rained on. But everything was wet. As we cleaned our plates, two young women who were camped across the creek came by to introduce themselves and to ask us to join them by their fire. From what we could tell, the two men with them had spent most of the time since their arrival cutting and gathering wood to keep the campfire going in the rainy conditions. I generally camp without a fire, not wanting to carry the extra tools, knowing from experience that fires typically produce more smoke than warmth, and simply being too lazy. We unhesitatingly benefited from someone else's labors.

Both couples appeared to be in their late 20s and were from a town nearby. They were attractive and friendly, but everyone seemed to be strained by the stress of dealing with the rain. Their men continued to make trips to and from the forests to gather wood.

We visited with them for an hour or so, and Whitney enjoyed a couple of s'mores — graham cracker, marshmallow, and chocolate sandwiches. I heated a pot of water on their campfire to wash my hair in comfort and did the same for Jane.

It rained much of the night, and Jane's sleeping bag was wet. Drips of condensate from the inside layer of the tent fell on my face. By morning, we were gleefully ready for our exit.

During the second-half of the four-hour walk back to the car, it rained, and the stream crossings were higher. At the car, we stashed our stuff and changed into dry clothes. I watched a rivulet of water dripping onto the dashboard from a leak at the top edge of the windshield. There was a puddle of wet carpet at the base of the driver's side door. I thought to myself, I should trade this car.

The Colt started dutifully, and we decided it might be fun to drive to the summit of Spruce Knob given that we were so close. However as we began to ascend on the dead-end spur road towards the peak, we entered a cloudbank. We couldn't see more than 50 yards. At the point where, according to our map, we were no more than a mile or two from our destination, we decided to turn around, reasoning there was no purpose in going to the peak if there was no visibility anyway.

We set our sights for lower elevations and began the long descent into the valley. The road was initially graveled, but after several miles it became paved and wound through a thick hardwood forest with occasional views to the east. Descending, we could see that the fog was an attribute of the grand peaks, whereas the valley was bathed in sunshine. The road had many switchbacks, and at the base of the valley we pulled into a country restaurant. When I emerged from the car, I could see that the front wheel was smoking badly. Something had evidently overheated on the long descent. Again, I thought to myself, I should trade this car...

I opened the cargo door of the wagon and rearranged the soaking wet backpacks to find the lug-wrench and the jack. The entire car was as humid as a rainforest, and the windows were coated with mist. When I removed the scorching wheel, I deduced the problem as either a blown bearing or a sticky brake. I had neither the tools nor the knowledge to fix it. Our only option was to continue on our journey, going easy on the brakes, and look for help later.

It was Sunday afternoon, and the restaurant was beginning to fill with the local after-church crowd. Three teenage waitresses and one woman in her 40s were staffing the restaurant. It was nicely appointed and relatively modern in construction, and the food was reasonably priced. Spending several days on the trail always makes the first front country meal more delicious.

Our destination was the Bear Mountain Retreat, just over the border into Highland County, Virginia. We stopped in the village of Blue Grass and bought groceries at an old country store. The young woman doing checkout calculated our purchases on an adding machine. Fortunately, the store accepted credit cards, as I feared we would need our modest reserve of cash to fix the car.

We continued to Hightown and turned right on US-250, crossing Lantz Mountain, and then ascended Allegheny Mountain. On the long dirt and gravel driveway to the Bear Mountain Retreat, mud puddles were frequent and voluminous.

We checked into a rustic pine-paneled cabin, which was to be our home for the next three nights. Our cabin had two bunks and one queen-sized bed, so there was more than enough room for the three of us. We left all our wet backpacking gear in the car and unloaded our suitcases in the rain.

Jane and Whitney took a nap, happy to be indoors and dry. I went with the innkeeper into Monterey, the county seat and largest community of Highland County, for an informal jam session. There were eight musicians playing in the barbershop waiting room, with guitars, banjos, fiddles, a base fiddle, and an electric guitar. The musicians varied in skill, but the music was entertaining. My favorite piece was Bob Dylan's "You Ain't Goin' Nowhere." It reminded me of my car.

The next morning while Jane and Whitney slept, I walked the three loop trails around the retreat, carrying my 25-year-old binoculars. Thick banks of clouds lay in the valleys below, and the green ridges protruded above like ships on the surf. The trails had a pleasant mix of forest and field. Songbirds were active. Near the spring that feeds water to the retreat was a small pond that had several warblers and a pair of indigo buntings. At one point, I tried to remove the rubber eyepieces from the binoculars in order to clean the lens. As I did so, I broke the plastic ring underneath. I thought, I should trade these in on a newer model.

After noon, I read and slept in the dining building while an intense thunderstorm hammered the tin roof above. What a pleasure it was to nap without the fear of getting wet! What extreme weather this mountain has!

We had pre-arranged dinner with friends that evening in Monterey. On our way back, we drove alongside the South Branch of the Potomac River north of town. At one point, about a hundred yards away across a field, two bald eagles pranced on the ground, evidently eating a carcass.

An increasing amount of noise bellowed from our exhaust system, indicating a leak somewhere in the pipe.

The next morning, I left the cabin again on the marked trails, but this day I did a more spirited jaunt, running the levels and downhills and walking the uphills. At a clearing near the access road where rusty tractor-driven equipment sat, I surprised four turkeys that quickly took to the air, one dropping a load of excrement in his haste. Near the equipment, I stepped across what I thought was a garden hose. It surprised me when it slithered; it was a 5-foot black snake.

Later I decided to see if I could get the Colt repaired. I drove to Monterey and found a downtown auto repair shop on Main Street. They did not have access to the parts necessary to completely fix the Colt's brakes, but they were able to provide a temporary fix by freeing up and lubricating the sticking brake pads. On my way back to Bear Mountain, the small exhaust sound had turned into a roar. I stopped the car and looked underneath to see the exhaust pipe had broken in half just behind ahead of the muffler. I had no way to fix it.

Jane and Whitney were reading and watching videos. I suggested they walk the trails with me, my third round-trip in two days. The black snake was still by the farm equipment. It was so startling to Whitney she didn't even want to look at it.

The next morning our vacation was done. We traveled over 100 miles towards home under the roar of a disconnected muffler. Conversation in the car was impossible. Upon our return home, we began shopping for a new tent, binoculars, and car.

Rock outcropping, Germany Valley

West Virginia

PENDLETON

POCAHONTAS

Monterey

HIGHLAND

BATH

Virginia

Highland County, Virginia

Highland County is entirely within the Appalachian Ridge-and-Valley to-pography of limestone mountains and boasts the highest average elevation of any Virginia county. Major mountains are Allegheny Mountain on the West Virginia border, Lantz Mountain, Monterey Mountain, Jack Mountain, Bullpasture Mountain, and Shenandoah Mountain on the eastern border. The northwestern part of the county is in the watershed of the Potomac River, flowing northwards (thus included here in Part 2), whereas the bulk of the county is drained to the south and east, a James River watershed. "Virginia's Little Switzerland," Highland is the least populated county in the state.

Monterey is the only incorporated town in Highland County, and it is the county seat.

Population

Highland County's population has steadily declined over the last century, from 5500 in 1900 to 2500 now.

Institutions of higher education

There are no colleges or universities in Highland County.

Traffic

Highland County has no four-lane roads and no traffic lights.

Today's...

Highland County, cold, wild, and rugged, has no industrial activity. The economy is solely farming and tourism. It boasts the southernmost extension of the nation's commercial sugar maple production.

Attractions

- McDowell Battlefield Trail, McDowell, to the core of the 1862 battle
- Buck Run and Locust Spring Run Trails, Blue Grass, beaver ponds, glades, cranberry bogs
- Maple sugar camps, various, maple syrup and other maple products

Rexrode Family
Blue Grass

One of the most famous events in Highland county is the annual Maple Festival. There were two maple farms near Blue Grass, the Puffenbarger Sugar Maple Orchard and The Rexrode's Sugar Maple Orchard.

"Rexrode's Sugar Maple Orchard," had a sign written in black block letters over the image of an orange-framed maple leaf. I drove up the steep driveway and parked my car alongside others in a muddy field. There were several small buildings nearby, seemingly built into the hillside, with steam pouring out of the roof of one. Inside there was a large, shiny metal apparatus almost blocking the door. Beyond it was a table, behind which stood several women, selling jars of syrup and pastries.

I entered the adjacent room through a dimly lit hallway and found smoke pouring from a roaring fire. Burning wood sat below a tray perhaps three feet by eight feet wide that was filled with a sweet-smelling liquid. Several older men were sitting around the room in what appeared to be time-honored tradition. I introduced myself to one of the men. He was a small man, about my height, husky with a salt and pepper beard and laugh-line framed blue eyes. "My name is George Taylor," he said. "I'm Everett Rexrode's son-in-law." Everett was the family patriarch.

A whiff of smoke from the fire curled into our eyes, and as we retreated a few feet away, George explained the process of making maple syrup.

"This is an older method," he explained. "Everett's grandchildren are the fifth generation on this place making maple syrup in the way they've always done it. It's called an open pan method, because it's just a big open pan over a wood fire. We bring the sap water in from the trees. And that's what it is — mostly water. The idea of the pan is to get rid of as much water as quick as you can and get it close to a syrup. After that is a final process of filtering, testing to make sure the syrup is of a given consistency. What actually comes out of the tree is almost water. If you could take a taste, it would have just a faint sweet taste. That's why you hear producers call it sugar water.

"In Highland County, about 90 percent of the trees you'll see are sugar maple. We had folks come in and do core samples and have estimated the trees at over 200 years old. The altitude, make-up of the soil, and climate are ideal for them, and they just grow like weeds. We don't plant, fertilize, or care for the trees in any way.

"To get the sugar water, you drill a hole in the tree about 4 inches, past the bark, and place a tap in it. It is then connected by long hoses to other trees into a collection area. At the end of the season when we remove the tap, you don't have to seal the tree; it seals itself. We try to get everything ready the last week of January for the first week of February, so sometimes we're out walking through the woods in the snow. The trees may not be producing then, but we get all our stuff ready. When we start to get some warm days and freezing nights, the sap starts flowing. Usually by the end of March it'll get warm and stay warm, and the trees will stop producing sap. So there's about an eight-week production period.

"We use clear plastic tubing to collect the water from the trees. In bygone years we used buckets at the trees. We have the tubing numbered, and we have the trees numbered so in the next year we know the tubing will match and be the appropriate length that we need for each individual tree. It's a huge job to clean the tubing. It takes about three weeks because we have to wash all those lines and soak them in a bleach and water solution and dry them in a special can so no impurities or bacteria can grow during the off-season. Getting them out in the spring also takes a couple of weeks.

"My wife and I live over in the Staunton area. I'm in the contracting business over there. My wife works for an insurance company. Another sister works for the city of Waynesboro. But we all come back and help during the Maple Festival.

"In good years, we make about 300 or 400 gallons. We have had years where we didn't even make 100 gallons. It's a good springtime activity and it is fun for all of us, but it's not a great source of income. Everett's primary source of income is raising sheep and cattle. Sugar-making has been an important family tradition throughout the lives of everyone in the family. We have a lot of the same folks who come every year to visit and shop, many of which we won't see until the same festival the next year. We sell everything we make during the festival. Sometimes customers, if they can't make it to the festival, will call and ask us to put some aside for them so we will have it for them when they get here. Unlike some other producers, we don't make enough to sell commercially."

To produce maple syrup, the Rexrode family boils off most of the water from the tree sap. This is done in large metal pans over wood fires. Final boiling is done over propane to control the heat more closely. They use a bottling machine to bottle it.

"This particular building has been in use for production for several decades. I married into the family about 26 years ago. For us, making maple syrup is a tradition. We enjoy people coming and sharing what we do here and sharing our family history. I think that's the same attitude all across the County. Family heritage here is still important. This is the 50th anniversary of the Highland Maple Syrup Festival, but the making of maple syrup long precedes the festival.

"We call these farms 'orchards' or 'camps'. The maple trees we call an orchard because it's kind of like an apple orchard.

"As you can imagine, we cut and burn a lot of wood. We typically burn a lot of maple because that's what we have. I think the wood influences the taste a little bit. We are conscious of taste. We can taste the difference between ours and the syrup made by producers across the valley. We can also tell the difference from one year to the next.

"If the trees are producing, we have to process every day. You can't store the water. On good days there are as many as a dozen of us working together."

He pointed across the room at a young blonde woman, "Here's one of our fifth-generation girls." George introduced me to his niece, Jamie Rexrode.

Jamie told me she was nineteen. She said, "I grew up about a half mile down the road. I have a younger brother, a senior in high school. When I was 12, my dad died in a farming accident when one of our outbuildings collapsed on him. My mom never remarried.

"I graduated from Highland County High School in 2006. I go to Blue Ridge Community College now. I think family is important, and I want to keep them close and I like them being close to me. I think most of my friends feel this way as well."

Jamie and I drove up the hill to her grandparents' house. It was on a bench above the valley, and it had a commanding view to the northwest.

"The house has been in the family for generations. I think the house was built in the beginning of the 1900s. My granddad talks about when he was younger, with snow blowing through cracks in the walls, he'd wake up covered in snow. My dad grew up in this house. My mother grew up in Bath County."

The house had modern vinyl siding and seemed solid, comfortable and warm, with an outdoor wood furnace simmering behind. We walked to a small outbuilding. She said, "This is our finishing room. Once we've boiled off most of the water, we bring the syrup here for final processing."

She showed me a small propane burner, a syrup thermometer, and what she called the press. "It's used to do the final straining of the maple syrup." She also showed me a filter, which looked like a piece of antique parchment paper. The thermometer was about 10 inches long and resembled a candy thermometer. She said, "If we cook the syrup too long it turns completely to sugar."

I smelled the sweet smell of maple syrup.

"I come almost every weekend. Lots of my friends come back during the weekends as well. Driving over those mountains from Staunton doesn't bother me anymore. I've had a driver's license for three years now, but it's common for farm kids to drive around the field in trucks and tractors."

We looked at a chalkboard where her grandfather tallied up each year's harvest. She said, "Last year we only did 211 gallons, but this year we made 359 with fewer trees. Everything depends on the weather. Weather conditions have been ideal." She talked about what she called the Hightown Breeze. "The wind always blows here."

On the way back down, she and I stopped to look at a couple of the trees close-up. She showed me how a larger tree may have three or four taps into it, spiraling up the tree, so the water can run from one down to the next through the hoses and eventually to collection tanks. The whole system uses gravity to move the sugar water.

I noticed how craggy the trees were. They weren't like rows of corn. Every tree had its own shape and personality.

Once back at the camp, I talked with George about the area's beauty. He said, "I was with Everett one morning working out in the field, feeding the cows. There was a foot of new snow on the ground you could see all the way to Blue Grass. The air was crisp and clean. I turned to Everett and said, 'My goodness, look at that'. I mean it was beautiful! He looked at me and said, 'What?' I said, 'Everett, you just don't realize what you have.'

"Country people do appreciate it. Everett notices too, he just doesn't have the words to express it. When you're around these folks, you know they're a part of the land. They can't describe it, but when you see how they live and how they work the land, you know that it's been life for them, and there's a love for the land and for the tradition.

"What I'm finding is that people tend to have places like this in the back of their minds, that they idolize, and yet they don't realize that for the people here, there are the same types of pressures in marketplaces and competitive business situations and development pressures that are everywhere else."

I bought some maple syrup and candies and bid my new friends adieu. "You'll be back next year," George said. "You're part of the family now."

Photo by Doug Puffenbarger

Sis and Ivan Puffenbarger
Blue Grass

The following fall, I was back in Blue Grass, this time as a guest with Ivan and Sis Puffenbarger. Their orchard had been in continuous operation for more than 100 years when it was destroyed by fire a year earlier, in February 2008. "It took 50 years to put our sugarhouse together and 50 minutes to lose it all," Ivan Puffenbarger told me with his signature gravelly voice as he stroked a grey goatee. He has close-cropped grey hair and peers through thick, scratched eyeglasses. "I started helping my father when I was too little to do much."

Puffenbarger was born in 1936. When his father operated the orchard, he drilled holes in the tree with an auger operated by hand, collected the sugar water in buckets, and carried the buckets by horse to the processing plant.

"I helped with that until 1955 when my wife and I got married. My wife, Sis, and I decided that we were no longer going to participate in the family sugar-maple business. About 1959 my father told us that he was no longer able to run the sugar camp. He wanted to know if we were interested in running it with him. I told him we would be interested so long as we could purchase it from him rather than working for him with the risk that he might sell it away. So we struck an agreement. Sis and I purchased the camp."

Sis Puffenbarger sat nearby, showing me old photos. She has blond hair, pulled back behind her head, and has the weathered face of someone who has always worked as hard as her husband.

Ivan continued, "In 1959 when we took over, we built a new sugarhouse. We began to use a tractor towing big barrels to transfer the water to the sugarhouse rather than using the horse. We immediately went from 250 buckets collected each day to more like 1000. It took about eight men most of the night to collect all this water.

"I began to use plastic tubing rather than buckets and collect the water in a centralized container. The first year we connected about half our trees by plastic tubing, and we were able to see how well that worked. The next year we went all plastic. At that time, we had only one evaporator, but we soon bought another. This new machine processed maple syrup continuously.

"Those days, Sis and the kids ran our dairy operation. We were milking about 50 cows. We decided to sell our cows and cease dairy production. It takes a long time for an evaporator to boil off enough water to concentrate the sugars into syrup. One night the wife and I were in the sugarhouse waiting for the evaporator to do its job, and I had an idea. I said to her, 'I am a'gonna hook that milking machine from our dairy onto the trees.' Sis said, 'You are way too sleepy. You have done lost your mind.' When we were collecting sugar water simply by the flow of gravity through the tubing, we would often experience airlock. It occurred to me that if the milking machine could collect a liquid into a bucket from cows, why could it not do the same thing from the trees?

"Everybody made fun of me and thought I was crazy. I told them that Ivan Puffenbarger was going to find out for himself whether it worked or not. That was the best day's work I have ever done in my life. The milking machine could typically milk from four to eight cows. But when I connected it to the trees it was effectively milking 800 trees at one time.

"By the end of the year I had cut eight men from my labor force and upped production by 25 percent. Not only did the trees give us more sugar water, but there was no spillage. The people who made the milking machine asked my permission to publish the story in a publication for the dairy industry. I said, 'Sure, no problem. If I can be of help to somebody else, that would be great.' They published this story and people came from all over the country to see what I had done."

Puffenbarger told me of many other innovations and capital improvements he'd made over the years to increase sales and overall production. "We sell perhaps 75 percent of our total annual production during the Maple Festival. We also sell to a few restaurants. We are now producing from the sugar water of over 2000 trees. We have over 11,000 taps.

"Everything was going really well until February 26, 2008, when disaster struck. Our neighbors were returning around 9 p.m. from a basketball game with their children. They pulled into our driveway and ran to our door, yelling, 'Your sugar camp is on fire.'

"I was already in my pajamas. I have a bad back and I walk with a cane but somehow I sprinted 100 yards up the hill to find fire destroying our building. The first thing I did was to move one of our trucks away so it wouldn't be destroyed. By the time I went back to move a second truck, the smoke was so black I could barely see."

Puffenbarger was able to save both trucks, but nothing inside the building. The dry planks burned quickly, fanned by strong winter winds.

"The rest is history," said Ivan. "The fire trucks arrived and began to spray water. Several firefighters told me they had never fought a fire as hot. Fire trucks arrived from Bluegrass, Monterey, and McDowell. They had six trucks here, but they couldn't do a thing. The boy who drove from McDowell told me he sped through downtown Monterey at over 70 mph."

It is likely the firemen saved the Puffenbarger barns and house. There was a fuel tank containing 6000 gallons of fuel oil next to the burning building and somehow the firemen kept it from spilling or burning. "They sprayed water on that tank, and you could see steam just pouring off it. There was another tank with 1000 gallons of propane nearby. Somehow, I had the presence of mind to shut it off. The man from the propane company told me that had I not shut off the valve, the tank probably would have exploded.

"We lost around $250,000 worth of equipment in less than an hour. We were devastated."

The Puffenbargers had only minimal insurance. The fire occurred about two weeks before the 50th Annual Highland County Maple Festival began. The story was printed in the Monterey newspaper, The Recorder, as well as several regional papers, but people came anyway.

Ivan said, "I sat in a chair to greet our visitors as they arrived to buy syrup. My back hurt too much for me to stand up. It was pretty tough for me to watch. People crawled out of their cars and wiped tears from their eyes. One after another, they walked over to me and said, 'You have got to put it back.' I told them, 'I don't know whether I can put it back.' One after another, they took out their checkbooks and wrote us checks. 'Maybe this will help.' We got checks for $100 and more.

"People said, 'You are the backbone of the Maple Festival. You have got to put it back.' I was 72 years old. In spite of my reluctance, we decided to move forward and rebuild. People came from all over to help us rebuild."

People from around the area helped with the foundation, the roof trusses, and the framing. Puffenbarger scheduled the rebuild on a Thursday, Friday, and Saturday in May. By Saturday evening their building was almost completed. "At various times we had upwards of 15 people working at one time, and I sat in my chair and told them what I wanted and they did it. It beat anything I had ever seen! Someone said to me, 'You have helped everyone in this valley for over 50 years. They have not forgotten.'

"Both young and old were still here for us when we needed them. Country people know how to get things done. In this day and time, you just don't hear stuff like this happening anymore. I cannot give my friends and neighbors enough praise for what they have done for me and my family. I never thought in my life I would see a building of the quality level of what is out there right now."

The Puffenbargers spent $95,000 on new equipment. Ivan said, "If the Lord gives us enough time to live and good weather to let our trees produce for us, we can get it mostly paid for before I kick the bucket.

"We still have people arriving at the house to buy syrup from us. When I tell them we have nothing to sell because we were burned out last year, they say, 'So be it. We are not going to buy from anybody else. We will come back in the spring when you have new syrup to sell.'

"One newcomer wrote me a check. He said, 'This is for you to use until you get back on your feet.' It was substantial. He said to me, 'You can't believe how many good things I have heard about you. Of all the good people in Highland County, people say you are the best.' I said to him, 'I appreciate all those kind words. If you ever need any help, I will be there. I try to help everybody.'"

Camp Allegheny
Allegheny Mountain

West of the sugar camps of Blue Grass was the ruin of a Confederate fort, Camp Allegheny. To get there, I drove through windswept Hightown with its forlorn, exposed country store, then over Lantz Mountain. At the base of the mountain was Back Creek, where beavers had built several elaborate dams on both sides of the road. The ascent of Allegheny Mountain was winding and intricate with terrific views northward. Just past the state line in an area of deep woods and snow, there was an interpretive sign for Camp Allegheny. I had to brush three inches of snow off the sign to read it.

It was shady and cold. I shivered leaving the warm car. But I knew the Confederates endured a winter here, and I thought I would try to experience their world.

The Confederate Army had built a camp here in the summer of 1861 in an effort to control the Staunton to Parkersburg Turnpike (much of which is now US-250) which had significant strategic importance. At 4500 feet on the top of Allegheny Mountain, this was the highest elevation of any fort east of the Mississippi River.

Colonel Edward Johnson had been assigned a Confederate force of 1200 men consisting primarily of Georgia and Virginia regiments, a detachment of cavalry, and eight pieces of artillery. The fort was referred to variously as Camp Allegheny, Camp Baldwin, and Camp Johnson. It was constructed on the farm of John Jaeger, and several cabins were built supposedly with the wood taken by cutting down a large sugar maple grove. One can only imagine the indignation felt by Mr. Jaeger at this imposition, regardless of his political loyalties. Confederate General Henry R. Jackson moved his forces to this position following the Battle of Greenbrier River at Camp Bartow on October 3, 1861, and joined Johnson.

Only sporadic skirmishes occurred at the encampment through the fall and approaching the winter solstice. The soldiers settled into a routine of drilling, combat exercises, and preparing for winter at a remote outpost. That relative calm was soon shattered.

Brigadier General Robert H. Milroy, commander of federal forces in

Photo by Doug Puffenbarger

the Cheat Mountain division in West Virginia, was determined to destroy the Confederate outpost. He assembled a force of about 1900 men at Cheat Summit and deployed on December 12, 1861. The next morning, a sunny but cold day with a bitter westerly wind, Milroy split his army about a mile from the fort and began his assault. His main column, which he personally directed, left the Turnpike and picked its way up a steep mountainside. Meanwhile, the second group, commanded by Colonel Moody, approached from the left. Milroy instructed Moody to attack first with Milroy joining the battle as soon as he heard the first assault. Unfortunately for the attackers, Moody encountered a Confederate outpost and was forced to begin the fight prematurely, sending a false signal to Milroy, who then began his attack. Ultimately, in close hand-to-hand combat where the Federals were unable to use their cannons efficiently, the Confederates gained the upper hand.

After several hours of fighting, Milroy retreated, gathering his dead and wounded from the open field. Finally, Colonel Moody made his appearance, but his late attack was hopeless, given that the Confederates were now able to commit their entire force against him. Moody's troops also were reported to have fought stubbornly but were also driven back. They soon rejoined Milroy's force and both retreated to the west. The battle had lasted from 7:15 in the morning until 2:00 in the afternoon. The number of casualties reported was approximately 20 killed and 115 wounded on each side. This was the only action seen by the Confederates in their lonely outpost. Confederates claimed victory; Colonel Johnson was promoted to brigadier general and his command received a commendation from the Confederate Congress.

The Confederates may have wished they'd lost. Through the remainder of the winter, they suffered more from their exposed position than they had from the battle. Pneumonia, measles, and dysentery swept through the camp. Many of the soldiers from Georgia had never seen snow and were miserable.

My mind's eye saw poorly clothed Confederate troops huddled around pitiful campfires in the snow, while comrades lay in tents shivering and delirious with the fever of measles.

In April 1862 Colonel Johnson's troops abandoned Camp Allegheny and soon afterwards local militias set fire to much of the camp. Nevertheless, the site was reputed to be one of the better preserved in the Virginias.

A guidebook described the presence of at least 35 cabins. The hillside above, the direction of General Milroy's attack, was said to still contain a shallow trench. I started off walking to the north in a thick copse of trees, evergreens, clearly planted long-since the War. I wandered through, looking for anything of note, and found only what appeared to be a more contemporary campsite with some broken beer bottles. I explored a large shallow valley that appeared to be nothing more than a pasture covered in a white blanket. Did the Confederate Army camp here? The only remnant I could find anywhere was an unusual tombstone for Milton Stout, a Confederate. The main part was a prone, cylindrical slab of granite, perhaps 10 inches in diameter, lying on a granite platform.

I shuffled through the snow and scrub grasses. It was warm in the sunny areas and cold in the shaded areas. I finally returned to the car for the last time, frustrated, and drove away. Descending Allegheny Mountain, it occurred to me that being cold and frustrated, if even for a couple of hours, gave me a more profound sense of empathy about the soldiers' misery than had I visited in fairer weather. And I didn't have to deal with dysentery.

Nicole Ballenger
Blue Grass

There is an annual motorcycle rally at a farm in Blue Grass, called simply Camp Night, held in support of the bookmobile for the tiny community. Admission is by contribution only, any amount the rider deems appropriate. Riders receive a picnic-style dinner, live music in the barn, and breakfast.

The weather that afternoon was sunny and pleasant, but by the time we'd retired to the barn to sit on hay-bales and listen to music, the sky let loose with a thunderstorm of biblical proportions. The next morning I met Nicole Ballenger, who helped to organize the rally. I heard she was a beekeeper, and I wanted to learn about that. Nicole is an attractive blond woman from southern Maryland. "My husband and I started coming to Highland County about 10 years ago. On our first trip, we were motorcycling. We were looking for a hotel near the Skyline Drive, but we found them to be booked up. We decided to go further westward to see what else we could find. We ended up staying at the Highland Inn in Monterey."

Nicole and her husband eventually bought a home in Highland where they split their time. Her primary income is from working both in Maryland and in Highland as a computer consultant. But beekeeping was her passion.

"Beekeeping started because I have an interest in gardening. Gardening here is no easy thing. Where I came from in Maryland, the soil is loamy sand. You can dig anywhere you want. Here the land is rocky. Our house is in a bottom, and when I dug the garden, all I found was river rock. So I spent a lot of time carrying river rocks. Back in Maryland, I started putting things in the ground in late March. Here, I can't plant the tomatoes until June 1. We get days in the low 30s in late May.

"We were told how cold it gets, but it was still a surprise. We planned to be here for spring, summer, and fall. All of the seasons are beautiful. Even in this starkness of winter, there is still great beauty.

"Beekeeping captivated me in a way that nothing else, except perhaps motorcycling, ever has. It is an incredibly fascinating hobby. All of my colonies originated from two colonies I bought several years ago.

The colonies are called nukes, from the word nucleus. I have split these several times and gotten more colonies. If you split a colony and leave the queen but take some eggs and put them into a new box, the bees will realize that they do not have a queen pheromone, and they will begin to feed those eggs and develop one or more of those eggs into queens.

"In order for me to keep more bees, I had to keep them protected. The biggest threat is black bears. A mom and two cubs live on our ridge and often pass through our property. A lot of beekeepers protect their hives from bears by using electric fences. If it fails, the bears are in and you can never get rid of them.

"We have a neighbor who loves honey and believes in the healing powers of honey. He has a sawmill and offered to help us build something that would provide a better home for the hives. So we cut some locust and hemlock trees on our property and hauled them over to his sawmill. We made all the posts and all of the framing from those trees. Now we have a 20-foot long bee shed. His sawmill is 21 feet long so the longest board he could cut was 20 feet so that is the length of our shed. It is 14 feet wide. All of my colonies live inside.

"Just having the experience of seeing this come literally from out of our place, and the relationship that we developed during the process with him, was gratifying and now we are friends. It is illustrative of country life at its best.

"I think nutrition is a big key to keeping the bees healthy. Just like humans, the bees need a balanced diet. The bees go into winter with a lot of young bees. They are strong, and they form a good-sized cluster. They are able to over-winter successfully because of that.

"Colony Collapse Disorder is largely affecting the migratory beekeepers, the people who are putting colonies on tractor-trailers and taking them from place to place. That handful of people is responsible for almost all of the commercial pollenization for all the crops that we buy in our grocery stores. This is industrial beekeeping. These bees are being affected by mites, and they have the additional stresses of constantly being reoriented at new places. Colony Collapse Disorder is a result of a whole series of things."

We talked more about mountain life. She said, "Living in rural, mountainous areas teaches you so much about yourself. You learn to rely on yourself and your neighbor. Back in Maryland, if something breaks you call a technician and pay them to fix it. Here, you need to involve more of your own ingenuity. You end up extending your skill-set and knowledge. You learn how to ask for favors and be grateful and gracious when you receive them.

"Let me give you an example. Last Sunday we began to get air in our water lines. We had guests coming. We called a man named Carl, who came over on Monday morning to help. We figured we had a problem with the check valve at the bottom of the well. We pulled out 260 feet of pipe. Carl and my husband made a shopping list of the things we needed. They went to a hardware store in Franklin and bought everything. Surprisingly, they had everything in stock. We worked to reinstall all the stuff, and by Monday evening we had running water again. If we had decided to call a well-drilling company, they would have taken many days to get here. Fixing your own problems gives you a sense of satisfaction.

"The people who visit here get a short glimpse of this ethic. I think the sense of friendship and fellowship they see sticks with them. It is one of the things that make country life special."

Stuart Simmons
Blue Grass

The first time I laid eyes on Stuart Simmons, I was in the passenger seat of a friend's car. The evening light was dim, but I could see in the distance a hulking, Terminator-like man, shirtless and riding a black steed. It felt like a scene from Braveheart.

Stuart Simmons is the self-proclaimed barbarian of Blue Grass. He is paid modest appearance fees for attending regional Renaissance festivals, brandishing huge swords he makes himself. This man with Popeye arms seemed unfazed by the cool evening air. He wore jeans and a belt with a pistol in a holster.

"I was born and raised here in Blue Grass," Stu told me as we sat on the uncovered front deck of his mobile home, just a mile or so from the Camp Night venue. "I have never had a reason to leave. Everything I like to do is here. My family is here including my parents and siblings, and even my grandmother.

"The beauty of this place is that I can pee off my porch and traipse around with my guns. I can ride my horse up and down the road. There is a swimming hole in the river nearby. There is a freedom that people who live distances from here pay to have access to every once in a while, and these things are always accessible to me. The trade-off is that I make $10 per hour with no benefits, and I work hard. There are few occupational opportunities here. If a person enjoys the things that I enjoy, they will be happy here.

"I could have made more money in the city. But if I had done so, I wouldn't be who I am. I enjoy traveling and going to beaches and stuff, but when I return and begin to see these mountains, I become over-whelmed with a sense of safety and security. If times get tough and mayhem breaks loose, I can go to places in these mountains where I will not be found. I would rather be here than anywhere else.

"I am not a bodybuilder, but I have done some power lifting. To me, what my body looks like is important. But I do not want it to look any stronger than I am. The substance has got to be there. Over time I have worked out what seems to work for me. I am 50 years old. At one point in my life, I was into being radical and fighting. The Mohawk haircut and Fu Manchu mustache was about being noticed and drawing attention to myself."

He spoke about his diet and workout routines. He said, "I train four to five times per week. My workout helps to calm my anxieties. This evening, I had some things bothering me before my workout, but now I don't give a shit. I am as mellow as can be. I have been through periods of deep depression in my life and have been suicidal as hell. I have a psychiatrist, and I am on medication. I only have to see him every four months or so. I can run my own medication up and down as I feel is necessary.

"I work for a company called Medieval Fantasies. When a community sponsors a Renaissance fair or medieval festival, they hire Medieval Fan-tasies, and I take on the persona of a barbarian. I will ride on my black horse, bareback, wearing nothing but a loincloth and carrying a sword. I am typically paid a small appearance fee, but it is a fun thing for me, and I would attend even if I weren't being paid. I really can draw a crowd. I think what draws them to me is my appearance and my unpredictability. I may go into the crowd and capture myself a maiden. I may hoist her over my shoulder and carry her around for a while or take her to the woods. If somebody didn't want the attention, I certainly wouldn't do it, but lots do. Sometimes some of the other performers can be on stage, and I can ride up on my horse and steal the show. That is what the audience wants.

"I have always been interested in the medieval period and in medieval life, especially the Knights. I have been going to the medieval festivals now for about eight years.

"I got my start by appearing in parades, which I did to promote my weapons business. I make knives, swords, and guns. I tried for many years to make my weapons sales into a legitimate business. I was never able to pursue it full-time. I continue to make custom weapons, and if someone wants to buy one I will make it. No two items I've ever made are the same. I enjoy improvising.

"One of the things I like about Blue Grass is the fact that it has changed little over the years. There are only a few businesses: the Country Convenience store, a computer store, and a metal shop. The cabinet shop was formerly a general store, and there were barstools inside. People would gather and hang out."

The village once had a jewelry store, a bank, and a movie theater.

Stu said, "In those days the roads were not improved, and Staunton was a significant trip. The people who lived in the area would patronize the businesses. The way gasoline prices are going these days, it wouldn't surprise me if the village saw a resurgence.

"I have a hillbilly friend, and he took me some places that your average citizen would probably not want to wander around. When I went to his folks' house, they were standoffish. But they offered me something to eat. If you are offered something to eat, eat it. Trust me. If you don't, they will feel that their food is not good enough for you. I went there on my motorcycle wearing a black leather jacket and no shirt and a skull hanging on a necklace. They didn't know what the hell to do with me. There is a whole different culture still hidden back in some of these hollows. You wouldn't want to go nosing around without someone who knows the area.

"One family took me to a church. It was a pretty rock church made of flat stones. I walked inside and saw that the pews were a mishmash of collected furniture. On the stage was a Lazy-Boy rocking chair. They had a baptismal tank which was a cattle tank with a lid on it. The preacher came in a great big Cadillac with stickers all over it. During the service they had a retarded girl sitting in the rocker and wailing incomprehensibly. The music was ancient. The musicians played on a guitar, a piano, and some other weird instrument that I didn't recognize. I went there simply for the experience.

"This area is somewhat frozen in time. I think in many ways we are 50 to 100 years behind much of the rest of the country. I like it that way. It is still a place close to nature. It is colder than hell in the wintertime. In years past it was common to be able to walk over fences because the snow was so deep. But even here, the winters are moderating.

"The first year I got married, we lived in a trailer park. My wife worked at a sewing factory in Monterey. They got really low on work, and she was not working much of the time. I didn't have work a lot of the time either. We existed on damn near nothing. We had electric heat in our trailer, and I can remember seeing frost on the inside walls. We couldn't afford the heat. I had started weight training, and I knew I needed carbohydrates. I was eating stuff that was being thrown out of grocery stores. Some of it I could keep down and some of it I couldn't. Anything that had fur on it, I ate. It was hard, and at the time I thought it was awful. But I will tell you the God's truth; that was the best time of my life. I had a woman, and we were struggling. But we were one. Together, we made only about $6,000 or $7,000 all year. We froze but we slept pretty close; we were newlyweds. When I saw a critter wandering through the woods, I didn't see a cute animal anymore; I saw dinner."

Stu never had children. "I have struggled with depression all of my life, and I wouldn't condemn Hitler to that. I was afraid of sending that down the line. I am suicidal, and if I killed myself, what kind of daddy would I be? It was that bad, and I took it that seriously. I am pretty happy with where I am at right now. I ain't got shit; I'll never have shit; I don't need shit."

I asked about some linear scars on his left shoulder. He said, "I did that intentionally. Sometimes when I get depressed, I cut myself a good deep cut and bleed it into a vodka bottle. I enjoy the hell out of it. This is not something many people understand. I haven't done this for a long time because it is really not acceptable. I have always been around sharp things. When I got cut badly, I always became happier than hell.

Photo by Doug Puffenbarger

"If you write about this in your book, I don't want people to think that all Virginians are like this. My behavior is nonstandard. You don't typically see people walking down the road leading a black horse and wearing a thong on a Sunday afternoon. Most people have never seen the likes of Stuart Simmons."

Lumbar

Watersheds of the Greenbrier, James, and New Rivers
Counties of Pocahontas, Bath, Alleghany, Greenbrier,
Craig, Monroe, Giles, Bland, most of Tazewell, and what was
left of Highland

You know, most reporters can't go back to the towns they wrote stories about. I never wrote that kind of story.[6]

— Charles Kuralt, reporter

The experience of the last five months in Alderson, West Virginia, has been life altering and life affirming.[7]

— Martha Stewart, ex-con, businesswoman

Summer

Jane and I left home on a rapidly warming August morning bound for Pocahontas County, West Virginia, on the Honda touring motorcycle I'd recently bought expressly for such trips. It is a twenty-year-old used bike, with ample storage space and a comfortable rear seat for her. The body work on the back end of the bike had a minor misalignment from perhaps a previous owner's mishap, but seemed insignificant when I looked it over before my purchase.

We entered Giles County on The Spine of the Virginias near Newport. In the village were several large crepe myrtle bushes with flamboyant red blossoms at the top. The village was as quaint and picturesque as always. A church sign boasted, "Free trip to heaven. Details inside." We rode northeasterly on SR-42, then over Johns Creek Mountain into the crossroads of Maggie in Johns Creek Valley. Puffy white clouds hovered over Potts Mountain to the north. The valley had several cultivated fields of corn, bright green plants with tan tassels atop. Cylindrical bales of hay sat in other fields, beige in color, sitting on seas of green. In one hay-field sat a solitary flagpole with the Stars and Stripes flapping in the light wind. By a house was another flagpole with an American flag strung over a Confederate flag. A driveway was flanked by a stone wall with six millstones embedded within it. A great blue heron flapped away from the creek.

We rode over Potts Mountain, the favorite amongst area motorcyclists for its smooth pavement, open sight distances, and sweeping curves. We encountered one other vehicle, fortuitously at the sole passing zone, and swept by rapidly.

We drove through Paint Bank, Sweet Springs, Sweet Chalybeate, and Crows, then the tunnel where the mainline C&O Railroad approaches its long Alleghany Tunnel under the mountain atop which is the state borderline. The roadway tunnel looks like a steel corrugated pipe. We passed a church with a sign that said, "Help me to be the person my dog thinks I am."

In downtown White Sulphur Springs, I stopped to make a telephone call. Jane sat on the curb and fingered the red mulch, lightweight shredded rubber. Downtown was quiet with several unoccupied storefronts.

Departing westward, we saw a sign in front of a church that read, "God answers knee-mail." We stopped in Lewisburg where I treated Jane to lunch at an upscale restaurant with items on the menu we didn't recognize and $6.00 slices of cake. Outside, I chatted with three motorcycle riders, all with expensive late-model BMWs, touring from Pennsylvania. One rider said, "This town seems different than others we've seen in West Virginia."

"How so?" I asked.

"Well, it's nice."

The state fair was underway in nearby Fairlea, and a policeman directed heavy traffic at Lewisburg's central interchange. He appeared to have been there for awhile; a half-empty bottle of Gator-ade at his feet.

Northward, through the Wal-Mart/Lowes/McDonalds madness, we swept past the tidy farms of Maxwelton, Frankford, and Renick before cresting Droop Mountain. A sign outside a church said, "Try Jesus. If you don't like him, the devil will always take you back." The curvy road made passing several dawdling pickup trucks a nerve-wracking affair.

We turned left in Mill Point, drove up Yew Mountain and stopped at the Cranberry Glades Botanical Area. The Glade is a high-elevation bog with many plant and animal species more commonly seen in Canada. During the last Ice Age, 10,000 years ago, glaciers never made it as far south as the Virginias, but the climate was cold, bringing Arctic plants into the area. These plants retreated northward with the glaciers, but they also migrated to higher elevations, now like cold islands in seas of warmer-climate vegetation. We strolled on a one-way marked boardwalk, examining the pretty wildflowers and ferns, and reading the interpretive signboards about insect-eating plants. We wondered whether the family we passed going in the other direction was illiterate or simply obstinate.

Back aboard the Honda, we rode the Highland Scenic Highway for its 30-mile duration, cresting over 4500 feet of elevation where pines and spruces dominate the stunted forests. Long, straight stretches of road begged for greater speeds than the marked 45-mph limit, but I held back, basking in the cooler air. From the overlooks, we could see isolated dark clouds and streams of rain amidst the hot, green valley.

The downhill run into Marlinton is 3½ miles with grades exceeding 9 percent, another motorcyclists' favorite. My windshield became splotched with sprinkles of rain, wetting the road and holding my speed in check. An Air Force jet swooshed low overhead. We parked by our bed-and-breakfast lodging for the night where parking meters requested contributions of a nickel for a half-hour or a dime for an hour. A passer-by said the town never enforced them.

As we unpacked, Jane discovered her nightgown had somehow been torn inside the trunk. I discovered the trunk was sufficiently misaligned with the rear wheel that the tire, at full compression of the suspension, had chewed a hole through the inside of the trunk. I said to myself, when you buy a 20-year old motorcycle for a pittance, you get what you pay for.

Patti Reum
Allegheny Mountain

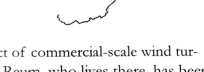

Highland County faces the prospect of commercial-scale wind turbines atop Allegheny Mountain. Patti Reum, who lives there, has been collecting data on eagles and other migratory birds in an effort to have the turbines banned.

In order to track the movement of eagles, Patti and friends raised money to put a telemetry unit on a golden eagle. "Even when hooded, these birds are pretty impressive. They have up to 6-foot wingspans. I sat holding this bird while the biologists attached a small harness with a solar collector and a telemetry unit. Not many people have ever held an eagle in their lap. We banded its foot with a U.S. Fish and Wildlife service band, and then we released it.

"When the wind turbine people came out here, they said, 'Because nobody lives out here, this is a perfect place for these turbines.' We protested, saying, 'This is a migratory raptor pathway. I had seen both bald and golden eagles. A friend and I started a project that we called the Highland County Eagle Survey. We collected data on sightings of eagles and searched for eagle nests. In our first year, we found three bald eagle nests. The bald eagles are fish eaters, and we typically found nests along the rivers. The golden eagles were found along the ridge lines.

"We were seeing golden eagles here summer and winter. We wondered why they were still here in the summer and not migrating northward. Golden eagles do not mature until five years of age. We were seeing mature and immature birds. We began to think there must be a nest here in Highland County. If there were a nest, it would be the first Appalachian golden eagle nest ever discovered.

"This is ideal eagle habitat because of the large number of exposed rock outcroppings and because of the remoteness. There is ample prey. Golden eagles eat carrion, groundhogs, fox squirrels, rabbits, and the entrails of deer."

They tracked the eagle through Pennsylvania, New York, and western Massachusetts, and then into Maine and finally into Québec for the summer. Will she ever return? A coup in the ornithological world would be if she nested here.

"Wind energy is cleaner than coal and nuclear energy. But the wind is inconsistent. It is not as high during the summer when most of the energy is needed. There is no plan for the storage of this power. So there has never been a definitive balance sheet of how much energy they will generate. I have never seen a published study of the return on investment or any other financial considerations. Why? If there were a lot of money to be made, I would think these studies would be well publicized and easy to find.

"Standing before an audience of well-dressed men and women in a courtroom in an air-conditioned building in Richmond, I heard a lot of people talking about an acceptable level of destruction of bald and golden eagles. 'What is the allowable take?' To me, killing one golden eagle is not allowable. The people in that courtroom were attempting to put a dollar value on the life of an eagle. Will $5,000 bring a dead eagle back to life?"

"Everybody in Virginia should be fighting to protect places like this so that we can tell our grandchildren that we helped to save the eagles."

Post Script: the State Corporation Commission of Virginia gave official clearance for the construction of 19 turbines on the state line of Virginia and West Virginia between Highland and Pocahontas counties in March 2010, with construction beginning in the spring of 2010.

Doug Gutshall
Monterey

Doug Gutshall is a farmer who lives near Hightown and is chairman of Highland County's planning commission. His ancestors have lived near here since 1750. He told me he cannot make enough money on the farm to support his family. In his case, the income of his wife, who works at the Homestead resort in Bath County, supports them and provides their medical insurance.

He chairs the Highland County Planning Commission that provides guidance to the board of supervisors with regard to various plans with respect to how they fit or do not fit into the comprehensive plan. He said, "I think our commission does a good job, and we are fair. If we lean one way or another, we lean towards the land owner because we believe in property rights. We believe in protecting farmland because many of us are farmers. But we also recognize that we must have growth to survive. Our emergency services are not adequately funded. The fire department in Monterey has, I think, only four responding members. The fire chief is over 60 years old.

"It costs more than $18,000 per year to educate a student. In Pocahontas, down in Tazewell County, it costs $14,000 per student, and that was so much that the county closed the school. We are on the verge of losing our entire school system."

At the time of this conversation, in 2009, Highland County's entire school system had 287 kids in K-12.

"We have got to have growth to support our schools and other county services. We will need some kind of industry. It will probably be something that a lot of people are not going to like. Near the Pendleton County line some citizens and the county got together to build a slaughterhouse. Of course, this is an agricultural business. That will help to provide jobs and is the type of thing we need to look into. The things we will fund will not necessarily always be pretty or please everybody. But we will need some new jobs if we continue to exist.

"I am in favor of the proposed wind turbines, but that is more of a tax issue than an employment issue. The money they will generate (excuse the pun) will ease the tax burden on everybody. They will undeniably have an impact on the environment, which I hope will be positive. It should benefit both the newcomers and the natives.

"If people want to move to Highland County, they better bring their money when they come. They ain't going to get it here. Throughout the area there has been a shortage of good paying jobs. This goes for both the Virginia side and the West Virginia side. We are looking to bring in the type of industries that will protect the environment and yet provide incomes so that young people will want to stay. Young people need to make enough money so they can raise a family with benefits and health insurance and to the point where they are not in debt to the system for their entire lives."

Pocahontas County, West Virginia

Pocahontas County boasts the highest average elevation east of the Mississippi River. Much of the county is within the Monongahela National Forest, and the county is generally thought of as West Virginia's wildest and most scenic. It is the location of West Virginia's second highest peak, Bald Knob.

There are 942 square miles.

Incorporated towns include Durbin, Hillsboro, and Marlinton, the County seat.

Population

Pocahontas County's population rose above 15,000 in the early decades of the 20th century, but has since fallen to 9000.

Institutions of higher education

Pocahontas County has no colleges or universities.

Traffic

Pocahontas County has four-lane highways and three traffic lights, all in Marlinton.

Today's...

Pocahontas County boasts tourism as the biggest source of its economy. Many out-of-towners own second homes in the county.

Attractions

- Cranberry Glades, Mill Point, scenic botanical area
- Highland Scenic Highway
- Pearl S. Buck museum, Hillsboro, birthplace of famous writer
- Droop Mountain State Park, Droop, battlefield and lookout tower
- Beartown State Park, Droop, limestone rock formations
- Snowshoe Resort, Snowshoe, ski and golf resort
- Cass Scenic Railroad State Park, Cass, steam locomotive railroad
- National Radio Astronomy Observatory, Green Bank, telescopes and visitors center
- Greenbrier River Trail, Cass to Caldwell (Greenbrier Co.), flat bicycle trail

Pamela Pritt
Marlinton

The *Pocahontas Times* is a weekly paper published since 1883, located in a small, two-story building in downtown Marlinton, a town with a grid of streets three blocks wide by six blocks long. Pamela Pritt is co-owner and publisher of the newspaper. Pam was born and has lived in Pocahontas County all her life. She said, "At some point in my childhood, I became quite the comic book fan. I wanted to be Lois Lane. I didn't necessarily want to be continually rescued, but I did become interested in reporting.

"In 1993 the *Pocahontas Times* hired me to cover a murder trial, which I freelanced. Two women who were here to attend a gathering of the Rainbow Family were shot and killed. For several weeks prior, all our highways had hippie-looking characters with their wild outfits. Marlinton looked like a medieval festival. There were jugglers on the street, and people were playing folk music and panhandling. It was all good.

"On June 25, 1980, a doctor found the bodies of these two women in his driveway. The murder went unsolved for 13 years. There were no witnesses and little evidence. The older one was a nurse, and the younger was on a mission to find herself. Thirteen years later, the police had enough evidence to make an arrest. They arrested seven men in 1993, and they got a conviction on one of them. [The detectives] determined the women were picked up, taken to a place where they were shot, and then dropped where they were found.

"The hardest part for me was that some of these people who were arrested were my neighbors. The man who was convicted spent 6½ years in prison, then he appealed. The judge granted him a new trial and at the second trial in 2000, he was acquitted. According to the way our legal system works, after the trial in 1993, yes, he murdered those two women. After his acquittal, then he didn't murder those two women.

"Our county had seen a mini-invasion of back-to-the-landers. The locals felt that these were rich hippie kids, moving here to drive up the price of land and take the county back into a less modern era. The kids didn't want electricity or bathrooms. They wanted to really rough it, at least until they found out how rough it could really be. Local people had just gotten these [amenities] and think electricity is a good thing. Today, the back-to-the-landers of the 1970s and 1980s are fully integrated into everyday life. But the Rainbow Family, in those days, was beyond what most of the locals wanted to accept. The murders occurred a few weeks before the grand gathering, which was at the Three Forks of the Williams River, in a remote area. The murders certainly put a damper on the festivities, which may have been part of the murderer's intent.

"As a matter of legal fact, the case is still open. It would have been easier for the community to have not looked, to have buried this under the carpet. Our [news]paper forced them to look.

"Floods have plagued Marlinton. We had a particularly devastating flood in 1985. The water was 6 feet deep inside the downtown buildings. The flood occurred on Monday. Our newspaper is typically distributed on Thursday, but on Friday, one day late, the paper was in print. I had the heartwarming feeling that everything was going to be all right because the *Pocahontas Times* was still in print.

"After the flood in 1985, people felt this was a once-in-a-lifetime thing. After it happened again in 1996, people were reluctant to rebuild and reinvest in downtown Marlinton. If it rains for several days, people are understandably nervous. Our paper printed several stories about how resilient people were.

"Another former issue was that of the presence of white supremacists. They came here from other places and bought property because it is remote and racially 'lily white.' A man named William Pierce ran the Aryan Nations from a compound in Hillsboro. He died in 2002. For all of his ideologically cruel mindsets, he was a civil human being; polite and straightforward. He could answer questions intelligently.

"When we interviewed Dr. Pierce, we were met at the gate to the compound. The gate was unlocked for us and then was relocked after we came through it. They took us into the main building where Dr. Pierce lived, and they locked the door behind us. Nobody knew I was there. I purposefully did not leave word with anybody because that word would have quickly spread. I did the interview and then they unlocked the doors and I left. At his core, William Pierce was a charismatic evangelist. We never published this interview because we felt it would be like making a big scene. We didn't want to give him that avenue of publicity. These people are not here anymore. His replacement left and runs the organization from Cleveland, Ohio."

Pam spoke of the value to the community she saw in her weekly newspaper. She said, "We were a few hours late this week. People were lining up outside our office waiting for the paper. This happens every week.

"I read a survey last week that said 53 percent of Americans would not miss their community newspaper if it was gone. This is not true here or for any small community. Pocahontas County is huge. It takes over two hours to drive from one end of the county to the other. There are no four-lane highways. The paper is what connects us from Durbin to Droop Mountain. People look forward to receiving their newspaper because it contains information about their neighbors.

"Since the Civil War, Pocahontas County has been the beneficiary of outside influences who came here for development. First it was the loggers. Fifty years ago a scientist drove through and decided this was a perfect place to receive radio waves from the universe. [Former Senator] Jennings Randolph decided the land between Cranberry Glades and Highway 219 North of Marlinton would be a great place to build a scenic highway. Doc Brigham came and decided that Cheat Mountain would be a great place to put a ski resort and that has become Snowshoe Mountain. From now on, Pocahontas County must be more pro-active in setting our own course, deciding what we want to look like. We must shape our future rather than having outsiders come here and shape our future for us. There is a risk to us if we fail to do this. The next thing that is brought to us by outsiders may not be such a good thing.

"There is some animosity towards the skiers. Pocahontas County people do not really understand recreation. How can you make a job out of taking somebody skiing or fishing? We don't play around. Fishing is survival around here. It has taken us a full generation or two to understand recreation and why people come here to do it.

"We have so many disparate communities. The three villages of Durban, Frank, and Bartow have a remnant industrial outlook. Green Bank is filled with scientists. Snowshoe is populated by young people devoted to recreation. Marlinton is the county seat, and it is the home of the lawyers and administrators. Hillsboro is a farming community. Each has different needs. We need to work hard to make sure that each group has its needs met and a piece of the economic pie. Each of these areas will respond to the future in its own way.

"We don't have a lot of racial diversity here, but we sure have diversity amongst our white folks."

Allen Johnson
Marlinton

Allen Johnson, director of the county library system, has been working in Pocahontas County since 1974, almost 35 years. He and his wife raised four sons, who now range in age from 33 to 23. None still live in the community. His take on the community is that people have a strong sense of core values. "They can be somewhat wary of strangers, but in many cases they have had a history of exploitation by strangers. If the locals feel that a newcomer is looking down his or her nose at them, they are likely to be standoffish.

"Life is really a struggle in many rural communities. It is difficult for young high school graduates to stay and contribute to their communities. Pocahontas County currently has no higher education offerings. Our two main universities, WVU and Marshall, are distant.

"There seem to be four things necessary to create dynamic communities. The first is creative people. There needs to be people who are able to think outside the box. Second, there needs to be an ethos of education, of learning, of knowledge, of exploring, because people want to be around others who are questioning and growing intellectually. There must be a tolerance for diversity and acceptance of different people. Third, there must be something unique about the area. We certainly have that! Finally, there must be actual physical places where people can hang out together. There must be theaters, coffee shops, museums, recreation centers, and bistros. People are attracted to and will naturally gravitate to communities that have these attributes."

He believes there were many public policy decisions detrimental to the needs of rural communities. "For example, there was a ruling many years ago whereby property taxes are paid to the state rather than to the local school district. The money is then redistributed back to the individual school boards, based on a formula allocating certain amounts per child. That drove a wave of consolidations across the state, all in the name of efficiency. The problem was that kids on the periphery of this county had extremely long bus rides. There are kids here in Pocahontas County that get on a school bus at 6:30 a.m. School starts at 8:20 a.m.

"When a community loses its school, it loses much of its identity. Dropout rates increase because kids are unwilling to endure these bus rides. Kids are less likely to become involved in athletics, school arts, and music because they have no transportation home once the bus leaves.

"I think we should be putting much greater emphasis in our schools on local traditions, history, culture, ecology, and citizenship. Typically, curricula are oriented around the needs of urban areas. Our kids need to know about themselves before they begin to understand the greater world. Our mathematics, science, and technology classes can be integrated with outdoor experiences. It is great to be teaching music from the perspective of a band or orchestra, but Appalachia is so rich in traditional music. In addition to teaching the clarinet and the trombone, we should be teaching the dulcimer and the autoharp. This would help to develop some pride in who we are as mountain people.

"Our children need to know that they can lift their heads up and look in the eye of any citizen in this country. Magazines and television these days always glorify Miami and Los Angeles. Appalachian people, if portrayed at all, are portrayed as a notch or two down on the level of humanity. Our children need to be able to say 'I am proud and glad to be from West Virginia. I respect who we are.' I am realistic about our needs and problems, but I have never been anywhere that had a deeper sense of place, family, and tradition.

"Many bright minds across our country are looking into ways to resuscitate and reinvigorate rural America, to move people back to farms and small communities. We need a new homesteading movement to bring families back to the country.

"We have from our federal government policies that do nothing to benefit independent farmers. Our policies shower the market with cheap and un-nutritious food. There seems to be no interest in quality of life or public health. Our only interest seems to be corporate profits. Massive corporate salaries are not even providing happiness to the people who get them. The happiness indexes are steadily dropping in our country.

"We need to have a new conversation in our country where we conclude that quality of life does not come from money, it is not going to come from blowing the top off a mountain, and it is not going to come from big agribusiness pushing out independent farmers. I want to pay higher electric bills and pollution taxes. We should be paying more for our food. We should be allowing the people who grow our food to make a living.

"I have been working with an organization called 'Christians for Mountains.' I have many streams in my religious background, but my primary roots are in the Mennonite and Brethren worlds. I have also worked with Catholics and other Protestants. I have been frustrated because I feel overall that the churches have been captivated by the culture. Since the time of Christ, his followers have continually splintered into groups and subgroups depending on the particular interpretations.

"I was asked to give an invocation at a rally near a mountaintop removal site. Normal channels of communication with public officials do not work in West Virginia because they are so beholden to the coal companies. I recognized that these people saw me, as I looked to them, as fellow soldiers in this struggle. I listened to the people whose lives were being ruined by this exploitation. One woman said that they didn't need [the coal] jobs. What she said they needed was their sense of place, their fresh water, and clean air.

"Pocahontas County is the gem of West Virginia's outdoor beauty. I would like to see this place become known as having a viable rural vigor, populated by people who understand the value of being able to hunt, fish, hike, camp, and grow a garden. I would like to see a strengthening of intellectual and cultural amenities. I would like to see people coming here to learn to live viable rural lives, for things like hospitality, ecology, and subsistence farming.

"In West Virginia and in this area in particular, you can be who you want to be. You don't have to look like the man you see in the television commercials. At its core, this is a place of connections. In our cities and suburbs, people don't even know their neighbors. Here, we are entirely dependent upon our neighbors."

John Swift
Mike Cecchini
Marlinton

On several occasions, I have attended motorcycle rallies in Pocahontas County. On my way to a rally one June, I encountered what seemed to be a constant stream of wild animals to evade, like the child's game of dodge-ball. Songbirds flitted along, and chipmunks and squirrels scurried across the road. I was heartbroken when I hit a squirrel. As I saw him, I lowered my speed and planned to zig in anticipation of his zag, but he zigged too, and I nailed him. I had been in such a cheery mood until that moment and was chagrined at how quickly it was shattered.

This rally gathered approximately 40 people. Among my old friends was Mike Cecchini from Maryland. Mike's riding jacket had a splotch of red near the shoulder. He told me it was blood from a bird he'd hit earlier in the day. Wildlife encounters were epidemic.

The following day on a ride I led, another rider hit a deer in Bath County and was flown to a hospital in Roanoke. After the ride, I sat with Mike and a mutual friend, John Swift from Northern Virginia, to ask their experiences.

John said, "What amazed me was that we could ride at 9:30 a.m.

and for an hour and half not see a car. Another nice thing is that there aren't many policemen here!"

We spoke about the deer encounter earlier in the day. Behind me had been John, another rider, then Mike, then the victim, then another rider — six total. Being in the front, I saw nothing. Mike said, "I was keeping an occasional eye on the fifth and sixth riders behind me. We were on a straight road in a deep forest on the top of a ridge. At one point, I looked in my mirror and nobody was there. I stopped and waited several minutes. I turned my motorcycle around in the road. I came around a corner, and [the victim] was lying in the middle of the road, spread eagle, on the yellow line, motionless. His motorcycle was badly damaged."

The victim was soon attended to by rescue personnel. I asked Mike if the experience changed his riding style. He said, "No, I just needed a few miles to clear my head. Within an hour or so, the original passion and flow returned. We understand that accidents can happen at any time, anywhere. None of us should live in fear."

Mike told me he'd always lived like a kid, excited about the next toy or new thrill. "John and I have ridden in uncountable wonderful places and been deliriously, wonderfully happy. There were times when all we had to do was look at each other and we would burst into uncontrollable glee.

"West Virginia is as good as it gets. Every time I leave Interstate 81 and go west it feels like a different planet. I feel my entire body begin to react to the peacefulness and serenity. This area is not a secret. It is in everybody's atlas just like mine. But I know a good thing when I see it. I am a lucky man to be able to ride these fine motorcycles on these roads."

Gary Oberlender
Allegheny Trail

West Virginia's Allegheny Trail is 330 miles long. While several thousand hardy "through hikers" attempt the 2100-mile Appalachian

Trail each summer, only a few dozen walk the entire Allegheny Trail. My friend Gary Oberlender and I started a four-day hike near Dilleys Mill. We began our northerly ascent of Thorny Creek Mountain amidst several small clear-cuts. The afternoon was humid, making the sweat flow, but the slope was easy on modestly graded logging roads. Then it started to rain. In moments we were soaked. We pitched the tent and called it a rainy day.

Gary uses the trail name Gob. Gob is adept at backcountry travel, and best of all, regardless of inclement weather or hardship, he is habitually congenial.

The next morning we walked along a ridgeline path on an abandoned fire-road. We crossed a gravel road that looked like it hosted only a few dozen cars each year. There was an elaborate log structure with picnic tables, an amenity of the Seneca Forest State Park, but inconveniently for us it had no water source. Had we hiked later and longer the previous evening, we would have camped without water and drunk only what we'd carried.

At the foot of the mountain, we crossed a single-lane road. Emerging from the deep woods onto a traveled road, no matter how remote, brings a quickening of the pulse rate, a shock of reality. Barking dogs, automobile engines, and voices interrupt the reverie of the woods. Gob and I agreed that while many folks view the woods as foreboding and scary, we regard the woods as gentle and inviting.

We descended to Route 12 above Sitlington Creek. Two handsome horses grazed in a pasture. Gob petted them and I took photos. In Sitlington, we met a livery operator who has established a business catering to horse lovers. He was a model for rural West Virginians: bushy beard, long dark pony-tailed hair, camouflaged green shirt, baseball cap with the logo of a farm equipment supplier, blue jeans, and work boots. He told us that during the previous weekend, his livery had hosted a caravan of 200 riders on the Greenbrier River Trail.

For three miles, the Allegheny Trail uses the flat Greenbrier Trail. Our walk was hot and monotonous. My feet ached. In Cass, we walked along the still railroad-tied grade and across a few back yards and finally the town's streets and plank sidewalks. By the time we reached the general store, I was knackered. Gob bought me a cold drink and some potato chips and soon rousted me for the final push of the day. We crossed the Greenbrier on an auto bridge and turned northward again on a gravel road, passing occasional houses for a mile or so. The last abode we passed before we reentered the woods was a mountain stereotype — a house with scores of wrecked vehicles amidst the weeds. Two large dogs — thankfully friendly — escorted us through the area. We camped at the first running stream.

During dinner, we listened to the birds, Gob telling me the calls he recognized. The wood thrush is his undeniable favorite; its song is "like a little man playing a flute." The scarlet tanager, he said, has always wanted to be a cash register, "ka-ching!" Growing up in the city, Gob didn't get the wilderness background I had, but he made up for it by being a better student. I could tell a maple from a hickory and a cardinal from a robin, but identifying birds by their song escaped me. Gob knew these things.

Although smart, unfailingly upbeat, fit, and accomplished, Gob was not without his quirks. His funniest habit was his use of the word "bundy" as a substitute for excrement. This was a multi-purpose word, both noun and verb. "Look, deer bundy." "I've bundied and I'm ready to hike."

By the second night, we still hadn't seen a single hiker nor even evidence of earlier camps, or a speck of trash.

Next morning, we ascended Little Mountain along a creek in a dense forest of emerald green, the profusion of leaf and vine dazzling in brilliant new luxuriant growth. The trail atop Little Mountain was level and pleasant, an abandoned logging road. We saw the radio telescopes at the National Radio Astronomy Observatory. The sight provided a strange juxtaposition of new and old to the relic railroad in Cass.

On night three, we camped just before the ascent from the Laurel Run drainage. My feet were painful, particularly on the descents when my foot crowded the front of my boots. Gob popped open a pill bottle and handed me an ibuprofen, what he called "trail candy." While most of our peers preferred carrying golf clubs to backpacks, we found no greater pleasure than being deep in the wilderness, regardless of the pain. By 9:30 p.m. we were in our bags.

Gob woke me early on our third morning. We hoped to finish in four hours. By noon, we were still on the trail. This section had no evidence of trail maintenance, but instead was simply a progression of yellow blazes. We often detoured around fallen trees.

We finally crossed the East Fork of the Greenbrier on an auto bridge and walked to the Durbin Train Depot. Gob bounded across the street to the general store and bought me a soda. When he changed his shirt, I could see red marks on his shoulders where his pack straps had dug in, but he never complained.

Fred and Gerri Bartels
Cass

From our hike Gob and I could hear the locomotives at the Cass Scenic Railroad State Park. Months later, I returned to explore. In one of the camp houses converted into an office for the park, I introduced myself to Fred Bartels, the train master, in charge of all railroad operations.

Fred said, "In years gone by, logging was a major employer in this county. At the turn of the 20th century, the people of Cass worked in the sawmill and on the railroad and shopped at the company store right in the center of town.

The timber barons found an amazing resource of timber here. The workers cut the trees as close to the river as possible. During the winter time, they dragged the logs across the snow and dumped them into the river. During the spring thaw, they floated the logs all the way to Ronceverte, to the sawmill. They were called riders of the flood. By late summer the water runs so low you can walk to the other side. The timbering began just after the Civil War. The railroad did not arrive until the early years of the 20th century, so in the meantime, the river was used for transport of the logs.

"After many years, all of the timber near the river was already cut. The 80-mile long float to Ronceverte was time-consuming, dangerous, and costly. When the owner of the timber in this area, the West Virginia Pulp and Paper Company, heard that the C&O railroad was going to put a branch line through this area from Ronceverte to Durbin, which is about 100 miles, they decided to build a railroad from Cass to Cheat Mountain to bring the logs down from that area. They also built a sawmill and a pulp mill here in the town of Cass. They started laying track for this line even before the C&O branch line reached town. This logging railroad has become the Cass Scenic Railroad. We have about 11 miles of track.

"For decades, the West Virginia Pulp and Paper Company took timber out of this region. Loggers first used horses, but soon realized that if they were going to navigate the steep grades in these mountains, they needed the additional power of steam locomotives. They needed a machine that would handle the steep grades, the heavy loads of logs, the rough track, and the sharp curves. The Shay locomotives were designed by a Michigan logger who solved those problems."

Fred told me in detail the unique design of the Shay locomotives. They had variable wheelbases. Shay put four wheels, two each on two axles, on a swiveling truck. Each locomotive had two or three of these trucks. Power was supplied to each of the axles via a drive shaft running longitudinally along the outside edge of these wheel trucks. Shay mounted three steam cylinders vertically and parallel to each other, like marine engines.

"Our guests run the gamut of interests. Some are railroad enthusiasts and are fervently interested in our locomotives. Some are simply looking to take the ride. Most of our tourists are average families. Many have never ridden any train before. Our interpreters try to relate the locomotives, the history, the timber industry, and the town in a way that strikes a balance for everybody.

"There is an intermediate stop half-way up the mountain at an area we call 'Whittaker Station.' Here, each engineer must take the time to lubricate his locomotive. During the brief stop at Whittaker, passengers can tour a recreated logging camp. Some of our excursions go beyond Whittaker Station to the top of the mountain [Bald Knob], and they have less time for tourists to see this camp.

"Our Shay locomotives have more motion [than typical locomotives] because of the configuration of the pistons and the driveshaft. The driveshaft spins 2½ times for every revolution of the wheels. They look and sound as if they are running extremely fast, even when the locomotive itself is moving slowly. Oil is the life of the engine, so the engineers typically lubricate their locomotives every hour or so of operation. Our biggest expense each year is parts and materials. Our oldest locomotive was built in 1905, and our youngest was built in 1945.

"What we do here at Cass is preserve history. Our goal is to enable people from all over the world to understand what life was like during the timbering era. We want people to understand the lifestyle, not just view artifacts. The machines are not meaningful without the people."

At times during the year, they do a murder mystery train where they dress as characters and act out a drama that actually took place in Cass. They try to illustrate the positive as well as the unsavory aspects of life.

"Because of the type of community this was, being an industrial company town, there were many interesting lifestyles that are not part of our modern experience. We want people to see that this was an intense but productive industrial environment in a wilderness."

Fred's wife, Gerri, works at Cass as well. She said, "West Virginia showed tremendous foresight in acquiring this community and preserving it as a state park. We have many buildings here that have not yet been refurbished. Every day that goes by, buildings deteriorate if they are not maintained. We need to preserve our history and our antiquities."

Gibbs and Cheryl Kinderman
Frost

Cheryl and Gibbs Kinderman run WVMR radio, a non-commercial radio station serving Pocahontas, Highland, and Bath counties. In decades gone by, every community had a radio station, with programming filled with local arts and culture. This relic of the past endures here. I met them in a modern building beside the Pocahontas County

High School.

Cheryl said, "Our call letters stand for West Virginia Mountain Radio. We have two other affiliate stations, all within the umbrella of Allegheny Mountain Radio. One is in Hot Springs and the other is in Monterey. We share programming from 6:00 a.m. until 6:00 p.m. After 6:00 p.m. each station has volunteer DJs who do their own programming. We are the headquarters station, and we do the daytime programming. The station in Monterey went on the air in 1995, and the station in Hot Springs came online in 1986. This station began operation in 1981."

Cheryl's husband, Gibbs, said, "Several people were talking about how great it would be to have a radio station so that everyone in the county could know what was going on. We set up a nonprofit corporation, and we began operations. It will be 30 years soon!"

Cheryl said, "Being a nonprofit community radio limits us in our programming and in our funding. We don't air any advertising. We have corporate underwriters who we thank with on-air announcements. We also accept private donations. And we get grants from the Corporation for Public Broadcasting. We do semiannual fund drives."

Gibbs said, "They are lots of fun. They are entertaining rather than agonizing like most fund drives. We get lots of entertainers to come in and play. We have ladies singing gospel music or bluegrass bands. Rather than laying guilt trips on people to encourage them to give, we provide a high level of entertainment.

"We do some recording here, and we take recording equipment to some live shows in the area. We go to local festivals and broadcast live. We tow our equipment in a little red wagon, a Radio Flyer! It is the world's smallest mobile radio unit.

"The original concept and core idea was to be a communication link for the county. My idea was to replicate the small town commercial radio station of the 1950s when I was a kid. Those radio stations played things like high school football games and community activities. They had their own studio where people could come and play music or talk. This is sort of a back-to-the-future idea. We have stayed fairly true to that original concept.

"We have at least one local news story from each county every day. We have volunteer reporters in each community. Radio stations don't do this sort of thing anymore.

"Our communities are isolated and cohesive. These communities have weekly newspapers, but they are not able to offer radio's immediacy. If someone dies on the day the weekly came out, he would be in the ground before the next edition. We coordinate with the funeral homes to air obituaries every day."

Cheryl said, "We broadcast lost dogs, cats, and kayaks. We have lots of church news and community events. We focus heavily on local impacts of big stories."

Gibbs said, "We have nine or ten people who call in every morning to tell us what the weather is at their home. This gives our listeners information on local weather patterns. One older listener almost became a star, calling us every day. We have the most fun when the weather is really bad. Several listeners call to report their temperature and compete over who has the worst weather. Some days, people get the notion to call and express their opinions. This kicks off a dialogue that can go on for some time. Conventional radio stations would never do this.

"One morning years ago I was the DJ. There was no coffee here at the station. I was moaning about it on the air. Ten minutes later, a man drove up, walked in the door, and handed me a can of coffee. That is community radio!

"When we have a disaster is when we are most useful. We had floods in 1985, 1995 and 1996. Our radio station became the communication medium for the entire county. For most of the county, there were no phones. There was only one working substation in the county and we were connected to it. We broadcast information on people who were dead and alive and who needed help. In each of the three counties, we became the communication centers.

"Radio waves do not recognize state lines. People in Pocahontas County have always bitched about what happens in Charleston. People in Bath and Highland counties have always bitched about what happens in Richmond. But you will find that people in Pocahontas, Highland, and Bath counties have much more in common with each other than any of these counties have in common with people in the more urbanized areas of either state.

"There are many old people who now live alone. They are isolated and they don't get out much, especially during the winter. We have become their family. They turn on our radio station in the morning, and it stays on all day long. Our listeners hear the voices of local people."

Cheryl said, "We have several local ministers who record sermons that we put on the air. For some of these people, church life is important but for various health or weather-related reasons they may be unable to attend. We are their source of information and entertainment. People recognize our DJs by their voices throughout the community."

Gibbs said, "I was once at a gathering at the Green Bank Elementary School. I was talking for a while and a woman came to me and said, 'You sound just like Gibbs Kinderman.' I said, 'I am Gibbs Kinderman.' She said, 'You can't be. He is a much better looking man than you!'

"This really isn't a radio station. It is a giant playhouse for adults!"

Karen O'Neil
Green Bank

There are few grander or more surprising sights in Appalachia than the huge Robert C. Byrd Green Bank Telescope, the world's largest fully maneuverable radio telescope. The GBT stands gleaming white amidst a pastoral green environment. Karen O'Neil, the observatory's site director, said, "We are the original site of the National Radio Astronomy Observatory. We have on our site many of the original telescopes in the field of radio astronomy.

"We do not do visual telemetry. The difference in radio telemetry and visual telemetry is merely the wavelength of the light observed. The electromagnetic spectrum spans from short to long wavelengths. The visual spectrum is a small sliver within it. We are looking at longer wavelengths than visual. Wavelengths that are shorter than visual are blocked by our atmosphere and must be seen by telescopes in space.

We look at the range greater than 2½ millimeters.

"I am a native West Virginian, born and raised near Charleston. I always loved astronomy, but I studied physics because I thought the job opportunities would be better. I got my undergraduate education at Marlboro College and did my graduate work at the University of Oregon. In graduate school, I decided there must be a job for me somewhere in astronomy, so I switched back to astronomy for my graduation project. My doctorate is in physics with a specialization in astronomy.

"This observatory was built in 1956. A lot of interest was gained in radio astronomy as an offshoot of radio communication. The early pioneers in the field stumbled on the discovery that celestial bodies emit radio waves. This was discovered in the 1930s, and most of the work in radio astronomy was done by amateurs in their own backyards. We have a display telescope at the entrance to our observatory that is a replica of one of the earliest amateur telescopes. It is the Jansky telescope named after Robert Jansky, who was the father of radio astronomy.

"In the early 1950s, a consortium of universities met and concluded that radio astronomy needed to be done at a national observatory rather than in back yards. That was the birth of the National Radio Astronomy Observatory concept.

"The Green Bank site was chosen because the mountains proved protection from radio waves and because of the sparse population here. It was also accessible to the major research universities and to Washington, D.C. Almost every project we do here is in conjunction with one university group or another. We have often worked with the Universities of Pennsylvania, Maryland, and California. We are getting more involvement from West Virginia University.

"The pictures we produce all are drawn by our computers from radio frequency spectrum waves. When you think about an optical telescope, you think about looking through an eyepiece and seeing into space. When you do optical astronomy, you employ a series of filters to pick the wavelengths of interest from the wide variety of incoming waves. Our telescopes see waves outside the optical band. Our computers take wave bands that your eye cannot see and convert them

GBT, the Green Bank Telescope

into bands that your eye can see.

"Many of our recent discoveries are in the field of chemistry. Traditionally the way astronomy has worked is that a chemist would find a molecule and would then challenge the astronomers to go look for it. Now we are inverting that process. We infer what these molecules are by the emissions we detect. We see spectral lines originating from space which will be embedded amongst other lines that we have already recognized. So we say, 'We recognize this molecule and this molecule, but here is this molecule that we don't.' The chemist in the lab will say, 'We know what atoms are out there, and we know how molecules are created, so through our various modeling techniques we can infer that it is this.' There are not any molecules that I know of that transfer only at one frequency. When excited, they transmit at several different layers. There are electrons coming out at usual frequencies, but electrons spinning in other exciting states can produce different frequencies as well. The chemists will say, 'If it is the molecule you suggest, then you should see this emission and this frequency as well.' The astronomers will then look for that frequency. If they find it, then they know they have discovered something new.

"We have also found what we call prebiotic molecules. Prebiotic means before life. These are things like glycols and sugars. These are things that chemists will say that if life is to be created, you first have to create glycols or sugars. We have seen some of these complex molecules in space where previously we didn't think stars would be able to form. This is giving the biologists and the chemists new ways to think about how life was formed here.

"When the GBT was first commissioned and put to use, much greater emphasis was put on outreach than before. Our stated goal is that every child in the state of West Virginia should visit this facility at least once during his or her secondary education. Our number of visitors has been increasing steadily. Last year we had roughly 50,000 visitors. We are trying to teach kids that science is about finding answers. There may be many answers to any given problem. We want kids to know that the journey is as important as the destination. That is a different way of thinking for a lot of kids. We try to show them what science is all about and how much fun can be found in discovering new things."

Laura Parquette
Snowshoe Mountain

Dentist Thomas "Doc" Brigham, often referred to as "The Father of Southern Skiing," founded Sugar and Beech Mountain resorts in North Carolina before setting his sights on Cheat Mountain in the early 1970s. By 1973, he had purchased the land which would become Snowshoe Mountain.

Knowing "Cheat Mountain Resort" wouldn't cut it, Doc Brigham searched for a new name, which presented itself in the unusual snowshoe hares which made their mountain home there. Because snowshoe hares require high elevations and abundant snow, Doc's marketing staff thought the name Snowshoe would conjure great skiing.

After two decades of financial tumult, a Japanese company bought the resort in 1990 and sold it five years later to the current owners,

Intrawest, which developed it into a modern, four-season resort. Today, Snowshoe is the largest ski resort in the mid-Atlantic and Southeastern U.S.A. and one of West Virginia's largest employers and most visited attractions. In-season, Snowshoe is the largest community in Pocahontas County. Laura Parquette is communications manager. Laura, a native of Boston, Massachusetts, had been at the Resort for a year-and-a-half.

"Snowshoe Mountain Resort has 60 trails and 244 skiable acres. We are by far the biggest, and we like to think, the best ski resort in the mid-Atlantic region. Our western territory has a vertical drop of 1500 feet. The rest of our slopes offer between 750 and 850 vertical feet of drop. The summit of Snowshoe is 4848 feet. Our Cup Run was designed by Jean-Claude Killy.

"We typically open at Thanksgiving and stay open until the end of March or the beginning of April. We see a lot of natural snow, but we depend upon snowmaking to build our early base.

"There are 2200 lodging units on the mountain. At full capacity, we can accommodate upwards of 10,000 people per night. About 1400 people work here during the winter. We become a good-sized town when we are at full capacity."

She told me business was good in 2009, their third record income year in a row. "We may in fact be benefiting from the downturn in the economy. Because we are a drive-to destination from many of the East Coast cities, people who in previous years may have flown to the Rockies have decided to drive to Snowshoe instead.

"In recent years, Snowshoe has become a four-season destination. We have a championship golf course at the base of the mountain, and it will open in May. It is a beautiful course, designed by Gary Player. What makes it unique are the huge elevation drops on the course. An individual hole may gain or drop 200 or 300 feet.

"We also have an extensive summer event program with such diverse things as a chili cook-off, the West Virginia Symphony Orchestra, and our Freedom Fest motorcycle rally.

"There is a sense of community and pride here that I have never seen anywhere else. We at the Resort are proud to be part of that. Many people outside of West Virginia come to the state solely to visit Snowshoe. Hopefully they are discovering other great things about this state."

Maggie Scott
Wildman Adams
Hillsboro

In 1998, Hunter "Patch" Adams became a household name by the release of the eponymous movie starring Robin Williams. The comedy-drama was based upon Adams' book, *Gesundheit: Good Health is a Laughing Matter*, about his struggle to replace the corporate, impersonal fixtures of modern medicine with generosity, respect, and compassion. Adams' Gesundheit! Institute near Hillsboro combines traditional and alternative medicine and integrates nature, recreation, crafts, and agriculture.

Maggie Scott calls herself the Land Mama of the Gesundheit! Institute. She said, "That moniker came from one of the volunteers to the Institute. I am a full-time resident, and I manage everything. The volunteer season runs from mid-April until October. Some volunteers are short-term and some stay longer."

We sat on a couch in the main floor of a whimsical structure called the dacha. It was triangular in shape, with each of its five floors being narrower than the one below. It had a rough, unfinished wood exterior with an onion-top roofline. There were lots of windows of all sizes, many with overhanging eaves. The interior had multiple stairways with railings made of tree branches, mosaic panels with tesseras of mirrors, broken dishware, and decorative stones. The entrance featured a wooden footbridge over an intermittent stream.

She said, "The dacha has many Russian influences. It has an open floor plan with five levels. The builder had to take down several trees, and the wood from these trees was used back in the house. Handrails are carved from tree limbs. We began using it in 2000.

"After medical school, Patch and a few of his friends started a free hospital in Fairfax, Virginia. Patch's philosophy was that people should not be charged for medical services. Recipients of medical care would be encouraged to donate money or goods. Nobody should be denied medical treatment due to inability to pay. Even if a patient had medical insurance, that insurance company would not be billed for services. Unfortunately, the model failed as most patients did not contribute anything.

"In 1981, one of Patch's friends was traveling through this area and found a 310-acre piece of land for sale for $80,000. Several friends pooled their resources and bought this land. The name, 'Gesundheit,' comes from the German word for good health. Patch became a full-time fundraiser. He hoped to raise the money to fully fund this place quickly. Patch was seeking $180 million to build his hospital and fully fund its endowment to keep it operational. Most people who have that kind of money either want executive control or a return on their investment. Minimally, a large donor may insist that his family would receive preferential medical care should they need it. Patch was not willing to do that. In Patch's mind, it is not about the money, and yet he needed money in order to fulfill his vision.

"At this stage, we do not have a hospital, we do not have a clinic, and we do not see any patients here. My job is to keep the land and the buildings operational. Our hope is that as investors come through they will see the potential and will look to contribute.

"For a number of years, this place had the reputation as being a rock 'n roll, hippie hangout. Some of our early scrapbooks show naked bodies frolicking on the lawn. We still run around in tie-dyed skirts, barefoot. The philosophy is of a happy, loving, thoughtful, creative, and funny cooperative community. People should be interactive and happy in their work. In that type of environment, the healer becomes taken care of too.

"At this time, we do not have healthcare services happening here, but the healing is ongoing. When a person puts herself or himself in one-half hour of free play in nature every day, it has healing effects on the human body.

"It is a relatively unusual experience for millions of people in our country. People need time to sit, read, be in nature, play music or play with one another. I have had groups who arrived here thinking this would be a 'Habitat For Humanity' type work experience. They thought they would work from 7:00 a.m. until 6:00 p.m. But here, it is about maintaining the balance.

"We have many volunteers who are college students here on their spring break. They are tired. They need to rest their minds. They need to learn the balance between work and play. For many people, life is no longer in balance. This place is about finding points of joy. Volunteers come here to work for 35 hours in exchange for a place to stay and for food.

"A typical stay can range anywhere from a single overnight to several months. Most people stay from four days to one week. They come from all over the globe. This place is all about the joy of service and of supporting each other. Patch's whole philosophy is spreading joy and love through service. Patch says anyone who has friends and food has everything he or she needs in life. There is no reason to be depressed if you have that."

Wildman Adams, Patch's older brother, is a staff member at the Institute. Wildman has a long, white beard and hair halfway down his back. He looked like Merlin, the magician. He said, "I do everything I can to give Patch the opportunity to explore avenues of harmony, medicine, education, and life.

"The core message of Patch Adams and the Gesundheit! Institute is peace, justice, and compassion in healthcare delivery and for the whole world. Every patient in need of medical services should want to go to the hospital. Today when people are sick, they do not go until the last stages because it is a nightmare to go to a hospital, especially if you are poor. Some rich benefactors have given the Institute money because they had their own nightmare experiences at conventional hospitals. They found chaotic and incompetent situations, totally lacking in justice.

"For 39 years, Patch has been in the process of raising money to build a hospital here to showcase his message of justice and compassion in healthcare delivery — appropriate and consistent care for everybody. When you walk into a hospital, the administrator, the nurse, the orderly, the anesthesiologist, and the doctor should all orient their level of care and attention around your need. It is important to eliminate hierarchy and rank, to eliminate rudeness from doctors to others.

"Patch is a voracious reader. He concluded this earth can be a paradise. It is only in societal decisions that it has become otherwise. Our current worldwide financial collapse is a result of greed. It will cause literally millions of people around the world to have much less than the whole life that they deserve because of greed, money, and power.

"There is not a living thing in the world that does not react well to human kindness. Trees. Flowers. Dogs. Cats. Rats. Zoo animals. Human kindness is a powerful thing; even the smallest amount can heal and change another life forever.

"We are beginning to move forward on our hospital. Just getting blueprints that have adequate detail to solicit bids and obtain a building permit will cost upwards of $1 million. We are currently preparing the land, and construction will begin soon."

Joel Rosenthal
Hillsboro

The Greenbrier River flows southward across most of Pocahontas County. In the area south of Marlinton, the west bank of the river is a mix of farmland and forest, all privately owned. The east bank is entirely publicly owned national and state forests, except Joel Rosenthal's land. And to get to it, visitors must ford the Greenbrier River.

In 2000, Joel, a native of Washington, D.C., bought several hundred acres of land bounded on three sides by forests and on the fourth by the Greenbrier River, over which there was no bridge. He established a non-profit wildlife rehabilitation corporation where he takes in birds and mammals of all types that have been incapacitated in some way and nurses them back to health. If they can be released, he will do so. Otherwise, he keeps them for the rest of their lives.

As Joel ferried me across the river in his tall pickup, a bald eagle flew overhead. A great blue heron stood immobile near the 8-acre wooded island. Joel's new home is built of contiguous octagonal timber frame pods. From inside, one can look through a multitude of windows and see a lawn where deer graze as placidly as cows in a pasture and a series of lakes Joel built to host migrating geese and swans.

Joel's yard has dozens of motorized vehicles, from lawn mowers to backhoes to four-wheelers. His library, in the basement of the largest pod, holds 4000 books. Hundreds of framed photographs taken during his many motorcycle journeys stand in rows on a shelf. A tiny screech owl flitted around the study.

By the barn were two turkeys, one in full strut. There were red-tailed hawks, great horned owls, black vultures, buzzards, and parrots. One black vulture was his favorite. He stroked its naked face and beak as he spoke softly to it. Back outside, Joel fed a small deer some grain, which it ate from his hand. All of us petted the deer, and I thought how muscular and sturdily built it was, ideal for doing maximum damage to motorcyclists.

Joel said, "This farm or something like it has been a dream of mine all my life. Since I am an animal person, I wanted to do some animal rehabilitation. The best method for me to do this was to set up a nonprofit charitable organization as the owner of the property. The organization is called Point of View Farm.

"All of the funding for the organization came from me. In essence, I gave away all of my own assets to the charity. In doing so, the charity makes better use of my assets and loses less of it to taxes. I can run it as I see fit. Because I had enough personal resources, I do not have to go around begging other people for funding.

"One of the reasons I came here was that a man can do what he wants to do. About the only thing the state is concerned about regarding a structure is where you put the water and septic systems. [When I built my house], there were no inspectors.

"I have found myself in frequent conflict with the hunters of this area. I am not against hunting per se, but there are hunters in particular who are cruel, pure and simple. They use packs of dogs to tree bears, where they shoot them. Even running a mature bear without shooting at it can cause it to become so exhausted that it dies. This is neither ethical nor moral. I have written many letters to the editor about this, and I have taken lots of flak. Beyond the hunters, people write back and question whether I, as an outsider, can come here and tell local people what to do.

"I consider myself to be a friendly guy. But I did not come here

Turkey in full strut

seeking new friendships. I like being alone. Most people have never spent a contiguous 24-hour period of time totally alone. I have spent up to a month completely alone at my house. There have been extended periods where the water is too high to ford the river. Every day, I jump into my projects.

"To do the things I like to do and to have the lifestyle I have, I could not have picked a better place than Pocahontas County. I think I could draw a roughly circular loop around my house, which encompasses 25 square-miles, and I would be the only permanent resident in it. Most people in America don't believe a place like this still exists, especially east of the Mississippi. There are more bears near me than people."

Joel had told me previously about a brush he'd had with the law. "In 2005, the State of West Virginia charged me as a criminal for taking care of an abandoned fawn. Since I run a non-profit charitable organization incorporated as an animal sanctuary, it was my belief that my business license provided me with the authority to take care of the fawn.

173

"Therefore, I decided to fight the charge. Furthermore, I decided to represent myself without a lawyer or legal aid. This led to a 3½ year odyssey that required me to spend thousands of hours learning how the law works in West Virginia.

"In short, magistrate court in Pocahontas County was a scam in that the judge had worked for the DNR, who had filed the charge. The prosecutor not only was the personal lawyer for the judge, but at one point was suspended from practicing law. My trials began with the judge proclaiming that I was guilty, but that she would 'allow' me to try to defend myself. Then she prevented me from even introducing my evidence. This led to my being convicted twice in Magistrate court.

"Ultimately, a Federal Judge ruled that my Constitutional rights had been violated, finally forcing the State to agree to all my demands, allowing me to take care of wildlife.

"It was an experience that provided me with a tremendous amount of insight and enlightenment on several different levels. First of all, it was a unique academic exercise for me, to realize I could learn the law and defend myself. Second, I learned to a disappointingly great degree, how poorly people who are entrusted in upholding the law actually regard it. Implementation of the law in West Virginia is a crap shoot. Lower courts tend to simply go with whatever the state wants. Communities with sparse populations treat issues pragmatically rather than with specific adherence to the letter of the law. Third, even the highest court in West Virginia, while acknowledging my claim, still violated my Constitutional rights. By the time all was said and done, at least the Federal judge in my case saw how poorly I had been treated and rectified the situation."

Joel Rosenthal
with captive
black vulture

West Virginia

Virginia

Bath County, Virginia

Bath County is entirely within the Appalachian Ridge-and-Valley topography of limestone mountains and is the most consistently heavily forested of the Virginia Counties. Major mountains are Allegheny [on the West Virginia border], Back Creek, Warm Springs, Little, Beards, and Mill Mountains.

There are 535 square miles.

Bath County has no incorporated towns. The county seat is Warm Springs.

Population

Bath County has always been sparsely populated. In 1900, there were 5,600 people, rising to 8,000 in 1930. Today there are about 5,000.

Institutions of higher education

There are no colleges or universities in Bath County.

Traffic

Bath County has no four-lane roads and no traffic lights.

Today's...

Bath County is bucolic. 90 percent of the land is under forest cover, the highest proportion of any Virginia county. Bath boasts one of the nation's premier resorts, The Homestead, which grew around one of the many natural mineral hot springs. Farming is done on small, local farms. The real estate market is dominated by new second-home vacation homes. Bath County has excellent golfing, hunting, fishing, bicycling, and motorcycling.

Attractions

- Douthat State Park, Millboro, boating, swimming, camping, mountain biking
- The Homestead Resort, Hot Springs, golf, spa
- Garth Newel Music Center, Hot Springs
- Jefferson Baths, Warm Springs, spa
- Lake Moomaw, Bacova, boating

Senator Creigh Deeds
Millboro

Creigh Deeds is a state senator from Bath County, Virginia. When we spoke on a hot summer day in 2009, he was running for governor. He told me, "I am as proud as I can be to live today four miles from the house my ancestors built in the 1740s. I would not want to be from anywhere else."

He explained his family tree, with ancestry of Scots-Irish and English roots, as well as French Huguenots. "My people never had any money. They were always farmers or they worked in the woods. Some may have been carpenters. Over in Greenbrier County, West Virginia, some of my people were merchants.

"I am proud of the fact that the last member of the state Senate from this part of Bath County was my seventh great-grandfather back. He was state senator before Bath County was even a county. My great-great-grandfather on my mother's side was a captain in the Confederate Army.

"My grandfather was chairman of the local Democratic Party in Bath County from the Depression until the 1960s. I have always known about politics and have always felt a responsibility to step forward. The house where I grew up was the first in the county that had electrical power through rural electrification. I grew up with firsthand knowledge of the power of effective government.

"I was in the House of Delegates for 10 years, and I have now been in the Senate for another seven. I was a Commonwealth Attorney before then. I have been in an elected position for over 20 years.

"Coming from an area like this which is so green, beautiful, and undeveloped and where people want growth and jobs, I see that unbridled growth sometimes can bring things that we don't want. In 1998, I was chairing a subcommittee on land conservation and state parks, and we were trying to figure out a way to conserve more land and more green space in Virginia. I worked to get a tax credit bill passed that put in place the most progressive incentive-based land conservation program in the country. Nine years later no other state has gotten it ahead of us. I am proud of it."

As he was actively campaigning for the governorship, Deeds was eager to discuss goals for the area and nation. "We in this country have failed to develop a comprehensive energy policy. We have started a statewide energy policy. I often speak about creating a research-based economy. If we have a plan for coordinating the research that is already taking place at our research institutions, we have a lot to offer. We also need to do what we can to attract energy-based research so that we can solve the problems we are beginning to face with energy depletion. I am convinced that we will need to develop alternative sources of fuel. If I am elected governor, I feel that I can do many things to conserve state resources. But at the end of the day we will still need to find new sources of fuel. We will need to develop more efficient wind energy and put more research into solar technologies. I believe people understand the urgency.

"I talk about three major issues. The first thing I talk about is transportation, not only providing enough money for the roads we need and the maintenance of highways we already have, but to put more people and freight back on the railroads.

"The second thing is this whole notion about a research-based economy and building a secure energy future.

"The third thing is using the community colleges to build the smartest workforce in the world and linking our communities with high speed Internet and growing a technology-based economy.

"I talk about what I think is important to the people of Virginia. It takes no talent to find social issues that divide us. These things don't create jobs or educate our children. There are several issues that we will never have unanimity on: abortion, prayer in the schools, gun control, death penalty, gay rights. These involve personal decisions that people have to decide for themselves. I prefer to talk about those things that I want to do to improve the lives of Virginians. What I want to do is make a large scale difference in people's lives. I will not change my views to get elected.

"People in Virginia are not as partisan as the pundits would have us believe. Once a governor is elected, everyone generally wants him to be successful. They are smart enough to recognize that their success is tied to the governor's success."

A few months after this meeting, Creigh won a surprising victory over two other candidates to become the Democratic Gubernatorial candidate in the 2009 election, which he subsequently lost to Bob McDonnell.

Keene Byrd
Warm Springs

Keene Byrd is the executive director of the Bath County Historical Society. "My family migrated here in the early 1740s. We farmed on the land. In the 1840s we moved to Byrd's Nest, which is in the northern part of Bath County. Highland County was formed from Bath County. Our family settled before the split. Andrew Hamilton Byrd wrote the legislation to have Highland County formed. He made certain that the dividing line was drawn such that his land stayed in Bath County.

"Prior, Bath County was part of Augusta County, as was much of the land all the way to the Mississippi River. The legislature decided at one point that people needed to be within a certain maximum distance from the courthouse in order to conduct business, and they set about to reduce county sizes by establishing more counties. Bath County was formed in 1790 out of Augusta, Botetourt, and Pocahontas counties. Highland County was formed later from parts of Bath County and Pendleton County.

"There is a fairly good high-speed Internet access throughout Bath County, particularly in Hot Springs and Warm Springs. Good Internet access is vital to the economic future of rural communities. The Homestead Resort and the Homestead Preserve have marketing programs that are deeply dependent upon Internet access. We have a great potential here to make a living using the access through the Internet if we can educate our kids and they develop the skills and talents. I believe the Internet will be an equalizer that will allow the linking between the rural and urban communities that in a previous era may have only been provided by highways or railroads. A lot of the new people who are moving in, particularly in the homes in the Homestead Preserve, are Internet savvy and have the caliber of intellect and education to be successful.

"Certainly farming and hospitality have always been the backbone of the economy, but there are other occupations. This area has three golf courses, and we contribute more individuals to professional golfing than perhaps any other small town in the United States. People who have learned the golfing business have taken career positions in Pro shops or as caddies or as groundskeepers throughout the country.

"I am a Peter Drucker disciple in his concept of having three separate areas that work together in economic development. You have governmental, societal, and business interests and you have to keep them working together in balance where neither of the three becomes dominant. If you get too much government, then they become heavy-handed and they lose track of what things cost. If you get too much business, you can find your society becoming dependent and susceptible to rapid changes in the marketplace.

"I am interested in building relationships between the communities in the area including Covington, Clifton Forge, and Marlinton. Communities throughout this region have a shared heritage and face shared challenges.

"We see some divisions between this part of Bath County and across the mountain on the east side of the county. I often hear from people on the east side that they are neglected in decisions that affect us all. Divisions are always there, but we are always looking for ways to bridge them. I still wonder about what a state we would be had we held on to what has become West Virginia. I feel a strong affinity for our friends across the border. I know we would both be better off if we were somehow able to reunify into one state, one Commonwealth.

"Even today, in some ways the connection that we have in Allegheny, Bath, and Highland counties with Pendleton, Pocahontas, and Greenbrier counties is greater than the connection we have with Richmond. In many ways we share a legacy, and it is in our best interest to share our resources."

Ian McIlvaine
Hot Springs

Ian McIlvaine is the Director of Sales for the Homestead Preserve. He told me, "Our company bought a little over 12,000 acres belonging to the Virginia Hot Springs Company. We immediately transferred 9,200 acres to the Nature Conservancy. This became the Warm Springs Mountain preserve. We transferred another 935 acres to the Virginia Outdoors Foundation. So over 10,000 acres have been permanently set aside as nature preserves. We are developing approximately 450 homesites on the remaining 2,000 acres.

"Each track costs between $250,000 and $1 million. People are then spending anywhere between $600,000 and several million dollars on the homes themselves. Not only that, but these are, by and large, second homes or vacation homes. [The wealth] is pretty amazing.

"I had a sales prospect here a year or so ago. He said to me, 'It took us forever to get here. When are they putting in a 4-lane highway?' I looked him square in the eye and I said, 'I hope never.' We do not have a Wal-Mart. We do not have a traffic light or traffic reports. It takes an hour and 20 minutes to drive from here to the nearest real shopping mall, in Roanoke. If there were a 4-lane highway from here to Covington, it would shave perhaps 10 minutes from the trip. If that happened we would become the place that everywhere else already is.

"When people first move here it is a little bit of a shock. The longer you live here, the more you appreciate the pace of life and living in a place that everybody else seeks on vacation. The Homestead Resort and the remoteness and the natural beauty are the three things that define the county. Most of Bath County is protected from development forever. Because of what landowners for over 200 years have done, because of what we at the Homestead Preserve have done, and because of what the Forest Service has done, there is little developable land. Yes, the Preserve is building a community that we hope will one day grow to 450 homes, but beyond that there will never be any large-scale development here.

"I think most locals either have a neutral or positive view of what we are doing here. Our Company has a longer-term, more holistic view of development than most developers. Our Company did an economic study before we started. It showed a net positive economic impact because it not only increased the tax base, but its residents would use public services at a lesser rate than local people. Because many of these homes are vacation homes, their owners are not sending children to the local schools or putting any additional strain on the infrastructure. We are paying our own way from a utility perspective. We have paid to renovate the sewage treatment plant and many infrastructure upgrades that otherwise would not have been done. In many cases we are adding additional capacity beyond that which we will be using. We have added many new jobs in an economy where the Homestead Resort is the biggest employer. The resort and the school system are the two largest employers. There is virtually no manufacturing done in the county.

"I am a motorcyclist. In other places I have lived I have planned my motorcycle riding around traffic. I never wanted to ride around five o'clock in the afternoon or during certain days of the week when I expected lots of traffic. Here, I literally plan my riding around the deer and will not ride near dusk unless I must. Almost everyone I work with has hit a deer with their car within the last six months. With farms and forests, this is perfect deer country. In living here, I have traded traffic for deer."

I realized the deer/motorcycle collision I've described previously was less than ten miles from where Ian and I sat.

Bicycle ride with Carolina Tailwinds
Bath County

One of the best ways to see The Spine of the Virginias is on a bicycle. Carolina Tailwinds has a tour through Bath County. Carolina Tailwinds owners Anne and Greg Fleming are perhaps 30 years of age. Anne is slender with chestnut blonde hair and light complexion. Greg is dark-haired and bespectacled and looked as if he could have once been a CPA. The tour guest list consisted of three couples and two single people.

Our ride was 62 miles long and formed a figure 8 pattern. It had been only a week since I had done a 55-mile ride, so I thought I knew what I was getting myself into, but every ride is different. Even the Carolina Tailwinds website advertised with some measure of understatement, "A few challenging climbs will punctuate the day's ramble. You will be pleasantly exhausted by the time you arrive back at Fort Lewis Lodge." Can the words "pleasantly" and "exhausted" commingle?

We began our journey under overcast skies on a rolling country road just east of Warm Springs Mountain. The road alternated from farms to deep sylvan forests, overwhelmingly luxurious in the late spring. Birds flitted to and fro on the pavement, and mockingbirds taunted me on the climbs. Occasional raindrops fell.

After 8 miles or so, we turned right on SR-39 and ascended Warm Springs Mountain. The summit pass was visible from below and seemed impossibly distant. The first 1½ miles or so were the steepest, after which the grade moderated until the final mile, which was almost as steep as the lower section. I attempted to ride slowly and steadily in my bicycle's lowest gear, typically moving only five or six miles per hour. A red-tailed hawk left his perch on the uphill side of the road and soared over the great valley. A deer ambled lazily across the road.

The last 200 yards had a stunning view to the right, with ridge upon ridge, each successively lighter into the distance, standing like congealed waves on an endless green ocean. The ascent took forty minutes.

The group rode from Warm Springs, through Micheltown and into Hot Springs, where we stopped to look at the grand Homestead Hotel. We descended to Bacova [from BAth COunty VirginiA] Junction, where we took another right turn and entered the Jackson River Valley, at the lowest elevation on the trip, and the town of Bacova itself. A middle-aged couple were tending a garden as I rode up the short steep hill into town. I commented on their fanciful scarecrow. The man said, "It doesn't scare away the crows, but it keeps them laughing."

We completed the loop to Warm Springs, then turned northbound on US-220 and went another 6 miles or so before turning right, riding a small chip-and-seal road through the woods, gaining elevation as we went. We cycled through Burnsville, then Flood. By this time the tight confines of the forest road had given way to a broad open valley with cows grazing peacefully in the pastures. Now headed southbound, we rode towards Williamsville along the Bullpasture River to the point where it joins the Cowpasture River. A mountain angled steeply down from our right, and the river was below us on the left until our return to the Fort Lewis Lodge.

Shelly Roberts
Burnsville

During the bicycle tour, I stayed at Fort Lewis Lodge where I met Shelly Roberts, who works in the kitchen and dining room.

When we spoke after a busy breakfast, she said, "I grew up in Burnsville, which you passed through yesterday on your bicycle tour. My grandmother and grandfather owned the country store. My grandma died two years ago. The store used to have a post office, but when she died, the Postal Service moved the post office to Williamsville.

"I have been in Bath County for my entire life, and I am 27 years old. I am trying to get accepted into dental hygiene school. There is only one school close by, in Roanoke. Each year they have approximately 350 people who apply and they only accept 12 new students. I am also looking at Virginia Western Community College. That is three hours from here, and I'm a daddy's girl. I am not wanting to leave. I guess once I get my education done I can always come back.

"I am part of a big family. My great-grandma had seven kids. At the time she died she had 89 great-grandchildren. Between great and great-great-grandchildren, there were 112 of us total. That was 12 years ago and there are more now. We all live in or near Burnsville. There are family relationships everywhere.

"We don't have bars, restaurants or movies, but in place of that we have bonfires and river parties. Somebody will just announce that on the weekend there will be a party at such and such a place, and by the time the weekend rolls around a crowd will be gathering. At these parties there are always guitars and banjos and singing and whoopin' and hollerin' and getting drunk and stuff like that going on. There are also lots of little carnivals in the summer-time. We always find fun things to do in the country.

"Last year my father got a new kidney from my brother, and surgery did not go well for my brother. So we have had a difficult year. Dad is a hard-working man, and he loves his family. But he has had diabetes since he was 17, and we have watched his body deteriorate. He gets down on himself when he can't work because he wants to be a provider. But we're all right. My brother is 24, and he and dad work together in their own carpentry business.

"I love it here. I feel safe and know everybody. There are not a lot of surprises. It's beautiful. Tell the world to come see us. Bring money. Don't stay very long."

Becky Skidmore
Hot Springs

Ingalls Field is surely the most dramatic — and perhaps the most remote — airport in the state of Virginia. It is perched literally at the top of Warm Springs Mountain, just south of the grand resort, The Homestead. Ingalls Field is the highest general aviation airport east of the Mississippi River. It provides service for privately owned aircraft and private charter jets. To reach it, you must drive on a small squiggly mountain road to a gap six miles south of the airport and then take a spur road through the woods along the top of the ridge. Not a single structure or habitation are along the spur road.

Manager Becky Skidmore has reddish hair and a bright smile. She said, "The Bath County Airport Authority is a separate entity, but they manage it as a political subdivision of Bath County. All of our customers are privately owned aircraft and private charter jets, anywhere from one or two airplanes per day to as many as 30, depending on the time of year and what is going on at the Hotel. One aspect of my job involves talking on the radio with incoming flights and making sure there is nothing that would impede their landing. We let them know about any other local traffic and any localized weather conditions. The elevation here is 3792 feet, and we can get some fierce weather. Our access road is one of the last roads plowed after a snow.

"I have to make my own decision on whether to try to drive up here because it is possible to get stuck and, if that were to happen, I could be stuck for quite a while. Sometimes we close the airport, but if a pilot is in the air he may not check and may land anyway.

"Landing here is tricky because of the crosswinds. Because we are on the top of a mountain, the ends of the runway drop off precipitously. Pilots need to be skillful and careful. The runway is 5600 feet long, so there is plenty of length. We can accommodate a plane as large as a Boeing 727 jet.

"We have had many famous people come through, including Smokey Robinson, Hank Williams Jr., Rusty Wallace, and Terry Bradshaw. Presidents Bill Clinton and George W. Bush, Governor Mark Warner, and vice president Dan Quayle have been here.

"Bill Clinton was president when he came, so the whole Secret Service was here. There was snow, and we had to plow down the snowbanks at the edge of the runway because we were afraid that the wings of the airplane might hit them. The Secret Service was crawling all over. During that time of year, the local hunters chase and tree bears. Their dogs wear collars with tracking devices with long antennas. I told the head guy from the Secret Service that we always see these dogs. If one of the Secret Service agents shot a dog, we would have some unhappy armed hunters. We might have seen the beginning of World War III. So we asked the head guy to let his agents know. Fortunately there were no incidents."

The view from the airport is expansive. "On a clear day you can see the Peaks of Otter from here." It was a bright day but the valleys were shrouded, shimmering in summer haze. "My partner describes this airport as being at the top of the mountain at the end of the road in the middle of nowhere."

From the southwestern end of the runway, we could see row upon row of mountains into the distance. In the valley we could see The Homestead. She said, "In the winter time when we have ice on all the trees it is absolutely gorgeous. One day I was really upset about something. I came out here to calm down, and there was a glorious rainbow. I was fine after that."

West Virginia

BATH

GREENBRIER

ALLEGHANY

Low Moor · Selma · Iron Gate

Covington

MONROE

Virginia

CRAIG

Alleghany County, Virginia

Alleghany County is entirely within the Appalachian Ridge-and-Valley topography of limestone mountains. Major mountains are Potts, Peters, Allegheny [on the West Virginia border], and minor mountains Fore, Lick, and Oliver. The James River and its tributaries carved an east-west route that provided a transportation corridor taken by the C&O Railroad (now CSX), US-60, and Interstate 64.

Alleghany County encompasses 449 square miles.

Clifton Forge, Iron Gate, Selma, and Low Moor are the incorporated towns. Covington, technically a city independent of the county, is the county seat.

Population

Alleghany County's population has risen and fallen with industrial activity. In 1900, there were 16,000 people, rising to 23,000 in 1950. Today there are about 16,000 (including Covington) with the recent fall due to job losses.

Institutions of higher education

Alleghany County hosts Dabney S. Lancaster Community College.

Traffic

Alleghany County has 40 miles of Interstate 64 within its borders, and there are dozens of traffic lights in Covington and Clifton Forge. Amtrak provides daily rail service along the CSX line.

Today's...

Alleghany County has the Spine's biggest employer, the Mead Westvaco paper mill along the Jackson River in Covington. Low Moor was once home to an iron extraction and foundry industry. Clifton Forge has been a railroad town. Allegheny County is building its tourism business with hunting, fishing, bicycling, and motorcycling all being courted.

Attractions

- Longdale (Green Pastures) Recreation Area, Longdale, former "colored only" park
- Falling Springs Falls, Falling Spring, falls and species-rich moist microhabitat
- Covington Depot, Covington, restored railroad depot
- C&O Railway Heritage Center, Clifton Forge, railway heritage museum and visitor's center

Jack Hammond
Low Moor

Jack Hammond is a retired corporate executive and the former plant manager of the sprawling paper mill of Mead Westvaco, along the Jackson River in Covington. Although Westvaco had relocated him away from the area years earlier, upon retirement he and his wife returned.

He said, "At one point, this area was highly industrialized. It had significant iron deposits. Most of the people who came here between the 1840s and the Second World War were involved in either lumbering or in the manufacturing of iron ore. In those days they cut the trees and took the bark and made tannic acid to tan leather. They used the wood to make charcoal. They mined the iron ore. With limestone, the heat from the charcoal and the iron ore, they were able to make high quality iron. It was called pig iron because the process of pouring the molten metal was done as if a mother sow was feeding a row of piglets. The molten metal would run down a narrow trough into wider gullies where it would solidify into ingots called pigs. There were probably 20 to 30 furnaces in this area. The Low Moor ironworks grew out of that industry. The main ironworks was probably a consolidation of several smaller ironworks tucked away in the local hollows. In the early days they took the pig iron and loaded it onto bateaus and shipped it down the James River to Richmond."

In the years between the Revolutionary War and the Civil War, the James River Canal extended from Richmond almost 200 miles upstream to Buchanan. "The canal was built with picks, shovels, and mules. After the Civil War, the railroad extended to Covington and ended the era of the canals. The C&O canal evolved into the C&O Railroad. So the combination of iron ore, limestone, trees for charcoal, and transportation in the form of a canal initially and later a railroad, led to the development of this area as a major iron producer. In fact, the lampposts on Park Avenue in New York were cast here in Low Moor.

"In the early 1900s, this plant in Low Moor produced over 130,000 tons of iron ore per year. Not only does that represent a tremendous amount of iron ore, but the production requires voracious amounts of wood."

During the 1920s and 1930s, the industry shut down due to competition from the upper Midwest and to the Great Depression.

"When I got here in 1961 there were perhaps 20 beehive style furnaces made of brick. None of them are left. One or two of them should have been saved simply for the historic value. We certainly should have hung onto something because the iron ore manufacturing was an instrumental part of the earliest migrations here. There were Germans and Scots Irish coming into the Philadelphia port.

"Clifton Forge became primarily associated with the C&O Railroad, Low Moor became identified with the iron production, and Covington became identified with paper manufacturing.

"The new dynamic is set against a background of old money amidst relative poverty. The wages paid at the Westvaco plant are competitive with anything paid anywhere in the state. A technician with three to five years experience and a two-year technical degree may make between $40,000 and $50,000. Hourly team leaders on a production unit may make over $100,000.

"The plant is unionized, and the work ethic is good. There is an independent streak in the workforce here, but at the same time it is almost like family. To me that was an interesting chemistry. I arrived right after I graduated from college with an engineering degree and worked in a technical unit. I learned that there is no monopoly on intelligence.

"During the 60s the plant needed to move into more automation. Today, this plant is as environmentally sophisticated as any in the world. With every expansion, we improved the environmental quality. The plant emits an odor that comes from hydrogen sulfides. It is impossible to build a paper plant that doesn't smell bad, but the locals cannot smell it.

"Implementing more automation caused problems because the number of jobs was reduced. At one point, I even received a bomb in the mail. You have a lunatic fringe everywhere. They were convinced that I was trying to make changes for my own personal benefit. The guy who sent the bomb was a Vietnam War vet. I think he is still around.

"The postmaster called me in my office. He said, 'Jack, I have a package and it looks strange.' He brought in the state police and the ATF [alcohol, tobacco, and firearms]. They blew it up. The perpetrator was caught because there was enough loyalty to have not tolerated that kind of behavior.

"Before our expansions we would bring all of our potential critics together. We would tell them what we planned to do and ask what they thought. We always achieved better solutions by working proactively and cooperatively."

Alpha Averill
Low Moor

Alpha "Granny" Averill ran the Low Moor Company store until the age of 99. When we met in 2009, she was looking forward to her 102nd birthday and was the oldest person I'd ever met.

"I was an employee of the commissary for the Low Moor Iron Company. I believe they got their start in 1907, the year I was born. My parents lived near the mine in Corbett. The mines cast iron at ten o'clock in the morning and again at four o'clock in the afternoon. Sometimes they poured a third time at midnight. They took the hot ashes and poured them along the river plain here in Low Moor.

"All the houses that you see here in the neighborhood were occupied. There were whites and colored people too. They weren't really integrated. The blacks had their own school up the road near Rich Patch. The school for whites was here in Low Moor. We walked to school every day, even in the snow. We didn't have good shoes or booties, and when we got to school our feet were wet.

"The manager of the store knew me when I was in school, and he let me work in the store. I usually waited on people. In those days, clerks waited on the shoppers. Everybody in town worked for the company. A colored man drove a wagon pulled by a mule to deliver purchased items to the customers' homes. In those days, almost nobody had a car. The store had a telephone and a man took messages for people in town.

"When the Iron Company closed their operation, my brother-in-law bought the store. I had married his brother. I ran it for many years after he died until recently when Mrs. Belmont bought the store building and wanted her people to run it. I enjoyed working, but I was getting up in age."

She worked 12 hours a day for five or six days a week. She seldom took a vacation and had never flown or seen the ocean.

"I spend most of my time sitting in this chair," she said. "I think I am the oldest person in Allegheny County. I still can't believe I am over 100 years old. I don't feel like I am. I used to play organ for the church. I always played by ear. I played piano until about three years ago."

Louise Belmont
Clifton Forge

Clifton Forge is the quintessential railroad town. The C&O Railroad was founded in 1836 as the Louisa Railroad, primarily to enable farmers to deliver goods to Richmond. During the ensuing years, it extended eastward to Newport News. Two lines emerged from Richmond west. One follows the James River through Lynchburg and the James River Gap to Glasgow, then through Buchanan into Clifton Forge. The other was more northerly but parallel. It goes through Charlottesville, tunnels under Rockfish Gap of the Blue Ridge into Waynesboro, then Staunton, and into Clifton Forge. The rejoining of these two lines has made Clifton Forge an important switching center. This work was done before the Civil War with the first train arriving in 1857, but further expansion westward was interrupted by war and completed shortly after its conclusion.

Eventually the line reached the New River and followed it downstream into Charleston and Huntington, West Virginia. Along the way, it passes through two significant tunnels, the Lewis Tunnel on the

Virginia side and the Allegheny Tunnel directly below the state line. Because more robust locomotives were necessary for the mountain sections of track, Clifton Forge was used as a staging area for that switching as well. Many manufacturing and maintenance operations were performed at shops in the town, and a fantastic culture of industrial craftsmanship emerged.

That the chosen corridor involved relatively modest elevation changes provided a competitive advantage. The C&O was one of many railroad chains from New York to Georgia that took advantage of the various natural corridors through the Appalachians.

Beginning in the 1960s and through the 1970s, the railroad began the process of transferring jobs from Clifton Forge, and the town fell on hard times. The diminishing economy was only a blessing in that much of the commercial and residential development was frozen in time. Much of it is architecturally significant and remains so today.

Because Clifton Forge is near the midpoint of the line between Newport News and Huntington, it became the natural location to place the headquarters of the C&O Historical Society. In its mission to preserve, archive, and disseminate the history of the C&O Railroad, it has become a collection point for photos, artifacts, and documents relating to the Railroad. Its new Heritage Center in Clifton Forge has in planning a replica signal tower, replica depot, replica engine house, and assemblage of locomotives.

Clifton Forge is emerging from its slumber with a number of new projects and motivated citizens. The future seems bright.

One of the people bringing new vision and energy to town is Louise Belmont, the woman who bought Granny Averill's store. Her grandfather was the founder of Reynolds Metals Co., now Alcoa. She has opened the 416 Gallery in downtown. She said, "I found a house that reminded me of the house where I grew up in Kentucky. It was for sale and so I bought it. Once I moved here, I kept looking around and seeing things I thought needed to be done."

She had no familial ties here.

"I had been through here several times before taking the children skiing at the Homestead. I lived in Powhatan, Virginia, at that time, but I also spent a lot of my time in Kentucky. I am in Clifton Forge

C & O Railroad near Allegheny Tunnel

full-time now. There are so many interesting people living here. I think the general public is unaware of that. I find pleasant secrets tucked away in these hills.

"I never came here with a vision or a grand plan for my personal impact on Clifton Forge. I simply got here and became inspired. This is a beautiful town and the architecture is fabulous. Many of the houses need to be refurbished; real estate prices are reasonable. People are polite, thoughtful. It is a totally different attitude than any place I have been in the last 20 years. This is a special place.

"Most of the people who are moving here, me included, want to keep it much the same but to simply fix things up. We would like to spruce up the buildings and make things livelier. The downtown is already nice, but it is quiet. We are trying to get more retailing downtown, and I think we will be successful.

"I think Clifton Forge is kind of magic. You will see it if you spend any time here. I have no plans to ever live anywhere else."

Bonnie Keyser
Kitty Fitzgerald
Paul Linkenhoker
Covington

I met Bonnie Keyser, Kitty Fitzgerald, and Paul Linkenhoker in the recently remodeled Covington railroad depot that now serves as a headquarters for the city's historical society. Each did volunteer work for the society. Paul told me, "The area was settled in 1746 by Joseph Carpenter and Peter Wright. They came from New York through the Shenandoah Valley and through Staunton and Goshen to settle here. In those days, homesteaders could earn land grants. Many of the descendents of Joseph Carpenter are still here today, living on the land he was granted. We call it Fort Carpenter."

He said the first industry was iron production, centered around Low Moor. "Before the iron industry, there were homesteads and plantations in the area."

Kitty said, "The mines employed more than 2000 people in their heyday in the late 1800s. The route which is now followed by Interstate 64 from the Great Valley of Virginia in Lexington into the area of White Sulphur Springs and Lewisburg and on into Charleston on the Kanawha River Valley has been used for centuries. It was originally called the Midland Trail, and it was one of the country's earliest major east-west roads. The rivers provided a transportation corridor that people have long traveled to make their way through the mountains."

Paul said, "We are the headwaters of the James River. The area and its natural resources brought settlers and homesteads. Then logging developed into a viable industry. The loggers floated logs down the river from here.

"All this time the iron industry was going on at the Lucy Selina furnaces below Clifton Forge. There was another mine at Longdale. They produced the iron that was used in the cladding of the Civil War ironclad, the Merrimack. The iron also was used for munitions during the Civil War. When the company went out of business in the late

1920s, it did so not because they were running out of ore but because of the discovery of richer, more accessible veins in the upper Midwest. These hills are still rich with iron deposits.

"In 1899 the paper mill was opened by the West Virginia Pulp and Paper Company. At one point, the two largest paper machines in the world were here. The primary reason they put the paper mill here rather than Caldwell, West Virginia, was because they got weaker pollution restrictions from Virginia than they did from the Greenbrier River area. Until the water quality environmental regulations were put in place in the 1970s, this was a heavily polluted river. Now there is aquatic life in the river again."

Kitty said, "In decades past, the first thing we did every morning was to go out of our houses and sweep all the soot off the porch and furniture. Not only did the plant smell and pollute the river, but it put a lot of particulate into the air. Happily, the Jackson River has been clean for many years and has fish in it. One of my friends who was an engineer said that, years ago, once it ran several miles below the city it wasn't so bad anyway, but of course it looked bad."

Bonnie said real estate was inexpensive. "Neighbors across the street just bought a nice house for $38,000. She probably put another $10,000 into improvements but it is a beautiful little house."

Both women made a couple of laments. The children want to leave after graduation, and the crime rate is increasing. Kitty said, "I lock my doors now when I never used to. Having more jobs would help everything. One area of potential growth is in serving the aging population. The natural beauty is enticing retirement people. Some prospective industries say that they do not see the labor force they need. I think that is ridiculous. If a company puts new jobs here then the workers will arrive to fill the jobs. People will come."

Greenbrier County, West Virginia

Most of Greenbrier County's residents live near an east-west line of Interstate 64 and the CSX Railroad. Much of the northern part of the county is within the Monongahela National Forest or owned by large private landowners such as Mead Westvaco and CXS.

There are 1,024 square miles, making it the largest county along The Spine of the Virginias.

Incorporated towns include White Sulphur Springs, Lewisburg, Ronceverte, Rainelle, Renick (Falling Spring), and Alderson.

Population

Greenbrier County's population rose from 21,000 in 1900 to more than 30,000 in the 1920s. The population has remained between 30,000 and 40,000 since.

Institutions of higher education

Greenbrier County has two institutions of higher education, New River Community and Technical College [Lewisburg Branch] and the West Virginia School of Osteopathic Medicine.

Traffic

Greenbrier County has almost 40 miles of Interstate 64 within its borders. Lewisburg and White Sulphur Springs have several traffic lights. Amtrak provides daily rail service along the CSX line.

Today's...

Greenbrier County is home of The Greenbrier, one of the nation's premier resort hotels. Lewisburg has a vibrant arts scene.

Attractions
- Lost World Caverns, Lewisburg, and Organ Caverns, Ronceverte
- West Virginia State Fairgrounds, Fairlea (Lewisburg)
- Lewisburg Historic District, Lewisburg
- Carnegie Hall and Greenbrier Valley Theater, Lewisburg
- Greenbrier River Trail, Caldwell to Cass (Pocahontas County), hiking, horseback, and bicycling
- North House Museum, Lewisburg
- The Greenbrier, White Sulphur Springs

Greg Johnson
Lewisburg

Greg Johnson, a retired social worker and writer who lives just south of Lewisburg, told me, "I grew up in Florida, but left when I was 20. I'd never seen a mountain or snow. I wanted a master's degree in social work and wanted to live in a small town, so I looked for programs that specialized in rural social work. I was accepted at West Virginia University."

Before graduation Johnson secured a job at the Greenbrier Valley Mental Health Clinic, where he worked for 25-years.

"When I left social work, I became more active in the community. Lewisburg is a hotbed for people with artistic interests. This town of only 4500 people has six art galleries and two arts organizations. The Greenbrier Valley Theatre started as a tent by the river. After that it was in what we called the Barn, a rickety wooden building by the airport. It was a summer operation, and there wasn't any way to cool it. But it was beloved. Occasionally the theatre flooded and the actors and technicians would walk through puddles that had tangles of live electric wires in them. One night, the light booth caught on fire in the middle of a show. We evacuated the Barn, fixed the problem, and then continued.

"There is a book on the market called *The 100 Best Small Towns for the Arts in America*. We're in it. Artists attract other artists, and we've become a magnet. One painting group has 75 members.

"The West Virginia School for Osteopathic Medicine has been a tremendous asset to the community. It brings hundreds of people here to work and study.

"Another thing that impacted our community was the 'back-to-the-land' movement in the '70s. A lot of young people fled urban life, looking for relatively inexpensive land where they could grow their own food. Initially the locals were a little suspicious of this influx of newcomers. As time went on they became very much a part of things, and many of our downtown shops are owned by folks who came here this way originally. Almost nobody ended up being a self-sufficient farmer like they imagined. Now our community is a seamless blend of '70s homesteaders and multi-generational farm families.

"Our community is also driven by agriculture. Lewisburg is the home of the West Virginia State Fair. Every year we have 200,000 to 250,000 people passing through town during the 10-day Fair. It gets better every year. Many of the people who live here are unaware of our agricultural community, except during the Fair.

"I read about a guy in the *New Yorker* who asked people to write their life stories in six words. Mine would be, 'Left Florida, lived happily ever after.'"

BJ Gudmundsson
Lewisburg

BJ Gudmundsson is a filmmaker in Lewisburg, originally from Marlinton. One of her first films was about Calvin Price, a founder of the West Virginia Wildlife Federation, who was involved in conservation his entire life. He died in 1957. She used all of his writings to create a one-man play. Bob Conte, the historian at the Greenbrier, played the part of Calvin Price. She filmed a performance of the play at the opera house in Marlinton, making a movie of the play. It won the best documentary of the year award in 2005, and she was named the West Virginia Filmmaker of the Year.

"I am involved now with mountaintop removal mining and with wilderness preservation. Back in the 1970s, Congress passed the Surface Mine Reclamation Act. Strip-mining is not new. There were strip mines in Pocahontas County in the 1930s and the 1940s. People started to protest this practice because it was so ugly. I protested that for a while like I was protesting the [Vietnam] War, but eventually I got out of it.

"Then in 2006, Allen Johnson, the man you met in Marlinton, got together with some friends and formed an organization called Christians for the Mountains. They were working to motivate Christians to preserve the land as part of the biblical ethic of stewardship of the land. Allen asked me to take a slideshow that a man had done in eastern Kentucky and build a film around it with a Christian perspective. I made some trips to the coalfields and toured a mine site that was reclaimed 30 years earlier. It seemed to me that everything the mining industry was saying about their reclamation efforts was a flat-out lie.

"These coal companies claim to have been pouring money into reclamation of these mine sites. But if this is all they have to offer after 30 years, then something is wrong. On this particular site, they had replanted the whole area with a weed that was imported from China: lespidesa. The gullies were all filled with rip rap. Everything else was a bright, cheerful green. When I got out of the car I could see that it wasn't green at all; it just appeared green. It was dry like sagebrush. There weren't any bugs. There weren't any birds. There was nothing living except the flies that would land on your skin and bite your flesh until you literally bled.

"What looked to be small rocks in the gullies were boulders. Gushes of water poured onto the community below during storms. There were no trees. It was sterile. Then I saw the tailing ponds where they clean the coal. All this stuff runs off and contaminates the drinking water. At Kayford Mountain, I walked to the edge of the cliff and looked out over that mine. I almost dropped my camera. I started crying so hard, and I couldn't stop."

She finished the film, called *Mountain Mourning*, and it was used by activist groups at community meetings. Her next film, *Rise up West Virginia*, was about taking on the government.

"I understand why we have relied on coal for power for so many years. I understand that if we stopped burning coal tomorrow, it would barely make a dent in what is being emitted into the air in China, Russia, and worldwide. I understand both sides of the climate change discussion. I see the same types of arguments from the anti-windmill people. Nobody seems willing to give a little. The electric utilities are now preaching conservation but not the coal industry.

"The coal industry, regardless of whether they are doing mountaintop removal mining, longwall mining, or subsurface mining, will figure out a way to extract the coal. They will continue to proffer the argument that it is all about jobs. The industry doesn't care about jobs.

If they are able to replace people with machines, then that is what they will do. Eighty-five percent of the children in McDowell County live below the poverty level. Am I upset that Caterpillar is about to lay off 15,000 people? Hell, no. Let them all go to work at McDonald's.

"Our coal severance tax barely repairs the damage of what the industry leaves behind. The schools are hurting. The roads are full of potholes. The drinking water is poison. We need to have people in government who will admit that we are glad to have all the money that coal has brought over the years, but we need to chart a new course for the future. We need to insist that our children will not live in poverty or go hungry. Our water will be safe to drink. Solving these problems involves changing mindsets. It means working with people and not against people.

"Why don't we have new manufacturing plants in West Virginia, western Virginia, and eastern Kentucky? We have outsourced our manufacturing economy to the developing world. I think this is a tremendous mistake, and it will come back to bite us. We live in a country that is unable [to reclaim our glory]. We don't have the spine to take it back!

"I think the fight against mountaintop removal has made Appalachia hip again. It has given Appalachia a way to put its best foot and our best people forward. This fight has taken everyday Appalachian people into the lobbies of the major energy companies in New York City and put them on stages in major state universities. America is taking notice, asking, 'Are we allowing the destruction of our mountains, streams, underground aquifers, and ecosystems to be destroyed in America in the 21st century?' It is unbelievable what citizens are forced to live with in these regions.

"We should start working harder conserving energy. When I have an audience, the first thing I tell them is that West Virginia is being blown off the planet, and our government is responsible for it. The second thing I tell them is that the government is able to do this because you continue to keep them there. The third thing I tell them is that if they want to do something about it right now, they can go home and systematically reduce their electricity consumption. I tell them it will not only save a lot of coal, but a lot of money. I tell them how they can save $50 in the first month alone."

I said, "I am envisioning that in my book I will issue a statement the first time I type the word 'coal': Disclaimer: the exploration, extraction, processing, transport, consumption, and residue disposal associated with the mineral resource we call coal is an intensely controversial topic. You will read things in this book that you will not agree with. I will strive to lend balance to this topic, but please do not expect to be fully satisfied. Beyond that, I think, if someone wants to get really angry about the story of coal in this country, they should start by looking in a mirror because consumers create the demand."

She said, "I encounter people all the time who whisper to me, 'I agree with everything you are saying, but I cannot speak out or I will lose my job.' Whatever the excuse is. My attitude has always been, to hell with that! I didn't have a job when I found this one. The people of the Appalachians, along your Spine of the Virginias, still fight for what they believe in. We can, and we must, teach the rest of this country something about freedom.

"We West Virginians are proud and patriotic. We are doers. We would make things again if our factories came back to us. I don't think there is anything wrong, demoralizing, or demeaning with being from around here, whether on the West Virginia or the Virginia side. I think it is something to be proud of. We are as good as anybody else. I am really sick of being from a place that has supplied what we have in this area to our country — and for this country to have socked us the way they have and to deem us unworthy of the fruits of the American dream."

Vernell "Bimbo" Coles
Lewisburg

Vernell "Bimbo" Coles was a basketball star who played for Virginia Tech and in the NBA. His wife, Weslea, runs a boutique in downtown Lewisburg. Retired from basketball, he is now director of fitness at the Greenbrier Valley Physical Therapy and Fitness Center.

Coles is a trim, 6'2" man with a "Michael Jordan" hairdo. "I was born in Virginia, but I am really proud to say that I am a West Virginian. I learned many of life's lessons from my people here in Lewisburg and in Greenbrier County.

"I am trying to have a positive impact on the fitness level of all West Virginians. I am doing what I can to improve the health of people here. The people of my hometown are not in the physical condition they should be. West Virginia is the second worst state in the nation for obesity. It is a huge problem.

"This is not just a PR effort. It is straight-up fitness. I am hands-on with the work I do. I teach fitness classes. I do assessments on body fat and blood pressure. I put people on fitness plans that dictate what they are supposed to eat and what they should avoid. I help people understand calories, vitamins, and minerals. I have only been at the organization for three months, and we have 350 new members. Some of my clients have diabetes, and I have gotten them to the point where they can do regular workouts. I have a guy who has Parkinson's disease and is working out. People see my commitment to a lifetime of good health. My customers are learning how to maintain better health and hopefully live longer and happier lives. My notoriety has helped me appeal to people who may not have come to us otherwise.

"When I was in high school here in Lewisburg, in many of my classes I was the only black student. It was difficult. One of the television networks showed the documentary *Roots* each year. I came to class every day knowing that many of my classmates had watched *Roots* every night. We were having discussions about slavery in class. As the only black kid in several of these classes, it was uncomfortable having this much attention directed towards me.

"Even as a minority black kid in a small town, I really never saw color. All I ever saw was people. I did not have to break any barriers. I am not sure whether this was more about this region or more about me as a person. I was determined in my life that if I was not going to see color, then I was not going to let the people I associated with see color. It was never a problem for me that the majority of my friends were white. My wife is white. If other people see color, then that is the way they are. I cannot change them, but I do not have to be around them. Why would I waste time on people so petty as to see color lines?

"My wife and I have been together since high school. We began dating when she was 15 and I was 17. Interestingly, I believe she dealt with it more than I did. People would never openly say anything to me. Even when I was growing up, I would hear people say that I was special because of my athletic talent. I have no idea what they said behind my back, but more things were said to Weslea. Around here, racism is hidden, and hopefully rare.

"I was a four-year starter at Tech. I started my first game as a freshman. During my sophomore year, I received an invitation to try out for our U.S. National Olympic team. I was 19 years old. To this day, I am the only West Virginian and the only Virginia Tech player to have ever played basketball in the Olympics."

About coming back to Lewisburg, Coles said, "It was Weslea's idea, definitely. I loved Miami, but Lewisburg is great. People still recognize me, but I have plenty of time and space for myself and my family. People respect my privacy and my eagerness to live a normal life."

Matthew Patterson
White Sulphur Springs

I met Matthew Patterson, a specialist in freshwater mussels, at the National Fish Hatchery complex in White Sulphur Springs. He said freshwater mussels are the most endangered group of organisms in North America today. Mussels are an essential component to our streams because they improve water quality by filtering bacteria, algae, and other small particles from the water. The quality of the water in a stream is indicated by the health of the mussels.

"There are about 300 species and 70 percent to 75 percent of the species are now in decline. In addition, freshwater mussels help keep our rivers clean by filtering large amounts of water on a daily basis. A large bed of mussels can filter over a million gallons of water per day.

"They are facing a loss of habitat. Many of the streams have been impounded. The Ohio, Mississippi, and Tennessee are essentially impounded from one end to the other. Mussels are fast water species. They like high oxygen, fast-moving water. When water is backed up behind dams, sediment accumulates, and the mussels struggle to survive.

"Another big problem is the overall degradation of water quality. They are sensitive to pollutants in the water. Things like ammonia, copper, and heavy metals can kill them. There is a lot of research going on now that shows that the EPA's standard limits for some pollutants are above what these animals can tolerate. For instance, the West Virginia Department of Environmental Protection recently discovered that the White Sulphur Springs sewage treatment facility is releasing a lot of phosphorus into the Greenbrier River, which can cause algal blooms."

Matthew said mountaintop removal mining has had a dramatic negative impact on mussels. "Dumping of fill material, whether it reaches the perennial streams at the bottom of the hollow or not, is still a problem because rain water trickles through it and leeches the bad stuff [to go] into the streams below."

Lynn Swann
Bob Conte
White Sulphur Springs

The Greenbrier, the grand old resort in White Sulphur Springs, is a sprawling complex of buildings painted in white. The main entrance resembles the White House. I was graciously welcomed to visit by Lynn Swann and Bob Conte, the marketing manager and historian, respectively. Lynn said, "This is the last hotel/resort that CSX has owned. The resort has not been profitable for some time. In fact, during the last six years we have lost over $90 million." As we spoke, the ownership of the resort was in transition.

Bob said, "These were all summer resorts. The 19th century business was characterized by wealthy lowland city dwellers coming into the mountains for the healing properties of the water. We say unofficially that this place began entertaining guests in 1778. There was not much here for the next 30 or 40 years. The primary reason, like all the other resorts, is the water. If there weren't any natural springs here, there would not be a resort. The water here has a sulfur taste to it, and it is not hot. But people both drank it and bathed in it. People drank it for the cure of digestive problems.

"The Railroad bought the resort in 1910. From there, we had a second history. The Greenbrier and the Homestead are the two remaining grand resorts from that era. For most of our over 200-year history, we have been successful.

"We have always had a considerable amount of our business from professional groups. We have records that show that the Virginia Bar Association came here in 1889. Prior to that, most of our business was wealthy individuals. During the Great Depression, all of the resorts looked to fill their rooms with larger groups. But the real upswing did not occur until the 1960s. At that point, the resorts were able to transition to entertaining large trade organizations and groups of professionals. In many ways it was the same people, the same clientele, but when they came with an organization, the people were able to deduct these expenses from their taxes."

A stay at The Greenbrier is expensive, often surpassing $600.00, sometimes up to $1000.00 per night per person. Bob said, "This is the opposite of a recession-proof business. This is something people who have a lot of money do when they have extra money to do it. Nobody needs the service we provide."

Within weeks of my visit, The Greenbrier got a new lease on life. Wealthy businessman Jim Justice stepped in and bought the place. Justice, a West Virginian, proclaimed in newspaper reports that success could be found even in the tight economy, saying his first priority was to reclaim the coveted five-star status and begin making investments for the future. Time will tell if success will come.

The Greenbrier Hotel

Craig County, Virginia

Craig County is entirely within the Appalachian Ridge-and-Valley topography of limestone mountains. Its long linear valleys are delineated by towering mountains, Potts, Peters [on the West Virginia border], Sinking Creek, and North [on the southeastern border] mountains. Much of the mountainous land is within the George Washington and Jefferson National Forest.

Craig County is 331 square miles.

New Castle and Paint Bank are the incorporated towns. New Castle is the county seat.

Population

Craig County's population has remained remarkably steady. There were [approximately] 4300 people in 1900 and 5200 today.

Institutions of higher education

Craig County has no colleges or universities.

Traffic

Craig County has no four-lane roads and no traffic lights whatsoever.

Today's...

Craig County is one of Western Virginia's least populated counties, adjacent to the most populous (Roanoke County, along with the cities of Roanoke and Salem). Craig is building its tourism business with hunting, fishing, bicycling, and motorcycling all being courted. There is virtually no manufacturing or industry. Farming is restricted to the tight valleys.

Attractions

* Paint Bank, restored town

Mikell Ellison
Paint Bank

Paint Bank was once a quintessential lost town on The Spine of the Virginias. In the early 20th century, the Potts Valley railroad ran from Ripplemead to Paint Bank. Two thousand people lived in Paint Bank. There were perhaps seven or eight businesses, including a hotel. When the railroad ceased operation in the 1930s, the town declined. The hotel was abandoned, and the general store sold little more than some canned goods and dairy. A few years ago, Paint Bank got unlost. A couple from New Jersey, John and Nancy Mulheren, bought almost the whole town and put everything back together.

Today, the General Store is the only retail establishment in town. There are Texaco gas pumps outside the hundred-year-old brick building. A new restaurant has been built on the back. There's a delightful mix of old ambiance and new funk.

There is a kiosk with ads for pickup trucks and property and a chain-saw bear holding a sign that says, "Welcome to the Paint Bank General Store." A stream of customers in camouflage and Carhartt bib overalls wanders to and fro. A pickup truck in the parking lot has a bumper sticker with a Confederate flag and the words, "This is our flag. If you don't like it, you can leave."

I met Mikell Ellison, manager of most of the Mulheren's ventures in town. She is another example of the kind of people who have chosen to live along The Spine of the Virginias and represents the back-to-the-earth culture. She said, "A lot of the people who live here now, including myself, were from a modern, metropolitan area, and we've had a decently sophisticated life. A lot of people thought I'd gone insane when I sold out. I ran like a crazy woman to these mountains.

"We chose that piece of land because it had not been tampered with since the 1950s, so the earth itself was probably pure at that point. We turned it into an organic farm. We raised dairy goats, we milked them and made cheeses and mozzarellas. We raised our own pigs and did prosciutto ham and sausages. We could squat in our field and eat (the vegetables) from it; there were no preservatives or chemicals on it. We canned lots of food and had root cellars so we didn't have to go off the mountain unless we really wanted to. It worked out well that we were largely self-sufficient at that time because we had to be.

"We spent ten years building the house, a round house. My husband is from West Virginia. He is immensely skilled as a carpenter, and he built it. We built a barn. He made a cupola that weighed one-hundred and fifty pounds. Even though he is a big muscular ex-Marine, he couldn't carry it up to the roof. So he tied me off and used me for ballast on the other end of the barn to get the leverage he needed to lift the cupola onto that roof.

"The first time we butchered a pig, I ended up shaving it with Barbasol [shaving cream] and Bic razors because we didn't have anything big enough to dip it in. The day we shot that pig, she had gone into estrus at two o'clock in the morning and commenced taking on with my pit bull in the doghouse. We couldn't control that pig; she was going to have her way with that pit bull. She had him cornered in his doghouse, and we couldn't get either out of it. We finally had to get a chain saw and cut the back of the doghouse out. We pulled the pit bull out to get the pig off him. We tried our best to convince that pig to go back to the pen so we could kill her.

"She was about 275 pounds. And of course we'd made the mistake of naming her. So when you've got to put a 45 [caliber bullet] in her head, it's not an easy thing to do. But at two o'clock in the morning when we couldn't get her out of that doghouse, it became an easy thing to do. We laid that pig out right there. We cut her throat, propped her butt on a cinder-block and let her bleed out the rest of the night. I'd gotten an FHA brochure telling us how. By the way, anything you ever want to do in life, you can go to the FHA and they'll have a brochure telling you how to do it. Brain surgery. Anything. They have a concise brochure on how to gut a pig. This is a farming area, and someday you'll have to butcher a pig.

"Anybody who has been raised on a farm knows that once you have eaten meat or produce grown on the farm, especially organic, you'll never taste anything like that again. It spoils you rotten."

She said, "My husband is considerably younger than I am. His grandmamma cobbled his shoes. They grew everything they ate. He's Arnold Schwarzenegger-built because as a four- or five-year-old kid he was picking up boulders and carrying them from the garden. Sure, they had electricity and one or two channels on TV because you can't get reception in those hollers, but he learned how to do everything for himself. His grandfather had set up a mill there and cut the trees down and milled all the lumber for their home.

"But anyway, we sold the place. We'd burned out from the lifestyle of living off the land. We came down here to Paint Bank. I got a job managing the store. The Mulherens have restored these buildings back to period looks.

"I manage the Lodge and do marketing for all the businesses. Ms. Mulheren owns six businesses within the Valley including a seven-thousand-acre buffalo farm. What's so neat about the Valley is it's kind of locked in time.

"The people who lived in this town knew it lost its population and vitality, but just like people in the city, you see changes and you accept things. We have to make people aware of their past. We love to read books about what happened in Europe or the Middle East because these places are romantic, but we don't pay any attention to the heritage that we have and are losing here. We fall into the trap of thinking culture is something other people have. We need to puff up our chests a bit more. People in these lost communities need to be aware and proud of what they have. The pride will lead to a successful future.

"If the world goes to hell in a handbasket, these are the people that will survive. These are the people you want standing next to you, I promise you that."

214

Bill and Ellen Wolf
Sinking Creek

Bill and Ellen Wolf in the Sinking Creek Valley of Craig County were into organic gardening and had a seaweed importing business from, of all places, Iceland.

"I was born and raised in suburban Connecticut," Bill told me. "During the early 1970s, my wife, Ellen, and I were farming in New Hampshire. I was milking cows at a dairy and working for Buckminster Fuller in Cambridge, Massachusetts.

"My parents exposed me to a wide variety of ideas. My real mother, who died when I was five, was an architect. She designed and built one of the first passive underground solar homes in New England. My stepmother who raised me was the first female producer/director on Broadway. After WWII, my father collaborated with Bucky Fuller on the Dymaxion Corporation.

"Buckminster Fuller was the Leonardo da Vinci of the 20th century, particularly in that his contributions were not fully realized or recognized until after his death. He had turned me on to seaweed in work I was doing for him in 1970 and 1971. That work is actually what got me into agriculture in the first place.

"From that research, agricultural practices have become my life's work. I particularly became interested in agriculture and food, primarily because I recognized that individuals can affect that pattern, certainly more so than energy or transportation. In the summer of 1971, I started a garden where I experimented with sustainable gardening methods.

"Ellen and I bought a farm in Back Valley, which is between Waiteville, West Virginia, and Paint Bank, Virginia. Our 40 acres was surrounded on two sides by National Forest. The house was appraised at $6,000 and the land was $100 per acre. So for $10,000, we bought 40 acres and a house.

"My intention was to move here and become a full-time farmer, learning by observation the basics of how farming really works in a natural setting. I had already studied agronomy on my own from the work I was doing for Bucky. I was already harvesting seaweed. I was looking at rock powders and biological systems.

"The essence of the decay and renewal cycle is that the waste product of one agricultural activity becomes the food stock for the following activity. It is the essence of life on our planet. There is a cycle of carbon renewal. There is a nitrogen cycle. It is the essence of sustainability. For us to buy fossil fuel-based nitrogen and to transport and apply to our soils that nitrogen is an arrogant embarrassment. It is devastating to our biological system and to the future of our civilization. There is more nitrogen in my hands than we will ever need to buy. Air is mostly nitrogen. The natural nitrogen cycle in a sustainable system uses legume crops to capture that nitrogen from the air by nodules on the roots of the legumes such as clover, peas, beans, and some trees such as locust. These plants have an extraordinary symbiotic relationship with the nitrogen-fixing bacteria that fix it into the soil and make it the nitrogen source for the next crop.

"We have put profit before ecology. For decades, yield has been the goal. Farmers were encouraged to get higher and higher yields by applying synthetic inputs.

"Fuller said in the 1930s that the petroleum industry was the pirate of the 20th century because they were not being charged for, nor were they charging their customers for, the cost of making the product. When you mine a resource you do not pay the earth for it. You are also not paying the community or society. The amount of physical energy in a unit of petroleum is far greater than the cost of removing it from the earth.

"Seventy and eighty years ago, Bucky was calculating the equivalent amount of human energy input in a barrel of oil. He determined that a barrel of oil should cost $200 then. If it had, then solar, wind, and other renewable energy sources would be fully employed today. He thought tidal energy was extremely consistent and reliable. He opined that first, there is a huge ocean resource that we do not understand. Second, he believed that local resources would become important. Third, he thought that composting and renewable agriculture would become essential.

"We need to be buying and selling and evaluating our food supply around the parameter of nutrient energy, not around tonnage. Synthetic nitrogen is perhaps the most egregious example of our current system. Most mineral supplements can be generated by local systems. We are pumping natural gas from the earth and burning it to produce urea or ammonium nitrate which is then applied to the soil.

"I have spent my career studying appropriate farming methods. Let's look at soil in its component form. First is the physical. Second is the chemical. Third is the biological. In each of those areas, what we are doing now is not sustainable. These days, I am a gardener, part-time farmer, and educator. I spend little time farming.

"Organic farming is the fastest growing segment of food interest in the country today, and yet the USDA is only giving a token amount of attention to it and only because organic farmers have forced them to. We need more money in research, statistics, and marketing for organic farming.

"The earthworm should be the primary driving force for how decisions in agriculture are made, our greatest measurement of fertility and crops and soils. We would evaluate the success of our efforts by the ratio of beneficial insects to harmful insects and by the health of the soil, the loss of erosion, and overall measurements of the fertility of the environment. Breaking the link between food and human health is the most ridiculous thing we have ever done in human history."

Tracy Roberts
Sinking Creek

Tracy Roberts, who trains and trades cutting horses and raises Australian Shepherd dogs, and John White, a physician, live in an historic house on highway SR-42 in the Sinking Creek Valley of Craig County. The home is a two-story brick structure, with painted wood trim, in the traditional "T" shape of houses from the early 19th century. "The house was built about 1826 or 1828," she said. "It was built by Oscar Wiley, who was a state congressman. The farm itself was originally a land grant from the king of England.

"The brickwork is the same as Monticello, so the craftsmen may have been the same. There's a pattern brought over from Italy. The kiln is still here where they made the brick. You can still see fingerprints in the brick from the man who formed it by hand.

"Wiley Jr. inherited this house and about 1200 acres. He married his first wife and they had a child. They were living in this house when the [Civil] War began. He was trained as a surgeon, and he served the Confederacy. He was transferred to the Western Campaign and was sent to Kentucky. While he was gone, his wife packed up the child and moved back to Charlottesville. She and her child got measles and died. Wiley came back and married a girl local to this area. She and her sister and friends were here.

"He came home for a while, doing surgeries and delivering babies. When West Virginia seceded, his land got split. He had thirteen slaves. So in or around the house were thirteen slaves, four white women, one white male, and too many children to count. The story we've heard is that at one point while he was gone for a few days, Averill's Raiders arrived. There was a natural spring right behind the house, and the Raiders camped there. From the descriptions in Averill's notes, they sent a Private to the house to take supplies. The Private knocked on the back door, and one of the slave women shot him in the head. It was too early in the war for things to get really ugly to the point where the soldiers would rape and pillage and burn the house to the ground. Nobody knew what to do. The dead soldier laid on the door stoop into the next day. Averill was afraid to send anybody else to the house because of what might happen. Later in the war, there wouldn't have been any hesitation in killing all the women and children.

"Averill wrote in his notes about wondering how to deal with this situation. He went to V.M.I. so he probably knew these people. Wiley returned home from his trip and Averill's people put him under arrest. They took him for eight months and never let him return to the house. It seemed to be a gentlemen's arrest. He worked for them and taught them some surgical techniques. There was a time when he was actually doing surgery on both Union and Confederate soldiers. The folks back home thought he'd been killed. Wiley came back eventually, built this little building, and continued his medical work.

"We were having dinner here one night with family and guests. This house definitely has ghosts. My sister's mother-in-law wanted to get away from this ghost talk, and she went outside and walked around the little building. She came back in and said, 'I love your guest house. Look at all these neat things we've found,' showing several objects. John, who is a physician, pointed at the vertebrae and said, 'Well, that's a vertebra. And these would be finger bones.' She was mortified."

West Virginia

GREENBRIER

ALLEGHANY

Union
🏛

MONROE

CRAIG

GILES

Virginia

Monroe County, West Virginia

Monroe County has a mild topography with many square miles of open farmland. Much of its southeastern border is dominated by Peters Mountain. A boundary anomaly takes in part of Potts Valley and Potts Mountain, which parallels and rivals Peters in length and grandeur.

There are 474 square miles.

There are two incorporated towns, Peterstown and Union. Portions of the town of Alderson, including the municipal government, are in the county. Union is the county seat.

Population

Monroe County's population has remained remarkably steady, vacillating between 12,000 and 15,000 for over 100 years. Approximately 14,500 people live there today.

Institutions of higher education

Monroe County has no colleges or universities.

Traffic

Monroe County has no four-lane roads and no traffic lights whatsoever.

Today's...

Monroe County is a quiet farming community with little manufacturing or industry.

Attractions

- Sweet Springs Resort, Sweet Springs, under development
- Moncove Lake State Park, Gap Mills, resort and wildlife management area

Craig Mohler
Union

Harrison Craig Mohler is editor of *The Monroe Watchman* in Union. He said in an email, "I was born in Union in 1961. I graduated from Union High School, from Virginia Tech, and from the University of Georgia as a doctor of Veterinary Medicine. I operated a mixed-animal veterinary practice in Union from 1988 until 1998 and was the primary veterinarian for the Hollow Hill Bison farm at Paint Bank for several years. I was elected to the county commission in 1994 and served two terms.

"My dad died of cancer in 1997, and I returned to the family business then as editor of *The Monroe Watchman*, a newspaper which has been printed in Union since 1872. I juggled all three jobs (veterinarian, commissioner, and editor) for a little over a year but closed my veterinary practice in 1998."

We met in his cluttered office on Main Street in Union.

About Monroe County, he said, "Groups and subgroups have formed and they disagree on certain issues, but if there is a perceived threat, it's amazing how the County comes together. People don't lock their doors and are always willing to help one another. The downside of that is that people often know a lot about what's going on in each other's lives.

"Monroe County was settled early. There were scattered cabins here by the 1750s. There is a house just a few miles south of town that supposedly contains part of the foundation of the original fort, the Burnside Fort, which would have been built in approximately 1770.

"It's a county that identifies itself closely with Virginia. The leadership during the Civil War was pro-Virginia. There was a division between the mountain farmers and the wealthy farmers. The remote mountain farmers had no affection for the wealthy planters who fought for the Confederate cause. They were either trying to avoid war or held to the sentiments of the Union side. Different branches of my family leaned different ways.

"Another thing that is unusual about the county is a touch of so-phistication. This is attributable to the mineral springs resorts. About 1780 the resort at Sweet Springs started operation, prior to the Green-brier. By 1820 there was another resort at Salt Sulphur Springs and another at Red Sulphur Springs. Throughout much of the 1800s and until the time of the Depression, there were lots of people coming here from all over.

"I think the presence of the springs and the tourists that were at-tracted to them made the area a little worldlier. That influx of people brought money and new ideas with them each summer."

Craig said he began his political efforts because he was an oppo-nent of a planned power transmission line. He concluded there was nothing the county would gain from it in local generation or new jobs. He said the project got people thinking about the notion of progress. Local people began to realize that the line was not about local benefit, but about corporate profits. Ultimately the opponents were success-ful, and a shorter line was built elsewhere. He said he thought Monroe County was the first to vocally oppose it, followed by other neigh-boring counties. It was one of the first times in West Virginia when citizen advocacy successfully blocked a development project.

"Union's retailers are doing pretty well because of the isolation. We have a hardware store and two or three restaurants. We have a local grocery store. These businesses do okay primarily because it is incon-venient to go elsewhere. If we had a Wal-Mart or a four-lane highway to Lewisburg, we would probably lose a lot of that stuff. I think we are better off as a community with local businesses because these businesses return their profits to the community whereas a Wal-Mart's profit goes to corporate headquarters. Also a lot of their jobs are part-time or minimum wage.

"Union is a bit like a Norman Rockwell painting. Or, maybe like Mayberry RFD. There is not a single traffic light in the entire County.

"The state of West Virginia treats its counties differently than Virginia. In Charleston, the senators and delegates are pushing hard to consolidate some of the smaller counties. You can imagine the out-cry from a county that's been in existence for over 200 years. To have the delegates around the capital tell us that we can no longer be an independent county would be outrageous. They tell us we're too small and we can't make ends meet. A lot of that from my perspective is the state's fault. In West Virginia they don't kick any funding into the counties. In Virginia the opposite is happening where the state government is kicking money into the counties, and the operating budgets of the counties are phenomenally better. Excluding the schools, our typical county government budget in recent years has been about $1.7 million. Craig County has fewer people than we have, and they have a $7 or $8 million budget. It's a world of difference."

Here was another West Virginian who thought Virginia government better served its citizens than West Virginia. Reunification anyone?

Monument to the Confederate soldiers of Monroe County in Union

Brian Wickline
Union

Brian Wickline is the Cooperative Extension agent for Monroe County.

"I serve homeowners in terms of gardening issues, and I work with farmers in livestock production, marketing, etc. We try to target niche markets for not only livestock but also vegetables.

"We are trying to start some organic farming. One problem we have as far as marketing goes is that a lot of our agricultural products have to go out of the area for producers to get a premium price, because there is not a big enough market here. Generally today the organic market is high-end, so we target the Charleston area and we are doing work in some of the central parts of the state.

"We are seeing growth. The farmers are receptive. They want to get involved in these niche markets and are thinking outside of the box to get involved in niche markets.

"I also work with livestock producers. I have about 22 producers within a two-county area, in Greenbrier and Monroe counties, where we have developed a marketing pool using a tele-auction to sell calves. We are beginning to see a trend for all natural products. We only started this concept about 18-months to two years ago. I think Monroe County is on the leading edge of this movement."

Larry Mustain
Second Creek

Though some individuals might think that the wheel is the greatest invention of humankind, many historians and anthropologists now point to the first agricultural revolution as being even more important. When humans subsisted on what could be hunted or gathered, their numbers were always kept in check by recurring famines and shortages.

Furthermore, little time was available to devote to the other issues necessary to build civilizations. When primitive humans learned that the seeds of certain grasses were edible and these grasses could be cultivated and harvested, the first population boom ensued.

However, these cereals are inedible in their raw form and must be crushed and cooked to obtain digestibility. So ancestral people learned to crush the grains between stones. The automation of this process gave birth to the industry of grist milling. By about 1000 A.D., Europe had thousands of gristmills, typically no more than a few miles apart. The Doomsday survey of 1086 in England counted precisely 5,624 mills in England, one for about every 300 inhabitants, a number that was similar to mills found throughout western and southern Europe.

The milling process requires a considerable amount of energy to move the stones. Throughout The Spine of the Virginias, water power has been used extensively. These mills are some of the finest historic architectural and engineering handiwork evident in the region.

The miller necessarily understood the intricacies of the technology. Mills were natural gathering places for isolated farmers and were the source of much socializing.

Monroe County still has a working gristmill, Reeds Mill, along Second Creek, operated by Larry Mustain.

"Second Creek is born in a series of springs on the slopes of Peters Mountain to the east of here, and it flows west through this valley to where it joins the Greenbrier River. At one point there were as many as 20 gristmills along the valley, all taking advantage of power supplied by the falling water. Reed's Mill was built in 1791. My uncle ran it for 70 years, and he never knew the stream to run dry to the point where it wouldn't power the mill. Even in its driest years there was some flow. Most of the mills were destroyed during the Civil War as one or the other army came through.

"I'm trying to rehabilitate the shop of a man who manufactured brooms. I knew him when I was a child. I remember him telling me that Second Creek was a bigger place during the Civil War. They had a home guard to protect the horses. I remember my grandparents saying that when the Yankees came everyone would take their horses into the mountains to hide them from the Union Army. Otherwise, the Yankees would steal them. The Rebels might steal them as well. The residents had guns they would use to protect the horses, and they had one cannon. The men practiced shooting the cannon by hauling it up into the field and shooting across the valley aiming at a particular tree. He would have been about nine years old during the War. He said he remembered the tree was finally shot down. He told me that story to explain why I was finding cannonballs when I would walk behind my uncle while he was plowing. Some of the cannonballs still had the drill hole in them. Some of them had green around them, meaning that they still had some powder in them."

"Another friend's father tells the story of his grandmother saying that she lived way back on this mountain during the Civil War. At one point they saw fires down here in the valley, and they heard shooting and hollering and carrying on. In a day or two later they came to the mill to get something, and they asked a guy at the store what it was all about. He said, 'They were celebrating the end of the Civil War'. They had heard the news that the War had ended.

"The milling business model is remarkably similar to what it has always been. We grind three different types of cornmeal. One is the open pollinated corn called bloody butcher. One is white and yellow hybrid cornmeal. Then we do some solid white native corn. We also grind whole wheat flour, buckwheat flour, and occasionally we will grind rye. It is all whole-grain. We don't sift any of it.

"Most of the people who will bring corn to make cornmeal are the older people who are raising the open pollinated corn instead of hybrid corn.

"I have three acres planted in buckwheat, and it should have generated 1,000 to 1,500 pounds but instead it only generated 400 pounds. The deer and the turkey ate the rest. There are also a lot of raccoons. I had one patch of corn that was entirely eaten by coons. I trapped 12 coons before I finally gave up. I just quit and let them have it."

Charlie Dundas
Waiteville

Before the dominance of the automobile for personal transportation in the mid-1900s, the United States at one time had the largest network of railroads in the world. Many small towns across the nation were linked to the city by a vast rail network. Paint Bank was one of those towns. With the emergence of cheap oil and the automobile, the railroads gradually diminished in importance, especially for passenger service. The rails were removed, and the rolling stock was often scrapped. Thousands of miles of abandoned rail corridors still exist. People across the nation have made a deliberate effort to preserve these corridors as hiking and bicycling trails. Monroe County is in the process of preserving a section of the Potts Creek line to Paint Bank.

I joined Charlie Dundas and several others on a frigid winter day to hike the abandoned grade. Charlie represented the construction company that had secured the bid to build the trail.

The Potts Creek Railroad had a short existence from 1909 until 1932. The route went from the New River near Ripplemead in Giles County, Virginia, on a northwestern path along the Big Stony Creek, through the villages of Kimbalton, Gold Bar, Interior, and Kire. From there, it went through the village of Waiteville, then re-entered Virginia and made its way to the terminus in Paint Bank.

The line had a consistent and gentle grade. When the train was discontinued, the rails were removed, and most of the grade had a road superimposed over it. One section near Waiteville was not used for the road because motor vehicles have different requirements. The road left the grade, taking a shorter, curvier, and steeper route on the other side of the valley. It rejoined the grade near Waiteville.

After the hike, Charlie and I spoke about his interest in West Virginia history. "I am 65 years old. I was born in the Huntington [WV] area. I have bachelors and masters degrees in history from Marshall University. I spent 30 years in the United States Marine Corps, and I retired May, 1998.

"My family is originally from the eastern part of Virginia, the Potomac River, Chesapeake Bay area. My family members were loyalists during the Revolutionary War. After the war, they bought five thousand acres in Cabell County near Huntington, which was then in western Virginia. They were slave owners. They built homes and mills.

"In 1858 my family manumitted our slaves. When the Civil War started, my great grandfather and my great uncle joined the Wythe brigade in the Confederate Army, the Eighth Virginia Cavalry. At the end of the war, returning Confederate officers were required to take an amnesty oath before they could regain full citizenship rights, including voting. When he refused, our family basically lost most of its land. So in my household, the views of who the good guys and who the bad guys were are much different than the conventional wisdom.

"West Virginia's creation was totally illegal because the Constitution says that in the creation of a new state, the mother state must give approval. The Federal government circumvented this law by considering an exiled government of Virginia, separate from the traditional and legitimate government in Richmond, to be the new legitimate representation of the state. This 'restored' government was in Alexandria originally and then in Wheeling. That new, 'restored' government agreed to allow the secession of the counties that are now West Virginia from the original state of Virginia. But the Richmond government never agreed to this. In 1863 when the vote to take this action was held, the only people who could vote were men who were sympathetic to the Union cause. [Even so, the vote was close.] People sympathetic to the Confederate cause were either away in the War or not allowed to vote.

"The western counties which now form West Virginia were, in effect, stolen from Virginia, and the federal government had the power to do so because they occupied the area. The people who pushed for this new state and for the illegitimate restored government of Virginia were looking to punish and weaken the Confederate-leaning people in Richmond."

This was entirely consistent with what Stuart McGehee had told me, but I'd never spoken to another West Virginian who understood it similarly. I asked if he knew why the border line was drawn where it was.

"I am sure it was at least in part because of the occupation. They basically took the counties they were able to control, which were all of the counties along the Allegheny Front. There are still many people in West Virginia who display the Confederate flag, but I don't think they are necessarily sympathetic towards the Confederacy itself. They are more likely sympathetic to Virginia. For them, the whole concept of the Confederacy was based upon states' rights. As a government itself, the Confederacy was never strong. Some Confederate states would not allow their troops to fight outside of the boundaries of their own state. The common perception is that the Civil War was almost entirely about slavery, but the issue of states' rights was equally important.

"[My family] felt the North was trying to impose its lifestyles and values upon the South. It was your typical culture war. This still plays itself out over and over again.

"Certainly I accept the fact that I am a West Virginian. I would rather see us still be part of Virginia. I still sometimes jokingly refer to myself as a Virginia irredentist. West Virginia is not a legal or viable entity. Our population has dropped to approximately 1.7 million people. We have an infrastructure that we can barely maintain. We don't have any kind of tax base. We are not willing to tax coal, gas, and oil at rates necessary to create sufficient income to provide governmental services. If you include the areas that are now in the Monongahela National Forest, something like 70 percent or 80 percent of West Virginia is owned by absentee landholders: the federal government or corporations. In many areas where this is especially true, for instance the coal communities, the people do not have a lot of respect for private property or ownership.

"I am proud to be a Virginian. My family was Virginian. As a Marine in Vietnam, I fought under the American flag. The other soldiers in my family either fought for the British against the United States or for the Confederacy against the United States. In the 200 plus years that my family has been here, I am the first to have ever fought for the United States. It feels all right…I get a retirement check."

Mark Soukup
Gap Mills

Mark Soukup is a chair maker and cabinetmaker in Gap Mills. His style and craftsmanship is of the caliber that he was commissioned to build antique reproduction furniture for Monticello, Thomas Jefferson's home.

Mark and his wife had grown up together in Cincinnati, Ohio, and had lived in Washington State before seeking an arcadian life in Monroe County. The stresses of isolation were evident. "After we were here for a couple of years, like many people early in their marriages, my wife and I began to face real life and our marriage fell on the rocks. It almost failed at that point. We split for a time, and after we got back together we were quite shaken by what had taken place. We truly loved each other, and it became as close to a death experience as I had ever had. It was extremely stressful.

"It is probably good for young couples to be around other young couples that have positive views about relationships. It takes help and care to have a healthy relationship and direction in life. A problem for us is that we were products of our generation. We grew up in the '60s and early '70s, and we weren't given a lot of guidance and direction in our lives. We didn't even get married until after my wife became pregnant with our first child. Suffice it to say that there was a lot we just didn't know about basic living.

"There is a local Amish Mennonite community here in Gap Mills. My wife and I were looking for something in the way of a strong community to help us better understand ourselves. This community existed in its most beautiful form within these Mennonites. We had never seen such responsible children. They often invited us to attend church with them. They seemed so foreign. The women wore dresses like the styles of the 1800s. When we got back together in our marriage, we began to attend their church. Frankly, that changed our lives.

"My wife and I had been indoctrinated in a secular fundamentalism with really no religious education and no church. I could be critical of the Bible, but I really knew nothing about it. When I heard about the teachings of the New Testament, it spoke to me and I responded to it as a truth about my life. That really meant that we found ourselves at home there. We eventually became part of the church. It was a long process because we had come from being total atheists and then converted to Christians. We had come from ultra liberal suburban American backgrounds, but joined one of the most conservative and traditional American churches. We attended that church regularly for almost 15 years.

"Our children have grown up largely within the Mennonite Church. The Mennonites had their own school, and our children went there. Our two oldest children are now strongly Mennonite, our middle daughter is straddling the fence, and our two youngest are more affiliated with the Episcopalians, where we now go to church. The point is that through the religious experience we had a lot of really good teaching about how to have a good family life and to act responsibly towards our fellow man. It really helped to give us a life.

"It also encouraged us to have a lot more children, but raising our family has truly been a blessing in our life. If you had asked me earlier in my life if I expected to sire five children, I would have thought you were crazy.

"I started making chairs for a living in 1983. A man in Lewisburg who ran a nice antique shop started selling my work. I make 18th and 19th century antique reproduction American furniture. I found myself being right where I wanted to be as far as having access to quality timber. I found sawmills that would allow me to go through their yards and pick out woods that I wanted, and they would saw them for me.

He picked up a piece of wood and said, "This is poplar, and it comes from a tree at least two-feet in diameter. A sawmill will typically not saw the wood for a wide board, but that is what I need. You can't just go out and buy that lumber.

"The quality of the timber in our forests has been increasing because our forests are getting more mature. That growth in volume of good quality hardwoods has meant that many entrepreneurs have come to set up big operations here. I don't want to be too critical. I have come to know loggers and veneer buyers and a lot of people along this whole chain of producing and using woods. I know what it is like to be around clearcuts. I have also tried to harvest wood myself in the forests.

"Clearcuts are not pretty, but small-scale clearcuts can be the best way to harvest hardwood forests because they allow for better regeneration of quality timber. One thing that has happened for too many years in our forests is that people go and take the best timber and leave behind the lower grade species and the lower quality wood. A knowledgeable forester can plan the cutting in such a way that the logger does not do unnecessary damage, and the regeneration will actually be improved.

"I love to walk in the woods. I grew up being a preservationist, and I still am. I understand the value of wood, and I can't help but think that in this country we are being too wasteful, and we have a lot of poor quality woodland management. We have so much land that we are not forced to take better care of what we have. This will sound funny, but sometimes I feel as though the wood I buy from the sawmills is too cheap. Because we have so much, we are careless with everything we do along the production chain.

"I come out of the house in the morning with my cup of coffee, work until lunchtime, and go back into the house and have lunch, come back to the workshop afterwards and quit my work at five or six o'clock and do not see another person. There are good things and bad things about that. I do need contact with other people, and my wife does too. That can be a drawback in working here. But on the other hand, I often don't appreciate how much time I have to work in peace here.

"I understand that some people cannot relate to my lifestyle at all. Even in my own family, sometimes my siblings don't understand why I would choose to live in this kind of a place.

"In the urban setting, I would probably be able to make more money, and sometimes I long for that. Still, after all these years, I have to continue to work harder to market myself and to make my work better-known. I have no pension. When I am sick or on vacation, I generate no income.

"We didn't come here because we felt the world was going to collapse, but we did want to live where we felt we weren't dependent upon the typical American consumer food chain. In that, we have been successful because we are removed from it to a much greater degree than my former classmates in Cincinnati. We have our own livestock for meat. We have always grown a lot of our own food and know other people we can get food from. I want my children to know what it means to grow food and not be wasteful. I want them to have those values.

"I think a lot of people are not mentally and emotionally prepared for the stresses of rural life. If they were forced into it, we would see a lot of divorces and suicides. To many people it would seem like a prison."

Hanging Rock Raptor Observatory
Peters Mountain

On fifteen miles or so of Peters Mountain is a section of the Allegheny Trail. From the trailhead I hiked steadily uphill towards the Hanging Rock Raptor Observatory to watch for migrating hawks. The early September sky hung anvil clouds at a ceiling just below the elevation of the ridge. I walked in fog. I reached a short spur, marked with a sign saying "Fire tower," which the observatory once was. The observatory itself, rebuilt in 1997 after a fire that destroyed the 1972 model, is dramatically situated. Hundreds of miles south of the Great Lakes, this area gets the wintertime weather phenomenon known as lake effect rain (or snow). Moisture-laden clouds seem to run into Peters Mountain where the sudden elevation uplifts, chills, and condenses their moisture, sending prodigious amounts of rainfall into nearby streams.

This uplifting scene also provides the thermal currents used by raptors for millennia as migration superhighways. Peters Mountain seems to be a convergence zone, producing strange effects. One is a bizarre and incredible natural wind tunnel. In springtime when conditions are just right, visitors have heard a great roaring wind, described by one as a thundering roar of giant waves breaking over rocky reefs.

Meteorologists love this stuff. Dr. W. J. Humphrey, born in 1862, a native of nearby Gap Mills, was a noted meteorologist, physicist, professor, and author of numerous publications on natural phenomena. He thought these Gap Mills Winds originated in the Atlantic Ocean, then traveled across upland Virginia and struck Peters Mountain and spilled over and caused the roar. Farmers on the West Virginia side have found ocean gulls that have been carried along on these mighty magic carpets of air only to land dazed and exhausted.

I reached the observatory and climbed the 20 steps to its platform. Photographs were tacked to the wall showing the most common birds seen, and a logbook with historic records of raptor counts lay on the table. The highest historic populations were from the middle to the end of September, so I was a couple of weeks before prime.

The most frequent sighting is of broad-winged hawks, followed by sharp-shinned hawks, Cooper's hawks, and red-tailed hawks. All I could see was a plastic owl atop a pole fifty feet away and lots of fog.

While the weather was awful for bird watching, I decided it was perfect for a run. Running mountain trails in the fog is a rare but welcome treat, almost dreamlike but fast and intense. I lumbered downhill to the junction, then west (southbound) on the Allegheny Trail. The early going was rocky and treacherous with the wet surfaces. The enveloping gray-green of the woods and fog lent a surrealistic feel as I bounded along, leaping fallen logs and mud puddles. At a football-field-sized moor, I slowed to a walk. The field was otherworldly, with a honey-hued iridescent glow, soft and sweet. The fog rose gently from the blades of grass, in reverse gravity. In a tree was a small insect trap, shaped like a pup tent. At twenty minutes, my legs aching, I turned and ran back. I dutifully left my name in the logbook and trudged back to the car. Descending the mountain, I quickly left the fog behind.

Months later, I hiked to the observatory again. This time, another hopeful sky watcher occupied it. As we scanned the sky together, he said wistfully, "There was a day last year when I saw 7000 hawks! From one o'clock until five o'clock in the afternoon, I never put down my binoculars. It was the most amazing thing I have ever seen. I hope I live long enough to see another day like that."

Ronnie Huffman
Warren Smith
Sweet Springs

Not a stone's throw from the state line and tucked into a hidden corner of the state of West Virginia, is the spa and resort at Sweet Springs. Of all the surviving resorts, this is among the most grand, rivaling the superstars: The Homestead and The Greenbrier. The "Old Sweet's" magnificent hotel was reputedly designed by a protégé of Thomas Jefferson.

The earliest settlement in the area of the eastern tip of Monroe County was in the 1700s. By 1792, William Lewis began developing the area as a spa. Visitors today are awe-struck by the size of the grand hotel. It was built in 1833 from brick and painted wood and designed in the Georgian Colonial style. The structure has a 300-foot front expanse. There are four separate porticos, each with four stout white columns. By the late 1800s, the resort could house 800 guests. Unfortunately, its heyday is long past, and it hasn't had paying guests in decades.

A number of cottages and outbuildings make up the resort. One is made of stone and was reputedly once a jail. The bathhouse and pool were in good condition until about 2005, when a deliberate demolition was initiated. Prior to that, it had stood since 1830. It is a delightful building in its own right, with a five-arch entrance and two rectangular two-story towers at each of the front corners. The water that bubbles from its base contains carbonic acid, which has fizziness like a soda and is reputedly responsible for remarkable curative powers over maladies such as neuralgia and rheumatism.

The guest list over the decades is impressive, including Presidents George Washington, James Madison, Millard Fillmore, and Franklin Pierce, plus luminaries Patrick Henry, Robert E. Lee, and John Marshall. General Lee even brought Traveler, his Grey Eagle American saddlebred gelding, to the healing waters. Jerome Bonaparte, Napoleon's youngest surviving brother, met his American wife, Elizabeth

Patterson, there.

The Lewis family sold it in 1852 and several different owners kept it in operation until in the 1920s. No record exists of a specific reason why it ceased operation. Certainly the lack of railroad access may have been a factor. The short-lived Potts Creek line would still have ended in Paint Bank, requiring a strenuous trek over Peters Mountain. By contrast, the Greenbrier has had a railroad adjacent to its entrance since the late 1800s.

In the last eighty years, the hotel was used for a variety of non-hospitality purposes. It was a sanatorium where accounts of rape, murder, and other mistreatment still linger. One story persists of an insane doctor in the 1940s who was particularly heinous. The West Virginia State Legislature took control of the site in 1945 and established a home for the aged and infirm. It was abandoned in the 1990s.

Warren Smith, a real estate developer from Fredericksburg, Virginia, acquired the property in 2005, and work is underway to restore the resort to its former prominence.

Ronnie Huffman manages the Resort's bottling plant. He told me they bottled under the name Sweet Sommers at Sweet Springs. "There is another bottling plant over in Gap Mills (ten miles away to the southwest) that has been bottling longer than we have, and it is called Sweet Springs. Since it had the name first, we had to use the name Sweet Sommers at Sweet Springs.

"The water does not require purification. It is 100 percent spring water, pure and natural. Our spring flows lots of water and will satisfy our needs for some time. The mineral pool produces a million gallons per day, and we're not using it at all yet."

Warren Smith said, "I absolutely love history. I was captivated by the thought of what this property had been beginning in the late 1700s. It is documented that six United States presidents stayed here, several of them frequently. Civil War generals, kings and queens, and people from literally all over the world have stayed here. I almost had goosebumps just standing outside in front of this cottage and realizing that not only were those people here, but that all the 14 buildings on this site that are on the National Historic Register, including the Grand Hotel, look virtually identical to the day these people stayed here. This is truly hallowed ground.

"It feels as if the prior owners simply turned the key, locked the doors, and walked away. Some of these buildings have been restored. We intend to restore all of them. Our vision is to bring this resort back so that guests can literally step back into history, seeing exactly what those illustrious guests saw back then. Plans are to create a family-oriented resort, self-sustaining and in tune with the environment. There will be a golf course, spa, fitness center, conference center, orchards, vineyards, and gardens. It will be totally modern in that regard. It will be a place where the nights are still fresh, clear, and cool. We will build an amphitheater on the hillside above us and have outdoor concerts and events, overlooking the Sweet Springs Valley.

"There is already a synergy developing between what we are working on here in Sweet Springs and what the Mulherens have developed across the mountain in Paint Bank. They are receptive to what we're doing as are we to what they have done.

"For many years people have thought of coal as being the precious resource of West Virginia. Actually their most precious resource is their water. The people of West Virginia are just starting to realize how precious it is."

Fred Ziegler
Greenville

Fred and Barbara Ziegler have retired to Greenville, living in a restored farmhouse adjacent to an historic but out-of-service grist mill by Laurel Creek. Fred worked as a geology professor in Chicago. He explained the forces that formed the Appalachian Mountains.

"I began my career in the late 1960s when the idea of plate tectonics became popular. We first focused on the generalities of the continental movements around the world. We attempted to learn where the various continental plates were during the successive eras of the Earth's history relative to the poles and the equator."

He told me The Spine of the Virginias spans the entire Allegheny Fold Belt. "The Fold created Peters Mountain on the border and the area's other linear mountains. The area by the Narrows of the New River is a region of unfolded rocks. The rocks around here are tilted to a degree but nothing like the Fold Belt. The line that in this area is on the front or west margin of Peters Mountain can be traced up and down the length of the Appalachian mountain range. There is a major geologic transition between the rocks that have been folded and those that have been stable, under the central part of the North American platform for one billion years.

"The rocks that were folded about 260 million years ago. Rather, the folding terminated 260 million years ago. That would have given us the forerunner of a zone of mountains of Himalayan proportions. Remember that at this time, the continent we now think of as Africa was contiguous with this region.

"The Alleghenies represent that portion of the margin of North America that had collected a series of flat-lying sedimentary rocks. Africa crashed in and pushed the margin and folded the mountains. Picture in your mind taking a throw rug that is lying flat on the floor and pushing one edge inward. It would create a series of ridges. This is exactly what happened when the continental plate of Africa crashed into this region.

"The mountains rose and then eroded. Sediments were being derived from them that flowed onto the coal-bearing regions of West Virginia, Western Virginia, and Eastern Kentucky. The upthrusting of the ridges created the basin which would become the entire Allegheny or Appalachian Plateau. Coal developed on the stable platform below the towering peaks, but it is derived from the effect of the collision of Africa with North America.

"In summary, the continental plates crashed together. The action of crashing caused folding, which produced long and immensely high ridges. The flows from those ridges sent streams of deposits over the flatter lands and alluvial planes to the north and west, alternating with periods of massive amounts of biological activity. Successive flows buried the products of those biological activities and converted them over heat, pressure, and time, into fossil fuels. What caused the alternating layers of coal with other non-mineral rock layers was not so much attributable to changes in climate but instead to changes in sea level, causing the base level to go up and down.

"The areas that now produce coal were once at sea level. Marine-based fossils are embedded between the coal seams. The reason for the cycles is the alternating levels of the sea."

Ziegler mentioned ominously that modern societies are consuming finite fossil fuel resources at a rate one million times faster than the earth is generating them.

"Much of the continent was covered by ocean. The ocean was on both sides of this great mountain chain. The Mississippi and Ohio River valleys were submerged. The Atlantic Ocean formed as the African plate began to drift away towards its current location.

"To the west, in areas that we think of now as being part of the Mississippi and Ohio River valleys, was a shallow sea. We live in a time today when the sea level is at or near its historic low with respect to the continents. The continents are like gigantic rafts sitting on the mantle, like pancakes on a greased griddle.

Introducing his interest in gristmills, he said, "I have twin interests in antiques and in energy." For about three years before he retired, he and Barbara searched the East Coast for a mill to purchase. "We became aware of this mill and could see that the potential was there to

Old store at Salt Sulphur Springs

turn it back into a working operation. We eventually bought it."

The Zieglers want to be involved with economic development and tourism, so they are restoring the mill. The mill itself is three-and-a-half floors including a large attic. The outside has wooden clapboards that have not been painted for years. There is a steeply sloped tin roof with several of the panels, perhaps 20 percent overall, showing some rust.

"One of the reasons we moved to West Virginia is that this is a relatively safe area. I can use the power of falling water to generate electricity. We are well away from sea level, so we will not be affected by rising waters.

"This is not an easy place to make a living. But on the other hand, being a long way from Wall Street has somewhat insulated this area from the current economic swings. West Virginia has not suffered as much as other states. In a sense, being backward has been good."

Aaron Elizabeth Broyles
Paul Leonard Broyles
Rock Camp

Paul Broyles is pastor of the Rock Camp Baptist Church. I watched as he baptized his daughter, Aaron Elizabeth, in nearby Indian Creek in the middle of winter when there were four inches of ice on the stream. A few days before the ceremony, he chipped a path into the stream, but it had frozen over in the meantime with another half-inch of new ice. So for the baptism, he started by inching his way into the flowing water chipping the ice again with a mattock. He returned to the bank where he took the hand of Aaron Elizabeth Broyles, and they waded into hip-deep water together. In front of perhaps 30 people, he spoke a prayer. He held one hand in front of her, clutching her hands, and the other on her back, and lowered her backwards until she was submerged into the icy water. Instantly, they scampered to the bank where they threw on dry jackets.

After a pot-luck lunch in the basement of the church, Paul told me about his life. He said he was born and raised in Ballard, in western Monroe County. He is fifty years old. "I graduated from Peterstown High School and went to work in the coal mines in Mullins, West Virginia. The next year I met a little girl from across the border near Narrows, Virginia. We dated for six months, and then we got married. I was 18 at the time and she was 19.

"A month after we were married, my brother asked me if I wanted to go fishing with him. I said being a newlywed I would stay with my wife. He and my father went without me. Within a couple of hours they had capsized their boat, and both of them had drowned. I could have easily been there and drowned with them. You will go crazy doing those what-if's.

"Within 18 months I learned that I was going to be a daddy. The next thing I knew the coal miners went on strike. So I lost my job and my income. My mother moved away to live with a brother in Oklahoma. So I was the only family member around when our first son was born.

"The next thing I knew my wife was pregnant again, with Aaron Elizabeth. I made $8 or $9 per hour working in a coal mine. When I lost that job, I found another job bagging groceries for $2.85 per hour, so we were having a hard time.

"I got a better job at a rubber factory for a while and things began to improve. Then I got a job at Celanese in Giles County. Sometime later, Celanese laid me off. Soon my unemployment insurance ran out. I was desperate. I had a wife and two children. I knew that Celanese had a program where I could hang on to my seniority if I were in the military. I decided the Army was my best bet. I was 22 years old. Two weeks later I was at Fort Lewis in Texas. I went from having long hair to having this," he said, pointing at his head, which he described as being a "Telly Savalas."

"My drill sergeants and all my fellow soldiers made fun of me with my accent and being from West Virginia. There have always been a disproportionate number of people in the military from West Virginia. For one thing, there have been limited employment opportunities here. For another, we are patriotic, and we are not afraid to serve our country. True, joining was partly about doing my patriotic duty, but the bottom line was that I needed a job. The Army shipped me overseas to Germany for three years. After eight months my wife and kids moved over to live with me. I had a wonderful experience and matured a lot.

"After I served my time, I came back to the states and resumed my job with Celanese. I saved $3000 in the Army. I began to attend the Church of Christ on Wolf Creek, where my wife was from. But within a short period of time I reverted to my old ways, drinking and smoking a little pot.

"After a couple of years being back, I got saved. I had joined the church when I was young and had been baptized, but I think I did it just to fit in with my friends.

"Then I had an experience that changed my life. We used to do a lot of camping. There was a children's home near where we camped, and they brought many of their orphans to the campground. We spent two weeks camping near them. I wanted to take some of them home with me. I had had a vasectomy, but I wanted more children. So I talked to my wife about adopting a foster child. We submitted our paperwork

"Our first foster child was a baby, just six months old. That was just the beginning. In the last 20 years, my wife and I have raised 52 foster children. At this point we have eight grandchildren. It is a miracle what God has done with us."

He told me his job at the church was only part time. He continued to work in the Celanese factory. He looked at his watch. "I work shift work at the plant. Right now I am working a 3 p.m. until 11 p.m. shift. As soon as I leave here I am on my way to work."

As he departed, he said, "I am a servant. I am a pastor, but I am a servant to the people. I am a servant to you. If we disagree, that is fine too. Now, if you ask me to do something to help you that is not in God's will, then I cannot help you. My first master is God. My second master is my wife. My third master is my children and my foster children. My fourth master is my parishioners.

"I am proud of who I am. We are patriotic people. We stand by our convictions. We are not perfect. There is theft and corruption in this state. If people want to laugh at us that is fine, but there are many great people in West Virginia."

Aaron Elizabeth Broyles said, "I have always forged my own way in life. I am 27 years old. These have been 27 years of hard life. As Dad told you, I grew up in a large family with one biological brother and lots of foster siblings. When a child has to share her parents and her house and her toys with lots of other children, it teaches her not to be selfish. It was hard sometimes, but my parents continually reinforced to us that they were not trying to replace us. We always knew we had our place.

"Christmas at our house is still huge. We visit each other when we can and we have stayed a close-knit family. Some have married and now have babies who consider my parents to be their grandparents."

Aaron admitted she was a hard-headed person. Once she graduated from high school, Aaron got married and had two kids, but the marriage failed. Then she had a second unhappy marriage and divorce, along with serious physical problems. "My parents have always stood with me even when I have made mistakes. I have been really lucky.

244

Baptism of Aaron Elizabeth Broyles in Indian Creek

"Before, I was living just for me. I got to the point where I had been through so many bad things and I had to ask so many people for help... I would go to my dad and ask him for help and finally it occurred to me that I was asking the wrong person. All along, I should have been asking God.

"To an outsider I'm sure my baptism appeared to be really crazy. That water was crazy freezing cold. But it was something to me... I just felt that I was going to be okay. Today was probably the coldest I have ever been, but I felt happy."

Her eyes began to get moist. "I have been carrying a lot on my shoulders for a long time. I have been through a lot."

She took a deep breath. "But not anymore. I am rejuvenated. Now I believe I can handle a lot more than I ever felt I was capable of. Today was the easy part. Now I have to commit my life to His work.

"I will be all right. I will go to heaven. I'm not afraid about that. Regardless of what I do for the rest of my life, everything will be all right."

Giles County, Virginia

Giles County is entirely within the Appalachian Ridge-and-Valley topography of limestone mountains. The mountains are distinct and linear, but all are dissected by the New River, which is the county's dominant physical feature. The northern border primarily follows the East River/Peters Mountain ridge, and the southern border primarily follows the Big Walker, Gap, and Sinking Creek mountain ridges. Other mountains are Wolf Creek, Pearis, and Brushy mountains west of the river and Butt and Salt Pond mountains east of the river. Much of the mountainous land is within the George Washington and Jefferson National Forest.

The county is 360 square miles.

Five incorporated towns make up Giles County: Pearisburg, Glen Lyn, Pembroke, Narrows, and Rich Creek. Pearisburg is the county seat.

Population

Giles County's population has remained steady. There were approximately 11,000 people in 1900, 19,000 in 1950, and are 17,000 today.

Institutions of higher education

Giles County has no colleges or universities.

Traffic

Giles County has about 55 miles of four-lane roads. There are many traffic lights in the county, mostly in and around Pearisburg.

Today's...

Giles County boasts about 37 miles of the New River, an American Heritage River and one of the oldest rivers in the world. The New provides bountiful water sports, including canoeing, rafting, bird watching, and fishing, and an extensive trail system, including 50 miles of the Appalachian Trail. Giles has a mix of industry, recreation, and extractive industries. Farming is largely restricted by the steep mountains.

Attractions

- Cascades Recreational Area, Pembroke, waterfall and hiking trails
- Mountain Lake Resort, Pembroke, hotel and hiking
- New River, various, National River
- Appalachian Trail, various, National Scenic Trail

Shawn Hash
Pembroke

Shawn Hash, owner of Tangent Outfitters in Pembroke, Virginia, working with New River Community Partners, organized a trip from the headwaters of the New River in North Carolina northward through Virginia and into West Virginia in June of 2008, in order to commemorate the 10th anniversary of the designation of the New River as the first National Heritage River. I met with him on a stormy night in a park alongside the river near Pearisburg where the group of eighteen or so individuals was completing their fourteenth day.

A tanned lanky man, Shawn said, "There are 14 National Heritage Rivers now, but the New River was the first. Ten years ago, President Bill Clinton and Vice-President Al Gore dedicated the New as a National Heritage River at a ceremony in North Carolina.

"The New River is special in several ways. It is an ancient river, predating the Appalachian Mountain chain, which is one of the oldest in the world. Due to its south-to-north orientation, it has played a large role in the historic development of this region. The railroad has been an integral part of the river's history for over 100 years."

The river provides a natural corridor for trains coming from the east to slice through the Appalachian Mountains. Two lines join in Montgomery County and use the grade created by the river.

"The railroads have been a mixed blessing. They have impacted the river negatively, from a serenity standpoint. But the railroad saved the river by effectively blocking development. Along much of its way, it is still wild and scenic.

"The New is just coming onto the radar screens of everybody. The Shenandoah River and the James River are close to large population centers. They are impacted pretty heavily. Now we are just beginning to see the star quality of the New River draw people in from greater distances. Sometimes I lead trips for an entire day and don't pass anyone.

"The River belongs to all of us, so we need to take care of it. From my experience, as soon as people touch it, they understand that

Giles County courthouse, Pearisburg

they must take care of it. If a person crosses it over the US-460 bridge a million times, it still may never mean anything to them. As soon as they touch it, everything changes.

"We have some contamination issues, but it is a healthy mainstem river. We are building an environmental ethic on this river, one customer at a time."

Pat West
Eggleston

In Pat West's life, everything is art. No trinket, knick-knack, or bauble is too trivial not to be stored away or closeted, awaiting its chance to be incorporated into a piece of art. Her home looks like a scene from *The Lord of the Rings'* Rivendell, of waterfalls, cliffs, and rivers. Decades before her arrival, her driveway was essentially the main highway from central Giles County to Blacksburg and beyond.

Now, the main road bypasses her by a couple of miles, leaving her in splendid isolation. A bend in the New River fills the view from her immense picture windows, shimmering with light.

Below the house is a grassy field falling away to the timeless New River. Cliffs 200-feet high overhang the waters, their white-rock surfaces painted in vertical stripes with black patinas of decaying vegetation. Hawks drift above, catching thermal updrafts, and ducks bob in the ripples.

The house is a marvel of serendipitous engineering and building code nonchalance. The foundation is stacked river stones, Dr. Seuss style, supporting a stone floor. Pat has painted virtually everything that doesn't move: floors, walls, chairs, and ceiling fans. Whimsical sculptures adorn the walls, interior and exterior, and the gardens outside. A school of plastic sharks skims above the mulch around a rose bush. A multi-level terrace cascades down to the largest of several outdoor goldfish ponds. Frogs leap in when anyone approaches.

Pat's studio is a barn. In the loft are pieces of art with price tags from a few hundred to well over a thousand dollars, stacked against the walls like paperback books on a bookshelf. Her work has overtones of blood and death, sexuality, mysticism, and comedy. The canvases are thick with paint, sometimes a quarter of an inch heavy. Many are glittering, with sparkle paint splashed on colorful landscapes. The sculptures are cartoon crazy, incorporating restaurant style napkin holders, plastic and rubber toys, and dolls of all shapes, sizes, and compositions.

One sculpture is of a young couple in foreplay. In it, an elongated woman sits propped on the floor on her knees, leaning backwards, her cascade of red hair resting against the chest of her standing lover. Her tight green dress left one breast covered, the other exposed. Her man stood behind her, pants unzipped, one hand on her breast. One of her hands reached behind to grab his penis. His head rested back, his eyes closed in a cat-that-ate-the-canary grin. Pat's work is distinctly non-subtle.

Pat said, "To be an Appalachian artist you need to be influenced by the Appalachian landscape. My art is impressions of everything I see: patterns, painting, constructions, manipulations, whatever moves me. I'm whimsical; I like the word.

"I love this place. One of the most wonderful things about living here is the bird life. I've become very interested in the birds. There is a great variety of songbirds, and the river attracts water birds too. I see lots of smaller songbirds. I saw an eagle last week over the river. I had sixty bluebirds over the winter.

"I love the growing zone. The length of the winters and summers and springs; nothing lags. I like the constant change. We have incredibly free, great water around here. From a human perspective, the river is as constant as anything can be. The cliffs are thousands of years old.

"I like being the local weird artist. It suits me."

H. M. "Buzz" Scanland
Mountain Lake

Ten thousand years ago, vast glaciers swept from the Polar Regions across the North American continent as far south as Ohio, Pennsylvania, and New York. The Great Lakes and the Finger Lakes of New York were scoured from hard rock by the glaciers and Long Island and Cape Cod were terminal moraines. The Spine of the Virginias was spared this onslaught. Therefore, there are no mountain natural lakes, except one. At an elevation of 3875 feet, Mountain Lake is unusual indeed.

A grand sandstone rock hotel sits at the southern end. It became the backdrop for the enormously successful and timeless 1987 film, *Dirty Dancing*.

Normally about 50 acres in size, Mountain Lake is frustratingly fickle, often shrinking to a much smaller size. In good, wet times, the lake drains from a small creek at the north end. In drier years, it simply wilts away. In 2009, when the lake was almost gone, Buzz Scanland explained the history of the Mountain Lake Hotel. It was originally a stagecoach stop between Christiansburg, Virginia, and Union, Virginia. "The road was completed in 1857, before the start of the Civil War. The lake was more of a stagecoach stop than a resort. Later on,

251

the lake became a destination of its own. People began to seek out the mountain areas to escape the summer heat. Mountain Lake is always cooler than the surrounding valleys and much cooler than the areas along the Atlantic seaboard. Just after the Civil War, the property was owned by a Union general named Herman Haupt. A white-framed hotel was built around 1890. It remained in use until this structure was built in 1936. The entire hotel of three stories was built in one year. It has 50 guestrooms, a 2700 square-foot dining room, a 2700 square-foot ballroom, and a series of other meeting rooms of various sizes. It is built with sandstone that was quarried here on the mountain."

The hotel went through a series of owners until the current ownership, the foundation of Mary Moody Northern. I asked what he thought people found so enticing.

"For most people, this is a step back in time. It is relaxing, and it seems far away. People often say, 'This is a family place, and we all talk and do things together as a family when we are here. We come here to forget how the world moves down below.'

"One family has been hosting an annual reunion here for at least 50 years. Other families have just started this as a tradition. There are many things that appeal to the kids. During the summertime, we offer magic shows, storytelling by the teepee, and roast s'mores on the campfire. We have many miles of mountain bike trails and a Frisbee golf course. We do more and more because we no longer have the lake.

"The 6-mile access road is gorgeous. There is a church on the road up the mountain that has a beautiful maple tree in front of it. The television stations use that scene as an intro to some of their programming. The view is spectacular at many places on the road. Many people come to walk and take in the scenery. We encourage people to come here to hike, ride mountain bikes, and explore. Bald Knob in particular is a wonderful hike.

"Filming for *Dirty Dancing* began the week I began working here, on September 2, 1986, the day after Labor Day. Originally, the producers had contracted to do the entire movie at Lake Lure in North Carolina. They were flying back to New York City on Piedmont Airlines, which was the regional carrier in those days. Mountain Lake had

252

Salt Pond Mountain, Giles County

an ad in the in-flight magazine which included a picture of the hotel. One of the producers thought the hotel looked more like a hotel in the Catskills than anything at Lake Lure. They came back and looked at our hotel.

"The production crew and actors were here for three weeks. It was really cold. The actors wore coats while awaiting their turn to be in the film. They dropped their coats in a pile just off camera and appeared in the scene dancing around and having fun.

"The Hotel actually has the autographs of Patrick Swayze, Jerry Orbach, and Jack Weston and a few others when they signed in. When we have *Dirty Dancing* weekends, we make copies of those ledgers to give to attendees.

"We got a lot of publicity and television coverage. We had no idea then that the movie would stay so popular and be a continuing source of business. Last year we looked at how much we did in foreign business with Europe and Canada. It was ten times as much business this year, maybe more. We have seen people travel from Europe all the way to the United States to come here for one night because they want to see the hotel used in the movie. *Dirty Dancing* has an appeal that transcends age ranges. Some of the newer fans are young teenagers while many of the older fans are now in their 70s."

The natural draining of the lake brought about another news item. A skeleton was found in the lake. Buzz told me, "Amateur sleuths have determined within a reasonable doubt that the victim was named Samuel Ira Felder. He had no children. He attended Clemson University in South Carolina and was from New York.

"There are so many wonderful things about Mountain Lake, but like any hotel, what makes this one special is the people who stay here. It is really enjoyable being in the hospitality business."

Lucille and Gary Griffin
Mountain Lake

The American chestnut is unquestionably the most valuable tree in the forest. Or it was, before it was decimated throughout its range by the chestnut blight, caused by an Asian bark fungus accidentally introduced in America in 1904. The blight swept through The Spine of the Virginias in the 1940s and killed virtually every chestnut tree.

The chestnut, a deciduous tree of the oak family, is broad and fast-growing, with a straight, massive trunk. It has a lightweight, dense, straight grain, reddish-brown wood that doesn't warp or shrink. Because it is naturally rich in tannins, it is highly rot-resistant and is thus ideal for furniture, home and barn construction, split-rail fences, roofing shingles, railroad ties, telephone poles, and even musical instruments. Significant quantities of pre-blight chestnut wood are still being reclaimed from old barns and storage buildings and are being recycled into new uses. Even "wormy" chestnut, which has had insect damage, is fashionable because of its rustic look.

Because it produced prodigious, reliable quantities of mast, it was the most important tree for wildlife, as well as free-range livestock. The seeds are encapsulated in a spiny burr, velvety smooth on the inside. Before the chestnut blight destroyed four billion trees, one of every four trees in the Appalachian region was a chestnut. It may have been the largest destruction of a forest resource in recorded history. For millions of families, the chestnut was the wood of their crib, their schoolroom desk, their log home, and their casket: a true cradle-to-grave resource. The loss of these magnificent trees is a story of heart-break and sorrow. The potential restoration is one of hopefulness and optimism. Professor Emeritus of Plant Pathology Gary Griffin at Virginia Tech and his wife, Lucille, have devoted their careers to the teaching, research, and experimentation in making it happen.

Gary told me the tragedy began in 1904 when chestnut trees in the Bronx, New York, were found to be infected by blight. The blight was caused by a fungus traced to Japanese chestnut nursery stock, import-ed to the United States. In Japan and China, the blight and the chest-nut co-evolved, so it was not fatal to those species, but in Appalachia there was no resistance. The fungus invaded the tree through wounds or broken branches and grew beneath the bark in yellowish cankers, blocking the passage of nutrients and water. Mortality was absolute.

Airborne spores wafted upwards of 50 miles per year northward into New England and southward through the Virginias to Alabama. Within 50 years, Appalachian forests were decimated, leaving hillsides covered with standing pallid skeletons, monuments of the tragedy. The devastating effect on wildlife was commensurate.

Professor Griffin showed me a sample of the blight fungus in a laboratory container. Even in a plastic dish it looked sinister. "The roots of older trees in the forest understory are still viable," he contin-ued "so they are still producing trees." But the fungus still permeates the air. New trees grow but invariably contract the blight and succumb within ten years."

Scientific understanding of tree pathology has increased dramati-cally in recent years and a multi-faceted approach using molecular biol-ogy, biotechnology, and conventional breeding has been implemented to restore the chestnut to its former glory. First, scientists are looking for ways to genetically engineer stronger trees with greater resistance to the fungus. Second, they are experimenting with ways to weaken the fungus through a virus that naturally infects the blight fungus on many large, surviving chestnut trees; in essence a "blight of the blight".

They have found that if the fungus is fighting a virus, it is less lethal to the tree. Third, they are using modern propagation methods, grafting, and forest management approaches that involve specific placement of individual trees to strengthen the stock in order to mass propagate the trees throughout their former vast range.

Weeks later, at a chestnut orchard near Mountain Lake, Lucille Griffin said, "This was originally a cultivated field. We planted some chestnut trees in the early 1970s. Trees with greater resistance are brought into the breeding program through grafting. We can place the same specimen in many orchards to achieve the best probability of success. We have both low-altitude and high-altitude orchards. We are enhancing the blight resistance through the generations."

A tree that was infected by the blight had a large area perhaps a foot and a half from end to end where the trunk material was blistered and split and orange in color whereas the unaffected trunk was smooth and browner. The blight had spread itself through the growth layer, the cambium, and then girdled the tree. This prevented the movement of nutrients and killed the tree. If the canker doesn't circle the trunk entirely, the tree will live for a few more years and produce more nuts.

"Even if we can limit the damage the blight inflicts, we still have to get to where the trees can compete in the forest and not just on open, cultivated sites. We already have reasonable success with growing trees in these managed plots and we can collect many nuts. But we need to get to the point where the trees can compete for the canopy in the forest by themselves.

"Successful restoration seems daunting, but we're optimistic. It is just a matter of staying with it. This is a lot of work but it is worthwhile. Right now I am tending more plots than there are days in the week." The site Lucille showed is one of their seed orchards. She collects seeds during harvest time and sends them across the country to growers who are raising chestnut trees. A lot of the nuts that fall from these trees have the potential to be more blight resistant than their parents.

"We only collect nuts from the mother trees that have passed blight resistant tests, no matter what the condition of the tree at this time. Before the chestnut blight the amount of mast in the forest was orders of magnitude greater than today. The degradation of the overall mast production in the forest was greater due to the loss of the chestnut than to human development. The food source loss to the wildlife due to the devastation of the chestnut trees was unprecedented and horrible.

"When I leave some of my plots, I am happy with the possibilities. I am always grafting with high expectations. I know that at most only 20 percent will be successful, but I am optimistic that I will have a better chance and every year I get a few more. Once we get into a generation where the blight resistance is handed down on a regular basis, and most of the nuts have higher resistance than we have now, we'll be able to reclaim the forest chestnut sites. My life's work will be rewarded. But really, the work is its own reward. I have a job that is interesting and it keeps me busy and I have confidence that it will amount to something."

Dale Smith
Rich Creek

Only a generation or two ago, virtually every community along The Spine of the Virginias, indeed across much of the United States, had a meat packing plant. Most have closed, with the industry consolidated into industrial operations generally in the Midwestern and Great Plains states, processing thousands of animals each day. Dale Smith, owner of Smith Valley Meats in Rich Creek, is a notable exception.

When I arrived for our pre-arranged meeting, the 61-year old Dale washed his hands, hung his apron, and escorted me into his office. "My wife Brenda and I started the business unintentionally in 1972. I've been cutting meat since 1963 when I worked in a supermarket in the meat department. I was still in high school. My father-in-law had asked me to do a couple of beefs for him and some friends."

One thing led to another, and the result is the busy company he runs today. He did a series of expansions, adding new capabilities. "In the early days we were processing beef, swine, deer, lambs, and goats. We started working with bison a few years later. At one point we even

THE SPINE OF THE VIRGINIAS

did ostrich. The bulk of our work these days is beef, bison, and hogs.

"We do gourmet cutting of any animal. We cut to perfection. We do custom slaughtering for Islamic and Kosher customers. Everything that isn't edible goes to a company that picks up from us. They take everything: the blood, guts, bones, skulls, and skin. There are many products like fertilizer, feed, and cosmetics that are made with the leftover parts of farm animals. Nothing goes to waste. Everything we do is clean and natural."

Dale and his wife now employ seven people.

"We are the only full-service meat packer in Giles County. My customers are the animal growers. A farmer raises a cow or a bison and brings it to me. I return to him the packaged meat, already weighed, labeled, and ready to sell at farmers markets, to restaurants, and to discriminating individual customers.

"We charge for each service: slaughtering, cooling, waste removal, individual packaging and labeling. Just as a for-instance, if the buffalo farm in Paint Bank brings us a 1400 pound animal, it will cost about $700 to have it slaughtered, cut, and packaged. A steer or bull will have approximately 60 percent yield to the hanging weight. This means our example will have a hanging weight of 840 pounds. From that, about 65 percent is actually edible, so this animal would return about 550 pounds in edible meat. The remainder is bones, fat, and lost weight in the cooler from moisture loss."

Dale told me about the slaughtering process. "We kill our cows, shooting him in the forehead with a 22 caliber rifle. The shot doesn't actually kill him, but it stuns him and makes him dormant and he falls to the floor. We then take a hoist and lift him by his back legs off the floor. We go up through the chest, above the breast bone, at the brisket, with a large knife. We slit his artery and his heart. Then all the blood rushes out of him almost like a fire hose. The heart is still pumping until all the blood drains out, and then it stops. At that point, the animal is dead. This is about as humane as any method for slaughtering an animal. We're conscientious about how we treat animals.

"The whole meat industry has changed in recent decades. There are no cutters in the stores anymore. Everything comes to the store already packaged at assembly lines in the big plants. I think of what we

Billboard near Narrows, Giles County

do as more of an art. There are, fortunately, enough people who are willing to pay us what it takes to keep our business alive. But our trade area is now throughout many states."

Dale showed me some workers cleaning a table with Clorox. He said, "One time some researchers from [Virginia] Tech took a swab from our table. The table turned out to be cleaner than the swab.

"The government has become masters of paperwork and not productivity. Especially since the food-borne scares of recent years, the paperwork has exploded. We do around 30 animals per week, but we have the same costs for an office and a bathroom for an inspector that a plant doing 3000 animals per week has."

He showed me a variety of saws, chillers, and other equipment, all expensive to purchase and maintain. He opened the door to the room where all the waste was stored. Heads of cows and bison sat over guts, piled in many large plastic trash containers. The room was refrigerated, but it was malodorous. He said, "If it weren't refrigerated, you wouldn't be able to stand the smell."

We then entered another refrigerated room where all the sides and quarters of the animals were stored. They were hanging from hooks on rollers, suspended from overhead beams. It reminded me of the scene in the original Rocky movie where Balboa went around punching animal halves. Dale showed me the relative sizes and different colors of hogs, cows, and bison. We walked through the main cutting room, already scrubbed down for the day. It was spotless.

I asked Dale his favorite meat. He said, "I like everything. I like a good steak and hamburgers. I tend to like beef ahead of pork and bison, but I really love all meats."

David Colatosti
Carrie Blankenship
Newport

The geologic formation of the Spine has created many caves. So exploring the subterranean world is an avid pastime for an enthusiastic group of adventurers. David Colatosti and Carrie Blankenship took me spelunking near Sinking Creek and the road leading to Mountain Lake. As we prepared, Dave asked me if I was claustrophobic. I said, "We'll see."

We climbed a small hillside where Dave unlocked the gate, and we descended into the earth. The initial maneuver was a contortionist's dream, steep and confining, but a mere precursor to what was to come. As I came to my feet in the first underground chamber, I stumbled about drunkenly, adjusting to the uneven floor and the utter absence of natural light. I never fully regained my footing. At the edge of the chamber Dave dropped to hands and knees and disappeared through a triangular crack perhaps 18 inches high. I peered ahead to where he had gone, completely convinced there was no way I could fit through. Nevertheless, I edged lizard-style until I reached an obstruction that I tried desperately to wiggle around, unsuccessfully. The ceiling was two inches from my eyelids. I retreated, stripped my jacket, and managed to squeeze through. Carrie slithered through easily.

We made our way through a series of tenebrous rooms, each with glistening monuments and columns of mineral deposits. Caves are devoid of wind, rain, or temperature fluctuations, perpetually dark and apart from circadian and etesian rhythms. Caves are mysterious links to pre-history.

The occasional bat hung from the wall as motionless as the stalactites. The going was always difficult, requiring continually weaving and scrambling through and over obstructions. In one area we walked a corridor where water from a stream poured into our shoes. Many caves are wet, and cavers become accustomed to being soaked.

While we rested in a large room amidst echoes of dripping water, Carrie told me, "I grew up on the family farm near Narrows. I started caving with a girlfriend when we were teenagers. I'm 27 years old. At one time I was caving almost every weekend, but then life happened."

Dave is 40 years old and is an electrical engineer for a Blacksburg company. He came to Tech for college from Connecticut and never wanted to go back. "I've been caving 20-plus years. I've been to places that no one else has been since time began. It's an incredible feeling."

Carrie said, "People who have been caving [in our area] for a long time take it for granted. A lot of people we meet in cave clubs from other areas are amazed when they visit, because they have nowhere near the riches to explore that we have. There are probably hundreds of caves within a 30-mile radius of my home in Narrows. I think Giles County is the most beautiful place on earth.

"Sometimes caves can be a little creepy. When I hear the gurgling water echoing off the walls, I envision voices in them. I never like to be the last one to climb out. I am convinced that there are creatures that live in the cave. The one I envision is a white wolf. When I get tired and I'm breathing heavily and sweating, I can see the steam roll off me. The steam, in my mind's eye, takes the form of this wolf. When I see the white wolf it is time for me to leave. He's the Lord of the underworld."

In March, 2007, a mysterious fungal disease called white nose syndrome appeared on the faces of bats in a cave west of Albany, New York. Since then, it has affected the bat population in Virginia and West Virginia caves. Invariably fatal to bats, the disease has caused experts to place a moratorium on human exploration of most caves through the area.

West Virginia

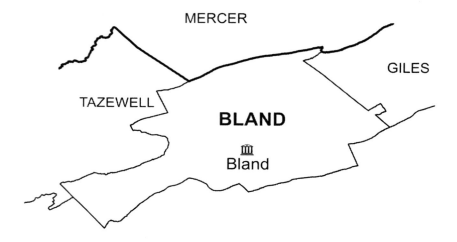

Virginia

Bland County, Virginia

Bland County is entirely within the Appalachian Ridge-and-Valley topography of limestone mountains. The mountains are distinct and linear, several of which extend for many miles, including East River Mountain (on the northern WV border), Rich Mountain, Wolf Creek Mountain, and Big Walker Mountain (on the southern border). Much of the mountainous land is within the George Washington and Jefferson National Forest.

Bland County is 359 square miles.

The county seat is Bland, but there are no incorporated towns or cities.

Population

Bland County's population has remained essentially consistent for a century, with 5500 people in 1900 and 7000 now.

Institutions of higher education

Bland County has no colleges or universities.

Traffic

There are 20 miles of Interstate 77 in Bland County but no other four-lane roads. There are no traffic lights in the county.

Today's...

Bland County is rural. The interstate brings many travelers through, but few stop. Much of the county is quite isolated.

Attractions

- Big Walker Lookout, Bland, lookout tower
- Appalachian Trail, various, National Scenic Trail
- Wolf Creek Indian Village, Bastian, outdoor museum

John Dodson
Rocky Gap

John Dodson teaches high school at Rocky Gap High School. For many years, John has been working with his students to record living histories of the people of Bland County. "I'm primarily a history teacher," he said, "but I've been working with our students to record oral histories since 1993. The inspiration for this was the Foxfire series of books, written (in that era) about country life.

"When we decided to interview local people, we decided that the Internet is free as publishing goes and we taught ourselves how to program websites. We got some grant money and began to send students out to do interviews. They talked with relatives, neighbors, and volunteers. We've done almost 600 interviews since 1993.

"The students have learned a profound connection with the past. One story I remember describes a little girl going to the outhouse and watching the sun come through the window and the colors would dance on the wall in the outhouse. We get lots of stuff like that.

"They have also learned to upload interviews and photos to the Internet and to make movies. They are doing something real and meaningful, as opposed to learning technological skills from some kind of workbook."

His program has become well-known and has received many awards. In the oral history business, subjects are dying continually, so there's always an urgency to preserve their memories.

"Bland County is not poor. For the most part, it's working people. It's not suburban, and it's not as rural as it used to be. When I moved from North Carolina, it was very rural. Everybody farmed or part-time farmed, but that's changed. In Rocky Gap, we now have several retired millionaires."

John introduced me to several of his students who talked about the living history work.

Ryan told me, "I got into it because my grandfather had always told me stories. I enjoy hearing what people did in earlier generations when they were young. They had to milk cows. They had to ride horses to school and some of them walked, which I don't have to do. A lot of roads were unpaved. When they got two or three feet of snow, and they had to walk to school, parents would cut down trees and get a team of horses to pull the tree to the school to clear the path for them. So I thought that was pretty cool, and I learned a lot of stuff like that."

Sean said, "It's interesting learning about people's lives, how they lived. For example, it only cost $0.25 to get into a movie, which would also buy you a hot dog and a pop. Nowadays, they cost $7.50. There is no theater now in Bland County. The closest one is in Bluefield or Wytheville. I really don't miss the movies or the malls. I like living in a rural area."

Josh said, "The thing I found most interesting about this class is how the towns have changed. When the Interstate came through, it brought more publicity and traffic. But there're less stores and gas stations now than there used to be. There used to be a barbershop and swimming holes and stuff. There were more people in Bland County in our parents' and grandparents' era than there are now."

Tyler said, "We all plan on leaving after graduation, but then everybody talks about coming back when we're older. We're happy for the people that did get out, but everybody comes back."

The only girl, Opie, said, "What I like about my interviews for this class is that you can see how traditions have changed. I interviewed a pastor's wife in Hollybrook. She was telling me about one time when she was in church and Elvis was real big at the time and they had just got a radio. Her and one of her sisters and a good friend snuck out of the back of the church and ran a quarter of a mile home just to listen to Elvis. I thought that was pretty funny."

Ryan said, "This school used to have a wood stove. It had pipes going through [to transfer the heat]. Well, some boys got there about six o'clock in the morning to get wood. One day, one of the boys got a gallon bucket of buckeyes and threw them in the fire. They started to get real hot and when class started they started to blow up. It busted all the pipes throughout the school and threw black soot everywhere. All the guys had to clean out the rooms. He was still laughing about it. He's in his 50s or 60s now, and this happened when he was in seventh grade.

"I believe [these interviews] help me relate more to my grandparents' time and what they had to go through. Some in their generation had to cut hay with a scythe and nowadays we have a tractor. I think we've got a lot easier than they did. My grandfather really likes it when I ask him stuff like that."

Tyler said, "As far as bridging generations, it does that. But the way people act is not much different. The only thing that's changed is the technology. We still do mischievous things like our parents and grandparents."

John said, "We need to find ways to have a sustainable economy while protecting our quality of life. We want our kids to be able to stay in the area if they wish."

Randy Newberry
Bland

Many of us have dreams of flying. Randy Newberry has taken his dream airborne. A thin, youngish-looking man in his fifties, Randy said, "I've been here all my life. I love it here. There's not a lot to do, in some people's eyes, but I can ride my bicycle to Rocky Gap or Holly Brook or Mechanicsburg ,and if I don't have any money with me I can go into any store in the county and say hey, 'I forgot my billfold,' and I could buy what I need. Of course they're going to stick a big IOU with your name on it up on the wall, so you gotta get back there and pay. They're only about 5000 people in the county. Everybody knows everybody.

"The Newberrys have owned land in this area since the 1700s, before this was Bland County. They were Irish immigrants. My grandfather had a farm nearby and owned a grocery store downtown called Newberry Brothers. When he passed away, my father and his brother ran the farm and the store. My Granddad had this house built in the '20s. My dad died when he was just 42; I was in the fifth grade. My Mom raised us and made sure we all went to college."

Interstate 77 runs through the center of the county, from north to south. Before the construction of Interstate 77, US-52 was the main north-south route through Bland. Randy said, "On a lot of old deeds, US-52 is referred to as the Raleigh Grayson Turnpike. Its nickname is Turkey Turnpike. Old timers said they gave it that name because they believed the road builders must have just let a turkey loose and followed it, it was so crooked.

"I've always wondered how Bland would be different today had the Interstate gone elsewhere. There probably wouldn't be any factories here, and we wouldn't have the tax base to support our schools and roads, not that we're rolling in cash now. If the interstate wasn't here and these employers weren't here, workers would have to drive either to Wytheville, which involves crossing a mountain, or to Bluefield, which has two mountains, and both would be a 30- to 40-minute drive.

"I was raised on a bicycle. When I was a kid, probably 9 or 10 years old, I'd ride to the Courthouse yard every afternoon to join 15 or 20 kids playing and everyone arrived on a bike. Bland's only State Trooper at the time always threatened to give us a ticket if he caught us on the road after dark because he was afraid we'd get hit. On hot summer days we'd ride 5 miles to a swimming hole. When we got back to Bland, we'd be so hot we'd ride back to the swimming hole.

"There are just a couple of locals besides myself that ride regularly, but Bland County has become really popular with nearby cycling clubs. Community organizations put on the Big Walker Century Ride to raise money for charity every July. It was voted one of the top ten favorite Century rides in five states by *Blue Ridge Outdoors* magazine.

"When I got out of high school I went to work for Seldon Stowers, who was the only airplane pilot in the county. He has a little grass landing strip on his farm because we have no airport. He taught me how to fly an airplane. I ended up buying his plane years later and still have it."

Randy told me of his near-death experiences learning how to hang-glide at Big Walker Mountain. "One guy from Beckley, who had a cast on his arm and no front teeth, said, 'It's a peeth of cake!' For the next six months, every chance I got, I was flying, working my way up to bigger and bigger hills. I flew off Big Walker Mountain towards what we called Whackertown. The residents are affectionately called Whackers. They are mountain people and just a hoot to be around. We landed at Andrew Houndshell's place. He was considered the king Whacker. We called the landing field, 'Andrew's Air Force Base'."

I'm still waiting for the glider flight Randy promised me...

Jonathan Sweet
Bland

Jonathan Sweet is county administrator for Bland County. He said he felt the people and culture were enticing. "It's their approach to life. We look at society and how it has changed over the years, and basically degenerated. I call it the degeneration of generations. Certainly we are losing ground in moral and ethical virtue, but I think we lose it a little slower here. We still have quality trustworthy people. There are a lot of people in Bland County whose word, handshake, character, and reputation still mean something.

"There are no cities or incorporated towns in Bland County. The Board of Supervisors is the sole governmental entity for everyone in the county. So they don't have to coordinate their work with separate town councils, and there are no conflicts between competing governmental entities.

"There are 359 square miles and no traffic lights. Some may look down upon us and laugh at us and call us bumpkins, saying, 'You're still on horse and buggy.' Well, that's fine. But when they're sitting at a red traffic light, we aren't. It's funny that some of our closest neighbors tease us about having a name of Bland. We are so far ahead of them in many ways. As we speak, we are installing additional capability to our last-mile broadband Internet connectivity and will soon cover a majority of the county.

"Every high school senior in Bland County has free college tuition to Wytheville Community College sponsored by The Wythe-Bland Community Foundation. It is an exceptional program that increases the probability for success of our offspring. For one, they are more prone to take advantage of college. Secondly, they go on to university where they have already matured a lot, and they have a foundation. And third, they have saved a lot of money on student loans.

"We have countywide trash service. For $10 per month the county provides household rubbish collection. We have programs that are second to none.

"Fortunately we're not in the recession bubble. In fact I think we are the escape from the bubble. We are seeing a lot of folks from New Jersey, Florida, Charlotte, and Northern Virginia moving here.

"We have a lot of good things in Bland. Free community college tuition for graduating seniors, low taxes, low-cost curbside trash pickup, access to wireless broadband Internet service, no stoplights. It's a great place to ride your bicycle or motorcycle. It's a great place to live."

Ron Kime
Big Walker Mountain

One of the most dramatic spots on The Spine of the Virginias is the lookout tower on Big Walker Mountain on the southern edge of Bland County. US-52 makes an impressive ascent over the mountain. Nearby, Interstate 77 tunnels underneath. For decades, Ron Kime and his family have run a mini-attraction at the crest of the mountain, with a store and lookout tower. A wonderful older store building, with exposed timber-frame construction and large picture windows, burned to the ground in 2003. A newer, simpler building has been rebuilt nearby.

Ron Kime said, "I have lived almost my entire life either on or near Big Walker Mountain. My family moved here when I was five years old. My father was a tool and die maker and an aircraft designer. He worked during World War II in several defense plants as a civilian. Before the war, he had worked for a man in the Ozark Mountains in Arkansas who had a tourist attraction with an observation tower at the top of a mountain. My dad fell in love with that kind of work."

As he spoke, I took in the view to the south of forested mountains and valleys sporting brilliant shades of newly emergent green. Hummingbirds darted from feeder to feeder. Small insects swarmed around me. I carelessly brushed them away and thought nothing of them until one stung me painfully on my forehead.

Ron continued, "Dad was an intelligent and industrious fellow. When he moved here after the war ended in 1945, there was already a beer joint called Jenk's Place. Bland County is on the north side, and Wythe County is on the south side of Big Walker Mountain. Bland was a dry county; Wythe was not. Jenk's Place was literally just a few yards to the Wythe County side. Dad bought Jenk's Place and built the roadside attraction he had dreamed about.

"In that day, this highway was a busy road, which was something he was looking for. It linked the population centers of Ohio in the north to the Carolinas. It is quite winding as it crosses each of these mountain ranges.

"Dad constructed the building that was our house and ultimately the gift shop and restaurant. I grew up in a house that at 3405 feet of elevation was probably higher than 99 percent of the people east of the Mississippi. This is the highest elevation on the Great Lakes to Florida highway. Everyone who drove from Cleveland to Florida came past our establishment.

"Dad put a sign on the building with a single four-letter word, 'Eats.' Mom did the cooking, and Dad did all the maintenance and construction. The original building was a small tin shack. Dad built addition after addition. Eventually, the building had three levels, each with about 4000 square feet of floor space. The main space had wormy chestnut wood and real plaster.

"Dad got plans for a tower. He was a machinist, so he bought raw steel and fabricated the first 50 feet of tower himself. Every hole in every beam he drilled in his own shop. Every set of stairway was hot riveted. He rigged up an A-frame on the back of a truck [as a crane]. He put a winch on it. Once [the tower] got beyond the reach of the A-frame, it was pieced together one beam at a time from the top.

"Our business was always known as the Big Walker Lookout. When fire destroyed our building, we had to re-think our business. We rebuilt the store and called it the BW Country Store. We decided quickly that we should not let a year go by without having some commercial aspect up here on the mountain."

The tunnel opened for business on July 2, 1972, and took so much traffic, and thus so much business, off the mountain, that the Kime family laid off 25 people. Ron said, "The business went from being strictly family when it opened in 1946 to having 25 to 50 people on staff in 1972, only to drop right back down to just family after the tunnel opened. Sadly, Dad died just a few months later in November, 1972.

"About half of what we sell is locally-made crafts. The other half is novelties, things we called memory starters. These are the types of things that help people remember their vacation when they stopped at Big Walker Mountain.

"We had been operating the business for only seven months out of the year. Last year, we decided to stay open year-round. Much to my surprise and delight, it was successful the first year. Today, business is fantastic. I am not having any of this recession crap. I refuse to participate in America's economic crisis.

"The biggest compliment we get is when grandpa brings grandson or granddaughter up here. He tells them about climbing the tower himself back in the 1950s. He tells them about going up the chair lift that isn't here anymore. He tells them about looking at the great view and about driving over the mountain. He reminisces. That our attraction has made a big enough impression upon him to bring his grandchildren here is as good a compliment as we can get. We have been a multi-generational part of many people's lives."

Tazewell County, Virginia

Tazewell County lies at the point on The Spine of the Virginias across the border from West Virginia's southernmost point. Most of the county is within the Appalachian Ridge-and-Valley topography of limestone mountains, but a small swath across the northwestern end is in the Cumberland Plateau coalfields, more resembling the topography of bordering Buchanan and McDowell counties. Burkes Garden is in the bowl of an oval valley, thought to have been formed in the collapse of limestone caverns underneath. Virginia's highest valley, it is completely surrounded by mountains.

Tazewell County has 520 square miles.

Five incorporated towns make up the county: Bluefield, Cedar Bluff, Tazewell, Pocahontas, and Richlands.

Population

Tazewell County's population rose from [approximately] 23,000 in 1900 to 50,000 in 1980. The current population has dropped to around 45,000 due to the loss of jobs in extractive industries, although the population has stabilized over the previous 20 years.

Institutions of higher education

Tazewell County is the home to Bluefield College in Bluefield, VA, and Southwest Virginia Community College near Richlands.

Traffic

Tazewell County has about 60 miles of four-lane roads and several traffic lights in and around the incorporated towns.

Today's...

Tazewell County's history is strongly influenced by coal extraction. Pocahontas, at the northwestern end of the county, was once its largest community. In recent decades, consistent with the drop in employment in the coalfields, Tazewell County has seen a diversification of employment and economies, with health care, education, tourism, farming, and transportation coming to predominate.

Attractions

- Crab Orchard Museum, Tazewell, pioneer museum
- Appalachian Trail, various, National Scenic Trail

Charlotte Whitted
Burkes Garden

From the sky, Burkes Garden leaves an indelible mark on the eye. What looks to be a volcanic crater, an oval of some five by ten miles, the valley is now thought to have been formed by the collapse of an immense system of limestone caverns. The limestone rock still contributes to outstanding soils; the valley's 300 people are primarily farmers. A country store is the only commercial establishment, and one paved road runs into the valley and, rather than following the valley's Burkes Garden Creek out the northeast drainage, it ascends Rich Mountain to the north. Another access road over Garden Mountain on the south rim, Virginia 623, is a remote and winding gravel road.

Burkes Garden was first surveyed in 1748. By legend, James Burke of that party is said to have discarded some potato peelings and covered them with dirt. The following year, they were found to have sprouted. The name Burkes Garden started as a joke, but it was never replaced. Nowadays the name acts as something of a novelty and its verdant tone is likely responsible for a sizeable percentage of its visitors.

During the Civil War, a number of valley residents became Union sympathizers. They were likely resentful of the powerful local landowners, the "Secesh" (secessionists) or "Copperheads," named as such because they clipped the words "United States of America" from the tops of copper pennies and wore them as lapel pins. One Union sympathizer was hanged for guiding troops of the Union Army through the mountains in 1863.

The reclusive nature of Garden residents remains strong. In 1880, industrialist George Washington Vanderbilt took a shine to the area and wanted to buy most, if not all, of it to build an estate. The locals refused to sell. He went instead to Asheville, North Carolina, where he employed a squadron of artisans who constructed the Biltmore Estate, the largest private residence in the country. Today the Biltmore has hoards of visitors annually. Burkes Garden has stayed blissfully quiet.

Only one paved road enters the valley, and it crosses a mountain.

Charlotte Whitted lives there with her family. In addition to her work on the farm, her day job is executive director of the Historic Crab Orchard Museum in Tazewell. She said, "My husband and I had been looking at the area because we were aware of its beauty and geologic significance. We had just come home from a trip to New Zealand and Australia. In the rain, Burkes Garden looks a lot like New Zealand. We were already sheep farmers in North Carolina, but the sheep like a colder climate and higher elevations. Burkes Garden is certainly the most appropriate grassland for raising sheep on the entire eastern seaboard.

"We have been in direct marketing of sheep, pork, and pasture-raised chickens for some time. We sell to farmers' markets and high-end restaurants.

"There were once thousands of sheep in Burkes Garden. They were easy to raise because there were no predators, and you could just turn them out in the pasture. Once coyotes showed up in the 1940s and 1950s, everything changed. It was not cost-effective for many of these farmers to stay in the sheep business if they had to invest in so much infrastructure. Our farm is small, based on the New Zealand model. It is low input and moderate output. To protect our sheep, we have four Great Pyrenees dogs and an electric fence. The dogs are formidable, and the fence works when it is on. The coyotes are quite bold, but we don't lose sheep any more."

One story of Burkes Garden lore is about the so-called Varmint of Burkes Garden. In 1952, an unknown animal was killing hundreds of registered sheep. Frustrated with the losses, the residents cajoled the Tazewell County board of supervisors into contracting with Dale and Clell Lee of Arizona to find and rid the community of this beast. Clell Lee answered the call and arrived in the valley to find a coyote print left in a block of ice. No coyotes had been seen in the area in decades, so the conclusion was met with skepticism. But Lee, accompanied by tracking dogs, presumably much of the Tazewell County law enforcement department, and dozens of hunters, tracked one down. Alfred Jones, a Garden resident, killed a 35-lb. specimen. The coyote was roped to a tree near the courthouse in Tazewell and reportely

7500 people came to admire it. The stuffed Varmint of Burkes Garden now resides in the Crab Orchard museum.

Charlotte continued, "We moved here on purpose. We did not have a family here. We were looking for something that was less high-paced and less frenetic. We wanted to be able to relax and enjoy our family and to show our kids the value of simple things. I know there are some trade-offs for that, but we believe they are turning out great."

Jerry Vencill
Tazewell

Tazewell County's Jerry Vencill lives on the land and earns some cash by acting in local outdoor dramas and in occasional movies. He is a big guy, with a big bushy auburn beard and rosy cheeks. He has a relaxed country drawl.

He said, "I'm a historian, actor, storyteller, and author. I am a jack of all trades and a master of none.

"In high school I enjoyed drama, and I continued to take drama in college. Since then, I have attended the school of hard knocks. In about 1978, I began doing storytelling. When I was growing up, that was still one of the major forms of entertainment. A lot of people in our area did not have televisions. So for entertainment, we would go and visit with people and they would tell stories around the fireplace or, during the nice weather months, out on the front porch. I realized from a young age that we needed to preserve that tradition.

"History was always my favorite subject in school. I became interested in the frontiersmen and outdoorsmen that first populated this area and all of the folklore and folkways: hide tanning, medicine, and preserving of food. People call me all the time to ask about how to do these things. I try to help them in any way that I can. I am almost 54 years old, and a lot has been packed into those 54 years.

"My great-grandmother on my father's side was full-blooded Cherokee Indian. The rest of his family was Scandinavian or German. Mom's side was pure Scots-Irish. My family had some involvement in the Civil War. My family is steeped in the art of blacksmithing. From what I have traced, several ancestors were in that trade. In those days, most farms had their own blacksmith shop, and most farmers knew how to do some blacksmithing.

"If it had not been for the skill level of the mountaineer, this country would not be where it is today. If a horse broke a bit or a shoe, they fired up the forge and made a new one. They grew almost everything they ate except for coffee. They also made molasses from sugarcane, and they had honey from their hives. I still raise bees myself.

"They would sit at the breakfast table and eat red-eyed beans, bacon, gravy, and biscuits. Even with all that salt they would go out into the fields and work it off and sweat it out of their systems. People sometimes died of cancer, and in many cases I suspect they didn't even know what it was. I do not think there was anywhere near the prevalence of cancer there is today.

"It is the same with cigarettes. I firmly believe that if the tobacco companies were not adding all sorts of preservatives, fewer people would be dying of smoking than are today. In those days, everybody smoked or chewed tobacco, but the health problems today seem dramatically worse.

"This was the mountaineer ethic to be able to do anything necessary to keep life moving forward. They were frugal and resourceful people. They patched their own shoes. They made their own rakes and other garden tools. In the 1700s it was not uncommon for a man to go work all day for the price of one metal nail. Most of the homes were pinned together with wooden dowels because metal was so scarce."

"I would much rather have lived back then than today. They had their troubles and trials, but they had each other and they stuck together. There was love and there was help. Today, a man can get hit by a car in the middle of the city and nobody will stop to help. People live close together in big apartment buildings and never know their neighbors. Even when I was a child, Tazewell County was very rural. By the time I was 14 or 15 years old, I had walked over all of the mountains in my area. The worst thing to worry about was perhaps a rattlesnake in some of the rock piles or perhaps a rabid animal. It was really an age of innocence. You could go away for an entire day without locking your door.

"When coal mines shut down and people lose their jobs, the media will come to town and interview the poorest guy with a broken pickup truck and the missing teeth. People watching will figure that everybody is like that. It is insulting to us, and I resent it.

"I know how to grow crops. I know how to cut up a deer or butcher a hog. I have a wood stove in the basement, and if the power went off I could cook my beans and bake my biscuits on it and I have many times. [Returning to a subsistence life] would be difficult, don't get me wrong. I am used to having a bathroom and running water, but I could do without these things if I had to. Most people in our society live on food from a can and they could not survive.

"What worries me is that people like me who can fend for ourselves are at risk from people who can't and who might come into our area to take what we have because we know how to survive. Country people are worried that marauding gangs will form and sweep through the mountain areas."

I asked him to tell me one of his audience's favorite stories.

He said, heightening his accent, "Folks like the story of the three little rabbits. It is a sad story, but they still like it nonetheless. The story is about the three little rabbits that lived at the foot of the hill. Once upon a time there were three little rabbits that lived in a house at the foot of the hill. There was Foot, and his son Foot-Foot, and his grandson, Foot-Foot-Foot. They were slow on names down there. One day Foot said to Foot-Foot and to Foot-Foot-Foot, 'Foot-Foot and Foot-Foot-Foot, I am an old gray hare. I ain't going to live much longer.' Sure enough, he died, leaving the family Footless. So they buried him in a grave that was one foot long and one foot deep. They put a foot-stone at the foot of the grave, of course. The little house at the foot of the hill was not the same without Foot. One day, Foot-Foot said to Foot-Foot-Foot, 'Foot-Foot-Foot, I do not feel well a'tall.' Well, Foot-Foot-Foot looked at Foot-Foot and he was turning pale. So they hotfooted it down the footpath past Foot's grave to where Foot-Foot could see the foot doctor. The foot doctor looked at Foot-Foot and said to Foot-Foot-Foot, 'Foot-Foot-Foot, I may not be able to save

Foot-Foot.' 'Oh, Doc,' said Foot-Foot-Foot sorrowfully, 'you have got to save Foot-Foot. I have already got one Foot in the grave.'

"Now ain't that the saddest story you have ever heard in all your born days?

"I get a lot of requests to do that story. One of the things about folktales is that they have been handed down from generation to generation. They have come over from Ireland, England, and Germany and once they arrive here, Americans have given them their own spin, butchered them, and in some cases made them largely unrecognizable from the originals."

Bob McGraw
Tazewell

Bob McGraw is well-known in town for his interest in history. His passion is the Civil War, and he coordinates an annual re-enactment across the highway from the Crab Orchard Museum. He said, "I am a fifth-generation McGraw right here in this town of Tazewell. My family [history] goes back six generations. I have documented the fourth, fifth, and sixth great-grandfathers who fought in the Revolutionary War. I have several great uncles and two great-great-grandfathers that fought in the War Between the States. All of them fought for the Confederacy.

"The war is still pretty real for me. The reason it is still real for me is that we are not yet out of Reconstruction here in the South. Reconstruction supposedly ended in 1964 with the civil rights agreement. The majority of the fighting men in all the wars since the War Between the States have come from the South. Even today, in the wars in Iraq and Afghanistan, most of the soldiers are from the South.

"People from the South have a strong belief in their heritage as well as in their states' rights and in their country's rights. And they are willing to fight for it.

"In my view, the Civil War was essentially about economics and about States' rights. Abraham Lincoln took away States' rights, the rights guaranteed under the Constitution for each state to have its own constitution. The Federal government was much weaker than today.

"The Federal constitution was set up to allow the states to govern themselves and to allow the nation to govern such things as international trade, piracy, and international conflicts. If the United States needed to be represented in an international conflict, the Constitution provided for the nation as a whole to do that. Each of the states that held secession votes did so by the legal vote given to them in the Constitution. The states were given the vote, the votes were taken, secession was chosen, and they seceded. According to Lincoln, a state could not do that. His interpretation was that the Union was indivisible.

"Our forefathers saw it to be important that each state should maintain its own ability to govern its own citizens. When General Lee resigned from the Federal army, he said that he could not fight against his own country and by that he meant the state of Virginia. Each of the original 13 colonies, when they became states after having won the Revolutionary War, was individually given a declaration of independence from England. It was their prerogative at that point to join into a confederation which became the United States of America.

"The other aspect, as I said, was economic. The northern industrialists wanted to control commerce throughout the states, as they seem to want to do today. It was cheaper for a merchant in the Southern states to have a plow manufactured in England and brought over than it was to have one made in the North because of an import tax imposed across the state lines. And the South could not have made it themselves because they were not industrialized like the North. The South became a better place to grow food. So the South fed the North and the North manufactured the implements used in the South. But the North needed the raw materials that were produced in the South.

"Prior to the Civil War the South was paying 80 percent of the taxes that went into the federal government. So the way things evolved in taxation were that taxation was primarily oriented around raw materials rather than finished goods, and therefore, the South was taxed unfairly. Someone suggested to Lincoln that he allow the South to secede and he said, 'My God, man, who will pay the bills?'"

Bob McGraw of Tazewell

Jim Kline
Burkes Garden

The Appalachian Trail is one of the oldest and most famous long-distance footpaths in the world. From its southern terminus on Springer Mountain in Georgia, the AT traverses fourteen states on its 2175-mile length along the long Appalachian chain to its northern endpoint on Mount Katahdin in Maine. Each year hundreds of "through-hikers" walk the entire distance, and thousands more walk smaller sections, anywhere from an afternoon to several days.

A full 25 percent of the Appalachian Trail is in Virginia but is east of The Spine of the Virginias. From Roanoke north, the Trail follows the Blue Ridge, the easternmost sub-range of the Appalachians. But a short section of the Trail beginning just north of Marion, Virginia, traverses several counties along the Spine including Tazewell, Bland, Giles, and a small slice of Craig counties before heading eastward.

I got together with my old friend, Jim Kline, for a three-day, two-night backpacking trip on the trail on the southernmost portion of this stretch. Jim is a schoolteacher with a gaunt face and a plethora of eccentricities. Other than the fact that his skin has the few wrinkles of age, he still has a chiseled physique resembling Michelangelo's David. He has a close cropped, spiked beard and graying hair showing no signs of thinning. He's a head taller than me with correspondingly longer legs and is a faster hiker. I would spend the entire trip trying to stay within shouting distance.

We began our hike alongside Wolf Creek.

The character of the trail in the area along The Spine of the Virginias can be roughly grouped into three categories: ridgelines, slopes, and watercourses. My guess is that 50 percent of the trail is slopes, either upwards or downwards depending upon your direction. Approximately 40 percent of the trail is on ridgelines, mostly flat or undulating. The remaining 10 percent is watercourses, along various streams, creeks, and other drainages. All have an almost continuous cover of trees preventing any significant views. As we climbed gently through a steamy forest, occasionally we found small rock outcroppings where

Jim complained sarcastically that nobody ever came along to cut down the trees and open up the views.

Our first day was scorching hot, on the tail end of a record-setting heat wave. The trail ascended for several hundred feet before leveling on a small ridgeline. Just as quickly, it dropped down a slope to Hunting Camp Creek. Jim and I took our first extended break alongside the stream and prepared for the ascent of Garden Mountain, which rims Burkes Garden.

During our lunch break, Jim dropped a piece of cheese he was eating and exclaimed, "Uff da!" which is apparently a universal expression of exasperation, with roots to the Norwegian language. A perfectly polite expression, it would be used the way most of us would say, "Good grief," or in Yiddish, "Oy vey." It became a theme for us.

The ensuing climb was an intensely difficult physical experience. The trail began ascending steeply, and with a southeastern exposure to the sun, the heat was relentless. Perhaps fortunately, the trail never allowed us enough of a view to gauge our progress or to see the top. As I trudged further uphill, straining under the weight of my backpack and the excessive heat, prodigious amounts of sweat streamed from my brow and splashed onto the trail. My right hip joint began to ache. Uff da! I stopped every fifty yards to catch my breath and quaff water. A pileated woodpecker, the huge black and white bird with the flaming red crest, pounded a hollow tree nearby. Known colloquially as the log god — the god of the logs — America's largest common woodpecker was the model for the cartoon character, Woody.

Jim strode ahead. I climbed for three hours. I finally reached the ridgeline, where I promptly collapsed into a heap.

After a rest, we walked along the ridgetop and found a spur trail to a campsite where we decided to camp. We descended steeply along the north side of Garden Mountain. The campsite was a hand-built terrace with a retaining wall perhaps four-feet high on the downhill end, twenty by twenty-five feet in size, wide enough for two tents, perched on a steep slope. We were evidently in an old orchard as there were unpruned apple trees around. The trees below had been removed to allow for a view.

Jim is originally from Southern California and has hiked throughout the Western United States. Jim complained as we set up camp, "It's ironic. Everywhere you go in the Rocky Mountains it's easy to find good free-flowing water although it seldom rains. Here in the Appalachians it rains frequently, and yet we are constantly seeking out the next available water source and planning our camps accordingly."

As we rested at our terrace, we watched ever-changing weather patterns emerge over Burkes Garden. Our vantage point gave us a 60-degree viewpoint on the valley. By dinnertime, full-fledged storm clouds formed, chasing us into the tent. A torrent rained for perhaps a half-hour.

Just as quickly as the rain had begun, it stopped again and sunbeams spotlighted the various farms and pastures in the broad green valley below us. Just before us in the valley was a creek, its waters reflecting the setting sunlight. In various areas within the garden were miniature forests, set atop minor ridges. In the distance was the ridgeline of the continuation of Garden Mountain as it wrapped itself around the eastern and then northern boundary of Burkes Garden. Puffball clouds hung above the gap in Garden Mountain where the access road entered. Behind it was the higher ridge of Rich Mountain over which the sole paved access road into the garden ran and further beyond was the horizon ridge, the wall of East River Mountain adorned with communication towers. As the sun sank further in the western sky, clouds painted themselves in pastels of pink and orange light. The braying of cows was unceasing.

As I looked to the skies and across the Valley, everything seemed transfixed, quite immobile. Yet if I looked away and looked back moments later, the shape and patterns of the sunbeams changed. The colors in the sky above continually shifted in shades of light. For a time, a red-winged hawk soared motionless above us. Fortunately, the temperature cooled after the storm, allowing for comfortable sleep.

The next morning dawned clear and calm with wispy clouds drifting over the garden. The scene was of complete stillness and pastoral quiet. Leaves rested, immobile, with nary a ripple. Behind us, songbirds flitted and sang. It was cool, giving us hope this day would not be as oppressively hot as the previous. Jim's shirt said, "Same shirt, different day."

I packed first and began by ascending the half-mile spur trail, switchbacking to the ridgeline where I rejoined the Appalachian Trail. I walked alone for a mile or so and then waited for Jim to rejoin me. For the entire morning, we walked the ridgeline of Garden Mountain, never falling below an elevation of 3500 feet. Although the hike was essentially flat, there were small ups and downs and many rock-strewn areas to negotiate.

Hiking is stressful on the body. The climbs require intense physical exertion, made no easier by the 40 or so pounds contained within the backpack. The descents are less taxing from an aerobic point of view but jarring to the joints. Uff da! Seldom is the Appalachian Trail completely level and smooth.

Finally we ascended to the highest point on Garden Mountain, Chestnut Knob, where the trail emerged into a grassy pasture-like field. At the summit was a stone building, once the residence for the keeper of the nearby fire tower which long ago was dismantled. This shelter is widely known for its outdoor privy which has no sides, allowing its user a grand view to the west as he or she bundies.

We stayed around the shelter for only a few moments, enjoying the views. We hiked southwesterly on treeless Chestnut Ridge with vast views to impressive mountains to the south and southwest, one with a distinctive plateau-like step towards the top. Ahead of us, we saw a deer bounding away. Jim wondered aloud by what cruel evolutionary scheme deer had been given a tall white tail to wag at its pursuers.

At one point atop Chestnut Ridge we approached what appeared to be a cultivated patch, with a red-tinged plant growing closely and intensely in what appeared to be furrows. As we approached closer, we discovered to our horror that it was a field of poison oak, perhaps the most magnificent patch I had ever seen. It gave us both the creeps, and walking the narrow trail through it felt like navigating a minefield. For hours we talked about how transfixed we'd become over the diabolical, malevolent horror of it, both of us previously having suffered the wretched agony of a rash. Jim said later, "When I saw it from fifty yards away, it looked like a garden plot." Uff da!

As the miles wore on, I came to realize how quickly my mind had settled into trail karma. There is monotony along the miles of the trail, and the challenge is not to allow that monotony to spawn boredom. Life on the trail has neither news nor media. There is food and water, companionship and loneliness, sun and rain, wind and stars. There is nature in abundance, with a profusion of growing, blossoming things. A brilliant patch of azaleas, colored in oranges, yellows, and all shades in between, glistened before us.

Other hikers had told us about a brackish tarn adjacent to the trail with a concrete springbox feeding it. The pond was shallow and perhaps 60 feet in diameter, richly organic with burping frogs and scores of insects. It was rimmed with reeds and cattails. Not wishing to leave the mountaintop, we decided to end our day beside this pond, finding a flat and previously used campsite near the earthen dam.

Unpacking my gear and setting up camp, I thought again about another aspect of trail karma, that being the self-contained nature of it. I was carrying everything I would need for several days and knew where every item was.

After dinner we walked from our secluded camp to the clearing above the tarn. The sky again was electric with shards of lightning emanating from two enormous clouds, one directly to our east and one to the south. The cloud to our east had craniated shapes and rippling features, illuminated by the sun. The cloud to our south was further away but equally impressive, casting shadows on its own varied surfaces. It was more active electrically with frequent bolts of lightning. The sun hid behind its own cloud, shooting sunbeams above and below in vibrant colors. Eventually, the gargantuan clouds merged into one another. Often the thunder settled into an amorphous timpani of lightning unseen. Both of us realized that our analytic brains had been lulled to sleep. It rained from the time we entered the tent at about 9 p.m. until perhaps 11 p.m. The frogs never stopped their croaking, a sound Jim said sounded like large drops of water landing in an empty copper bucket.

We awoke by 6:30 a.m., and as we packed our things and prepared for the final day, both of us were encouraged to think that the air would be cooler still. Over breakfast, Jim commented that many people have a difficult time understanding the attraction of backpacking because it is so far outside their personal reality. "I like knowing I could live for several days if not several weeks in the wilderness. I get a great sense of self-containment and independence. After every trip I make notes and reevaluate what I carry."

Within hours, we found ourselves crossing Lynn Creek on a wooden footbridge, perhaps 60 feet across. The stream below was, in places, a couple of feet deep. We both got naked and bathed in the stream (sans soap, of course). We had some lunch and continued on the final 6 miles or so of our hike.

We climbed and descended a couple more minor mountains before our hike ended. On one ascent, I saw and listened to a dazzling hooded warbler. The final descent back to the car was along a sylvan ravine. Our car was the only one in a lot, as it had been when we left it three days earlier.

The following day, my back ached and my calves were as tight as the strings on a banjo. Blissfully I had no poison oak rashes, but I counted 14 insect bites. Uff da!

Sue Carr
Tazewell

Sue Carr operates Sandy Head Ostrich Farm on SR-61 in Tazewell County. Sue said, "There are few women in the county that are the sole farmers on their property. My husband works out of town and is only here every five or six weeks. The majority of time I'm on my own, except for wonderful friends and neighbors that help out. I've been here on the farm since '81, but only raising ostriches for five years. My first husband and I ran a motorcycle repair shop here, fixing Harley Davidsons. This garage behind me was our repair shop and showroom for aftermarket parts.

"We had customers from four states shopping with us regularly," she said, proudly. "He taught me the repair trade because I was always interested in it. He died years ago in a motorcycle crash. After he died, I kept the place going for a while. I hired some men to do some of the repair work, but none seemed to work out. Finally, I ended up hiring women and that worked great. One woman was new to me-chanic work but had an aptitude for it. Besides, having an all-women repair shop was fun; we'd joke around as only a bunch of women can do together. I thought for a while the men would quit bringing their bikes out. They'd think women weren't supposed to work on Harleys. But we had a steady business. We weren't trying to become known as women mechanics, just as mechanics. Clear Fork Cycle earned that reputation.

"In the mid-nineties, I closed down. I decided that running a farm would be much less physical than running a mechanic shop," she joked, erupting in a gut-splitter. "So I learned the hard way. I'm outside all of the time, and I love farm work."

While she retrieved something from the barn, I studied the ten ostriches standing sentry in the pasture nearby. We've all seen them in photos or on television shows, but their ungainly substantial reality is still a shock. The legs are hairless and featherless, taller than a bar-stool's, with wrinkly earth-toned skin. The foot has a huge toe, with a puffin's beak-shaped toenail, and another vestigial toe alongside. The body resembles a plump pillow of feathers, with laughably useless wings occasionally flapping. Feathers are gray, darker towards black on the males. The neck is as long and substantial as a baseball bat. Heads are more beak and eyes than anything else. The beaks' gaping nostrils lend a menacing look. There's little hair atop, making them look like a sexagenarian who's just stuck a finger in a light socket. I wondered how a butcher went about executing them. Would he behead them with a hatchet? Shoot them? If so, where?

She continued, "I'm from Illinois and I grew up west of Chicago. When Don died, I wouldn't have made it without the support of all the neighbors. Everybody pitched in and helped out. They were just there for me. My family was still in Illinois, and they could only be here so much. It taught me what giving and sharing was about, some-thing I didn't really understand; I was so young and self-centered. I was a twenty-eight year old widow. I would never have made it with-out all the love and caring that people here showed me. I try to help people as I was helped when I needed it.

"Let me tell you a couple of stories about perspectives that people

Muffler sculpture in North Tazewell

have about this place.

"We're going to have what we call an Ostrich Fest in October, a benefit to help all the people that have been flooded out the last couple of years. We're asking people to bring as admission non-perishable food items, cleaning supplies, baby items, and similar supplies. Then we'll donate everything to the Bluefield Mission to be distributed to the different areas that have been so hard hit. We've been doing this for four or five years now. Last year we collected about 400 pounds of items. This area isn't thought of as being particularly prosperous, but people have already started bringing stuff to donate, and the festival is still two months off.

"Here's my favorite. I was sick years ago with cancer and going through chemotherapy. My sister wanted me to go to Chicago for the best treatment. We found out that one of the absolute top cancer specialists in the country is [fifteen miles away] in Richlands. You couldn't find a better doctor. We're not supposed to have that kind of thing here; it's backwards."

Johnny Hagerman
Claypool Hill

Johnny Hagerman is a professional brick sculptor, one of only perhaps a few dozen in the nation. His raised-relief designs grace some of the most distinctive buildings in Southwest Virginia and throughout the country. He said, "I grew up in a village called Compton Mountain. The access road is literally along the state line separating Buchanan County, Virginia, from McDowell County, West Virginia.

"My father worked in the coal mines for probably 45 years. The earliest lesson I learned in my life was that everything around you has value and a function. We learned how to multitask well before multitasking became a word. We grew our own food. We were enmeshed in the barter system. We raised our corn, and when we sent it to the mill to be milled, the miller would keep some of it for his payment. We bought minimal groceries. It was a typical mountain farm.

"We were at the top of the mountain, and there was some fertile and flat ground up there. We tilled with a horse-drawn plow. As kids, we followed my dad and his plow, and we looked in the ground for arrowheads. The view from the mountaintop was grand, and we could see several mountain ranges.

"I went to school in Whitewood. The school was open from about 1940 until about 1986. As the economy began to grind to a halt in the 1980s, people were leaving the area in droves. The school board began to shut down many of the schools and consolidate them with others. I went to school from 1st grade until 12th grade all in that same building.

"When I graduated, I attended Southwest Virginia Community College. I was the youngest of 10 children, and by that time my family was financially able to send me to college. I either wanted to become an artist or a cowboy. My mother supported these career options, but other people ridiculed them.

"Growing up, we wasted nothing. When momma returned from the grocery store I would slit open the grocery bags, which made great drawing surfaces. It was a stable life. I always felt secure. I was always surrounded by family and friends. Everything I did seemed to have a purpose.

"I attended Southwest Virginia Community College, which had just opened. I decided I wanted to teach. When I finished, I transferred to Radford University and got a teaching certificate. At age 23, I got a job teaching art in the same school in Whitewood where I went to school myself. I soon recognized that when schools faced budget cuts, art was typically the first thing to go, then music. My wife was a music teacher. During one extended snow closing, I began to tinker with some unfired brick material. I went to General Shale Company and learned they could alter size specifications at will. I began to produce some sculpture.

"The city of Richlands commissioned me to work on a piece about the local history. I worked on it at nights and during the weekends. On the snow days I would load up my van with sculpted bricks and would drive them to Kingsport to have them fired. One of their vice presidents happened to be in the research lab the day I was there. He became interested in seeing what the medium would allow. We started communicating."

As Johnny tinkered, he realized this was what he wanted to do for his career. "For the type of person who can spend lots of time by himself, this is a great job. My audience these days is two dogs and three cats.

"Brick is of the earth. It is a natural and ancient building material. The fact that I can take these rectangular shapes and connect them all and by sculpting and organizing them, can create a piece of artwork on something that separates the floor from the ceiling, is very appealing. The story of the Three Little Pigs is great marketing for the brick industry. Every child has an image of a brick house as being bulletproof. Brick has a longevity and permanence that I find appealing.

"God has helped me to be humble. *Southern Living* magazine did a feature on me back in the year 2000. When I got that edition of the magazine in the mail and the pages were clean and perfect, I turned to the article about myself and I said, 'This is so good.' Sometime within the next two days I was working on a large piece on my easel.

I stepped outside to take a break, and I heard a loud crash behind me. I went back inside, and it looked to me as if a bomb had gone off. I had undercut too much of the brick at the bottom. Everything came crashing to the floor, including the scaffolding and the easel. I would gladly have given up that feature article in exchange for this panel not having been destroyed. I had been working on that piece for about three months and it was completely ruined. It took me almost another full week to clear out all the rubble.

"I learned a valuable lesson, not to get overly proud of myself. Gravitational pull has a way of humbling all of us. People who live here in the central Appalachians have equal or better skills than people anywhere I have encountered. There is also a sense that if the Stock Market crashed and the economy collapsed, it would matter less here.

"I am fifty-something, but I still feel like a child. Work and play are together. Each job has an element of adventure, something new and different. Things stay fresh and challenging.

"[Being an Appalachian] has absolutely been a benefit to me. Everything I see has value. Every thought I have has to do with efficiency, making the most of what I have. We live in a throw-away world. I am not a throw-away person. Appalachian people are humble. It is a personal trademark, and I seek it in others as well. The work speaks for itself.

"Time, work, and mistakes are the best lessons. You need to have a passion for what you do."

Detailed brick sculpture by Johnny Hagerman

Part 4
Sacral

Watersheds of the Clinch, Big Sandy, and Tug Fork Rivers
Counties of Mercer, a smidgen of Tazewell, all of
Buchanan, and McDowell

People may not know West Virginia. But they know what Take Me
Home feels like. Country roads, I think, are part of everybody's life.[8]
— John Denver, singer/songwriter

The green rolling hills of West Virginia
Are the nearest thing to heaven that I know
Though the times are sad and drear
And I cannot linger here
They'll keep me and never let me go
— Emmylou Harris, singer/songwriter

Fall

Morning fog is a sign of the coming autumn along The Spine of the Virginias. At my home in Blacksburg, a cool day started with bright blue sky and high wispy clouds. Cresting Brush Mountain and then Gap Mountain into Giles County, fog appeared, gently blanketing the Sinking Creek Valley in cotton candy. The fogbank gave Salt Pond Mountain a more impressive presence and grandeur.

The most direct route to the day's destination, the far southwestern point on The Spine of the Virginias, was US-460 to Tazewell, but the parallel road from Narrows to Tazewell, SR-61, bypasses the traffic and confusion of the Princeton/Bluefield area. So I left US-460 and drove through the town of Narrows, past the town park where geese lounge beside and in a small pond, an impoundment of Wolf Creek. SR-61 is pancake flat for 20 miles to Rocky Gap, a favorite amongst the area's bicyclists, as it is one of the few flat roads around. I rode my geriatric but capable Honda motorcycle alongside the Creek, appreciating the changing colors of the leaves, shrubs, and trees. Backyard gardens had wilting ecru cornstalks and bright orange pumpkins on the ground.

The fog broke ten miles west of Narrows, and I took in the splendid views of the parallel ridges of East River Mountain to the right (north) and Wolf Creek Mountain on the left (south). Vast patches of kudzu, a non-native ground plant, were turning yellow. The road was nearly deserted, allowing me to fully enjoy the curves. I overtook only one vehicle in nearly 50 miles.

All summer, the trees have been like choir members, all dressed in shades of green. Now they seemed compelled to be soloists, with dazzling oranges, yellows, and reds, singing forth with exhaled chlorophyll. The autumn sunshine lends a crisp clarity to the changing foliage that always delights me. The fecundity of summer is over, and nature begins its seasons of dormancy.

Near the community of Clear Fork, a shirtless man with a distended belly stood tending a rubbish fire. Ostriches at Sue Carr's Ostrich Farm grazed in a pasture, contextually out of place. Near Tazewell, I saw the first signs of coal country: retailers of mining equipment. The town of Tazewell has an unusual layout, with a central business district and two outlying districts, one to the east and another to the north. My chosen route went through both the latter, but bypassed downtown. Beyond North Tazewell, the road ascends Stony Ridge, the last of the limestone, non-coal mountains. The border itself feels like it should be at the summit, but isn't. Instead, it's just beyond in the hamlet of Bishop.

I continued through the coal camps of Squire, Newhall, Cucumber, and War. In spots, the road is extremely curvy, with cliffs overhanging the inside lane. Trucks swing wide on the turns while the back wheels of the trailers kick gravel onto the asphalt. A man stands on the shoulder of the road, shoveling coal into his pickup truck. The coal had evidently been spilled there earlier during a wreck.

In Yukon, my friend Benton Ward and four of his friends joined my expedition. We departed westward to Bradshaw on SR-83. In a couple of spots on this busy, 2-lane road, the surface of the road had collapsed, the foundation underneath swept away by flooding months earlier. Warning signs demanded that vehicles make complete stops to allow for alternating, one-lane passage, but nobody did.

In contrast to the northeastern extreme of the Spine upon Cacapon Mountain, the southwestern-most point is difficult to pinpoint and more difficult to find. The final few miles of the border run for approximately four miles down the middle of the Tug Fork River.

The grittily named Tug's headwaters are in the McDowell County highlands. It flows generally northwest, where it first forms the state line of Virginia and West Virginia and then for the next 100 miles or so, forms the border between West Virginia and Kentucky. The Tug, the infamous river of the Hatfield and McCoy feud and the Matewan

Hotel Fretwell, War

Photo by Tracy Roberts

Coal Mine Wars, is synonymous with violence, insularity, and lawlessness. It's the very depth of Appalachia.

We crossed a one-lane bridge near Panther and stopped to take photos of it. Chunks of the concrete were cracked away in disrepair, held aloft by dangling re-bar. We reached an intersection of Panther Road and Four Pole Road, the latter numbered CR 1/1 to consult our map. West Virginia tertiary roads are often fractionalized. In Mohawk we stopped again, at a spitting distance from the border, where another one-lane bridge sat beside the construction of its own replacement. This old bridge was of steel girder design and wooden planking. Several steel struts were bent and rusty; others were absent entirely.

Between Mohawk and Isaban, we turned onto a narrow but paved country lane with a destination of War Eagle, a nearly deserted former coal mining town. The lane switchbacked over a minor but steep mountain pass. The hamlet of War Eagle was woebegone. Absent of any commerce, it was a smattering of homes, mostly trailers, many in unspeakable, numbing squalor. While certainly not every resident was indolent, I got the impression from some that lassitude was an art form here. When we stopped to take a photo of a hand-painted sign outside the tiny white-framed War Eagle House of Worship, Benton remarked, "Even the non-religious people around here are religious. Religion is deeply rooted."

Our final destination was a mere 2 miles downstream by the Tug, but it took us more than 20 miles to get there by road, through Isaban, Baisden, Wharncliffe, and to Wharncliffe Station. On the downhill side of a mountain pass was a gorgeous modern home. When I spoke to Benton about it at our next stop and the juxtaposition of ramshackle dwellings nearby, he said, "There are no fine neighborhoods around here. The guy who owns that place must have done well for himself, but he might have grown up in the trailer next to it."

He told me few people build fine homes in McDowell County. "For one thing, the only places flat enough to put homes are in flood plains. If the insurance companies won't insure them, the banks won't lend the money. But worse than that, if a man puts $100,000 into construction of a home, the area is so depressed that within three years it'll be appraised at half that. Banks will loan an employed man

$40,000 to buy a pickup truck but not for a house."

At one place, the road was high above the creek, which was to our left. Across the creek and high on the other side, steep on the hill, was a cemetery. At our next stop, we wondered aloud how any corpse, not to mention a burial party, could be delivered to such an inaccessible location.

The road from Wharncliffe to Wharncliffe Station followed a tiny creek that showed signs of flooding a few months earlier. In several places the narrow paved road was cracked and torn. Debris was omnipresent. Nearing the Tug, the road and the creek swept under two impressive steel railroad bridges, both adorned with profanity-laced graffiti. At the Tug, the road simply ended. Nearby was a wrecked pile of steel girders and wooden planking, the remains of an auto bridge over the creek at its mouth. Benton said it likely belonged to the Railroad, used for maintenance access to the tracks. The river itself was peaceful and pastoral, notwithstanding the occasional train. Two men pulled ashore in a john-boat from which they'd been fishing for smallmouth bass.

I walked the trash-filled shore of rock and mud and waded into the Tug. As I stood atop an ottoman-sized rock, Benton took a ceremonial photo of me.

The author in the Tug River.

Photo by Benton Ward

King Coal

To the southern arch of The Spine of the Virginias, coal is as elemental as air and water. Coal is a noun, a verb, and an adjective. Coal is profit and loss, agony and ecstasy, hope and despair, power and powerlessness, life and death. Hardly a sentence can be written about the history of Buchanan, Tazewell, McDowell, or Mercer Counties without the word coal in it. Without exaggeration or irony, coal is everything.

Coal deposits underlay fifty-three of West Virginia's fifty-five counties. Of the counties on The Spine of the Virginias, Mercer County has coal on its northwestern edge, under perhaps 25 percent of the County, on a line from Bramwell to Camp Creek. The entirety of McDowell County has coal under it.

In Virginia, Tazewell and Buchanan have coal. Tazewell's coal deposits lie under a sliver of land at the county's northwestern edge, from Pocahontas to Richlands. Like McDowell to the northeast, the entirety of Buchanan County has coal.

This rich blessing has proven to be decidedly mixed.

Coal is a combustible rock, comprised of primarily carbon, with encapsulated hydrogen and oxygen. All life forms contain hydrocarbons. Coal, along with natural gas, oil, and oil shale, is a fossil fuel. Scientists agree that fossil fuels originated from ancient life that decomposed under compression and time. The decomposition progresses in stages, from peat, to lignite, sub-bituminous coal, bituminous coal, and anthracite. Anthracite has the highest fuel value, nearly twice that of lignite, and has physically the hardest surface. Coal is one of the most efficient fuel sources ever discovered and is the most abundant. However, it is not the cleanest, densest, or most transportable.

Coal use is almost as old as history itself. Aristotle, the Greek philosopher and scientist, referred to a substance that could have been coal in northeastern Italy. Historians believe that coal was first commercially used in China. Coal became increasingly important in Europe and Asia through recorded history because of its abundance and high heat content, primarily for metalworking.

Coal deposits are sprinkled throughout the world. The United

Kingdom led the world in extraction prior to the 20th Century. Its fields extend from southern Scotland through Wales and into western England. Geologically, the mountains of that area are linked to the Appalachians. It's no coincidence that due to the familiarity they found, many people from these regions settled in the Appalachians after arrival in the New World.

The United States has six major reserves. Two are east of the Mississippi: the Appalachian region and the Illinois Basin.

The central Appalachian coalfield encompasses a vast area at its widest in the north, where it rises from the Western New York and northern Pennsylvania border and begins its southward sweep. It takes in most of western Pennsylvania, most of southeastern Ohio, and perhaps 75 percent of West Virginia. The coalfield takes in Virginia's westernmost counties, a large portion of Eastern Kentucky and parts of Tennessee, Georgia, and Alabama.

The primary contemporary domestic use of coal, accounting for roughly 85 percent of overall consumption, is in generation of electricity. This coal is referred to as "utility coal." Most of the remainder is used in the manufacturing of steel and is referred to as "metallurgical coal" or "met-coal".

Coal-fired power plants take raw coal, pulverize it to the consistency of talcum powder, and then spray it into a boiler where it is burned. The heat is transferred to water, which boils into pressurized steam. The steam spins a turbine, which in turn spins an electrical generator creating electricity. Oil-fired, gas-fired, and nuclear plants also produce electricity by generating heat that boils water, generating steam that powers a turbine. Regardless of the heat source, all commercial power plants require a cooling mechanism, either a river, lake, or cooling tower, to condense the steam back to water to continue the cycle.

The steel industry converts met-coal to coke by heating it in the absence of oxygen, resulting in almost pure carbon. Combined with iron ore and limestone, the mixture is heated to produce iron, which through alloying processes produces steel.

Mining accelerated in the early 18th century, when foundries in England used coal in the manufacturing of iron. In 1712, Englishman Thomas Newcomen invented the first device to harness steam to produce mechanical work. James Watt, a Scottish engineer, invented an improved version and became more famous.

Prior to independence, the American Colonies imported coal from England or Nova Scotia. Conflict with England spurred domestic production and led to the formation of small mining companies in Virginia's bituminous fields.

By the 1830's, mining companies had emerged throughout the Appalachians and into the Illinois, Mississippi, and Ohio River Valleys. The Civil War accelerated industrial development by magnitudes, with the need for steel becoming vital to the war effort.

Until the mid-1800s, mining in Appalachia was often a seasonal endeavor. Settlers hunted and subsistence farmed during the growing season and mined in the winter to gain additional cash. Only local blacksmiths used the coal commercially. Homeowners consumed small amounts for heat.

After the Civil War, the commercial demand increased dramatically. Many companies were organized to build the infrastructure to handle this emerging extractive industry. Extraction was heaviest nearest the factories of Ohio and Pennsylvania. The southern fields opened around 1870, with the most productive being the Flat Top–Pocahontas field in McDowell and Mercer Counties. Pocahontas Fuel Company, founded in 1907, owned the richest coal seam in the world and soon became the preeminent company in the region.

From the nascent days of commercial mining, railroads and coal have a codependent relationship in Appalachia. Coal fired the locomotives of the era and railroads allowed the coal to be shipped to distant markets. In the 1870s and 1880s, a race ensued between the Chesapeake and Ohio Railroad to connect central West Virginia's fields through Covington to Richmond and the Norfolk and Western Railroad connecting southern West Virginia's and western Virginia's fields through Roanoke to Norfolk.

The arrival of the railroad in coal-rich areas typically spawned economic booms. When the N&W arrived in Pocahontas in 1882, for example, the town exploded with new population. Many of the coal towns were populated by an influx of immigrants, first from England, Wales, and Scotland, and later from Eastern Europe. To the boosters of the era, this industrialized community was infinitely superior to the prior wilderness.

Once the Industrial Revolution gained momentum, the rush of speculators to coal-bearing regions was on! It is difficult to imagine the challenge faced by cash-strapped subsistence mountaineers to understand the ramifications of the insatiable appetite for the resource beneath their feet.

Early mining was hugely labor intensive. Miners excavated tunnels, placed timbers for support, and laid tracks both inside and outside the mine. Large mechanical cable spoolers called "steam donkeys" lifted coal upwards to the surface while beasts of burden pulled laden cars inside the mine. The coal seams were undercut with picks, then blast holes were bored. The holes were filled with explosives. The explosions broke loose the coal, which was then loaded by hand shovel into mine cars. Equally labor-intensive, although less dangerous, was the separation of coal from unusable rock. Miners' efforts were weighed, and the miners were paid by what they could load.

Miners had to pay to rent tools, have the tools maintained, and purchase the blasting powder and equipment, leaving only a portion of their wages for the staples of life. Because coal companies were essentially monopolies in every village, they provided a complete environment for their employees, including the homes, stores, churches, schools, and recreational facilities. This built a dependency that was both a blessing and a curse. Purchases at the stores were made by a token system called "scrip," where credit was issued on purchases of everyday necessities and deducted from wages. Coal companies used scrip to reduce the need for cash in remote locations. In many cases, scrip was location-specific to the particular camp.

Most mines were owned by distant companies. The ability or willingness of a company to provide a satisfactory life for its workers varied greatly. Once an immigrant arrived, he had little choice but to stay put, not having money, knowledge of the new language or surroundings, or options of any kind. Poor living and working conditions and inadequate medical care were not uncommon. Workers were expendable, more so than even the goats and mules used to pull loaded wagons from the mines. Rachmanism, the exploitation and intimidation of tenants by landlords, was rampant. Accidents were frequent, and when fatal, grieving widows and families were summarily evicted from company-owned homes.

West Virginia hired its first mining inspector in 1883 and established its first set of regulatory and safety rules. The United Mine Workers of America was established in 1890 in Wheeling to allow miners a collective voice in what became an ongoing fight for better pay and conditions.

Through the years of this country's industrial development, coal played an active role in steel and power production. Able-bodied miners were often exempt from wartime service due to the importance of ongoing production.

Methods of coal mining are dictated by the orientation of the geography and of the particular seam. Traditionally, most mining was done sub-surface, either drift or deep. In a drift mine, the seam is exposed on a mountain slope. In a deep mine, a shaft is dug to reach the seam. In either case, miners and equipment go underground to dislodge the coal and transport it to the surface. In modern times, surface mining has emerged, using gigantic earthmoving equipment to expose the seam. Each has inherent advantages and disadvantages, from the standpoints of cost, danger, and environmental degradation.

Sub-surface mining can injure or kill a miner in many ways. Chemical fires are a constant danger. Methane, a colorless, odorless gas, is naturally encapsulated in all coal deposits and is liberated in mining. It is dangerous because it is combustible and can ignite with any spark, either electrical or mechanical in origin. Adequate ventilation is essential to safe operation of a mine. Mine ventilation pumps it into the atmosphere, where, incidentally, it is a virulent global warming gas, ten times the intensity of carbon dioxide.

Coal itself, when pulverized into dust, is flammable, igniting in violent explosions. Mine fires are virtually impossible to extinguish. They create hellish conditions in local communities as smoke and combustion gasses waft from underground shafts, burning for years or even decades.

Other poisonous gasses such as carbon monoxide, hydrogen sulfide, and carbon dioxide may be present in a mine. Many miners have died from asphyxiation.

Working with equipment such as continuous miners, roof bolters, conveyors and other transport equipment, all in dark and cramped environments, is always hazardous. Heavy equipment is powered by electricity rather than internal combustion engines in order to lessen the risk of sparks. The electricity is supplied in phenomenal voltages that can electrocute.

Some mines have significant amounts of water. Many deep mines are below sea level. Floods can occur at any time and can trap or drown miners.

Modern mining methods include extensive precautions to prevent catastrophic collapses. But there are always geologic forces below ground which can cause shifting of rock. Resettling of ceiling rock can destroy a mine and everyone in it.

Black Lung disease, pneumoconiosis, or in the vernacular, "rocks in the box," is caused by ongoing inhalation of coal dust. The dust blocks the lung's capacity to process air and eventually leads to suffocation. Pneumoconiosis is increasingly painful and debilitating.

Working in cramped spaces can wreck a miner's posture. Thicker coal seams have been depleted, so today's miners often spend entire shifts crawling, as if continually working underneath a table.

In spite of improvements in mining methods and increasingly stringent regulations, mining remains among the most dangerous occupations in America.

Surface mining, also called mountaintop removal mining, has its own set of maladies. It involves the displacement of "overburden," a euphemism for everything above the coal, including trees, soil, and rock, to expose the coal. First, the mountain is stripped of all vegetation. Blasting turns the rock into removal chunks. The overburden is placed in nearby hollows, resulting in the alteration of the mountain.

The vigor under which federal reclamation laws are enforced varies from one administration to another. Proper reclamation is often predicated on the goodwill of the mining company. In better situations, the mountain is returned to its approximate original contour, re-graded with softer rock that will relatively quickly support topsoils, and replanted with hardwood trees. In worse cases, the land is left littered with rock, then reseeded with lespedeza, a non-native grass with no nutritional value to wildlife and no value whatsoever to humans. The forests cannot recover for centuries. If proper procedures are not followed, groundwater supplies become polluted and wells dry up.

It should be noted that many mountaintop removal mines are superimposed over previously mined areas. When the contemporary mining company is granted permission to work, it assumes responsibility for the environmental issues in place following the earlier effort when controls were less stringent.

Once aboveground, coal must be washed and separated from the unusable rock before it can be weighed and shipped to customers. The residue is a material called gob, consisting of clay, shale, and low-quality coal. It is laden with hazardous materials and heavy metals. Gob is placed in ponds which drown scarce bottomlands and are impounded by earthen dams, which are susceptible to breaches.

One of the worst mining disasters in history was caused by a breach in a gob pond. On February 26, 1972, after several days of heavy rain, a dam at Buffalo Creek in Logan County, West Virginia, broke, sending a torrent of wet gob into two other ponds, breaching all of them. Approximately 132 million gallons of black goo rushed through the hollow. It swept 125 people to their death, injured 1100 more, left 4000 homeless, destroyed 546 homes and damaged another 943. Total property damage was estimated at $50 million. Imagine the horror experienced by a survivor, huddling in a cold downpour, watching this black wave, often 20 feet tall, permeated with toxins and debris of cars, homes, and furniture, sweep down the valley at seven feet per second, obliterating everything in its path!

During combustion, coal releases carbon monoxide, sulfur dioxide, nitrogen oxide, mercury, arsenic, and lead. Before the emergence of air pollution restrictions in recent decades, coal-fired powerplants belched millions of tons of ash into the atmosphere. The ash is now captured and sent to landfills. While it is mildly toxic, with trace amounts of lead, barium, chromium, manganese, and arsenic, power plants generate lots of it.

The cruelest irony is this: almost without exception, there is a strong inverse correlation between the value of the resource and the wealth of the citizens. McDowell County has produced more coal than any other east of the Mississippi River, yet today is by far the poorest in West Virginia. The benefactors of the mineral wealth are seldom local.

Coal companies actively discourage innovation, economic diversity, and competition. New-economy companies shun coal mining regions. Young and able workers depart for better opportunities. Newcomers are few.

In spite of these issues, coal mining continues apace!

For decades, increases in oil and gas consumption outpaced coal, but that reversed in 2000. Since then coal has expanded at a yearly average of 4.8 percent. Looking to the future, the U.S. Department of Energy predicted consumption to grow by 2.5 percent annually. However, two recent studies done in Europe, one by the Energy Watch Group and then confirmed by the Institute for Energy for the European Commission Joint Research Centre, concluded that world proven reserves are decreasing fast, the bulk of extraction is concentrated in a few countries, and production costs are steadily increasing. Coal may not be as abundant as conventional wisdom espouses.

With oil's international peak nigh, and with natural gas and coal to follow, prices for energy, and everything that has an energy component to it, are likely to escalate dramatically. The implications for the global economy are devastating. The implications for the coalfields – and for that matter all rural areas – of Virginia and West Virginia are less clear and perhaps the realm of speculators, investors, and futurists.

The sacrifices made by the people and the destruction of the landscape of the coalfields of Virginia and West Virginia to provide for affluent lifestyles of people across the nation and world are incalculable. Those sacrifices have historically been poorly rewarded. This seems unlikely to change. The people who daily risk their lives mining coal are met more often with derision and scorn than appreciation.

Wendy B. Davis, former Assistant Professor of Law and Dean of Students at the Appalachian School of Law in Grundy, Virginia, is scathing in her assessment in the 2003 article, "Out of the Black Hole:

Reclaiming the Crown of King Coal." She said,

> Coal has made, and kept, the people of Appalachia poor…
> For decades, the four-state Appalachian coal fields region has
> been the poorest in this nation. The percentage of persons
> below the poverty level in the coal counties is nearly twice the
> national average, with a median household income of between
> one half and two-thirds of the national average." With coal
> being the region's only industry, the dependence upon it and
> its health and environmental effects have weakened real estate
> values, education levels, and depressed the standard of living
> below any other area in the nation.

Her solution was to insist on governmental reparations, similar to those paid to Japanese Americans, Native Americans, and others for past injustices.

> Those who benefited from the coal should now repay the
> people of Appalachia.

While my own thoughts will emerge during the following pages, I will rely primarily on the words of the people along The Spine of the Virginias to bring the story of coal to life and give it its place in contemporary society.

John and Nannie Hairston
Amonate

John and Nannie Hairston are an elderly black couple who live in Montgomery County, Virginia, but grew up in the coalfields near Amonate in Tazewell County. They have won many awards for their work in civil rights.

John Hairston, a large, strapping man, was born in Pocahontas, Virginia, last of ten children. "My father and mother moved to Pocahontas because there were opportunities there. Wages were poor before the 1920's when the Unions came in. But blacks were moving in from all over the South."

"My dad worked the mines. He died when I was five. Two years later, my mother remarried the Reverend Purcell, who already had eight children. Between the families were sixteen children. We actually had two houses side by side, rented from the company. Reverend Purcell, who was a custodian at the company store, moved us to Amonate, in Tazewell County, Virginia, a mining town with both blacks and whites."

John pronounced Amonate as "amma-notta" rather than "ammonate."

John continued, "When we finished grade school, we had to go to War, West Virginia, because Tazewell County had no high schools for blacks. I had to walk three miles to the West Virginia line where the bus picked us up. The buses wouldn't carry blacks and whites together, so they picked up the black kids first, took us to school, then picked up the whites and took them to their school. Then at the end of the day, the whites got to go home first and us last. So we left for school at seven in the morning and didn't get home until nearly five in the afternoon."

I'd learned from earlier reading that after emancipation, blacks neither owned land nor had access to means to improve their economic standards. Many were transported to the coalfields in little better than railroad cattle cars.

Mrs. Hairston said, "I was born in Bottom Creek in McDowell County. My father moved us to Amonate when I was in the fifth grade. John and I were classmates through school but we didn't date. We graduated in 1939, during the Great Depression. We were poor like everybody else, but we had a good life.

"We had to go to school in Berwind, which was six or seven miles away. The Board of Education office was in Iaeger [in northwest McDowell County]. My mother didn't like how far away our school was. She decided to talk to the Board concerning her children. She pawned her sewing machine for five dollars to get the money to pay someone to drive her to Iaeger. My father said to her, 'If they don't do anything within a year or so, we'll go back (and ask again).' A few months later, I saw a truck that said, 'McDowell County' on it carrying lumber. The Pocahontas Fuel Company donated some land. The county built us a schoolhouse in Amonate. She convinced the Board of Education to build a school all by herself!"

John said, "I started working in the mines when I was still in high school. I went to school during the day and worked in the mines into the evening. The best money was made underground. Man-trips were the carts we took into the mines, sometimes up to seven miles underground. Sometimes the seams we were working on were nine, ten, twelve feet tall. I'm six-foot-five and a half. There were several seams stacked like layers in a cake. We'd shoot the coal [blast with dynamite] once per shift, and then load it up. The area we'd work was only about sixteen feet wide. There was a prescribed pattern of the mining so as to allow for the airflow and prevent the buildup of explosive methane. But we'd have an explosion every so often anyway.

"The company and the Union were both safety conscious. The company wanted to keep their men safe and as a result everyone worked towards being safe."

Nan said, "The Pocahontas Fuel Company was a good one. They made money and provided for their workers. We had beautiful frame houses with fences around them and sidewalks along the street. Every five years, the company painted the houses. They were white with green trim."

John said the company didn't care what color a miner was; only what he could produce. Coal mining was a great equalizer. "The community wasn't integrated. There wasn't any tension, but there was segregation. There were white people right across the street and we were all friends. Race relations were good in those days. When you worked in the mines, you went in black or white, but everybody came out black!

"We had a car in those days, but the company had buses to pick up the miners. There were also passenger trains once a day, with coal-fired locomotives.

Nan said, "During the depression there was more hunting and fishing done to feed our families. My father hunted rabbits and sometimes we would have enough to give to the neighbor's children. A good-sized rabbit has enough meat for four people. Sometimes John would be on a shift in the mine where he'd have two or three hours of daylight after he came out and he'd hunt.

"Our family always had a cow. So we had fresh milk and butter. The ice man would come and put fifty pounds of ice in the icebox. Daddy would go to the side of the mountain and dig a hole and line it with sawdust. That way he'd preserve some of our butter. We'd churn butter just about once a week. During the Depression, everybody suffered, but we didn't suffer to the same extent as others, because we raised much of our own food.

"Our houses were heated by coal. We had what was called 'Heat-strollers,' not a pot-bellied stove. We had a fireplace too, with a chimney."

John chuckled, "The town smelled of coal burning all winter, but nobody complained."

Nan said, "There was a slate dump behind our house. It burned all the time. The mine operators removed the slate from the coal and dumped it there. Dust covered everything: porches, banisters, and railings. We made a point to stay clean."

John said, "We went on vacation every year. I had a brother in New York. We went there, or Philadelphia, Washington, or Huntington where Nan had relatives.

"When I returned from the army in Korea, we left the coalfields. It wasn't a hard decision. The mines were playing themselves out, and there were no jobs."

Nan said, "Let me tell you a story about those days. The next family beside us was black, but then the family after that was white. The water line came right by our house. The whites had water in their home but we didn't. It was that way for three or four years after we moved there. But when John knew he had to go to Korea, he spoke with the superintendent of the area, telling him that he was going overseas to serve his country. He said, 'I don't mind carrying water when I'm here, but I'm asking you to connect our home so when I'm gone to war so my wife won't have to carry water.' It wasn't two weeks when the superintendent had water plumbed into our house. We learned to ask for the things we needed.

"Some towns were worse than others for blacks. We knew not to go to Grundy. Grundy was a prejudiced community.

"The things we've done, we don't think much about; we're just being who we are. We've never tried to make a name for ourselves. We've always felt that to make a better world, let it begin within me. That's our motto. So you can take it from there."

Coalfield equality

So there was a sense of equality and of the ability of all races to achieve a satisfactory life in the coalfields. I spoke again with Stuart McGehee for insight. In addition to being a history professor, he is also the curator of the Eastern Regional Coal Archives located in the public library in Bluefield, West Virginia.

He said, "Just about nobody lived in the Appalachian coalfield region prior to the 1880s. The land is too rugged for anything more than a subsistence farm and therefore has no value in a pre-industrial society. In 1880, all of McDowell County had 2000 people. Once industrial mining commenced, people needed to be brought in to sustain an industrial enterprise. Most of the labor in the Appalachian coal fields came from two human migrations.

"The first was an internal migration of black people leaving the Jim Crow South. Some of them came from parts of the South that had mined coal. Others were delighted that the Pennsylvania and New York coal operators didn't care what color you were. Southern West Virginia soon became one of the black centers of America.

"The other was European immigrants. A lot of them came from coal-bearing parts of Europe. They found the terrain familiar and set about replicating the same communities they remembered in Europe. Southern West Virginia became ethnically diverse.

"The reality of the coal industry in this area is first, the people who invested in it made a fortune, second, it provided the energy that made steel that transformed America and helped the country transition from being a rural to an industrial power, and third, it provided jobs and homes for people fleeing persecution, revolution, racism, and instability. I believe that the quality of their lives was better than what they'd had before. Most people want to see these people for their own political purposes as oppressed, downtrodden, and manipulated."

Stuart said the miners generally weren't beholden to the company store, as the story often goes. "It's a myth. I can show you hundreds of payroll books right here in this office, and I never see miners 'owing their souls to the company store.' I feel like I have become more of a pariah for saying this than I have ever become for telling the controversial story about the formation of the state. The people who have built a history of coal mining are the labor historians. They see in the mine wars the proletariat seizing the means of production and a real chance of Marxism in American history.

"I believe that the real blame for the fact that you have a fabulously wealthy state filled with poor people dates back to Reconstruction and the West Virginia Constitution. This Constitution had no provisions for [managing] an extractive resource. West Virginia didn't enact a severance tax until 1971. Imagine how much coal had left in a hundred years without ever being taxed. These taxes would have greatly benefited our communities and our people. This is why our schools and roads suck.

"[In the last fifty years] increasing mechanization allowed for far more productivity with fewer miners underground, and it began to erode the population base. Some of the old company towns look decrepit. Perhaps some people superimpose today's poverty and social statistics on the past and assume it was always like that. I try to humanize people in the coal camps, instead of making them as pitiful pawns. I recognize their true dignity and worth.

"When we started this facility, the Eastern Regional Coal Archives, we timed it just right. The last generations of men who mined coal by hand and women who taught in company schools were dying off. The last generation of independently owned coal operators was dying off.

"I began to interview the old-timers. They said, 'Dr. McGehee, I loved coal mining. I'd do it again in a heartbeat if I could. I loved the men I worked with and the sense of community'. It was like combat soldiers talking about being in a war together. Even the danger was something they spoke about favorably. They said, 'Dr. McGehee, Gary Hollow was a beautiful place. We had electricity and running water before anybody in the other towns.'

"Then I began to look at payroll books and the secondary literature. Everything I could find was associated with the West Virginia mine wars, and everything was written from a Marxist point of view. There was a disconnect between what people were telling me.

"My interpretation of coal mining was positive. The energy that came from the coal these miners extracted enabled us to win two world wars and created modern America. Those jobs provided opportunities and homes for people fleeing persecution and their lives were of higher quality than most.

"Black miners had as good opportunities here in the coalfields as in segregated America anywhere, because the coal operators were all from New York and Pennsylvania and were not quite as racist as people in the South. They just wanted the coal. Tell me a place anywhere else in America where black people and white people worked the same job and got paid the same and worked essentially side-by-side. Coal camps were residentially segregated by race and ethnicity, but the two most important institutions, the company store and the coal mine itself, were integrated. That point can't be overstressed because racism is such a prevalent factor in American history.

"Like Lincoln said, this is the last best hope on earth. The 1860 census revealed that there were 4 million slaves in America. That makes my beloved United States the largest slave owning nation in human history. You can't understand America without grasping that fact. You sure can't understand the Civil War. And you can't understand America without understanding the Civil War, as my friend Bud Robertson says all the time."

Frank Tanner
Brad Jones
Glen Lyn

Tiptoeing my way towards the coal country, I decided it would be educational to see how coal was consumed. So I arranged an appointment with Frank Tanner at the coal-fired power plant at Glen Lyn, Virginia. Owned and operated by Appalachian Power Company, a three-state power company with 8000 megawatts of capacity, their Glen Lyn station is as tiny as commercial plants go. But it is the only commercial electrical generation plant on The Spine of the Virginias.

The Glen Lyn plant sits on a narrow strip of flat land, a coal lump's throw away from the border. Even as a small plant, it was imposing. It had two smokestacks, with neither billowing smoke. A billboard outside showed a middle-aged man wearing a white hard hat and a blue workingman's uniform on a black background. In the upper right was the logo for American Electric Power, parent company of Appalachian Power. In large yellow letters was written, "COAL Keeps The Lights On!" The main office, with its tile floors and walls, reminded me of my elementary school.

Frank Tanner told me he was originally from Appomattox and was a Virginia Tech Engineering graduate, as am I. Frank's first and only job was with Appalachian Power. He said, "American Electric Power serves over 5 million customers in 11 states. It is primarily in the generation and distribution business. Although our plant doesn't power a particular city or region, our generation would service the equivalent of a city the size of Roanoke. The grid is a nationwide interconnected power supply system. Power flows wherever it is being used. For all intents and purposes it cannot be stored.

"We have a legal obligation to supply the customers within our area. Once we meet that demand, we are free to sell our excess power on the open market. The current rate for a kilowatt hour in the state of Virginia is, I think, 6.7 cents which is among the lowest in the

At Appalachian Power Company's Glen Lyn Power Plant

country. Our Title Five permit stipulates that we burn low sulfur, bituminous coal which is mined primarily in southwestern Virginia. We can burn up to 3000 tons, the equivalent of 30 coal cars per day, if we are running both of our two power plants.

"The plant began operation in 1919. Virtually every mechanical aspect of this plant has been replaced at least once during those 90 years. The environmental regulations are much tougher today. Part of my responsibility is in dealing with environmental aspects. We have electrostatic precipitators to take the particulate matter out of the flue gas. When coal is burned, not everything burns. The unburned portion is ash, the non-carbon content of the coal."

In an earlier time, ash streamed from the smokestacks. Now ash is caught and sent to landfills. However, the gaseous chemicals, primarily nitrous oxide, carbon monoxide, and carbon dioxide still reach the atmosphere.

"As an engineer at a commercial power plant, I am on the front line in taking care of our environment. The environmental protection solutions used at a plant like this, if they are to be workable, must be pragmatic. The next generation will have to make some serious decisions. Demand for electricity is continuing to rise, but we are not building new generating capacity. Fifty percent of our nation's electricity is generated from burning coal and another 20 percent is generated with nuclear. Another 20 percent is generated with natural gas. A few percent are generated with hydroelectricity. Only two or three percent are from renewables like wind and solar.

"The nonrenewable fossil fuels — coal, natural gas, and oil — face their all-time international production peak within the next few years to a few decades. If we were to remove these sources from the mix, we would need to replace around 70 percent of our current usage. It is not technically feasible to replace those watts solely with solar and wind. People need to be reasonable with their expectations.

"Appalachian Power Company is involved in promoting conservation. New solutions must make sense technically and economically. I am convinced that the best solution is conservation. We will need to continue to make coal burning cleaner and more environmentally sound. I am convinced we will need new nuclear plants. But conservation is easy. Everybody can do it themselves.

"I love my job. I learn something new every day. I feel good about what we are doing here because we are directly contributing to the quality of life and economic prosperity of everyone around us. We take these things for granted here in the United States of America. But reliable electricity is a luxury in many countries. I feel that I am in a noble profession."

I also met Frank's boss, Brad Jones, director of the plant. We talked about a controversial plan to use the ash generated by his plant as fill material for a new industrial park near the plant. Opponents were worried about environmental risks. He said, "We generate about 90,000 tons of ash per year. There are some risks in land-filling. But I think the concerns are greatly exaggerated. Neither this plant nor my office had any particular stake in where our ash was sent. The original plan was not ours. We were asked if our ash could be used. We thought it would be helpful to economic development. We suddenly became the villains."

As Frank and I began our tour of the plant, I donned a hard-hat and safety glasses. The plant is filled with thousands of pipes of all sizes, running in a seemingly helter-skelter way. Frank said several welders work continuously repairing pipes. From an outside catwalk, I got a good view of the two electrostatic precipitators. The larger looked to be forty or fifty feet square and as tall as a three-story building. The stacks produced no visible emissions or thermal waves. A large storage mound of coal, jet black, was under a dusting of snow. There was a fenced-off area with an array of electrical transformers and other equipment. From it were tentacles of wires stretching towards transmission towers arching over the nearby mountains.

Inside, an extensive machine shop shared the largest room in the facility with the dynamos. They looked like face-down clamshells, where half was covered in a form-fitting insulated metal casing and the other half was below floor level. The sound level was high and steady.

The control room had a semi-circular wall of gauges, levers, and electronic displays. A mix of modern and old-fashioned instrumentation, some likely from the installation days of the 1957 boiler, filled the room.

At the completion of our tour, I spoke again with Brad, who said, "Our company recently did a survey which found that Western Virginians had a high rate of usage of compact fluorescent light bulbs. People here have a tremendous awareness of energy efficiency. I talk to people often, formally and informally, about energy use. If someone complains about a high electric bill, I tell them how to cut their usage. My opinion is that there is no cheaper kilowatt than the one you never use."

Susan Lapis
Over the Sacral region

My next goal was to take a better look at coal mining for myself. One outspoken opponent is Susan Lapis, a pilot for the non-profit advocacy group SouthWings, dedicated to giving politicians, writers, photographers, and concerned citizens aerial views of environmental abuses throughout the South.

Susan, a spunky, motherly, redheaded woman, told me when we met at the Mountain Empire Airport between Wytheville and Marion in Southwest Virginia she was SouthWings' first volunteer pilot. "I am not the person who makes things happen. I enable the people who make things happen.

"Laws have been passed based upon SouthWings flights! Robert Kennedy Jr. flew with me last fall. He has a phenomenal mind, and he has been a tremendous influence on any number of lawmakers. He works with the Natural Resources Defense Council and the Southern Environmental Law Center.

"I cannot stop mountaintop removal mining myself by waving a sign, but Kennedy and the NRDC can by forcing the enforcement of laws that are already on the books. My passengers see things that can't be seen any other way.

"Of all of the SouthWings pilots, I am the one who lives closest to the mountaintop removal mines, so I spend an inordinate amount of time flying over them. This sentence, 'I had no idea,' is almost the logo of SouthWings.

"I think the key issue hinges on the historic concept Kennedy speaks about: the idea that ordinary businesses or individuals do not have the right to despoil the water and the air and the mountains that belong to everybody. Some time after humans are extinct, the air will become clean again. The rivers will flow clean again. But nobody will ever put those mountains back again." She said the filling and contamination of streams with heavy metals like mercury, arsenic, cobalt, cadmium, and zinc is an invasion of the commons.

"In medieval days when the concept of the commons originated, the concept of an ecosystem had not yet been developed. I think humans have always felt the earth and all its resources were just for them. The Bible speaks of 'dominion thereof'. We are now beginning to realize it is more complex than that. We are part of a larger world where all of life is linked. We cannot despoil earth's ecosystems and expect to survive.

"When we get into the air and fly over these mines, you will see these enormous drag lines and earthmovers. They use an explosive called ANFO. Every day 4,000,000 lbs. of ANFO are used to destroy the mountains of Appalachia.

"Let's get into the air."

We flew to the northeast where we got a nice view of Ron Kime's tower on Big Walker Mountain, along with Interstate 77 and its tunnel. The area was dominated by woodlands with small patches of pasture mixed in. The land was sparsely populated, only lightly disturbed by human activity. The mountains below looked like fat snakes slithering under green carpets. The sprawling Celanese plant near Pearisburg was our next landmark. It occupied a significant plain and stood boldly against the surrounding mountains.

We flew over the power plant at Glen Lyn where Frank Tanner worked, but wispy low-hanging clouds hid all but the taller smokestack.

We then turned west and flew over the north edge of East River Mountain. Beyond Bluefield, also mostly hidden by low clouds, the first of many mountaintop removal mines came in sight in eastern McDowell County. It looked like an enormous construction site with no construction, a blob pastel of grey and tan amidst a sea of green. We could see where on several edges, terraces of overburden had been placed, each with a central spillway for rainwater, and a series of roads contouring around the rubble. Nothing was in black, no areas that looked like actual coal. We saw several trucks and earthmoving machines.

The forested mountains nearby were laced with dirt roads.

Further westward was another mine just north of Hurley, Virginia. This one had a couple of ponds at the base of the rubble. There were others to the north and west, not isolated or uncommon, but recurring features of the area.

We finally headed southeast, back to the airport, and we landed. As we taxied back to the terminal building, Susan said, "The passengers in my airplane are judges, legislators, and lawyers as well as journalists, activists, and writers. I can tell them about what they are seeing, so I am not just the airplane driver. They take the story back to their own audiences. We all work together."

West Virginia

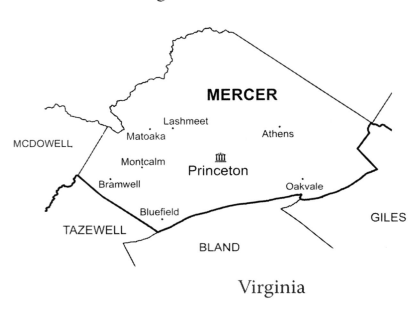

Mercer County, West Virginia

Most of Mercer County's population is on the southern edge, against East River Mountain, which forms most of the southern border. The northern two-thirds of the county is in the Cumberland Plateau topography and bears coal. The southern third, including East River Mountain, is in the Ridge-And-Valley formation.

Mercer County has 421 square miles.

Incorporated cities are Bluefield and Princeton, the county seat. Incorporated towns are Bramwell, Oakvale, Montcalm, Athens, Lashmeet, and Matoaka.

Population

Mercer County's population soared from around 7000 at the start of the Civil War to 75,000 in 1950. From there, population dropped somewhat, then stabilized in the range between 60,000 and 70,000 to today's 63,000.

Institutions of higher education

Mercer County has three higher educational institutes: Bluefield College, Bluefield State College, and Concord University.

Traffic

Mercer County has about 60 miles of 4-lane highways, including Interstate 77. There are dozens of traffic lights.

Today's...

Mercer County's two largest communities are Bluefield and Princeton. Princeton was founded first, almost a quarter century before the Civil War, and became the county's pre-eminent community. Bluefield was a planned city, founded as the staging area for the Norfolk and Western Railroad's operations in the nearby coalfields. Bluefield's fortunes have since been tied to the railroad, seeing a rapid expansion in the first half of the 20th Century, followed by a decline. Princeton's growth has been steadier and is now more tied to the transportation network of US-460 and Interstate 77. Princeton sits on a higher, flatter topography than that of Bluefield.

Attractions

- Bluefield Historic District, Bluefield
- Bramwell Historic District, Bramwell
- Pinnacle Rock State Park, Bluewell, dramatic rock outcropping

Ramona Shook
Princeton

Ramona Shook and her companion, Bill Sowers, live on a quiet street in Princeton. Mona grew up near Welch, the county seat of McDowell County.

"Dad was a coal miner for sixty-plus years, all underground. Miners made good money. When I was small, he got paid in scrip and we shopped at the company store. So we had little cash. We weren't well off, but were prudent. In World War II, he was exempt from the draft because he was a miner. He was needed as badly in the mines, because coal was used in the production of steel.

"I started in the first grade when I was four. In this area, country music is big — Bluegrass. But they played classical music for us in the first grade. My school was wonderful because the teachers were committed to the children, absolutely. I was a good student. We had no discipline problems. We had school nurses and dentists. The teachers sponsored clothes drives and gave the poorer kids clothes. We had home-cooked meals at school every day. The teachers made sure even the poorest kids had good food. We had good water, provided by the coal companies. They dredged the river every year so we wouldn't have much flooding. They didn't know how to do dust suppression or filter the water, so the Tug River ran black.

"My home was a duplex, brick, but it burned down. We had sidewalks, but some didn't. The houses were built on what we called 'red dog.' It was the refuse from the mining."

Homer Hickam, who wrote the 1998 book *The Rocket Boys*, upon which the movie *October Sky* was based, lived in Coalwood, not far from Welch. Mona said, "I didn't know Homer Hickam. I was in the tenth grade when he was shooting rockets. But what he and his friends were doing was known throughout the county. My father thought they ought to be whupped and go to work in the mines. Anything new or out of the norm was looked upon as bad by my parents.

"[Mining was] the only way of life they could do. Without going to college, without an education, which my father's family was not able to afford, mining was the best paying job they could have. Sometimes miners made more than the college graduates. Dad was fortunate not to have had a major accident.

"My friends could tell you more [about teenage life] because they got to run around more and free-willy everywhere. I couldn't even get out of the yard. My parents were strict. My mother would have been perfectly happy if I'd not done anything but stayed and worked at J.C. Penney.

"I wanted to be a biochemist. When I told mother, she didn't know what I was talking about. She said, 'That means you'll have to go to college for four years and then maybe four more after that. Well, you can't do that. I ain't going to pay for that.' I didn't know I could do it on my own. Everything else I tried to come up with, they beat me down. My mother said 'There are three things you can do. You can be a teacher...' and I didn't like kids. 'You can be a nurse...' and I didn't like that. 'Or you can be a secretary.'

"My parents didn't want me to do better than they did. They stifled me. To this day it is crippling: no encouragement whatsoever. Talk about being defeated all the time, no matter how hard I tried. I didn't want to be a secretary. I wanted to fly away.

"All my friends went to college. I was accepted at WVU and Marshall. My mother said, 'If you don't make straight A's this first semester, I'm not paying for it any more.' So why bother? You know, I had to work hard to make good grades. She was serious. So I thought, 'Forget it.'" Mona ended up going to New York and worked for Pan Am, but she hated it. When her marriage failed, she moved to Prince-ton.

"Now the area [near Welch] is depressing: little sky, bad environment, dirty. If I wanted to go anywhere from Welch, it took forty-five minutes to get to Bluefield. Then I felt like I was leaving; climbing up out of the hole. I always felt like I lived in a hole. Bluefield was out where you could see the sky. To me, Bluefield was the gateway out of the hole, and I like Princeton even better because it is more level."

She said being a West Virginian means freedom. "I think West Virginia is the backbone of the way a lot of people think in this country. I'm proud to be a West Virginian. The people here are strong, of the earth. They will survive."

Jeffrey and Susan Greenberg
Princeton

Another Princeton resident, Jeffrey Greenberg, is a neurological surgeon and an accomplished pianist. While lots of people move away, he moved into Southern West Virginia. He and his wife Susan spoke with me.

A native New Yorker, Jeffrey said his reasons for moving to Southern West Virginia were about the quality of life and his desire to remove the level of fear of being sued under which he lived. "I'm a neurological surgeon. I operate on disorders of the central nervous system, the brain and the spinal column from your neck down to the rear end. There are infinitely more variables out of my control than in my control.

"West Virginia had just gone through a crisis because their malpractice situation had gotten so Draconian that docs were leaving at a desperate pace. West Virginia passed significant model tort reform that made life reasonable, just reasonable, for doctors. Now I'm semi-retired. I'm here with my family for dinner every night.

Jeffrey, who is Jewish, said, "Many doctors who saw this area as interesting are Jewish. They are the people I have the most in common with. I learned recently that Kimball, in McDowell County, once had the largest per-capita concentration of Jews outside of New York City in the entire nation.

"I just had a session of bluegrass jamming (at the house) this afternoon. I don't have a background in it, but several guys came over, from all walks of life, and we had a great time jamming. I love all kinds of music."

Susan said, "One of the things I've encountered many times here is that no matter how bad somebody's situation is economically, how poor they are, they're not moving! Their grandma's here, their mother's here."

We spoke about issues of health in West Virginia. Jeffrey said,

"Obesity is a problem. It's malignant. This will break the bank of health care in America today. It creates hypertension, diabetes, and heart disease. It has to do with total lifestyle. It comes down to discipline."

Susan said, "Some of these kids who die in car accidents have autopsies done, and the examiners find coronary artery disease and circulatory issues of the type we used to associate with fifty-year-old people. The parents of these kids have no idea how unhealthy their kids are. People have serious health issues in their thirties. Their knees hurt, they have high blood pressure, and they are diabetic. But getting them to change is hard. A friend of mine has a gym where they try to help people change and lose weight. They have a group of twenty people who have signed up to try to get in better shape together. So far, one person is actually following the program."

Jeffrey added, "When you have a father who went on disability at age thirty-five and got paid handsomely, because he worked in the mines and it was gawd-awful dangerous, and now the father has a cane and the son at age twenty-eight has a cane, it's like imprinting: do nothing and get a check."

Susan, "Our PTO president is a hard-working local woman. Her husband also works hard as a mechanic for $8 per hour. She volunteers at the school, too, one of five or six parents in a school of seven hundred kids who are active and contributing. We do everything. I said to her, 'Well, everybody else is working, they've got jobs.' She said, 'No they don't. I'll tell you right now what they're doing. They're sitting on their couch watching Oprah and eating donuts.' This is coming from her, not me. I said, 'No!' She said, 'I'm tellin' ya, that's what they're doin'".

"Most parents want their children to do better than they did. But here, many parents don't encourage achievement in their kids. [Years ago] lots of people got an eighth-grade education and then went to work in the mines, because then the mines paid pretty well. Now the mines are mostly automated, and they don't need so many people. So now you have these people with eighth-grade educations, and they don't value education. It's been a real problem of local populations. Education is the key to achievement."

Dreama Denver
Princeton

Before we get coal dust under our fingernails, I'd like you to meet Ms. Gilligan. Yes, Gilligan!

Bob Denver was one of the most beloved and recognized comedic actors ever to have graced the little screen. For the last fifteen years of his life before his death of cancer in 2005, he lived with his fourth wife, the former Dreama Peery, and their son, who is severely autistic, in the shadow of East River Mountain near Princeton.

Denver's first big role was of the archetypal beloved beatnik, Maynard G. Krebs on the 1959 to 1963 show *The Many Loves of Dobie Gillis*. Denver set the stage for the hippies of the '60s and made slacking and bongo playing trendy.

But in *Gilligan's Island*, Denver's role as second in command of the crew of the ill-fated Minnow made Denver's face one of the most recognizable in the world. The show aired from September 1964 until September 1967, but its amazing popularity was such that 98 episodes have been in syndication ever since.

Gilligan's Island left Denver the actor typecast forever. After less successful shows and many stage appearances, he, Dreama, and their son departed Hollywood and the left coast in search of a quieter and more private life and found it near Dreama's hometown, Bluefield.

In Bob's last brush with fame, he was arrested for a miniscule amount of marijuana in 1998, when he was 63.

Dreama Denver is pert, loquacious, and appealing. She has a short, bobbing hairdo and effervescent blue eyes. She runs The Denver Foundation she and Bob established to assist and enrich the lives of disabled, disadvantaged, and autistic children in West Virginia.

She said, "During the last 20 years of Bob's life, he set aside everything, including his career, to take care of our autistic son. He had two children before we married, and he was my second husband.

"The Foundation gets most of its funding from the sponsors of Little Buddy Radio station, which features less-known artists. Music has saved my life since Bob died. The radio station runs on a computer in my house. I roll out of my bed every morning, grab a cup of coffee, and go to work right in my jammies. Today the playlist has probably 4000 or 5000 titles.

"Bob and I met when I was in Orlando, Florida, visiting with my parents. A friend called and said, 'You know, they're doing the play, *Play It Again Sam*, over in St. Petersburg. I auditioned and I got the part. I asked the producer who the star was going to be. She said, 'Bob Denver.' I said, 'Gilligan?' She said, 'Yeah.' I went, 'I am going to have to kiss Gilligan?' Little did I know I'd be kissing 'Gilligan' for the next 30 years."

"Bob loved being Gilligan, but he also loved being Maynard G. Krebs. Bob was accused many times of starting the hippie movement. I loved Gilligan too, but Maynard was my fave.

"Bob was only 32 when *Gilligan's Island* ended. He was a good [actor], much better that he was ever given credit for. As time went by, he really learned to embrace his role as Gilligan. He always said, 'How many actors get to be in a series that's loved by people all over the world?'

"One of the things I loved the most was that he never lost sight of the child inside himself. Once, when we had been married for about 15 years, Bob said to me, 'Dreams' — he always called me Dreams — 'Do you ever give little Dreama a hug? Do you ever think back to when you were a little girl and remember what she liked and what made her happy and what made her laugh and what made her sad? Do you remember what her friends did to make her feel great or to hurt her?' I said, 'No, I never do that. Do you do that?' He said, 'Yeah. I think about little Bobby. I sit quietly by myself, and I really allow myself to remember that little boy that I used to be. And I give him a great big hug for making me that man that I am today. Without that little boy and his experiences, I wouldn't be the man that I am today.' I got a bit teary-eyed. I said, 'That is so sweet!' He said, 'You really should give little Dreama a hug every once in a while. You should tell that little girl that you used to be how much you love her.' I said, 'Okay, I will.' Since then, I do take the time to love and thank little Dreama.

"Bob wasn't a perfect person. He had faults, weaknesses, and shortcomings like everybody else. But he was one of the smartest people I have ever known. He was extremely well-read and could talk intelligently with anybody about just about anything: politics, world events, and issues. Gilligan was a nebbish, that is all there is to it. Of all the teachers I had in school, nobody taught me as much as Bob.

"Bluefield was a great place to grow up. In those days Bluefield was small-town living at its best. Parents never worried about where their kids played, even though we were supposed to let our folks know where we were going. It was bustling in those days, a cool place. I think the little triangular area in downtown is charming. I think you could make that downtown so quaint and lovely. I believe there are many old movie theaters around the area that are crying out for refurbishing. It is sad.

"Bob Denver loved West Virginia! There was quite the fervor when we moved here. People that we didn't know from Adam would routinely show up at our front door. Bob never went anywhere without being recognized. But he loved that he could hang out at the computer store, go to Lowe's, and run to the post office. He loved the fact that as people built their familiarity with him, he was just a regular guy. There are downsides to everywhere, but small towns are lovely places to live."

About Bob's arrest, Dreama said, "Bob smoked grass on occasion. We didn't grow our own. We never smoked in front of anyone. We only smoked in the privacy of our own home. Bob and I devoted 20 years of our lives to taking care of our disabled son. Our son has never had a sleep schedule, no circadian rhythms. He sleeps five minutes here or an hour there. Bob and I took care of him in shifts. If it was my turn to take care of him and he fell asleep, I would try to sleep at the same time. Sometimes if I took a hit of marijuana it would help me fall asleep. Grass was therapeutic, a way to be able to sleep in a situation that was often sleepless and exhausting."

The arresting officers followed a delivery package containing marijuana to their door, where they arrested him on charges of possession. When all was said and done, Denver was given a suspended sentence and a fine and was put on probation. It was a traumatic incident for

Dreama.

"Initially I was upset, angry with this area. Bob loved it here as much as I can ever imagine anybody loving a place. I brought him back to the place where I grew up, to a place where I thought we could be safe, where we could raise our son in peace and security. I never envisioned anything like this could happen to him here. I'm not sure he felt as angry as I did, but I took this personally. Bob never missed a chance to talk about not only the beauty of the state but about the people who lived in it. I just couldn't believe this could happen.

"About a week after the bust, my hairdresser in Bluefield called me. She said, 'Are you doing okay?' I hemmed and hawed. She said, 'You come over here right now. We are going to give you a facial. We are going to do your nails. We're going to feed you some wine.' When I got there they had the gift baskets for me, filled with lotions and bubblebath. They gave me the works, and it was all free. We giggled and cried. Women were coming and going all the time while I was there. I could not have been more shocked by what they said. 'Oh darling, we are really so sad that this happened to you.' I'm sure there were many people throughout this area who were critical of us, but not one ever criticized me.

"As time went on, whenever I got out into the community, all I ever found was support. The people on the area you're calling 'The Spine of the Virginias' often said, 'Please do not let this reflect on us....We don't care what you do in your home....We don't want people to care what we do in our homes....We are proud that Bob Denver chose to live here. We are proud that he considers himself to be an adopted West Virginian.' I realized the fault didn't lie with the good folks who live in the area. I actually grew to love it here even more when the shock wore off and I understood that."

Bob Denver died a few years later of throat cancer in a North Carolina hospital. Dreama said, "Bob and I had a great love story. The instant we met and shook hands it was like, 'Whoa! There you are.' We were together 24/7 for the rest of his life. I never doubted his love for me. He never doubted my love for him."

The Marriage of the Bluefields
As told by Stuart McGehee

A hundred and fifty years ago, there was no city of Bluefield at all. A town called Graham was on the Virginia side of the state line in Tazewell County. It was the center of the agricultural economy for a lightly populated area north of the East River Mountain.

After the Civil War, the technology to mine and transport coal was developed. The Norfolk and Western Railroad sought a place to put its regional headquarters. They chose this valley because it is flat with a gentle rise in the center that allowed gravity switching of trains. The N&W named the new city Bluefield, after the blue fields of chicory that flourished.

In 1889 Bluefield was incorporated. By 1900, the population skyrocketed to 10,000 people. They built a city of wood, but in the 1920s it was torn down and the big buildings in the center of Bluefield were built to house coal company headquarters, insurance companies, utilities, banks, and warehouses.

Bluefield continued to grow and eventually expansion reached the state line. In a fateful decision in about 1921, the people of Graham held an acrimonious election and with a narrow plurality decided to change the name of their town to Bluefield, Virginia. And to celebrate it they had an actual wedding that took place on the state line. The Chamber of Commerce sponsored an elaborately staged, "Wedding of the Bluefields." Emma Smith from Bluefield, West Virginia, married a man named Wingo Yost from Graham, Virginia. The wedding was in City Park in the largest civic celebration this area has ever seen, even to this day. The governor of Virginia was the best man, and the governor of West Virginia gave away the bride. This is the only time until recently that both governors have been together in Bluefield. The bride stood with one foot on either side of the state line. When she took her vows, the results of the election were certified and they cut the ribbon. Mr. Yost and Ms. Smith became husband and wife and Graham became Bluefield, Virginia. The high school is still Graham

High and the rivalry with Bluefield High School is fierce.

As coal mining became increasingly mechanized, the population decreased. Since 1955 Bluefield's population has dropped at every census. Now there are people in Bluefield, Virginia, who want a divorce, and they want to rename it to Graham. There are still businesses there — Graham Hardware, Graham Animal Feed and Seed — and the high school is still called Graham High.

Collapse of the Milner-Matz Hotel, Bluefield.

Milner-Matz Hotel
Bluefield

The Matz Hotel was built in Bluefield by Samuel Matz in 1911, who also built the adjacent Colonial Theater in 1916. The Matz was located on Princeton Avenue, busy US-19, the road that parallels the railroad tracks, at the base of downtown. These were heady days for Bluefield, as the city was growing rapidly, with several buildings that were more than a dozen stories tall. The businesses in those buildings brought travelers, many who stayed at the Matz.

By 1927, Matz' son Max had taken over both the hotel and the theater from his father. Max was active in the Republican Party and represented the fifth congressional district at the 1932 Republican National Convention, where Matz placed Herbert Hoover's name forward for re-election. The Matz Hotel had hosted Hoover himself in 1928.

According to reporter Bill Archer in the *Bluefield Daily Telegraph*, Senator Robert C. Byrd said, "Simply put, the Milner-Matz was the place to be. [Union president] John L. Lewis stayed there when he came to Bluefield in 1920 to begin organizing miners in the southern coalfields, and train crews knew the place as home-away-from-home as they worked that route. I remember fondly the news stand there as a place you could get a good cigar and spirited discussion about the latest goings-on in the area."[10]

Bluefield's fortunes waned. The Milner Hotel chain, based in Detroit, acquired the hotel in the early 1970s, which from then on was known as the Milner-Matz Hotel. With revenue diminishing, the hotel went out of service in the early 1990s, and the utilities were disconnected. Portions of the roof failed, and water entered the structure, leading to its collapse in 2009.

By this time, many of the buildings nearby were decrepit and unoccupied. When I viewed the partially standing edifice, an unattended police car sat askew, blocking traffic, and signs indicated the required detour. It was astounding to think that because of the railroad and coal industries, Adolph Hitler had listed Bluefield as one of his 50 places to bomb in the United States during World War II. Cheery banners hung from nearby light poles, announcing "Welcome to Bluefield" with an iconic oncoming red and blue steam train superimposed on a deep blue background. I walked past a three-story, steel-beam parking garage that had no cars in it. The beams were unpainted and rusty. The street had a yellow "crime scene" tape across it.

Although there was a huge pile of rubble, mostly red brick, in the road, The Matz hadn't fully collapsed. Perhaps two-thirds of the building was still standing and intact. Upper floor rooms stood with the near wall ripped away. As I stood and watched, a few bricks fell from an upper level, bounced against a lower level floor, and crashed to the street.

The next time I was in town, the remainder of the hotel and those buildings around it had been demolished and all remnants were removed. The lot was seeded in new grass.

Richard "Buz" Wilkinson
Bluefield

Buz Wilkinson was a basketball star at the University of Virginia in the 1950s. This product of the coalfields of Southern West Virginia earned a law degree and made a life-long career at the First Century Bank in downtown Bluefield, West Virginia. His resume is long with directorships of charitable organization and memberships in honorary societies.

Buz is trim, 6'2" tall, bespectacled, with grey hair and the distinguished look of an accomplished man. In his office, surrounded by photos and mementos, he said, "The University of Virginia retired my jersey in 1955. This was the first jersey they ever retired in basketball. My career average was 28.6 points per game, a record that still stands throughout the ACC. If we had had a three-point line I would probably have added six to eight points per game. I had a two-hand set shot. I had a jump shot. I could drive to the basket with either hand and shoot with either hand.

"I was born in Welch, but I grew up in Pineville (about 20 miles north of Welch in Wyoming County). I attended school in Pineville until the 10th grade, at which point I transferred to the Greenbrier Academy which was housed in the building that today is the School of Osteopathic Medicine in Lewisburg.

"In those days, kids did not sign a grant-in-aid. There were fewer regulations. You would talk to the coach, and if there was agreement, you could go to that school. I was interested in the University of Kentucky and the University of Virginia. My father was the town physician, and my mother worked with him. So it fell upon my brother to take me to school. When we got up that morning, he said to me, 'Are we going east or are we going west?' My mother and father had both grown up in Virginia. I said to him, 'If I am going to stay in this family, I had better go east.' So he took me to Charlottesville. I have never regretted this decision. I got a great education."

After a stint in the army, Wilkinson returned to UVA and got a law degree. Then he returned to southern West Virginia, just as the economy began to decline. He has been involved with revitalization efforts ever since. "I am chairman of a foundation that is trying to put broadband high-speed Internet access throughout downtown Bluefield. Some of these old large buildings could easily be converted into modern office space. If we could do that, we could bring some high-tech businesses here. The cost of living is modest. Home ownership rates are high. None of the banks that I know of participated in the subprime lending process. So there have been many fewer foreclosures than elsewhere in the country.

"The economy here has worked in reverse to the national economy. When oil prices go up, when the Arabs are doing well, we are doing well. When oil prices go down, the rest of the country does well, but we do less well. Just in recent years we have begun to see some parallels between the national economy and our economy. The national economy began to sour in 2007. This is only just beginning to happen now in Bluefield. When gasoline was four dollars per gallon and a barrel of oil cost close to $150, coal went up to $300 per ton. Anyone who was willing to work in a coal mine could earn a good living.

"Historically, Virginia has been a better managed state than West

Virginia. If we are going to change the laws, we do not have to reinvent the wheel; we just need to copy what others are doing better. Virginia has been ranked the number one state in the nation for business. We are right beside them. Why can't we do just as well?

"There is a close relationship, obviously, between West Virginia and Virginia here in the Bluefield area. As Bluefield, West Virginia, has declined, Bluefield, Virginia, has continued to grow. Princeton has grown. I'm sitting here in the middle in Bluefield, West Virginia, watching population grow on both sides of us."

Bill Archer
Bluefield

Bill Archer is a reporter for the *Bluefield Daily Telegraph*, a newspaper with a circulation of around 26,000. As a news writer, Archer had an intimate look at the area's most interesting stories, including two he shared with me, the awarding of the Nobel Prize to native son

Bill Archer

John Nash and the collapse of the Keystone Bank twenty miles to the north. Bill is a jovial man, an accomplished folk and traditional musician, with a head of auburn hair and thick eyebrows.

"The phone was already ringing one morning when I arrived at 8:00 a.m. in 1994. It was a woman who worked for the police department. She said, 'Have you heard that a boy from Bluefield has won the Nobel Prize in economics?'

"This man turned out to be John Nash, about whom the book *A Beautiful Mind* was written, and a movie of the same name was produced. All day I talked to various people who knew Nash. His sister, Martha, who lived in Roanoke, called and said she had talked with his wife, Alicia, and told me to call him that night.

"[When I called him], we talked about things in Bluefield that I was surprised he knew. He always kept track of the goings-on in the city and the various people in the news.

"For the next two or three months, I did a series of interviews with people who knew him, and I learned as much as I could about his career. He never granted interviews to any other reporter, but he was motivated to speak to his hometown newspaper, and I was the lucky reporter.

"After the movie came out, he spoke at our Chamber of Commerce dinner. There are signs approaching Bluefield that say, 'Welcome to Bluefield, home of John F. Nash, Jr., Nobel Prize winner.' We had a community celebration in 1995 that Martha attended. Every community struggles with keeping its students motivated and moving forward in their academics. The message that our educators were able to make to their students was that even if you come from southern West Virginia, you can still do great things."

Archer's other signature story was about the fraud and embezzlement at the Keystone Bank in Keystone, a former coal camp between Welch and Bluefield, that in 1999 shut down the bank and incurred the largest payout by FDIC in that agency's history.

Archer said, "This was the biggest story in my entire career. I knew [former president of the bank] Knox McConnell from the time I moved here. Knox was filled with braggadocio. He knew some important people in the Republican Party, including George H. W. Bush. He was not afraid to use those contacts. The subprime markets were hotly inflated in 1990. McConnell was able to keep the regulators at bay for years, but the office of the Comptroller General and the FDIC were looking into his bank before he died.

"There were some articles in the Associated Press around 1995 discussing problems with a bingo operation in Alabama that Mc-Connell was affiliated with. I drove to Keystone and I spoke with [bank V.P.] Billie Cherry. I looked at her square in the face and said, 'You tell me right now that there is nothing to it. If you tell me that, I will walk away from here.' I learned later she had lied to me."

Four years later, Archer knew unequivocally of the betrayal. "After that I refused to hear anything else Cherry had to say. When she passed away in prison, I wrote only factual things about her career and life. What would have happened if I had not believed Billie and pursued the story vigorously at that time? Would that have unraveled the story years earlier? Untold numbers of people lost their life savings because of what Knox and Billie did. I do not personally feel guilty about not following up the story. Our entire American system and way of life is built on people telling the truth. But once I understood that I had been betrayed, there was nothing that was going to derail me from moving forward aggressively. Within six weeks of the collapse of the bank, it was becoming clear the extent of the losses to all the depositors. This story has never been fully adjudicated because much of what went on was so far away from here."

In terms of his reporting style, he said, "I try to be as thorough as possible. I try to not just report the facts but also to explain things in ways that everyday people can understand complex issues."

Gary Bowling
Bluefield

Gary Bowling founded a gallery called "Gary Bowling's House of Art," across the street from Buz Wilkinson's bank. Located in what once was a department store, the gallery featured whimsical, eccentric, and eclectic art. Strings of flashing lights illuminated papier-mâché caricatures and sea monsters. Canvases of dread, enlightenment, and everything in between, adorned the walls. There was a café inside, so patrons enjoyed great food while viewing the art. Gary, an exuberant, expressive sixty-year old man with a grey goatee, began talking about the city. "I was born and grew up here. After I graduated from high school in 1967, I went into the Air Force. I moved back in 1973.

"Bluefield has been kind to me. I have world renowned friends since I have traveled a lot. Because of what we are doing here, I already have New York artists who are internationally recognized and want to work and show their stuff here in Bluefield. When I grew up here I thought that being an artist here, well, you might as well be on Mars. Since then the population has plummeted, yet I am still putting in a major art gallery. In a couple of years it will compare favorably against anything on the East Coast.

"We help young people, encourage them, showcase their work, and build their esteem. So many of the kids are ensconced in the drug culture. We're trying to help them see another alternative, the art culture, which will be more meaningful, positive, and productive through their lives. We provide a place where people can not only do painting and drawing but also writing, theater, and music. We call this a "house" because it is for everybody. Everybody who walks through the door will become part of the family. This is a house of diversity; it is of every culture. Bluefield has always been a diverse place, especially for this part of Appalachia.

"Once we get recognition and get things moving, people will get off the Interstate and make the effort to come and see us. West Virginians are proud people. We need to be proud of what we contribute to our society.

"Art is a reflection of my everyday emotions and thoughts. Every day I create fun and whimsical papier-mâché pieces. I do what I call my Gary-glyphics — my version of hieroglyphics.

"I am unashamedly a dumpster diver. I go around town and take things that people have left outside in their trash. I bring those things in here and convert them to art.

"People need to stop sitting on the couch complaining about how desolate it is downtown. People tell me they can't believe that I would be wasting my time, money, and effort on this gallery when the downtown is virtually dead and they need to hang a tombstone on it. And I tell them, 'Until I stop breathing, it ain't over.' It's not that things don't bother me, but every day I see people in wheelchairs or people missing arms or they are homeless, and I thank God that I have my health and that I'm still able to make a difference.

"Some people say, 'I don't really understand what you are buying and selling.' To a business person what we are doing is a weird concept. To several wealthy people I have spoken with, what we are doing is a waste of time. I tell them that our goal is to enrich our community and to do so we need to keep the door open. We know we have to pay the electric bill. The café is making money. We are hosting a variety of musical events of every genre. These things will help us make ends meet. We know we have to make this a viable business, but we are driven to enrich the community.

"We need to see what God put here in the first place, our mountains and our scenery and our air and water. No, it's not an industrial city anymore. The cities in West Virginia that are transitioning well are showcasing their natural environment and the quality and creativity of the people. West Virginia is still a wonderful place and an inexpensive place to live. If people can see that, they can provide a whole new beginning. The structure of the whole country is changing.

"There are lots of people from what I will call 'the old guard' who talk about 'their' town. They speak of it as if it were a church to which you must be a member. I don't have all the answers, but I tell them that if they don't welcome new people and ideas, we will die. Sometimes new ideas seem flighty, extravagant, or uncomfortable to the old way. Doing things in the future the way we did things in the past is a dead end."

Marshall Miller
Ron Mullennex
Bluefield, Virginia

Marshall Miller & Associates serves the fossil fuels, transportation, and land development industries with a number of engineering and geological services. Their office is in an industrial park near the state line in Bluefield, Virginia. MMA has more than 200 employees in 12 offices in 10 states. MMA is a diversified company that helps other companies find coal, oil, and natural gas resources underground. Its other services are groundwater remediation, site assessment, characterization and cleanup, and other things that improve the quality of our water and land.

I met with Marshall Miller, Chairman and CEO, and Ron Mullennex, Vice President.

Marshall said, "In this part of the world, when you go far below the surface you find high-quality coals. The problem is some of those seams may not be thick enough to justify mining. Much of the coal is metallurgical coal, used in the process of making steel. Our customers are the major coal companies. They desire to safely mine their coals and to produce as much as they can from the resource. Our job is to tell them where that coal is, the quality of the resource, and the sustainability of it. We produce relatively detailed mapping, graphical representations of the position, thickness, composition, and quality of the strata."

Ron said, "In our 30-plus years in business we have applied geological sciences to the understanding of how these coal seams are distributed and what makes them good or bad in terms of mineability. Our expertise is in helping miners and mine owners understand what problems they are likely to encounter and how to deal with those problems."

Marshall said one of the problems was the release of methane gas. In prior years, miners vented the gas to the atmosphere. "Particularly in the mid-Appalachian coal regions where you have these high-quality metallurgical coals, the methane gas is a valuable resource. [Capturing it] is a winning proposition in two ways. First, we remove the methane gas, which is a potential explosion risk, thereby increasing mine safety. Second, we capture the energy of the gas to sell on the market."

With their knowledge and expertise about the coal industry, they were intimately familiar with the risks and controversies, including accidents. Ron said, "Every industry that is subject to industrial accidents should do everything it can to minimize or prevent those accidents. Nobody in the coal industry would ever argue against that. That doesn't mean that we should not mine coal for the benefit of our nation. The United States has more coal than any nation on earth. President Bush talked about us being addicted to foreign oil. What we are really addicted to is inexpensive energy. The one ace in the hole that we have is coal. I believe it is the responsibility of the mining industry to mine it in the safest, most environmentally benign way it can.

"All industries have their own sets of environmental effects. The coalfields, both on the border you're studying and beyond, are populated largely because of the presence of coal. There generally isn't anything else that would provide economic livelihood. The topography does not allow for any significant industrial development."

Ron said he was particularly interested in underground water. "Water is a big issue in this country; really in every country. It is a challenge to preserve and maintain the quality of our water. Subsurface mining can actually increase the storage capacity of underground water. There is a huge potential water resource that has been created unintentionally as a byproduct of underground mining. Is this good or bad? I will say that there are instances of both. In some cases there can be some acid generation. The coal in this part of the country does not produce acids. There are a lot of municipalities in this region that use those mines as underground reservoirs for public drinking water. It is naturally good quality water.

"At the headwaters of Elkhorn Creek is a gushing spring that you can see from the side of the road on US-52 between Bluefield and Welch. You will often see people filling up water jugs from the back of their pickup trucks with that water. This is a discharge from an abandoned mine, the Pocahontas #3 coal seam. The seam has primarily played out, but the void within the mountain is collecting water and is discharging it at this spring where it then becomes a major tributary of Elkhorn Creek. The Elkhorn is the premier trophy trout stream in the state.

"There is a large underground water resource that has a great potential to help our country. West Virginia is concerned right now about its water resources and is starting to quantify this resource. There are severe droughts in surrounding states, primarily to the south. There is tremendous population growth all around West Virginia. There is growing interest and potential in mining this water resource and sending it via pipeline to some of the rapidly growing areas.

"Our water resource can support a multitude of uses: industrial, recreational, and just general use. The water is also at a consistent temperature and therefore can be used as a heating or cooling sink for geothermal energy. The bottom line is that the water resource is there now because the coal resource has been removed. I am not trying to paint a picture that is slanted one way or the other. Mining has certainly had its negative effects."

Marshall said, "One of the best things the coal industry has done, to its credit, is work to preserve the environment. During the process of inspecting mines, the rules, regulations, and expectations for maintaining the environment have been clearly defined and emphasized. Miners know now they need to protect the water, avoid degradation of the value of neighboring properties, and do proper reclamation."

Ron said, "There is some fluctuation in tonnage production from year to year, but generally the last five years have seen the greatest production of all time. Economic conditions and technologies dictate what new coal is mineable. We are able to reach and extract seams today that were impossible years ago."

Both men were intimately familiar with the controversy around mountaintop removal mining. Ron said, "I am sure this is what many environmentalists or 'so-called environmentalists' would prohibit altogether. I use the word 'so-called environmentalists' because I think some people are really anti-industrialists. I will be the first to admit that our industry has had some environmental problems and excesses in the past. I see both sides of the issue every day. I split my time between mining work and environmental work, so I'm vitally interested in maintaining the quality of our land and water."

Marshall said, "We have seen a change in the mindsets of those who have survived in the coal mining industry. Those that have survived are now working hard to protect the environment. Those that never gave a damn are not here anymore.

"There have been several recent articles about the strength of the West Virginia economy and the capabilities within the state. The capabilities have been extraordinary. West Virginia has had a good economic year whereas most of the traditional economically powerful states have been suffering. I think it is largely because of the abundant natural resources we have in West Virginia."

Danny Smith
Bluefield

Pocahontas Land Corporation is Norfolk Southern's natural resource subsidiary. Pocahontas owns or manages a million acres of coal-bearing property in West Virginia and other Appalachian states.

Danny Smith is senior vice president of Norfolk Southern and the president of Pocahontas. Danny was born in Bluefield, West Virginia. "I have been with [Norfolk Southern] for 33 years. When I was in college I also worked for U.S. Steel at its Gary Number 4 coal mine in Gary, West Virginia. I am a third-generation railroader. The railroad provided a great living for my grandfather and father.

"The Norfolk and Western built a line along the New River in the late 1870s. They loaded the first carload of coal and delivered it to Norfolk for export in 1883. The company built a coal loading facility at Lamberts Point in Norfolk. Today it is the largest coal loading facility in the world. In 1992, we shipped 40 million tons of coal through there. Last year we did 17 million tons of coal. The downturn is primarily about the competition."

Almost 2 billion tons of coal have been mined from Pocahontas and affiliated properties. While Pocahontas continues to purchase new lands and mineral rights, they admit being on the downside of potential coal extraction, with 1¾ billion tons remaining. Smith said Appalachian coalfield extraction was several years past peak. "The peak for Central Appalachian coal fields, which include West Virginia, Virginia, and Kentucky, was sometime in the late 1980s.

"The Pocahontas Land Corporation was formed in 1901 when the Norfolk and Western Railroad bought some property. The original purchase was for 300,000 acres, and it has been expanded over the decades. Most of the land is in West Virginia, but we also own land in Kentucky, Southwest Virginia, Illinois, and Alabama.

"'Pokie' was originally formed to manage mineral rights. These days, we lease those extraction rights to mining companies to mine the minerals. We have sold the gas rights and the timber rights, but we still own surface rights. For years we have replanted timber on previously mined land and have overseen the harvesting of the timber to ensure that it was being done in the proper manner."

As head of Pocahontas Land Company, Smith explained the issues of mountaintop removal mining from the company's point of view. "Critics will show active mine operations, but they never show the results of our reclamation efforts. We are not really filling in running streams, as critics often assert. During a rain, water will fall more or less uniformly over a mountain. When we do mountaintop removal mining, we have to find a place to put the excess rock. We prepare the hollows, and we begin to transport rock to them. As the water falls, it flows through these new rocky areas. These areas are not as steep as the mountain was originally, so the water lingers and more of it seeps into the ground. The overall elevation across the mine is lower when we finish than when we began. But we do not make it as steep or as hard as we found it. There is typically no topsoil when we began because the land is so steep the topsoil is continually eroded away. Mountaintop removal mines leave the land with the potential for more topsoil, better wood production, and more ecological diversity than when we start."

Smith feels that his company is doing the right thing because it is good business. "Look at it this way. We not only own the mineral rights but we own the land. We are looking to do something with the land afterwards. We have worked with economic development people and with recreational people. We are always looking to leave the land better than we found it."

I said, "I think you will agree with me, Danny, that the coal industry has not always been a good corporate citizen."

He said, "Citizens of the United States have not always been good citizens, either. We have never missed a tax payment. We have every incentive to do something [valuable] with the land. We have employed people in timbering. We employ people in the railroad. People work for us, and we care about them.

"The railroad industry is a good industry that has provided excellent employment for thousands of intelligent and dedicated people. Norfolk Southern has provided for my family for three generations.

Coal mining provides for many good-paying jobs.

"Many people are still employed in coal mining. When an auto plant shuts down, the people often move away. When the automotive industry was in its heyday, a lot of people from West Virginia moved to Detroit and the other automotive cities. This is the way the United States is.

"This area has an exceptional quality of life. There are economic development people working in this region who are constantly searching for jobs that will keep people employed. If you have a pool of people with a strong work ethic, you have an excellent foundation."

Dana Stoker Cochran
Louise Dawson Stoker
Bramwell

The sister towns of Bramwell in Mercer County, West Virginia, and Pocahontas in Tazewell County, Virginia, grew around one of the richest coal deposits on earth in the 1880s. Nowadays, both towns are off the beaten path and are set in pleasant mountain coves.

Bramwell was once home to many coal barons and still boasts a dozen mansions. Pocahontas was larger and more vibrant, and one of the most ethnically diverse towns in the nation, but has suffered greatly during the decline. It is wracked with decrepitude and its general store, synagogue, opera house, and many churches are literally in ruins. An impressive graveyard wrapped over a knoll marks the entrance to town, sporting tombstones in a half-dozen languages.

Louise "Lou" Dawson Stoker is the current mayor of Bramwell. Lou is a vivacious woman, thin as a split-rail fence, with traditional elegance and style. Her daughter Dana Stoker Cochran has flowing red hair and a quick wit. She teaches at Bluefield State College and is working on her doctorate at Virginia Tech. They wrote a book together, *Bramwell, A Town of Millionaires*.

Dana said, "There is a certain mystique about Bramwell. Growing up here, I always knew it was special. Our high school principal, Mr.

Photo by Tracy Roberts

Downtown Bramwell

Dwight W. McCormick, was imbued with the importance of history and place. We all grew up with the sense of history that Mr. McCormick impressed upon us.

"The town of Pocahontas itself is the heart of the great Pocahontas coalfield. By 1883, people were flocking here. The people who came to own the mines and become millionaires gravitated to Bramwell, which became the enclave of the professional classes."

Mayor Lou said, "Bramwell was and still is populated by a diverse group of nationalities. They were from England, Wales, Germany, and Italy. Wales was highly represented because of the already established mining industry there.

"In 1884, a second mine was opened by a man named Mr. John Cooper in Coopers, between here and Pocahontas. This was the second mine in the Pocahontas coalfield, but it was the first in West Virginia. Before he died in 1899, Mr. Cooper was president of the Bank of Bramwell." She pointed directly across the street to a stately old gray stone building which housed the bank.

Pocahontas, Virginia, ironically, is west of Bramwell, West Virginia, just three miles away. Dana said that, during this 1880s period, "Pocahontas was a bustling place with tremendous commercial and mercantile activity. As close as Pocahontas and Bramwell were to each other, there were marked differences in them culturally and economically.

"In the heyday, from the turn of the 20th Century until the 1920s, there were 14 passenger trains from Bramwell into Pocahontas and into Bluefield. People were surprisingly mobile; they traveled all the time."

Lou said, "After that, the automobile and eventually the airplane began to dominate travel. There were still passenger trains coming through Bramwell until 1954, but for decades they were diminishing in importance. Since then, Bramwell went to sleep."

Dana said, "West Virginia still sees diminishing population. The population that has remained behind has aged. West Virginia has the oldest population in the nation. Many of the new people who move into the state are retired, so this statistic is likely to remain for some time."

Mayor Lou said the mansions built by the coal barons at the turn of the 20th Century are still there. "There is a magnificent stone house on the market for $325,000. There is a lovely Victorian house that is currently on sale, fully furnished, for $225,000.

"I was elected to my first term two years ago. I had 104 votes, and my opponent got 94 votes. I ran for mayor previously but was defeated. I have never run for, nor have I ever desired to hold, any other office."

Dana said, "Mom is running for re-election right now, unopposed, something that never happens in Bramwell. Bramwell has always had a history of activism. I have read that people in lower economic strata did not participate in political processes. That has not been true in West Virginia. This has always been a highly political state, and people are historically engaged in elections. In the election between George W. Bush and John Kerry, the number of people voting across the country was pathetic, but West Virginia was among the highest. This has always been a highly unionized state, and the union has traditionally encouraged voter participation."

Lou said, "Sometimes I say that progress has passed us by and we are glad. I joke that it only looks asleep when outside visitors are here. After everyone leaves it returns to Bramwell-doon [in comic reference to Brigadoon, the mysterious village in Scotland that appears only one day every 100 years]. There have been ups and downs in the economy, in the houses, and in the people, for different reasons over time. The last of the grand houses was built in 1914. The heyday of the community was in the 1920s, a vibrant time all over the world. This abruptly ended when the stock market crashed in 1929. Approximately 40 grand houses were built. Not all of them are still in existence.

"The Bank of Bramwell continued to function until 1933. Eventually, even the coal operators began to fail. Men begged to work for one dollar per day.

"In the early 1940s the United States entered World War II. The

Bramwell Mayor Lou Stoker

demand for coal skyrocketed, and people began to return to the mines. The coal from the Pocahontas Field powered the furnaces that made the steel that won the war. After the war, the demand for coal dropped off again. There was a major outmigration of people from the coal fields.

"Life was still good here in the 1950s. One of the things that made life so pleasant was that we had our old school, first grade through 12th grade. There was a tremendous amount of community spirit that was encapsulated around the school. This was a desirable community. We had a couple of gas stations and a movie theater. Even when the passenger train stopped, we still had bus lines serving the area.

"As far as our schools were concerned, school officials took off one finger at a time until they finally lopped off our hand. When there was first talk of closing our high school in 1988, we fought it like crazy until we finally lost in 1991. The school where our students were moved was down the river, and it was not accredited. It was not even located in an incorporated town. A few years later, our junior high school also closed. Finally, in 2004, our elementary school was closed. When a school leaves the community, the heart of the community goes away."

Dana said, "This community has always suffered from economic ups and downs, but the closing of our high school was probably the worst thing that ever happened here. Growing up, I assumed that everybody lived so wonderfully. It was a stable community. All of the kids I went to school with have remained friends. Even if we don't see each other for many years, we take up conversing as if we had never left. There is a closeness that many people in our nation have never experienced. We have a reunion every year for all graduates of Bramwell High School. It is a return to roots that is not duplicated anywhere. People who graduated here and moved away tell their friends about it and the friends say, 'I wish I had something like that.'

"Our population in West Virginia and in southwestern Virginia is rural. Our schools should naturally be smaller because the communities they represent are smaller. The notion that everything needs to be bigger and everything needs to be consolidated might work in urban settings, but it has not worked in this region. The children are on school buses for hours every day. It is not economically efficient, fuel efficient, or community efficient. It lowers the property valuations and that lowers the tax base. Prospective incoming families are often dissuaded from communities that have no schools.

"There is a total dichotomy of blessings between inside and outside Appalachia. We see family. We see place. We see our own home, even if it is a shack on the side of a hill, that at least it is ours.

"We don't mind being passed by or left alone. We are independent, and we can take care of ourselves. An outsider may think that because we do not have McDonalds or Wal-Mart we are not progressive. These things are not progress to us; they mean nothing. We value the things that lip service is paid to by everyone else. Family values are not a political slogan here. They are real everyday experiences.

"What has taken over our country? What is out there in America that Appalachia doesn't have that we could possibly want? Don't give us that commercial crap! Give us the things that mean something culturally. Give us back our community post offices. Give us back our general stores. Give us back our schools!"

Father Dan Brady
Pat Hurley
Pocahontas

Pocahontas' Hungarian Cabbage Roll Dinner has been held annually since 1936 in mid-October. Pocahontas, called Little Hungary in its heyday because of the influx of immigrants from that Eastern European country, is surrounded by low tree-clad mountains. The town, actually in Virginia's Tazewell County, has seen better days, and much of it is in an advanced state of disrepair. Buildings, residential or commercial, are crumbling, some with little more than exposed skeletal beams protruding through tattered shells of wood or plastic siding. Several downtown storefronts have intricate impressive European-inspired facades, backed by decaying structures. Nicely kept homes are surrounded by others almost buried in trash or burned rubble.

On a hill at the eastern edge of downtown is St. Elizabeth's Catholic Church, which hosts the culinary event. The church is an elegant white-framed building, from where there is a sweeping view of town. The front had an inviting set of stairs to a gabled door, flanked by steeply gabled windows. Above is a modest steeple with a tiny cross.

Dinner was served in the church basement.

Cabbage Roll is a classic Eastern European dish: meat mixed with rice and spices, wrapped in a cabbage leaf provided with a tomato-based red sauce. Side dishes included potato salad and overcooked green beans. From 1:00 p.m. until late afternoon, the women of the church served hundreds of all-you-can-eat meals to townspeople and visitors. Admission was $7.00. Several diners were in their Sunday finest, paper napkins tucked protectively into collars. Others were less formal, mostly wearing denim and flannel.

I met the parish priest, Father Dan Brady. We sat on the wooden steps of the rectory next door. He said, "I'll be the spokesman for this, but it is really the parishioners' event. This started out as a thank-you from the church to the mine owners. They invited family and friends. It opened to the whole town, and eventually visitors from all over came around. We'll serve around 500 sit-down dinners, and there are fewer people than that in town, so we're pulling from the surrounding areas."

"The church began before 1896, with the congregation meeting wherever they could. With the help of the Pocahontas Coal Company, [parishioners] were able to build the church primarily for the Hungarian community, but there were also Italians and Polish. The church is named for St. Elizabeth, the patron saint of Hungary.

"There was a tremendous influx of Eastern European people during the late 1800s. Owners of the mine literally scoured the world in search of people to work the mines. The mine was vast. It was one layer, up to twenty feet thick. It was once the richest seam in the world.

"The mine owners liked the Eastern Europeans because they didn't wander. In Europe, people were used to being in a town and staying there; this is where they're born, where their children were born, their grandchildren, so the owners had the mentality that if they brought those people here they'd stay. The families came and grew, the merchants came, and it was a true melting pot, very diverse. The workers lived here, within walking distance of the entrance of the mine, while the owners lived to the east in Bramwell.

"The town has few Catholics any more, about eight to ten. The church draws from Bramwell, Bluewell, from Princeton and the Bluefields, even. We have around 50 worshippers each Sunday, more on holidays — up to 70; sometimes as few as 35 or 40.

Originally from Long Island, New York, Father Brady said, "I love it here. It's been challenging. It's not challenging from an ecumenical viewpoint. In fact, the Baptists had a minister who 'put down' Catholics, and they fired him. The Baptists told this minister, 'These are our neighbors. You can't talk about them like that.' The challenges have been more personal. When you've been in front of people for sixteen years, you can't pull out homily number 634. Every time I get up there I have to start from scratch, and I have to think about where we are and where we've come. I've matured and I've grown here. It's an ongoing constant challenge."

The mayor of Pocahontas, Pat Hurley, was at the Cabbage Roll. He added, "Our population is diminishing. There are vacant houses all over town, properties that are not being kept up. When we lost the coal company, everything got worse, because this was a company town, and it provided well. Now that we don't have it, it's hard to change that mindset. Generations have been used to someone else taking care of things. Now too many things are left undone.

"Some economic development officials feel that our economic future is centered on tourism. Look down Main Street. We're losing our historic appeal day by day, brick by brick, window by broken window. So to get turned around, to be able to restore these buildings, we need to rebuild one brick at a time, one thought at a time."

The mayor told of one way that the town of Pocahontas got some civic improvement from a community in eastern Virginia. "We were flooded in July, 2002. The canal became filled with mud and debris. FEMA made promises. The Virginia Department of Emergency Services made promises. They were going to dredge the canal but never did. I never gave up the faith. Years earlier, the town of Franklin in eastern Virginia was flooded by Hurricane Floyd. The people of Franklin owed a debt of gratitude [to those who helped] and wanted to repay it by helping another town in need. Franklin is nearly seven hours drive away. Yet they came and dredged this creek for us. God's working here. We need to give him praise and glory for that."

Steve Mooney
Blacksburg (Montgomery County)

Steve Mooney is a Senior Instructor in English and a faculty member in Appalachian Studies at Virginia Tech. He has written extensively about the coal regions of the mid-Appalachians, on mountain life and coal societies. Steve's career started in journalism, covering the Virginia coal industry. He later got his Doctorate in English and began to teach at the university level. But all his people were coal miners.

"A common impression of Appalachia is based upon a set of ideals, both textual and iconic, that date largely from the Local Color Movement in American literature. This was from about 1875 until about 1920, the era when Appalachian culture was discovered at a national level. The Local Color Movement's intent was to appeal to its audiences' sense of the other, of the different, and of the strange and exotic. Coincident with this literary movement was the great shift in America from agricultural work and rural living to industrial work and urban living. Many of those people who had moved from rural areas into the cities of America began to long for that old rural way of life that they had known or perhaps their parents had known. There was more Local Color literature written about Appalachia than any other region.

"One of the ideas promulgated by the Local Color writers was that Appalachia represented a region that had never changed. It was supposedly a timeless static place where people lived the same way they did during the Revolutionary War. And according to the local colorists, all of those qualities that made America what it is — ruggedness, independence, strength of character, and a willingness to stand and fight, were still part of this land passed over by time. So almost by default, for those Americans casting about for a new wilderness, Appalachia becomes the last great frontier. It became the last repository of all of those great Anglo-Saxon virtues.

"The truth is that the development of America as a world-class superpower is directly indebted to the people of Appalachia. These are the people who dug from the ground the fuel that made the infrastructure of modern America possible. From coal we make steel and from steel we make skyscrapers, railroads, automobiles, and ships. People owe all these things to the labors of central Appalachians. And in postmodern America, people owe cheap and accessible electricity to Appalachian labor and — far more sadly — to the literal destruction of much of Appalachia's landscape.

"Both a beautiful and a problematic trait of mountain people is that they are characteristically humble. There are historical and cultural reasons for this humility. People began to arrive from Europe to the central Appalachians from about 1650 onward. They left mountains and they sought mountains. For mountain people there is a sense of sublimity and awesomeness in being on the top of a 5000-foot mountain and looking down a massive gorge to the river below or being at the bottom and looking up and seeing the top of the mountain lost in the clouds. Accompanying this sense of the sublime is a sense of the insignificance of the individual human being compared to the grandeur and majesty of the natural world. And to act prideful or arrogant in the face of this is the crossing of a line that cannot be crossed.

"There is something extremely satisfying in recognizing your own limitations, your own lack of importance compared to a much larger universe. And I think other people respond positively to this ability of mountain people to see their own insignificance.

"Personally, I am literally scared [of non-mountainous places]. I feel vulnerable and naked. Ridgelines make me feel protected and give me grounding. If there is only open space around me, I get the feeling that in any moment I could disappear into the universe.

"There are many Appalachias, with many subcultures within this larger cultural area. The different subcultures grew out of different ways of life. However, the thing that connects the subcultures is the essential ruralness of Appalachia as a whole and also to a degree, isolation. When people came together in any kind of collective way, they formed extremely strong senses of togetherness. Community has always been a defining feature of Appalachian life on both sides of the coal line.

"What is different is that from the last part of the 19th century for people in the coal areas, life became dominated by the rapid development of coal and timbering. Miners identified themselves, and they became identifiable by others, as coal miners because their entire life whirled around the development and production of coal. They became industrialized workers, even though the area remained largely rural. By 1910 there were about 600 coal towns throughout the mid-Appalachians. Life became urbanized, even if 'urban' meant only 300 people in a coal town.

"Most Americans, including many Appalachians, do not realize that most of the peoples' rebellions of the 20th century occurred in the central Appalachian coal fields. The single largest insurrection in American history outside of the Civil War occurred in the coal fields of West Virginia. As a result of actions like this, people became shaped by a sense of powerlessness, an unending struggle against a larger force that dominated their lives. What else could happen when people saw, on a regular basis, coal companies and private police and Army regiments that were ostensibly acting on behalf of law and order, browbeating them into submission?

"They asked, 'Why is it that with the arrival of this type of work our overall quality of life has decreased?' They asked, 'Why is it that when the nation has asked of us to provide the toil to produce this resource that the nation so desperately needs, are we so poorly rewarded?' On many occasions mountain people rose up and rebelled. They were always crushed. The world view of a person in the coalfields became different from that of an agrarian agricultural Appalachian.

"I want people to understand that contemporary conditions in the Appalachian coalfields are the result of actual, definable, traceable, historical, and cultural progressions. Things aren't the way they are because they were somehow meant to be or because there is an ingrained culture of poverty where people are so bound to place that they would rather suffer generations of abject poverty than to pick themselves up by their bootstraps and move to Houston. These people don't want to live in Houston. Mountain people may be characterized by some of the worst faults and flaws of humans, but they are also in possession of some of the greatest dignities and decencies. Things are the way they are because of reasons."

West Virginia

Kentucky

MCDOWELL

BUCHANAN

Grundy

TAZEWELL

Virginia

Buchanan County, Virginia

Buchanan County is at the southwestern end of The Spine of the Virginias. The county seat is Grundy, the county's only incorporated town. The county is completely within the coalfield region of the Cumberland Plateau and is characterized by modestly sized, irregularly positioned mountains encapsulating deep valleys.

There are 504 square miles.

Population

Buchanan County's population rose from approximately 10,000 in 1900 to 39,000 in 1980. Current population has dropped to about 25,000 due to the loss of jobs in extractive industries.

Institutions of higher education

Buchanan County is the home of the Appalachian School of Law in Grundy, which opened in 1997, and the Appalachian College of Pharmacy in Oakwood, which opened in 2005.

Traffic

Buchanan County has about twenty miles of four-lane roads and several traffic lights in and around Grundy.

Today's...

Buchanan County is revitalizing its economy, which was formerly deeply dependent upon the extraction of coal and timber. The law and pharmacy schools are bringing new ideas and vitality to the region. Many of the communities have been devastated over the decades by horrific floods. Because of the rugged topography, virtually every citizen lives and every business operates in a flood-prone area. The town of Grundy is undergoing extensive reconstruction as a means of flood control.

Attractions

- The cliffs of Grundy, Grundy

Big Sandy and Cumberland Railroad
Buchanan County

William McClellan Ritter's Lumber Company was at one point the largest producer of hardwood lumber in the world. He first became involved in timber operations in 1880 with a small circular sawmill at Oakvale in Mercer County, West Virginia. In the early 20th century he owned and operated several lumber mills in West Virginia, Virginia, and Kentucky. He died in 1952. Georgia Pacific purchased the mill in 1960. The town of Hurley in the northern corner of Buchanan County was intimately involved with the W. M. Ritter Lumber Company.

Ritter founded his own railroad line, the Big Sandy and Cumberland Railroad, in order to provide transit for his products to outside markets. The BS&C ran initially from Devon, West Virginia, southward, following Knox Creek into Kentucky briefly, then into Virginia just northwest of Hurley. This phase was in operation in 1903. Further extensions made a clockwise fishhook through Matney, Grundy, and eventually curved back to the Kentucky border.

Hurley became the core of operations for Ritter Lumber throughout Virginia, West Virginia, and Kentucky at the turn of the 20th century. In its heyday the company owned 300,000 acres of land and 72 locomotives.

Prior to the industrialization brought about by Ritter, nearly all of the timber in Buchanan County was cut and assembled alongside tributary streams. Without the power equipment of today, logging could only be profitable where transportation of the felled tree to market could be done economically. During the winter months, crews felled trees and used the snow cover to either slide the tree trunks themselves, or slide sleds loaded with tree trunks, to the drainages below. During mild winters without sufficient snow, logs had to wait for the following year. Using the freshets in the spring, logs were floated into deeper water to the Big Sandy River and eventually to the large sawmills along the Ohio River. Transportation was a significant cost to the lumber business.

Given the overall ruggedness of the area, railroads played an inestimable role in the development of Buchanan County. The arrival of the railroad in 1903 turned Hurley into a boomtown. The town boasted not only a large lumberyard and a terminus for the Big Sandy and Cumberland Railroad but also a hospital that served the greater community.

By 1905 the rail line extended from Hurley southward to Blackey, another 3½ miles. The line was then extended south from Blackey over Rock House Mountain at Rock House Gap with an impressive 6-percent grade and then steeply downward to Slate Creek to the village of Matney along current SR-83. Additional logging operations were established along Slate Creek, and another sawmill was built at Blackey. Passenger service was included in the rail operations.

The first train arrived in Grundy in 1916. The last major extension of the Big Sandy and Cumberland line turned back westward again and extended down the Levisa Fork to Kentucky.

The Railroad was essential to the development of this extremely mountainous region. Over 90 percent of the line was curved and grades were extreme. Photos show specially designed locomotives, like the Cass Scenic Railroad's Shay locomotives, navigating rugged terrain.

The Big Sandy and Cumberland railroad was eventually purchased by the Norfolk and Western and was incorporated into its overall operations in 1923.

Vern Presley
Grundy

Vern Presley is a lawyer in Grundy. His office in an industrial shell building turned into a retail and commercial shopping center.

Grundy and the entirety of Buchanan County are often beset with dreadful floods. Hurley's last flood in 2002 destroyed virtually every commercial structure and residence in the valley. Many residents rebuilt, moved to higher ground, or simply left town. Grundy had another plan.

After a particularly devastating flood in 1977 (photos show cars floating upside down, pressed against the upper windows of two-story buildings), town fathers got together with the U.S. Army Corps of Engineers and the Virginia Department of Transportation to forever alter the downtown.

The rescue plan envisioned for the town was four-fold, beginning in 2002. First, most of the downtown was razed. Second, three mountainsides were sculpted into cliffs, providing fill for a new, 13-acre flat site above the floodplain. Third, a four-lane road was built through what was the downtown, atop a raised embankment which would do double-duty as a floodwall. Finally, a new downtown was to be built. Amazingly, Wal-Mart, which is sometimes blamed for the demise of most American downtowns, was courted to build a superstore on this site.

The project involved moving 2 million cubic yards of rock. With demolition, new roadway construction, and erosion control, the tab has already exceeded $100 million. Grundy's population was around 1100 at the time, making the cost over $90,000 per resident. Work continued into 2009.

The day of my visit, work was ongoing on embankments and final grading and paving. Nothing was under construction on the new site; Wal-Mart had not so much as a sign expressing their intentions. Three immense cliff walls were marked by striated levels and vertical, exposed drill bores.

The shell building where Vern worked was the home of many of the displaced companies from downtown. He said, "In 1977 there were many strip mines, what today are called 'mountaintop removal' mines. We did have an exceptional amount of rain but without the vegetation at the top of the mountains to hold the water, it all came gushing off so fast that it overwhelmed the river's natural channel. We still have some mountaintop removal mining going on, but not to the extent that we had in 1977.

"Those of us who have lived in this county for our entire lives can tell you where the strip mines have occurred. When the reclamation laws came into effect, the mining companies did a better job, including the planting of many trees. A casual visitor may simply see the mountain and the vegetation and not realize that strip-mining had ever been done. If a tree was planted in 1977 it would already be 30 years old.

"Most of the mining in this area is done subsurface now. As far as I know, we only have one mountaintop removal project going on right now. It is in an area called Poplar Gap. The coal company is leaving behind several hundred acres that the IDA can use for residential and industrial development sites. The only flat land that you will see in this county is along the streambeds. These are where all the little hamlets and villages are located. Large tracts of flat land are rare.

"What you see across from the courthouse in the center of Grundy is a large flat tract of about 12 acres. It was formerly only about four acres but the rest was formed by the Army Corps of Engineers. That is where the redevelopment is planned. They have designed the road in such a way that the road grade itself will protect our courthouse from flooding.

"The decision to move forward on the project was controversial. There were people who wanted many of those buildings preserved and they were not in favor of the project. But I believe that the community was behind the project. The favorable sentiment has waned because of the delays.

"Most of the businesses that intended to stay in business during the project relocated to this building, the Grundy Plaza, which is owned by the Industrial Development Authority. Some business owners took a buyout and simply closed their doors. But perhaps half the buildings were already empty.

"The reconstruction plan is to erect what is called an urban design Wal-Mart. It will be a three-story retail and commercial building instead of a sprawling structure. VDOT will be building a parking structure and the Wal-Mart will be built atop that. No concrete has yet been poured [as of 2009].

"The Bristol paper ran an article recently contrasting the two towns of Abington and Grundy. Abingdon sees Wal-Mart crippling its downtown. Grundy is looking at Wal-Mart as being the saving grace for the town.

"The Appalachian School of Law has progressed well since its opening. Its admissions standards have improved. It has not actually received its full accreditation from the American Bar Association but that is soon to come. The Appalachian College of Pharmacy in Oakwood is seeing strong applications for enrollment as well.

"The overall population of the county has dropped over the past few decades. The students who are here for the law school and the pharmacy school are transient; only a few of them will remain behind. However, the law school has done a great deal to broaden the diversity in our community. I think in the early days its goal was to serve as an educator of Appalachian regional people from West Virginia, Kentucky, and Western Virginia. They are now getting students from all over southeastern United States and beyond.

"Several wealthy people invested a considerable amount of their own money in the formation of the schools. The county contributed as well. There was some resentment about that. Many people felt that if the county was going to invest millions of dollars into something it might be into manufacturing facilities that would put blue-collar people to work. Very few of the professors are local people.

"When we get the downtown finished, everyone will be pleased. These new academic institutions are giving our children something to aspire to. I think it has begun to change the attitudes of the parents. But these things take years.

"Both the law school and the pharmacy school encourage community service. Some of our school kids are seeing the graduate students at these colleges interacting in a community. They are coaching kids' sports. They are refereeing ballgames. The schoolkids have people they can look up to."

Appalachian School of Law
Grundy

The idea of the law school emerged from the mind of Joe Wolfe, an attorney in Norton, Virginia. He thought there should be a law school more accessible to the people of this region and that, as a business, the school would generate economic development. Grundy was selected because it had a suitable building and the Buchanan County Board of Supervisors was so completely supportive. The Board had the foresight to realize that the coal industry was on the downswing and that the economy needed to diversify. Fortunately they had adequate funding at the time.

Founded in 1994 and admitting its first students in 1997, the law school now admits 110 to 140 students each year. In addition to the typical law school topics, the school offers clinical programs for the exploration of ownership rights and mineral rights issues for indigent victims in Appalachia. The school also differentiates itself from others by its emphasis on Alternative Dispute Resolution, to help clients resolve differences without having to go into the courtroom. The school fosters a sense of collective achievement as opposed to the competitiveness that is common at other law schools.

The school has an emphasis on community service and leadership skills, because it recognizes that lawyers are often called upon to be leaders in their communities. Many students are from small towns and return to those small towns to practice law. The school has provided a viable economic benefit. Most of the students live in the community, paying for housing, food, fuel, and other products. Tuition is $20,000 to $22,000 per year and the school has 15 to 17 faculty members, who are paid salaries commensurate with their profession.

In 2002, three people were fatally shot by a disgruntled student who is now serving a life sentence. As horrific as it was, ironically, it helped the school to gain national recognition. Applications to the school actually increased.

Frank Kilgore
Lebanon (Russell County)

Frank Kilgore is an attorney with a practice in St. Paul, Virginia, and is a founder of the Appalachian School of Law. Kilgore is one of the few attorneys who passed the state bar exam without attending law school. He read the law and successfully passed the test. He has been practicing ever since 1982 while working on conservation, youth development, and health care issues in the coalfields.

About the Law School, he said, "It struggled initially both in terms of getting teachers and students. It was difficult to bring quality professors to the area. It has a great faculty and staff now, but it took a while. It has 360 students. We have well-credentialed and well-published faculty. The school now generates between $10 million and $12 million annually in economic impact. It gave a lot of people in Buchanan County an optimistic spirit that they could do anything if they set their mind to it.

"Based upon that success, the Board of Supervisors asked me if I could generate ideas for similar schools. We began to look at healthcare colleges and opened a pharmacy school. We recruited a Dean and support staff and in August of 2005 we had a grand opening and welcomed our first class. Last year we had 1300 student applications for 65 slots. This year we will have even more than that. We have sixteen on the faculty now and we need eight more."

The University of Appalachia with its Appalachian College of Pharmacy gives an umbrella for creating additional colleges. He said, "There are plans to establish other healthcare-related colleges. I am looking now at a Masters program in natural resource development. I believe this would be an ideal place for that type of college. Every kind of land-use issue possible is now going on somewhere in Appalachia.

"Our future is definitely brighter than it used to be. One of my main goals is to retain and educate our best and brightest students here in Appalachia. Eighty-one percent of our first graduating class at the pharmacy school stayed in Appalachia. We give priority admission to mountain residents.

"Lots of people look at problems and complain about them. I look at the source of problems and fix them. Failure happens often when the goals are set high, but without setting them high, nothing gets done."

Patrick Owens
Grundy

Patrick Owens is owner of Terra Tech, a civil engineering company in Grundy. He told me, "We started our company to provide services that would allow things to be done the way we thought things should be done. One of our major customers is the Buchanan County Industrial Development Authority. Another is Buchanan County itself. One is a company called Paramount Virginia Mining Company, which is a division of Alpha Natural Resources.

"The County Industrial Development Authority in conjunction with Paramount has taken on a tremendous project southeast of town called Southern [formerly Poplar] Gap. When the project is completed, there will be approximately 1600 acres of flat ground that will never flood. This is only available for development because of mountaintop removal mining. The Industrial Development Authority is compensating them for placing their excess material in certain places and in certain ways and in developing roads that ultimately could be converted into commercial access roads.

"In my opinion the enormous amount of money that was spent on this project through downtown could have built a road through Southern Gap, and have created much, much more developable acreage. And it is only about 10 miles from downtown.

"There is no flat land in Buchanan County unless we create it. The county's early development arose from timber extraction. Development relied on access to the water because the logs were floated downstream. There was considerably more water in these rivers in that era.

"The only flat ground we have already has something built on it. If something is torn down or burned down or flooded out, nothing can be rebuilt in its place because it is in a federally designated flood zone. The only way we will ever develop anything here, and if we don't develop something we will eventually perish, is to put it on a reclaimed (mine) site. We need to develop some flat ground. And, we must develop roads to get there.

"However, in my opinion, what we have done to downtown Grundy is way less desirable than most mountaintop removal mines."

Arlene Justus Stacy
Hurley

For two reasons, I was apprehensive about visiting Hurley, one of Virginia's most remote communities. First, they had had a flood in 2002 and I wasn't sure what level of recovery the town had seen. Second, I was aware that the Confederate Rebel, the symbol of intolerance, was the mascot of their high school.

I arrived on a hot summer day and met Arlene Justus Stacy at her brother's restaurant, the Rebel Café. She told me, "I have lived in Hurley all my life. Everybody knows everybody, and we are like family.

"Hurley sits at the junction of Knox Creek and Lester's Fork. They join right here in the center of the village, and they flow to the west into Pikeville, Kentucky. Both of the creeks are prone to flooding. In the flood of 2002 the restaurant was lifted from its foundation. Trailers were swept downstream in the creek. The market was completely flooded out."

Two houses across from the Café were ruined. "When the floodwaters began to rise one resident was unable to escape. He climbed into his attic and had to knock a hole in his roof. He was rescued by a helicopter. He had called his son with a cell phone and bid him farewell, he was so convinced he was going to drown.

"The flood was from an afternoon storm in May of 2002. It came right out of the blue. I don't know if it was a cloudburst or what, but it just kept coming. My husband had a family member who lived in a trailer. The flood swept the trailer away with him in it and it killed him. The other fatality was a young man who was just walking down the road. The waters rose so rapidly that it literally swept him away.

"We watch and evacuate if we have to. When it was a'floodin' my brother had to put his wife on his back and carry her into the hills. I looked out from my house up in the holler and I looked out to the stream and there were trees and boulders being swept away in it. I didn't know which way to go. It was really scary.

"My family that I come from, named Justus, we were outlaws. Our family seemed to have been cursed. My great-grandmother was murdered. She lived about 6 miles down the road, up in a holler. Her name was Elizabeth Baker Justus. She sold her trees to the Ritter Lumber Company, which was a big operation here. There was a man who worked there as a foreman named Harold Little. At one point in 1909 she sold some lumber and was paid over $1000. Elizabeth's husband, Hiram, was deceased.

"Elizabeth and Harold Little were friends. He made up a reason to spend the night on her sofa. During the middle of the night, he was rifling through her pocketbook looking for the money. When she woke up, he killed her and cut her up with a hatchet. She was in her fifties by then. He then shot and killed the son-in-law, who was probably in his thirties. Then he set the house on fire, killing her daughter and her daughter's three sons. Harold Little was the first man to ever be electrocuted in the state of Virginia. They were hanging murderers before that. I suppose that electrocution was thought to be more humane than hanging. A beautiful monument, about 8 feet tall, was erected at my old homeplace where the remains were buried."

"Elizabeth had a son who was murdered. She had cousins that were murdered. It's really scary, all of my family members who were murdered. It has been a long time since anyone was murdered so in a sense, these are better days. When I go to the cemetery I see the tombstone of my uncle Delbert Justus, who was murdered. He was with another man's wife. His sister, who is buried down below him, she was shot and killed. She was a-cheating. I have two cousins who were buried together, and one was killed in a hit-and-run and the other one was apparently stabbed. I could keep going but it is getting embarrassing.

"I was seventeen when I was married and eighteen when my first daughter was born. It is typical for people here to marry young, sometimes even younger than I was. It wasn't nothing to be married at fifteen and be having children right away. Nowadays we are strict on education so you don't really see too much of that.

"My daughter had three girls and right now she is getting ready to be a grandma. When that happens I will be a great-grandma. My mother is living and her mother is living. We are getting ready to have a sixth generation family picture. My daughter is thirty-three and I have two sons. My granddaughter will be eighteen in October. Everybody is still here in the Hurley community. My granddaughters are all smart, and I want them to get a good education so they can go far."

Polly Justus
Hurley

Polly Justus, a retired schoolteacher, was in her late 60s. She had a gentle manner and spoke with an absence of any accent, even though she was born and raised in Hurley.

"I can remember when we first got electricity," she told me. "I was only a schoolchild but I remember the man who worked on putting up the poles and stringing the powerline. He would come to our house to get water. Our water came from an open well.

"We raised our garden. We had a smokehouse. We killed our hogs and cured the meat with salt and pepper. We dug our onions from the garden and we hung them in bunches. We had chickens and cows so we had both the meat and the eggs and milk that they produced. And our neighbors did okay as well because neighbors always helped neighbors. We had several acres planted in corn and when it was time to hoe out, each neighbor would go and help each other hoe out their fields. We had one neighbor who slaughtered the beef. He raised the sugar cane and made molasses. He gave my mother several jars each year. My mother would make popcorn balls using the molasses, and we had popcorn balls in the wintertime.

"I was a schoolteacher. My early education was right here in Hurley. I was valedictorian of my graduating class. I went to Pike-ville College for my degree. From there I went to Morehead State College in Kentucky and got my masters degree in education and psychology.

"The 2002 flood was absolutely devastating. Floodwaters literally ran through my house. It took the brick foundation from under the house and swept the porch furniture off the porch.

"I still can't go to bed at night without having nightmares about that time. It took at least six months before we returned to any semblance of normalcy. We had no bank or post office. Our store was destroyed so we couldn't get groceries. I give kudos to Appalachian Power because they really did a wonderful job restoring our electricity within six to ten days.

"I think people in Hurley today are prouder. We weathered that storm. My brother has gone through three floods. He lost everything he owned each time.

"I really don't want to live in any other place. But if you saw what I saw and experienced what I experienced in the flood you would understand. We have rebuilt now better than we were before. We have now a Dollar Store, a pharmacy, a clinic, and a beautiful park. We have a wonderful grocery store and café."

About the Rebel, the school mascot, she said, "I taught for years under the Rebel flag at Hurley High School. There is virtually no racial diversity here. Over time we have had a few black students. Those I taught never seemed to be uncomfortable. But of course, I can't know their personal feelings. I think the mascot should be changed. I think it takes us back to a time I am not proud of; it makes me cringe.

"I can tell you for a fact that this community is not racist. People are no more racist here than anywhere else."

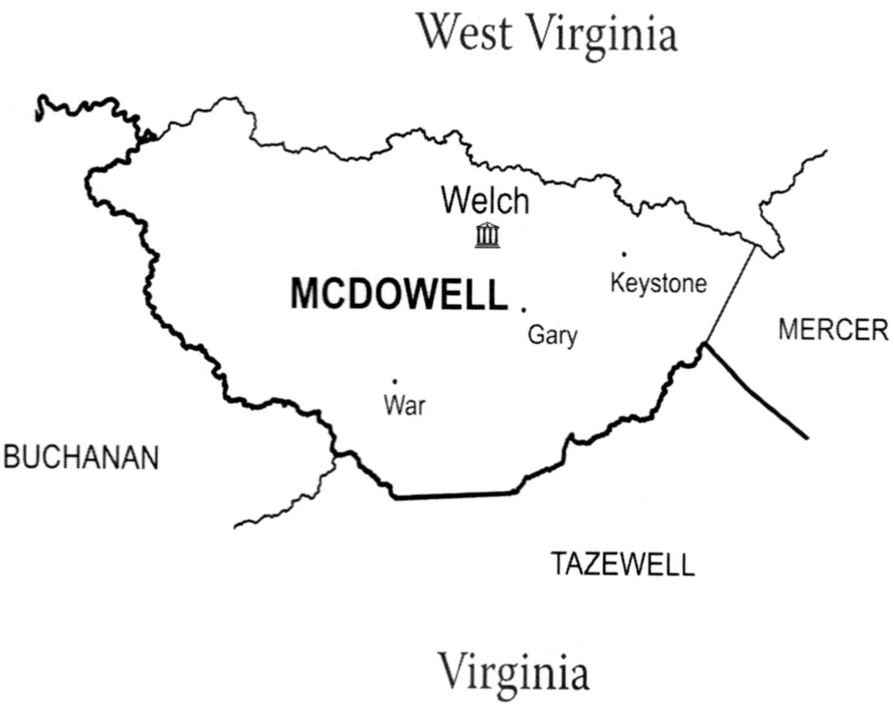

West Virginia

Welch

MCDOWELL

Keystone

Gary

MERCER

War

BUCHANAN

TAZEWELL

Virginia

McDowell County, West Virginia

McDowell County is wholly within the Cumberland Plateau and is deeply corrugated, with steep mountains and narrow valleys. Most of the population lives along the streams or in the hollows. Referred to as "The Free State of Mc-Dowell", it boasts a social and political environment thought not to be matched elsewhere in the state. It has by far the state's lowest per-capita income and the highest minority population, at roughly 12%.

McDowell County has 535 square miles.

Incorporated cities include Gary, War, Welch, and Keystone. There are another 83 unincorporated towns.

Population

McDowell County hosted dramatic rises and falls in population. From an estimated 2500 in the 1870s, McDowell grew to 19,000 by 1900, then 48,000 by 1910, at which time it was The Spine of the Virginias' most populous county. By 1950, at 99,000, it was West Virginia's third most populous county. From there, it plummeted to about 23,000 today. The population decline continues by several hundred people annually.

Institutions of higher education

There are no colleges or universities in McDowell County.

Traffic

McDowell County has no four-lane roads and two traffic lights. The county is laced with railroad tracks, many abandoned, and there is no passenger service.

Today's...

McDowell County has suffered mightily from the downturn in coal extraction employment. Once the home to 40,000 miners, there are perhaps only 1500 today. McDowell has yielded more high-grade coal than any county east of the Mississippi. Because of the difficult topography and exodus of people, diversification of the economy has been largely unsuccessful. Flooding, often severe, is a constant threat, causing significant numbers of fatalities, great economic losses, and personal trauma.

Attractions
- Anawalt Wildlife Management Area, Anawalt
- Berwind Lake Wildlife Management Area, Berwind
- Panther State Forest, Panther
- Hatfield-McCoy trail, various places, four-wheeler trail

McDowell County

Exploring McDowell County is an intensely riveting emotional experience. McDowell County is a cultural maelstrom and a jolt to the sensibilities. It is a woven texture of human triumph and tragedy. McDowell is not for the faint of heart or mind. In the process of researching this book, I often commented, "I began the process thinking I had 19 counties to cover; I came to realize I had 18 and McDowell."

The story of McDowell County, pronounced by the locals as MAC-dal, is the story of coal in Appalachia, told in its most grandiloquent and raucous way. Mac-dal is coal and coal is Mac-dal. McDowell is part of a six-county region straddling the southwestern tip of The Spine of the Virginias, which includes Mingo, Logan, and Boone in West Virginia, Buchanan in Virginia, and Pike in Kentucky, that has produced the most coal in the Eastern United States.

The actual border of Virginia and West Virginia as it extends to the north and east of Bluefield, follows an almost continuous line along the great ridge of East River Mountain and then Peters Mountain and then Allegheny Mountain for 150 miles. Between the Bluefields, the border swings abruptly northwestward on an arrow-straight line across the Bluefield Valley and then separates Pocahontas, Virginia, to the west, from Bramwell, West Virginia, to the east, before regaining its bearing and heading west again, forming the southernmost cupped palm of West Virginia.

Almost everyone in McDowell lives in one of the confined villages, former coal camps, or in the tight hollows. In most villages, many residences are occupied and in decent to fine condition. Some are crumbling piles of rubble, with exposed beams and plumbing, drooping asphalt tile shingles, and sheets of fiberglass insulation waving in the breeze. Roadside trash is ubiquitous, especially in the streams. The high-water flood-mark can be seen by where the rubbish line ends on the overhanging shrubbery. Forests and shrubbery grow profusely in the coal-enriched soils.

However insufficient they may be in describing the mosaic of life,

The Tug River bridge

statistics tell a story themselves, and three are worthy of mention here. McDowell County is the epicenter of the richest of the Appalachian coalfields and has given our nation more coal than any in the Eastern United States and has thus produced immeasurable wealth. West Virginia leads the nation in sub-surface mining. And yet McDowell is the poorest county, per capita, in one of the poorest states.

McDowell has a topography resembling the deep recesses of the brain. Mountains form the backdrop to every outdoor photo I've ever seen. The continual sense of being within the folds of the earth is palpable.

Like Buchanan County, everything is so steep that almost all commercial and residential developments are within a stone's throw of a watercourse. Most have railroad tracks snaking alongside. The railroad claimed the best land early on, with the commercial developments associated with mining second in line. What was left was fought over by stores, schools, and finally the homes. Few homes are built on flat land.

There are seemingly three types of McDowell Countians: those who grew up and stayed (some), those who grew up and left (many more), and those who grew up, left, and came back (few), but virtually nobody in decades has moved in. McDowell has thousands of vacant structures and is littered with millions of pounds of abandoned industrial equipment and household stuff.

Pete Ballard
Welch

Welch, the county seat of McDowell County, is situated at the confluence of several creeks, the largest being the Tug Fork of the Big Sandy River. Steep mountains surround the city on every side and tightly confine it. Houses and stores hug the roads that emanate like tendrils from the downtown hub. Being the center of a once-thriving area, there are many grand houses. Welch is steep and dense. Houses on hillsides above the street have dozens of stairs up from the road to the front porches.

The most detailed account prior to my personal visit was from Welch native Pete Ballard. Pete is currently a resident of Peterstown, in Monroe County, where he makes exquisite fashion dolls from the 1800s by hand in his apartment. In his resonant, nicotine-laced voice that sounded like the radio announcer for the Metropolitan Opera, he said, "I was born in McDowell County, which I still believe is the most intriguing place in the world. When I grew up in the '30s, McDowell County was as cosmopolitan a place as you could find outside of Manhattan. I was related to everybody in town one way or another.

"The coal resource meant there was a lot of money. Welch in the '30s was a community of 6000 people that had two ballrooms and had tea dances once a week. It had vaudeville houses. It had two top theaters with excellent stages for vaudeville; a vibrant scene. It had the Zigfield Follies. Culturally it had everything, from Fritz Chrysler to the ballet to the symphonies. The theaters were highly supported and every performer you could think of came to Welch.

"The Jewish population of Welch was extraordinary. There was class. My mother said that Northfork in the '20s had the best ladies' shops anyplace including Manhattan. It all came down by train.

"My grandfather owned the bank. A lot of the people who settled the area were expatriated Southerners. They had to go someplace else to start over after the (Civil) War. A lot of them went to the mountains but they were educated; they were lawyers and doctors. And so they just resumed their practices and they got in at the ground floor of the coal industry.

"Welch was exactly like Virginia City and Butte, Montana, and all those other Wild West (boom) towns. They all had whorehouses. One of the most notorious red light districts was in Keystone. It was called Cinder Bottom.

"Keystone was one of the small feeder towns that surrounded Welch. Others were North Fork, Gary, and Coalwood. Each community had its individuality because of the nationalities that lived there. My cousin was the head of the U.S. Coal and Coke Company in Gary, which was a lovely mining camp — gosh it was a beautiful camp! There was extraordinary diversity. There was no racial prejudice that I could tell.

"We were all raised in this potpourri, this melting pot. Everybody contributed. It was good. Of all the places God could have let me be born, I was born in Welch.

"Now I'm in Peterstown, which was named for my ancestor, Christian Peters, in 1793. After the Revolutionary War, he had what was then referred to as a house of private entertainment — a whorehouse. It seems that such a house was a family occupation until about 1840. When the courthouse was established in Union in 1820, many members of the Peters family kept getting hauled up for operating illegal houses of private entertainment."

Pete showed me one of the dolls he'd just finished. "In the 18th century the dolls were made by fashion houses because there was no media to advertise their work. They were shown to prospective customers who would then place orders for their dresses. This doll is wearing an afternoon costume from 1831. I copied her from a fashion magazine from that year. Her dress is made out of green satin and antique black lace. Her muff is made from Hudson Bay seal. The hat is a typical hat from the period with a high crown and lots of froufrou, ostrich feathers and chicken feathers.

"I donate the dolls to historic houses, to small museums that can't afford costume collections. I have probably from 250 to 300 hours work in each. I get materials anywhere I can. Once I found an 1845 ball gown of my great, great, great, great grandmother's that was made of silk. I was able to take the silk dress apart, wash it carefully in a bathtub, and I had just enough material to sew it back into a new dress for one of my dolls. This doll is wearing an 1845 ball gown made of 1845 silk. It's worth $10,000.

"I think for any artist, this part of southern West Virginia is perfect. All creative people need their solitude."

Martha Moore
Welch

The courthouse in Welch is on a hill. This grand structure was designed in the Romanesque Revival style. It has a square cross-section tower with a pyramid on top, with each face featuring a handsome clock. It is infamously associated with the assassinations of Sid Hatfield and a companion, Edward Chambers, in 1921. Hatfield was former Police Chief of Matewan and a central figure in the Coal Mine War, also known as the "Matewan Massacre." Earlier the same year, Hatfield had allegedly killed a private detective of the Baldwin-Felts Agency. A well-known and flamboyant labor leader, Hatfield boasted of killing three men. He was in Welch that day to stand trial. Several Baldwin-Felts men met and shot him on the courthouse stairs. None of the detectives was ever charged.

The grand main entrance is no longer in use and the new entrance is on a breezeway on the side. The inside is antiseptic and unremarkable.

Most of the storefronts downtown are vacant. There is a lunch café, a flower shop, and a Chinese restaurant. The Welch Municipal Parking Garage, when completed in 1941, was the first municipally- owned parking garage in the country. Nowadays it is unnecessary, as there is ample on-street parking. There is a modern multiplex movie theater and a small coal heritage museum.

The former First National Bank, Iaeger

I had scheduled a meeting with Welch's mayor, Martha Moore. On my way to her office, I was met outside by a flamboyant black man who introduced himself as Clif Moore. He told me he was the state delegate from this region and was running for re-election. I told him the reason for my visit and of my appointment with Mayor Martha Moore. "Come see me after you see Mayor Martha. I'd love to speak with you."

Mayor Martha Moore has a nice, modern office. She said, "I've been the mayor of Welch since 1986."

She said there were many challenges. "The coal companies made dependent populations. I couldn't know whether that was done purposefully. They took care of their people and when they left there was no one other than the government to step in and the government was not equipped to do so. After the big companies left, so did much of the population. Those who wanted to work found jobs elsewhere. The people who didn't want to work were those who were left behind.

"We are building a new federal prison near here. The construction alone, through Business and Occupational Taxes, will provide revenue for us to do a number of things I wanted to do twenty years ago.

"Floods have always plagued this valley. We actually had two 200-year floods within 10 months of one another in 2001 and 2002. This room was under three feet of water.

"We lost around 1700 or 1800 people throughout the County who moved away after the floods. Their homes were gone. They weren't going to deal with it."

About Welch's gloried past, she said, "If it was going on in New York, it was going on in Welch. It's hurtful that we aren't any more than we are now. But we continue to strive to do better. There are a lot of good people here working to make a difference and become more environmentally conscious and do things the right way.

"We have 90-some structures we are preparing to demolish in Welch. Until now, we simply haven't had the money. This is the stuff that will help us improve cosmetic things and take better care of our appearance."

I thanked Mayor Moore for her time. I entered the library and found Delegate Clif.

Clif Moore
Welch

Clif Moore is a delegate to the state Legislature from McDowell County, representing the 23rd legislative district, including the city of Welch, the city of Gary, and all of the communities along US-52 towards Bluefield. He was thin, with kinky jet-black hair swept back into a pony-tail, a Yasser Arafat beard, and wire-rimmed glasses. He wore designer jeans and a t-shirt that acted as a political billboard for himself. "Get Moore for your vote!" He told me, "This is a part-time legislative position. We meet from January 9th for 60 days. We are constitutionally bound to do that. My family has always been involved in public service. This ethic has been instilled in me since day one.

"McDowell County is an amazing place. It went from boom to bust on many occasions. At one point we had the highest income per capita of any county in West Virginia and now we're the lowest. We are at the top of every negative and at the bottom of every positive indicator of economic well-being."

I asked how it felt to be at the bottom of income statistics.

"Anger. Sadness. It is the whole gamut of emotions. I don't like to dwell on the negative. But you have to understand the negative in order to turn it into a positive.

"This county has always been ethnically diverse. I remember going to the company store on Saturdays and hearing Hungarian, Czechoslovakian, Russian, Italian, and Spanish spoken. I remember walking down the street and seeing different types of dress or smelling different kinds of foods coming out of people's houses. I remember different kinds of holidays being celebrated.

"Living here is almost spiritual. It has nothing to do with the economy. It has nothing to do with the social life because there isn't any. It's spiritual. It's almost like getting addicted to some kind of drug. I can't get it out of my system. People here have an indomitable spirit that no matter what happens, we will overcome. It's a spiritual experience being here.

"Growing up, I didn't know that families didn't get along. I didn't

381

know husbands and wives fought. I didn't know that mothers hated their children or children hated their parents. I always thought that everything was right, wonderful and beautiful. And I still think that today. And those things that are not right, wonderful and beautiful, I think we can fix them. I do.

"We never talked about the disparities and the racial thing. We never used the word 'minority' in my house. We thought everybody was the same.

"This place has often been referred to as the Free State of McDowell County. It was called this because people of all stripes could move here and be free. The people from the South could come here and be free. The tired immigrants could come here and be free. The Yugoslavians could come here and be free. They could be politically, socially and economically free. You have to understand that coal mining was a dangerous occupation. Your livelihood and your life depended upon working with other people.

"Back then, mining was a money maker. It was a great occupation. Given the dangers, the diseases, the health problems that people could get in the mines, probably 75 percent of the people I've ever talked with said if they had it to do all over again, they would've done the same thing. It bought health care, food, education, vacations, homes, and cars. It provided for families. Everything was about providing for your family.

"When you write about us, tell your readers not to feel sorry for McDowell County. We don't want sorrow or pity. We want partnership. We want people to come here and bring a business. Bring dollars, minds, and talents. We offer scenic beauty. Serenity. Low crime. Cheap housing. You can buy a house here for $75,000 that would cost you $400,000 or $500,000 in any city. Come to McDowell County and make this your home."

Coalwood

Coalwood is perhaps the most famous hamlet in McDowell County. It is the setting of the *New York Times'* bestselling memoir, *Rocket Boys*, by Homer Hickam, Jr. Hickam, "Sonny" to his friends, was fourteen years old when the USSR launched the satellite Sputnik. When he and his school chums saw it streak over the McDowell night sky, it captivated them and fostered a dream of building and flying amateur rocketry. The story is about his upbringing, his father's stern and unsupportive attitude, and his vision to pursue a career beyond the mines. The popularity of *October Sky*, the movie adaptation of *Rocket Boys,* has brought more tourists to Coalwood than perhaps anywhere in the County and is the subject of an annual festival which Hickam often attends.

The town sits two miles west of Highway 16, where a sign reads "Coalwood Unincorporated. Home of the Rocket Boys." During my visit, an earthmover sat in a huge pile of brick rubble, shuffling debris around, while a smoldering rubbish pile sent acrid smoke into the valley. I learned later that it had once been the Big (company) Store of which Hickam often spoke. Alawest, the absentee owner of the camp, had ordered it destroyed, much against the wishes of the townspeople who had hoped to restore it for tourism.

Across the way is a large, two-story white building with a drooping black shingle roof that serves as the Club House. The Coalwood Community United Methodist Church sits nearby and is a well-kept, traditionally styled, white-painted building with an impressive, pointed steeple. The former mine's machine shop has hundreds of broken windowpanes. Everything is rusty and damp. There are several nice houses in excellent repair nearby, but just as many in shambles. A pleasant structure with Tudor influences that appears to be a company bunkhouse or apartment building had a truck from a roofing company parked in the front and new tiles on the roof. I wondered what, if any, restoration may someday be done.

Tom Hatcher
War

Tom Hatcher is mayor of War, West Virginia's southernmost city. Although it has a city government, War is a mere village with fewer than 800 people. Tom's office is the former railroad station, a single-story white-painted wooden building. Outside is posted a large, stencil-lettered sign with each of the Ten Commandments. Tom's late model Buick sedan has a vanity license plate stamped boldly with the word "WAR."

Mayor Tom said, "About 1960, the mines started laying off people and then closing. One reason cited by the mine owners is that the unions got too strong and demanded too much and so there were some profit problems. Then in the 1970s, our country was importing coal that was cheaper to buy than domestic coal. Then there was the energy conversion when people were trying to eliminate pollutants and coal was a heavy polluter. So a lot of people switched to oil and to natural gas. All of those factors caused the big owners to close. The mine owners had provided the homes, stores, schools, and churches throughout these communities. They were involved in the miners' lives in almost every facet.

"This isn't a big coal area anymore. Even though more coal is being produced here than ever before, its impact on our economy and on the people has diminished.

"Our two biggest exports are coal and children. We make fun of ourselves sometimes because our kids, when they graduate from high school, take the Hillbilly Highway southbound. That's Interstate 77. That's a sad commentary on what's happened here.

"Before coal mining got underway there were only 2800 people in all of McDowell County. Although there was little farmland, some people were doing some meager farming. They were pioneering Virginia stock, primarily Scots-Irish by descent. But there weren't enough people here to mine the coal. The mine owners went to North and South Carolina, Georgia, and Alabama and recruited people to work in the mines. I would think that most of these were poorer people in the South. They latched onto many African-Americans. War in particular had a large number of African-Americans from Alabama.

"In 1906 the Norfolk and Western Railroad came. It formed the Pocahontas Land Company that became the land agent that bought up all of the land around us.

"This town was formed by five coal mine operators that came here after 1906. At one time there were about 4000 people here. Our home-owners own only 6 inches of dirt. The homeowner gets the sod and

Photo by Tracy Roberts

Mayor Hatcher and the jar of drinking water.

the grass and the coal company owns everything below that. This was established in state law and it has been upheld by court decisions. The coal companies bought up the lands in the early 1900s when people didn't really understand the value of the land. Today about 92 percent or 93 percent of the land in this county is owned by outside energy companies. It's a stunning statistic."

The mayor told me of the funding problems local governments have. "West Virginia has a homestead exemption which exempts the first $25,000 of property value. Since most War homes are valued at less, they pay no property tax at all. The land owned by corporations is outside of the tax structure. And traditionally, the coal exports have not been taxed. Although the land is extremely valuable for coal, timber, and more recently natural gas, the communities habitually struggle for revenue. The state legislature provides money for the school board authority to provide for schools.

"When I first became the mayor in 1997, the city had no sewer system and a water system that had been constructed in 1920 and hadn't seen any improvements since then. When the coal companies built these houses [in the early 20th century] there were no sewer systems. Their solution was to pipe the sewage to the creek. When the coal companies began to diminish in their contribution to civic infrastructure, there was no other entity in place to provide these services. So we got grants and so forth for the sewer system. But we're sitting in the middle of an area where the streams run north and there are communities to the south of us that do not have a sewage system, so we get all their sewage anyway. Sixty-seven percent of all the homes in McDowell County still straight-pipe to the creek. I'm working with a group that is trying to put a sewage system throughout the entire County.

"In the 10-year period I've been here, we eventually forced the company that owns the water system to sell it to the city because they were not making improvements. Pick up that bottle on the shelf behind you." He pointed to a mason jar, which I picked up. It was filled with a clear fluid. "It's not moonshine. Shake it." When I did, a sediment layer in the bottom began to mix throughout. The liquid turned as dark and thick as coffee. "That water came out of a house on the hill behind City Hall. We had a public hearing. The man who owns the house brought this in. When he got before the judge, he shook it and he said, 'Would you like to drink this? This came out of my kitchen tap.' The city bought the water company and it has taken us four years to get to the point where we're going to get a new system. From 1920 until we purchased it, they made no improvements.

"All of this goes back to some extent to the large landowners. When the coal companies left, in many cases they [abandoned their civic infrastructure]. Here in War we have a town government that assumes responsibility to provide for the citizens who live here. But in Coalwood they are unincorporated and there was nobody to take control of the water service. Within five years, the system entirely failed. It took them five years to get the authorities to move to get them a new water system. The principal at the high school here lived in Coalwood. He had to go to Welch to wash clothes. Residents had to buy bottled water because they couldn't drink anything that came out of the tap. It should be a birthright of every American citizen to be able to drink the water that comes out of his or her tap."

Public health is also an issue. "We are the poorest county in the State. Many people are without health insurance. They often cannot afford the treatments they need. If children don't have health insurance, they don't get started on the right track. It's not a good scene. We have a lot of overweight people. Poor people don't have access to quality food.

"At one time there may have been 40,000 miners in the County. There are probably 1500 today. But [because of mechanization] they are extracting more coal. Most of our mining is still subsurface mining. Some of the seams being worked today are so shallow that the miners work on their knees."

I had mentioned to the mayor my interest in touring a working coal mine. Tom was able to facilitate that for me and guided me to the mine entrance. Before we departed, he said cheerfully, "Many people love it here. These mountains are beautiful year-round, even in the starkest wintertime. Right now we are in the spring. Everything is beginning to bloom."

We drove northward on SR-16, past several mine sites, both operational and abandoned. The road narrowed and asphalt gave way to gravel. We climbed for several miles with poor quality forests of hardwoods and rhododendron around. Nearing the mine, I began to see piles of mining detritus alongside the road: cables, conveyer belts and rollers, coils of wire, chemical drums, and mining vehicles. Tom and I ran from our cars in the pouring rain into the largest building.

Frankie Ward
Caretta

The mine was operated by three brothers, John, Frankie, and Robbie Ward. The coal seam here was evident from the outside. This was a drift mine, where the entrance was exposed aboveground without the need for vertical tunneling. Tom Hatcher introduced me to Frankie Ward. Frankie described mining as being like taking the icing out from between layers of a layer cake without disturbing the layers of cake above.

The entrance tunnel was the height of the seam, about 48 inches, and perhaps ten feet wide. There were two other penetrations into the seam, one on each side. The one on the right had a fan that blew ventilation into the mine, removing any combustible gasses. The other had the

Photo by Tracy Roberts

Coal miner, Caretta

conveyer that transported the coal from inside the mine to the outside.

Frankie and I bounced along in an electric cart in darkness punctuated only by our headlamps over an uneven and frequently wet mine floor. In some places, there were puddles 10 inches deep and 20 feet across with water splashing over the floorboard of the cart. The ceiling was never more than an inch or two above my hard-hat and often bounced against it.

Frankie said, "My father worked hard, sometimes two jobs, in order to save some money. After many years and with a couple of partners, he saved enough money to start his own coal-mining company.

"I've been doing this for most of my life," he said. "I'm 39 years old. I have a wife and two girls." Frankie wore a knit sweater and a hard-hat. He spoke with a laconic, casual mountaineer accent. "There have been some tough times. But we all persevered. Now it's pretty good money in coal. An average equipment operator will earn about $72,000 to $80,000 per year. Sometimes more.

"The conveyor is continually advancing, so it's difficult to say how much it's worth. The conveyor belt itself is $13 per foot. The top supports are $79 each and the bottom one is $35 each and they work in pairs. We have a pair of those every 10 feet into the mine. The two most expensive pieces of equipment are the continuous miner and the roof bolter. You'll see them."

We splashed through another huge puddle of water. The cart was powered by an electric battery. We got a couple of hundred yards into the mine and Frankie said, "This battery is dying. We'll need to find another cart for our way out."

Frankie said their bigger pieces of equipment were powered by high voltage electricity. Nothing is powered by gasoline or diesel because internal combustion engines can cause sparks that can ignite fires.

He stopped and pointed to a string, suspended in the tunnel just above my head. He said, "This is a lifeline. If there is an explosion in the mine and the miner loses his light, this will help him find his way out." It had a series of cone-shaped bobbins strung along it. He said, "If you run your hand on it and you feel one of these you'll know by the direction it points whether you're going out of the mine or into it. If you're going backward your hand will bump into solid. As everything advances further into the mine, this advances with it."

He pointed down a nearby corridor at what looked to be a cinder-block wall. He said, "That's called a stab-in. That blocks the air. It's just like channeling water. We had to carry the cinderblocks in and build the wall in the corridor. It's sealed and airtight on the other side.

"Mine regulation is strict. The regulators designed laws to protect people against anything that's ever happened. There are regulations on air quality, roof support, bolt placement, and all aspects of our work. Regulators come on a regular basis and monitor our work. See this dust?" he said, scraping his fingertips along the ceiling just above our hardhats. "It is pulverized limestone. It is sprayed on the walls and ceiling throughout the mine. Even that is strictly regulated, in its composition, how we apply it, and how much we apply."

Our cart's batteries ran out of juice so we continued on foot, hunched over. The floor in most places was reasonably consistent and level, but in some places was six-inch deep mud and standing puddles. Frankie said we were almost a mile into the mine. We had about 200 feet of cover over us. "You want a lot of cover," he said. "If you get too shallow, the rock that forms the ceiling becomes less stable.

"This is called a check curtain," he said pointing at a curtain of heavy fabric. "Because it has slits in it, you can travel through it but it still blocks airflow. See this car that is parked half-way through it? It's parked that way so that someone approaching it from either side will see it and won't run into somebody coming towards them."

He pointed at the floor where a large electrical cable stretched along the corridor. He said, "This means that a shuttle car is going to be coming through here. The shuttle car backs up to the continuous miner and catches the coal as it is being mined. Once it's full, it pulls away and shuttles the coal to the beginning of the conveyor. It dumps the coal onto the conveyor, which carries it out of the mine. The car has a reel that automatically spools out its electrical cable as it advances away from the power source and then automatically retracts the cable as it gets closer. That way it never runs over its own cable."

At the beginning of the conveyor, there was a wide belt running inside a channel on the floor with a series of panels running across it that pushed the coal forward towards a crusher. He said it was important that the coal was not too large in chunks as otherwise they could jam the conveyor. This system allowed for smooth and consistent loading of coal onto the conveyor.

We approached the continuous miner. This was a massive, worm-like earth-eating machine reminiscent of the movie Transformers. The business end had three contiguous drums about a yard in diameter with rows of carbide-tipped teeth, each 8-inches or so long with the teeth rotated to get the maximum bite as the drums spun away and over the top. The entire drum apparatus was movable vertically by hydraulic lifters to allow for clawing of seams of various heights. Below that was a motorized scooping system which collected and then funneled backwards along a conveyor the length of the machine the coal that the scraper deposited below. The operator's chair was in a near-reclining position behind one of the drive wheels, necessitating nearly blind operation. Frankie told me the operator can sense variations in the rock by feel, much the same as someone driving a car can sense the smoothness of a highway surface.

"A new continuous miner like this costs about $3 million. We can get as many years' use as we're willing to put parts into it. This one is probably 15 years old."

Two miners were working near the machine. One, named Worm, said, "I love mining. I can't think of anything else I'd ever want to do. I worked in a factory for a while and a little bit of construction. When you are backing out of the mine you engineer a series of collapses."

Frankie explained in more detail. "The mine is cut out in corridors like city blocks. When you reach the property line, you start cutting into the pillars that you've been cutting around and you allow the ceiling to fall. The continuous miner marches 180 to 200 feet per day."

He used the ceiling as if it were a chalkboard to illustrate. What he described was an intricate dance between removal of the pillars and controlled collapses of the ceiling. He said, "Sometimes the collapsing material covers a portion of the machine. It's pretty exciting."

Wendell, the other miner, said, "I can do anything I've ever tried to do. But I like mining. I take pride in what I do. Most of the people that I know who mine coal would love to bring visitors into the mine and show them that it is not what it is stereotyped to be."

In a nearby area, two men were working a piece of equipment that places large bolts into the ceiling. The machine appeared to be almost as big as the continuous miner. It had a hydraulic support that held the ceiling while it was being drilled and prevented chips of rock from falling onto the operator. The operator placed a 4-foot-long drill bit onto a spinning chuck. As the drill spun, its own arm swung it upward, forcing it into the ceiling. Frankie told me that the machine feeds water to the drill bit and removes shards as they are generated. Once the bit is fully inserted, it is then fully retracted. The operator then shoved by hand what appeared to be a 4-foot long, 1-inch in diameter, clear plastic tube into the hole. The tube contained glue comprised of two parts, a resin and an epoxy held in place side by side. The operator then placed a bolt that resembled Rebar on the chuck, which forced it upward into place, splitting the glue container and allowing the resin and epoxy to mix and harden. At the bottom of the bolt was a metal plate perhaps 8 inches square that then supported the roof. Mine regulations dictated that these bolts were placed every 4 feet on a grid and the machine was equipped with a measuring device to help the operator quickly and accurately step off the appropriate distance.

Months later when I visited the area again, the recession had devastated the demand for metallurgical coal. Frankie and his brothers had shut down the mine and his workers were unemployed.

Norman Clark

War

Mayor Tom invited me to attend a meeting of his Kiwanis Club, which met in a church. Both men and women were in attendance.

Kiwanian Norman Clark said, "If there had never been one ounce of coal under this County, it would have become a huge National Forest preserve. There's really nothing else here. 80 percent of the land has a 60 percent grade or more. And the small portion of it that is flat is owned by big corporations and there is typically a railroad or a road on it. The rest of it is in floodplains."

Most images of Appalachia are rural, with plenty of land separating one homestead from the next. McDowell is anything but rural. As the coal boom developed, McDowell transitioned to one of the most urban environments anywhere. 100,000 people living in a county doesn't seem all that crowded unless they're all jammed into less than 10 percent of the land, the only land that is flat enough for building. Layers of creek, railroad, road, house, and then mountain put dwelling after dwelling shoulder-to-shoulder with the next.

"So we could never have a manufacturing plant that would employ 400 or 500 people. There is really no possibility for any industry other than coal mining. Originally there were 17 billion tons of coal in this County. There are an estimated seven or eight billion tons left.

"Today a significant number of the people in our County are living on welfare checks, pension checks, Social Security, or stuff like that. In 1960 we had $65 million in checks coming into the County. Now that number is about $32 million, but since the population has been cut by 75 percent the per-capita is in fact larger.

"[A century ago] many people from the northern states who had money to invest, invested it in these coal mines. They went to Ellis

Island and recruited workers who were arriving as immigrants from Europe. They brought them to McDowell County and put them to work in the mines and housed them in specific communities. War was primarily comprised of Italian immigrants. Gary has a lot of Polish people. Davy has a lot of Germans. Kimball and Keystone were primarily black communities.

"The only thing that I could hope for is for McDowell County, other than being in the inmate housekeeping [prison] business, to develop its tourism. The place is absolutely running over with history. Not twenty-five yards from where we are sitting is the junction of Warrior Creek and the Dry Fork. Two Indian tribes fought a battle here in 1788. The whites named the creek Warrior Creek after that battle."

Legend has it that so many people were killed the creek ran red with blood. The N&W Railroad built a small building in 1906, a station, and put the word "War" on it. That same year, the Post Office was established under the name of War. The founding fathers retained the name when the town incorporated in 1920. It is the only place in the United States named War.

Norman continued, "We furnished the coal that made the steel that won our wars for this country and we've got nothing out of it. I'm angry about it. You can understand the situation that got us here. But it can never fully be fixed. We will never get rid of the large land companies and energy companies and their heavy hand on our people. If you were interviewing me on radio or TV, I would tell you that I was an optimist. But the problems are intractable."

Carolyn Muncy Owens
Annie Muncy Muncy
War

Carolyn Owens, whom I also met at the Kiwanis meeting, gave me another view of life in War. She took me for a drive to the rustic mountain cabin where she was raised, what she now called The Nuthouse.

Along our drive in her four-wheeler to a place called Shop Hollow, I saw abject, wrenching poverty. There were about 30 habitations of every shape and construction. Some were nicely kept and attractive, while others were tarpaper. There was rubbish everywhere, from automotive tires and batteries to soft drink bottles, discarded mattresses, sofas, children's toy guns, bicycles, refrigerators, and things indistinguishable. Grass was in short supply. Mud ruled the day, and rivulets of water streamed across it.

Carolyn often pointed at a residence, saying a sibling or cousin lived in it. There were two fundamentalist churches in this tight hollow. Nearing the gap atop the hollow, the houses became fewer and the woods regained their dominance. We crested the gap and descended the other side, where countless four-wheeler tracks angled through the woods. A few hundred yards beyond we parked in front of The Nuthouse.

The Nuthouse itself is a large, wooden structure, neat and appealing. There is new planking on the bottom of two balconies. The structure had seen several enlargements over time, and it was difficult to tell what portions were built in what order. A hodgepodge of chairs in plastic and steel surrounded an outside fire pit. Nearby was an outhouse.

We toured the inside of the Nuthouse. There were half-staircases leading from floor to floor. The bedrooms were tidy, musty smelling. Walls held photos of friends and family. One set of photos showed all the male offspring together. Beside it was another, showing all the female offspring. The kitchen was huge. In its center was a large, home-made table that looked to be able to seat 18 or 20 people. There were two stoves, one gas and one wood.

In the living room was a bound scrap-book with "Visitors" on the front. There were hundreds of names inside of people who had come. There were groupings of names from various universities, including Notre Dame, which had sent students on Appalachian field trips. Many people wrote sincere, heart-felt letters.

Carolyn and her older sister Annie gathered some chairs on the front porch. Carolyn told me about her family: "Our mother was May Muncy and our father was Roosevelt Theodore Muncy, but nobody called him Roosevelt. Everybody called him Rose. Even on his Social Security card he was Rose. He got confused as being a woman if you didn't know. He was a big guy and he was wonderful. My brother Boo-Boo is named after Daddy. His name is Theodore Roosevelt Muncy."

Annie said, "There were eventually 13 of us. One year we moved way back up the hollow and lived in a cabin. My grandmother and her oldest son and one of my aunts and uncles and all their kids all lived in one house. At one point there was a big snowstorm and we ran out of food. We all about starved to death. We didn't even have flour in the house. There was 3 feet of snow or more. My uncle looked up on the hill one night and saw a light. He walked up to the light, which turned out to be a house. He borrowed some flour and my grandma made biscuits. We had biscuits and water gravy and that's what we had to eat. When we could finally get through this snow, we left that place and even left the furniture. It was really cold. My older sister Shirley and I would sit in the loft near the stovepipe. We just had an old barrel for a stove. The pipe went straight up through the ceiling. I think we even slept up there because we didn't have a lot of covers and we needed to stay warm. When you think about it later it seems like fun.

"Mommy used to make us clothes out of feed sacks. We'd buy feed for the cow, and flour sacks, and you could get a real pretty pattern on the flour sacks. Momma would sew skirts and tops to go with it and I remember wearing them to school and the kids made fun of me. I thought they were real pretty. When we'd get a new sack, we used to fight over who would get a dress made from it.

"There was one boy who was calling me all kinds of names. He was having all the other kids make fun of me. So I took all I could take. I never bothered anybody. But I got up out of my seat and I walked over to his seat and I picked it up and dumped him into the floor in the class-room. It was a wonder I didn't get in trouble. I couldn't even hardly go to school for a while. I know a lot of times I would cry. There's one lady still here. She works at the Dollar Store. She made fun of me because of my underclothes. They were made of feed sacks too. I still don't forget it."

Carolyn said, "When Daddy got hurt, he couldn't work in the mines no more and he worked for the town doctor doing handyman work. He was also on welfare. For some reason in those days when you were on welfare you couldn't even have a cow. You think they would want you to have a cow, but the welfare people wouldn't allow you to have any livestock. You had to tell lies in order to keep a cow."

Annie said, "We had a good life and we had a good family. But we had a terrible looking house. Y'all know what pasteboard boxes are? That's what we had on the wall. We used to be able to get flour sacks and they were blue on the inside. My older sister and I would paper the wall with it. We thought that was the prettiest thing. Some of the social workers came out while we were papering the wall, and I remember them laughing at us. It was hard to stay on welfare. Daddy wouldn't have had us on at all, but there were 13 kids and he had to feed us somehow."

Carolyn said, "Dad didn't allow us to date. My husband was raised in the same hollow as us but he lived on the other side of the hill. I didn't know him that good when we were growing up. I met him at school and he'd walk down the hollow with us to catch the bus. He went away in the Army to Vietnam, and when he came back we was grown-up and then we got together. When he and I would go out together, we'd have to have one of my older brothers or sisters along with us. We didn't ever get to be by ourselves. I never saw a movie until I was married. Daddy didn't allow movies. He objected on religious grounds."

Annie said, "I don't think he got religious himself until he got older. Our grandmother was very religious. She felt that women shouldn't have earrings, cut their hair, go to movies or dances, or go on dates."

Carolyn said, "I've never been to a football game in my life. None of my brothers were allowed to play football. And high school football is real big here."

Annie said, "It seems real cruel now, but I don't remember ever wanting to. We did want to go to a few dances, though. But we wasn't deprived because we had so much fun playing in the mountains with our brothers and sisters. My brother Melvin made up the best playhouses. He'd find a little level spot and he'd build us a little furniture out of rocks and logs and stuff. Then we had a little playhouse with little bitty dolls. We'd get real pretty moss and we'd lay it down in the dirt and play like it was a carpet.

"One year, everybody was getting flip-flops. We couldn't afford them so we made our own with pasteboard and string. We did the same thing with hula-hoops that we made from grapevines. They worked! They were pretty rough on us, though."

Carolyn said, "One of my favorite things to do in the spring when the creek was pretty high was put two cans in the creek and race them down to the bottom. We caught tadpoles and we'd see who could catch the most. Every year we'd fix a little pond and we'd see how many turtles we could get. We'd see if we could get the same turtles every year. One of them had a little busted shell and we'd look for this same one every year. We'd do that every springtime."

Annie said, "I wish I could've gone to college. I didn't get to go to high school. I only went to seventh grade. I like checking out stuff about herbs and all that and dinosaur bones. I wish I could've done something like that in my life. Now I'm too old."

Carolyn said, "We were poor but I loved my growing up. I always wanted to be a writer, actor, or entertainer. I love to entertain people. But I've done a lot of good things. I worked at the Dollar Store for a while. And I had a job at a bank where I was actually an assistant manager. So even though I don't have a college education or even a high school diploma, I did get my GED. I think being an assistant bank manager was a pretty good job.

"I belong to the Kiwanis Club, which I consider an elite thing for our town. There's not a whole lot of people that gets to do that. I'm with the higher ups now. The way we was raised helped us appreciate what we have. The stuff that my Daddy couldn't get us, I wanted my kids to have. My kids had everything they wanted."

Carolyn told me many universities send students there on field trips and for charity work. "It excites me when the college kids come to visit. I tell them how lucky they are that they got to go to college. All of our kids have not made it real good. But we've got kids in our family who did. We got teachers in our family. One sister is a professional photographer, one sister has her own catering business, so we're just smart people, ain't we Annie? One brother Melvin is an evangelist who goes around with the gospel tent, he's real famous.

"This little area is us. It's right here. Welch and other areas of McDowell County seem distant. McDowell County is put down a whole lot because it's a poor county. We were raised really poor but right now we have plenty. We don't never go in need.

"We go to a Pentecostal Holiness Church. We don't handle snakes but we do speak in tongues. That's the evidence of the Holy Ghost. You can't just do it, but you've got to be in the spirit. If you sat and talked to my mom about the Lord, she would get so happy that she would go into doing it right there. My mom is one of the most religious people around. She's too bashful to talk to you for your book. Most times when we'd get sick and we couldn't afford to go to the doctor, Mommy would just pray for us and we'd be better. But Mommy has so much faith in God and is such a powerful Christian and that's where we learned it from. Every one of us grew up religious. Church has to come first."

Annie spoke about medicinal herbs, saying, "I used to go ginseng hunting with my grandma. She was 102 when she died. She would take me with her and she'd pick up something and say 'taste of this and taste of that'.

"I used to think that all the teachers and everybody were so much better than me. We've had a lot of college kids and different people come up here. God helped me realize that everybody was created the same. I can talk with anybody now. Used to be, I would be embarrassed to even say a word."

Benton and Frances Ward
Yukon

On my second visit to the Nuthouse, I met a couple in their sixties, Benton and Frances Ward. Coincidentally, they were the parents of Frankie Ward, the man who escorted me into the coal mine. Benton, candid and outspoken, became a good friend. He offered to escort me to a mountaintop removal mine.

We got into his red late-model diesel pickup truck. I sat alongside a metal lunchbox and his spare jacket. Ashes from his cigars filled the tray. We headed north towards Welch, then east towards Gary. The day was overcast and dank, but without rain.

Past Gary, we stopped to take a photo of some abandoned coke ovens. They were a long series of arched caves, built of brick, perhaps 8-feet across, and burrowed into a hillside. They were significantly overgrown with plant matter, but easily discerned from the road. Between the ovens and the road was a railroad track. On the other side of the road was a row of former company houses. Benton asked me to imagine the amazing smoke and stench the former owners endured during the operation of the ovens.

We left the paved road and drove uphill on dirt. We passed a sprinkler set-up, running continuously, where departing vehicles were sprayed to reduce the dirt transferred to the road. We stopped at a 4-way junction. Another pickup arrived bearing a man Benton knew named Buck. His white truck was beyond filthy, with mud splattered above the roofline from ebony to lighter shades of grey. Buck told us that the mine was not operating, a victim of the recession, and that a watchman would be there but we could talk our way in.

We reached a mountain pass, and then continued upwards to the ridgeline. We stopped beside a mobile office. Inside, a woman sat, talking on the phone. Benton went inside to ask permission to drive the mine site. Returning to the truck, he told me he didn't know the woman, but in dropping some names to her, she let us proceed. There was nobody else around. We drove slowly through the muck. It was austere and barren, largely colorless, moonlike. The sky was featureless, white and grey. Nothing moved.

Benton explained that mine operators must file detailed excavation and reclamation plans. One ravine to our left was being filled in a crescent pattern, similar in shape to the original, simply with more material in it. At the bottom was a runoff pond which would ultimately be drained and removed. A bulldozer sat below us on a bench on the ravine where new material would be transferred and then compacted awaiting additional layers.

We stopped our truck alongside a large dump truck. Each wheel was about eight feet in diameter. Trucks like these are transferred over the highways with the wheels and bed removed, and are assembled at the mine site.

Nearby was an uphill mound where new grass was growing. Benton explained that as the mine progresses and soil can be placed in its permanent position, the new soil is re-seeded to retard erosion. What was surprisingly absent was any actual coal. Benton explained that many feet of rock are typically removed relative to the thickness of the coal seam. We finally found an exposed seam of coal which Benton measured with his ruler at twenty-five inches. He said it would be excavated as soon as the mine re-opened.

Mine operators were not allowed to impact flowing streams or rivers. The ravines we saw were steep, with intermittent watercourses. The new fill made the ravines steeper but mimicked their original shapes.

We walked over a flat area where dozens of turkey tracks were embedded into the surface of the mud. We saw some deer tracks as well.

Benton said, "Wildlife continues to use this area. Once grass and new trees are planted, the wildlife will return in full force."

Benton said all of McDowell's land has been logged or mined before, sometimes many times. After reclamation, according to the

Benton Ward on a mountaintop removal mine

pre-defined plan, the area would either be left essentially flat to allow for industrial or residential development — or even a golf course — or returned to a more natural, hilly contour. If there was to be no further development, it would be reseeded and trees would be replanted. Biological diversity can return if the mine is properly reclaimed.

Every industry looks for ways to cut costs in order to remain competitive. If it is cheaper to mine underground, that's where the miners will work. If it is cheaper to surface-mine, they'll work in that manner.

We drove a short way away into a circular-shaped depression, per-haps 75 yards in diameter. Rocks tumbled from vertical walls repeatedly. Eerie. With the featureless sky and the confining dampness, it was a sinister place, unearthly, and unsettling. In the distance over the cliffs stood some spindly trees, the only living things in sight.

We drove over a large, somewhat flat area upon which was parked the skeleton of a dump truck. It had no wheels, no engine, and no bed. Benton said it had been cannibalized for parts and would sit until the conclusion of operations when the metal of this and all equipment would be salvaged.

We left the site and turned downhill from the mountain pass away from the direction we'd come. We stopped at a tipple, under construction. We went inside the office and introduced ourselves to two men in hard-hats and coveralls. Both were happy to show diagrams of the tipple and its various components.

We spent the next 45 minutes exploring the tipple. It was comprised of structural steel members reaching five stories tall and a series of machines for sorting, cleaning, and separating the coal. It was evident the tipple would be a considerable consumer of electrical power.

As we departed, Benton said, "There were two reasons the tipple was not in operation. One was that they did not have the adequate supply of electrical power. The other reason was they didn't have the proper refuse permit. You must have a plan and a permit for everything you do in this business. Before miners do anything, they must file detailed engineering plans that are closely scrutinized by the regulators.

"We have so many mountains around here that we can destroy some of them without hurting nobody. The good of the people is represented by getting the coal out and putting the mountain back, not necessarily in exactly the same way as it was. The strip jobs don't go all the way down to the original creek. The only thing that is stripped is the upper portions of the mountain. If a stream is big enough to support fish then I do not believe it should be filled up. Any stream that runs intermittently, just when it rains, is not a stream. I have no problem with filling them."

"We are losing habitat when we operate a mountaintop removal mine, but we ultimately reclaim it back to productive use or turn it back to nature. The problems that we have down here are not the problems these well-intentioned [opponents] are trying to fix."

"In spite of the poverty, people in McDowell County have a good life. It is a relaxed life. It don't take much to live. Anybody can own a house. You can buy a house for $10,000 and put $40,000 into it and have a decent house. But you need a job. The only good-paying jobs are in coal mining. I have more money in my house than it is worth. My house may be worth $15,000 or $20,000. I have put $17,000 into my garage and it may be worth $10,000."

Benton admitted he was wealthy enough to live anywhere he wanted to. But, he said, "You couldn't replicate this environment anywhere else. Where else could you leave your garage door open all day long without having to worry? Where else could you leave for two weeks and not worry about your house? My wife and I leave for two weeks' vacation in Florida and don't even think to lock the door. Kids are always riding up and down my road on bicycles. Where else can kids do this in America today? Where else can their parents feel that their kids are safe under the supervision of the rest of the neighborhood? This is the way a community is supposed to work.

"We have been stereotyped forever. There is a T-shirt that is popular that says, "Everything is relative in West Virginia," speaking about incest and intermarriage. We do have some of that but other places do, too.

"There are no gangs and much less crime here. We are surrounded by the beauty and grandeur of nature and we have a more cohesive society where people help each other. A man who is not capable of working and is living on SSI [Supplemental Social Security] is better off in War than in Newark, New Jersey. The people around him in War will take care of him. Children can walk up and down our street at any time of the day or night and feel completely secure. People read about us and say how sorry they feel for us. We are depressed economically but we're okay."

Frances was active in a volunteer organization that helps to feed poor people, called The Hands of Hope. She got involved with them when they requested the use of a building she and Benton owned. "I never dreamed that I would become personally involved in anything like this. I was the one that got our church involved with it. The Hands of

Hope has furniture, food, and clothing. A lot of their furniture comes from hotels that are remodeling with new chairs and beds. They acquire this stuff, then warehouse and distribute it.

"The director said that he was brought here by the Lord to help the people of McDowell County. He probably learned about us on CNN or some other network station. We got our soup kitchen underway, and it varies from serving five people to 40 people a free hot meal. We also do 144 bag lunches and we deliver them.

"We did a home visit to a woman who had four or five of her own kids plus many of the neighbors' kids running in and out of her house along with assorted dogs and cats. There were infants, several babies. The animals were defecating in the house and the stink was awful. Oh, gosh it was filthy. I was thinking to myself, how could you raise kids like this? The bassinet had... I can't even describe it. I couldn't even sleep that night.

"Then I went into houses that were even worse. In some of these houses there is a naked lightbulb hanging on its wires in the middle of a room. Sometimes you can see outside through the walls. We have cold winters! Some of the ceilings are falling in. I have lived in this area all my life, and I knew it was bad, but I never dreamed it was this bad.

"There is one little boy who sticks out in my mind. The first time I went there, this boy ran down the driveway to greet us, yelling, 'Here are the ladies with the yellow shirts bringing our lunch.' It broke my heart. He was so delighted that we were bringing him something to eat because I'm sure he hadn't eaten. In the school program they get two hot meals everyday. But a lot of times on the weekends they do not get food."

She believed that there is a pattern of inability to make changes. "Many of the best and brightest have left. People who stayed are more ensconced in poverty and hopelessness, less intelligent and ambitious.

"God has given us many charitable organizations with food, clothing, and school supplies. The negative side is the lack of work. I was born and raised here. I am not a highly educated woman. I did not finish high school but I did go back to complete my GED. I have good common sense and I know the way the world works. My mission in life has been to be a mother and wife.

"Benton and I have worked hard all of our lives. We could live in a fine house. You can see how many kids there are in my yard. If I lived in a fine mansion I would be afraid the children would mess up things. In this house, I don't care if they come in with dirt on their shoes. My floor is washable. I am not a fancy person. I know how to be if I need to be, but fortunately we don't have to be fancy very often.

"People can improve their lives, but many choose not to. There are programs and opportunities, even here in McDowell County. We are in one of the poorest counties in the country and yet anybody can put clothes on the backs of their children and food on their plate if they choose to. The people that don't, they drive me crazy.

"There are a lot of people in this area that I call 'hollow people'. I don't mean that disrespectfully. They have lived their lives in these isolated hollows and are shy. They lack worldliness and knowledge. And sadly, a lot do not want to better themselves.

"The people we take lunches to generally live up the hollows. My organization cannot reach everybody who is in need. I think that for every family we are reaching there may be five-hundred more that we are not reaching. It is frustrating."

Minister Izalliar Dalton
Paula Branch
Kimball

Izalliar Dalton is a minister of a black church that meets in what was a theater in Kimball. It is called the Miracle Mt. Carmel Church. When I met her on a sunny Sunday morning before services, she said, "The founding apostle of this church is General Bishop Arnie H. Joyce. He has been preaching in Kimball for 38 years. When Bishop Joyce first came to Kimball, some of the local townspeople didn't want us here. But the Lord worked it out. We had a big green bus at the time with about 60 young people in it. We traveled from church to church, praising the Lord. The Lord showed us this theater building in Kimball.

"My pastor does not worry about opposition. When the Lord is on your side, everything works out. We have been here ever since, praising the Lord. We have several musical instruments and musicians that perform during the service. We have drums, keyboards, saxophones, clarinets, and guitars. The Bible says in the Psalms 150, 'Praise him on a stringed instrument,' all kinds of instruments, and that is what we try to do.

"[We have] about 100 parishioners and our population is holding steady. We have a number of young people coming in to the congregation. Many are going off to college now. A lot of the people in our congregation live and work in other places because there are so few jobs around here. We have a lot of people who live in Winston-Salem and they come home on the weekends to attend."

Winston-Salem is three hours away. She explained they didn't find what they looked for in a religious experience there. "They don't feel what they feel here. And they have been going here for all their lives. They get up around five o'clock each Sunday morning to get here on time.

"Everybody is welcome. Sometimes the church is jam-packed. You can't even get through Kimball because there are so many cars. There are several other churches in Kimball, and we fellowship with all of them. We all get along like one big family."

Minister Dalton told me her church was devastated by the same floods that hit Welch in 2001 and 2002. "People from all over the world came to help us and sent us money and did things to help us. A church in Princeton gave us all the pews. A church in South Carolina sent members of their congregation to help us. They brought equipment and helped us repair and put the stage back. They wouldn't let us pay for nothing. Another church bought the carpet."

The service itself got underway, and Minister Dalton put me in a front pew. The service included minister after minister giving praises to the lord. Glory hallelujah! At one point, Reverend Joyce stepped to the base of the pulpit and met with several parishioners individually, placing his hand on their foreheads one at a time, giving blessing against the droning backdrop of music. He shouted a prayer, and then gave him or her a gentle shove. The parishioner fell backwards to the floor, attended by large men to catch him or her, and another attendant to cover with a light sheet for the sake of modesty where a woman with a dress was involved. One of the female pastors came to me and placed her hand on my forehead and yelled a prayer in my ear. When in Rome, I thought to myself, closing my eyes. When she lightly shoved me, I fell promptly into my pew, stunned.

The quote that stuck in my mind for days came from a young male minister. He said, "We are the blessed people of the Lord." I was incredulous that these people, who had suffered the indignities of being black in America, in having their church ravaged by floods, and in living in the poorest county in the third poorest state in the nation, still felt so blessed. What did this imply about his expectations?

After the service, Minister Dalton introduced me to a woman named Paula Branch who had driven from Winston-Salem. "We like our home church," Paula told me, matter-of-factly. "I grew up here. We leave at seven o'clock on Sunday morning. Once the service is over, we turn around and drive home. There are typically one or two other cars that make the trip as well. We love West Virginia.

"When I grew up here there were more people. It is sad for me to see that the area has gone into decline. But many people come back frequently to get together. All of the movement away from this area has had to do with jobs. We would move back in an instant if there was work."

Clara Thompson
Ray Williams, Sr.
Kimball

Clara Thompson is the Executive Director of the McDowell County Museum Commission, located across the street from the Miracle Mt. Carmel Church. The Museum honors black soldiers of World War I and is the only one of its kind in the nation. The museum is a stately structure of yellow brick with four grand white columns on the front portico. Surprisingly, inside the building, there were no interpretive displays or artifacts.

Clara said, "I am a retired elementary educator. My last position was at Welch Elementary School. I was born in Gary, the 12th of 15 children. My dad came from Georgia when he was 16 years old. He migrated here because of the mines and the work. He lived first in a coal camp called Mohawk which is near Ieager. He met my mother and together they moved to Gary where he worked in the mines.

"Most of my upbringing was in Gary and I loved living there. Everybody had large families. We lived in double-sided houses, duplexes. There were only three bedrooms, one for the girls, one for the boys, and one for my parents, a little room under the stairway. My family had nine boys and six girls. The older kids began to migrate away. I was one of the younger ones so I really didn't get to know my older brothers and sisters well at all.

"We had one sidewalk in Gary,

Clara Thompson, Kimball

and we had one little highway that ran through town. One side had houses, and the other side had the embankment. All the kids played in the street. My parents planted a garden, and we raised our vegetables along with chickens and a pig. People went onto the mountain behind the houses and found a spot and planted a garden. Nobody owned their own house; all of them were owned by the coal company."

Eventually, her father lost his job and the family was evicted. He moved to Kimball and found a lesser paying job with the highway department. "He spent many hours standing in the road holding a caution flag. He was probably in his 60s by then, and he didn't like it as well he liked coal mining.

"I am so thankful for my raisin'. My mother was a housewife.

When the miners were on strike, many of the wives would go to the cities to get work. My father would not allow her to do that."

Dr. Ray Williams joined the conversation. He was also a retired educator and on the board at the Memorial. He said jocularly, "I have been black for 87 years. Since day one! I was born in South Carolina. My parents moved here because they heard there were five black high schools here in McDowell County. They wanted all of us to get good educations.

"This building was built in 1928. It was put here because of segregation to represent the contributions that black soldiers had made in the First World War. McDowell County was largely built on the backs of the blacks who worked in the coal mines. When the war started, a large number of the blacks went to fight in the war. When they came

Ray Williams, Kimball

back, there was a monument being built for the whites in Welch. [The blacks] wanted their own place in Welch, but Welch had crowded out. A family here in Kimball offered this property. Several men including my father-in-law, Harry I. Neal, went to the county court and argued that there were laws calling for separate but equal treatment.

The World War I Memorial, Kimball

'We fought in the War. We need something to represent what we have done.'

"This was a memorial not just for the blacks of McDowell County but for the 400,000 blacks across the whole country who volunteered to fight in the First World War. I believe there were 1500 from McDowell alone.

"When I went off to war in the 1940s this building was still considered a monument for black soldiers of the First World War, and it really pretty much remained that way. It was burned out in 1992. Prior to the burning there were many more artifacts, interpretive displays, and a library. Now it is as much a community center as a museum.

"It was rebuilt in 2003, but in the meantime the building was essentially a ruin to the point where trees were growing up inside of it. The destruction of this building was a source of deep sadness for people throughout the community, both black and white. In the later years, white people used the building as a community center as well as blacks."

Dr. Williams mentioned specific new plans, including interpretive displays and a contemplation garden. But money was always in short supply.

"There is still hope. Because of socialization and culturalization and of family values, there is always hope. We must always do the best we can with what we have. We have lost so many people, both black and white, from this County. The greatest natural resource that any place can have is its people. Of the investment my wife and I put into our children through their upbringing and their education, none of it is benefiting McDowell County. It is tragic, sad.

"Black Americans have come so far in many ways, yet we've regressed in others. We are still not equal citizens to the whites. We have to emerge from the locks that so many years of denial have put on us. But today, the only barriers are the barriers we hold ourselves. Our inferiority, where it still exists, is more in our own minds. In decades before, others put chains on us. Now we have only the chains we carry ourselves.

"The change we must see now will come from within. The blacks in McDowell County are empowered because we have always felt ourselves equal. My father spent his life on his knees mining coal so I would have the opportunity to get four degrees."

Epilogue

Gary

On my way home from my final trip, I toured Gary. SR-103 from Welch is like so many other roads in McDowell County, with a creek below, a railroad track constantly nearby, and clusters of houses on hillsides and embankments. Christmas lights shone in several windows, even in this morning. Frost clung to the grass in places yet to see the sun's rays. Some of the houses in tight hollows or clinging to the slopes of the north face of mountains appeared to never see the sun's warming rays at all during the winter months.

At one point, a huge conveyor structure angles steeply across the road from the mountainside above on my left to the railroad tracks below on the right. This massive work in steel is perhaps 200 feet above the road at its highest and is suspended by four towers and countless steel cables. I envisioned the inevitable collapse during some unfortunate, future day, and the enormous liability risk.

Gary is more topographically open than perhaps any other place in the County. There are several impressive churches in town, one with the characteristic onion-top steeple of Eastern European lineage. The elegant Roman Catholic Church has impressive stained glass windows. At the far end of town is a stone stairway leading into brambles, what was presumably formerly the entrance to a grand home.

I saw a young fellow riding a bicycle, the first person I'd seen anywhere in the county engaged in any form of recreational fitness; no runners, no bicyclists, no walkers.

I backtracked to Welch and drove US-52 southbound towards Bluefield. The villages along the way were strung like tarnished beads on a rosary. I began a benediction of reflection.

Maitland … Superior … Big Four …

Not surprisingly, lots of negative ink finds its way on paper with regard to McDowell County. Given the abject poverty and bottom placement on so many quality of life listings, it's a seductive trap. Yet doing so misses wider, more complicated points and robs current and former residents of their due.

Kimball ... Bottom Creek ... Vivian ... Landgraff ...

All of us judge our experience by our expectations. Everyday American life was considerably different a century ago, as McDowell began to grow and develop. Blacks from the Deep South faced discrimination, hopeless poverty, and illiteracy, but in McDowell County found adequate wages, acceptance, and a measure of the American Dream. Similarly, Europeans escaping persecution, pogroms, and intolerance found a new start in West Virginia. Expectation was decidedly more modest for them than for contemporary Americans. Those of us who feel that drinkable water from the tap and watercourses free of raw sewage should be a birthright are justifiably appalled at the McDowell experience, in spite of the fact that these necessities are unfathomable luxuries in much of the rest of the world. But however abhorrent these conditions are, the positives of close family life, natural bounty, caring neighbors, and a relaxed pace is enough to provide a measure of satisfaction and human joy in McDowell. It's not a perfect place. But nowhere else is, either.

Eckman ... Keystone ... Kyle ...

Is there a criminal in the McDowell crime? Coal companies built dependent societies in the coalfields because it was expedient and appropriate at the time. Is it not the American way for the free-enterprise, corporate system to seek opportunities, to exploit resources and labor in the name of profit? Pitiable McDowell is a living example of unrestrained corporatocracy.

Powhatan ... Upland ...

America has worked best with a marriage of corporate, social, and governmental power. Such things as libraries, roads, police departments, and armies are best funded by governments, collectives of the people. The McDowell experience illustrates the problems of corporations running everything. And yet the zeal to privatize increasingly permeates our society.

Elkhorn ... Ennis ...

As this odyssey wound to a close, I was swept with empathy. Would I have answered the call to fight Northern aggression in a great Civil War? Would I have walked from South Carolina to West Virginia and descended into the bowels of the earth to shovel the black rock that burns? Would I have fought the coal mine wars or protested the demolition of our mountains? Would I have fought to save my high school? Would I have sung the songs of freedom and equality?

And what of this area, loved by so many? Would The Spine of the Virginias sink into an economic quagmire or would the strength of the people and the benign nature of the land make Appalachia trendy and successful? Perhaps we need to puff up our chests a bit more.

Switchback ... Maybuery ... Coaldale ...

What has the McDowell County experience in particular and the Appalachian experience more broadly shown us? For one thing, we must increasingly chart our own course, based upon our shared values of community and cultural respect. For another, we must increasingly respect the land because from it emanates our sustenance. We must care for each other and practice good mental and physical health.

Freeman ... Simmons ... Bluewell ...

I drove past still another vacant store, this one with the corporate sign still in place but the merchandise long gone and a "Closed" sign on the entry door. I saw another burned-out home, charred timbers still in place. I remembered a spray-painted message I'd seen, graffiti on a wall near a flooded downtown. It said, "Tough times don't last. Tough people do."

Notes

1. John Alexander Williams, *West Virginia, A History* (W. W. Norton and Company, 1984, 1976), page 85.
2. Michael F. Doran, *Atlas of County Boundary Changes in Virginia, 1634–1895* (Iberian Publishing Company, 1987), page 50.
3. West Virginia Tax Commission Report: Report on State Development, 1884, West Virginia: Documents in The History of a Rural-Industrial State. On Internet: http://www.as.wvu.edu/WVHistory/documents/064.pdf
4. Ibid, page 184.
5. Dave Barry, on Internet, http://www.brainyquote.com/quotes/quotes/d/davebarry163468.html
6. Charles Kuralt, on Internet, http://en.wikipedia.org/wiki/Charles_Kuralt
7. Martha Stewart, on Internet, http://www.washingtonpost.com/ac2/wp-dyn/A5497-2005Mar3?language=printer
8. John Denver, on Internet, http://gb.cri.cn/11344/2006/07/31/2005@1155156_2.htm
9. Wendy B. Davis, "Out of the Black Hole: Reclaiming the Crown of King Coal," *American University Law Review*, 2002, page 906.
10. Bill Archer, "Memories of the Matz," *Bluefield Daily Telegraph*, March, 2009.

Index
of persons interviewed for this book

Michael Abraham

Photo by Steve Brightwell

I am a businessman, adventurer and writer. I live in Blacksburg, Virginia, with my wife, Jane, three dogs, and a garage full of motorcycles and bicycles. I have one adult daughter.

My other books are:

Union, WV, A novel of loss, healing, and redemption in contemporary Appalachia

Harmonic Highways: Exploring Virginia's Crooked Road

For updates on my books, excerpts, and sample chapters, please visit my website at:

> **http://www.bikemike.name/**

I can be reached by email at:

> **bikemike@nrvunwired.net.**

I welcome your feedback!